I0644004

ASIA for the ASIANS

China in the Lives of Five Meiji Japanese

Weatherhead
East Asian Institute

Studies of the Weatherhead East Asian Institute, Columbia University

The Studies of the Weatherhead East Asian Institute of Columbia University were inaugurated in 1962 to bring to a wider public the results of significant new research on modern and contemporary East Asia.

ASIA for the ASIANS

China in the Lives of Five Meiji Japanese

Paula S. Harrell

A Study of the Weatherhead East Asian Institute
Columbia University

MERWIN
ASIA

MerwinAsia
Portland, Maine

59 West St., Unit 3W,

Portland, ME 04102

USA

Distributed by the University of Hawai'i Press

Library of Congress Control Number: 2001012345

978-1-937385-20-0 (Paperback)

978-1-937385-21-7 (Hardcover)

Printed in the United States of America

The paper used in this publication meets the minimum requirements of the American National Standard for Information Services—Permanence of Paper for Printed Library Materials, ANSI/NISO Z39/48-1992

In Loving Memory
of My Mother and Father

Contents

Acknowledgments

Writing *Asia for the Asians* has been a fascinating and exciting journey from start to finish. I embarked on it with the same broad aim in mind that I had in the case of my previous book, *Sowing the Seeds of Change*: to challenge historians and others to look at the opening phase of China and Japan's modern relationship in new, less conventional ways.

The two books approach this period from different perspectives. *Sowing the Seeds* probes into the meaning of Japan to the thousands of Chinese youths who studied there in the early 1900s then returned home to try to remake China through reform and revolution. *Asia for the Asians* shifts the focus from the group to the individual and from Chinese perspectives on Japan to Japanese perspectives on China. It examines the Meiji view of China, imagined, real and evolving, through the eyes of five Japanese who worked directly with Chinese counterparts on various modernizing projects thought to be in the interest of both sides. Reliving the lives of these individuals—and a dozen others who did not make the final cut to become characters in my book—in order to understand what China meant to them, how they viewed Japan's place in Asia, and what they saw as the potential and limits to Chinese-Japanese partnership, has occupied much of the research side of my life for more than a decade.

Research is a solitary pursuit. But *Asia for the Asians* is about people. Reading accounts by them and about them, my five central subjects began to come to life, to become three dimensional figures instead of a few lines of bio and sometimes biased characterization. I began to understand something of their personalities, motives, and hopes and could at least imagine their failures and disappointments. I was delighted to discover rare photos to fill out the pictures of them I had formed in my mind. In the end, as is often true of new acquaintances, I liked some of my subjects better than others. Konoe Atsumaro, the idealistic consensus builder, struck a more sympathetic chord with me than the ego-driven, irascible Kawashima Naniwa. Yet in all cases I came to appreciate the immense energy these people expended over their lifetimes to achieve the goals they set out for themselves and Japan. They gave life their best try. No substitute for real friends, of course, but getting to know them and coming to inhabit their world in Meiji Japan and China was a source of true enjoyment for me as I labored away in solitude on my overarching theme of Chinese-Japanese interaction.

There are many individuals other than my five subjects that I would like to acknowledge for their contributions to the final product. When I presented a talk on Konoe a dozen years ago at Columbia University's Modern Japan Seminar, I was greatly encouraged by the members' enthusiastic response to both my Konoe interpretation and the project as a whole. James Morley was especially generous with his continued interest and support. At this same early date, Doug Reynolds commented in detail with keen insight on my first version of the Hattori chapter; Joan Judge did the same for Kawahara Misako. Much more recently, on short notice, Tom Burkman kindly read and commented on Chapter V, "Ariga Nagao and Japan's Internationalism." For sustained help over many years, I am immensely grateful to Edgar Harrell, Matthew Harrell, Philip Harrell, Erik Harrell, Veronica Li, Morris Rossabi, and Eiji Seki who reviewed all or parts of the manuscript as it emerged. Not only did they provide helpful comments and queries, they did so cheerfully, taking time from their own busy schedules to respond quickly and with evident interest in the themes that so engaged my imagination. Finally, I would like to extend my thanks to other family members and friends, young and old, who might have been puzzled by my long hours in front of the computer, but obliged me by very kindly asking from time to time about progress on the book.

In the final phase of bringing *Asia for the Asians* to publication, I would like to express my great appreciation to my editor and publisher Doug Merwin, who was enthusiastic about the project from the outset and a real pleasure to work with throughout, and to Carol Gluck and Dan Rivero of Columbia University's Weatherhead East Asian Institute, who moved rapidly to review the manuscript and issue a most welcome invitation to include the book in the Institute's study series. Credits for the photographs, brought to light by scouring through old books and Library of Congress collections, are duly noted in the captions. I have in this regard made every possible effort to trace and accurately cite the original copyright holders; if any have been omitted, I would be glad to hear from them.

Acknowledgments

As *Asia for the Asians* goes to press in the spring of 2012, the Government of Japan has just issued a new set of visa regulations intended to encourage foreign students to study at Japanese universities and find employment at Japanese companies after graduation. An aging Japan in need of young high tech professionals is reaching out in particular to surging China nearby as the most likely and culturally compatible source of supply. Chinese youth are attracted by Japan's good schools, the comfortable standard of living, and the prospect of future jobs in a structurally advanced economy. This is life in the new China-centered Asia, in which Japan is still powerful and technologically innovative, but by certain measures no longer number one. In 2010 China surpassed Japan in overall GDP (*not* per capita GDP) to become the world's second largest economy after the United States. In 2011, though still far behind the United States, it overtook Japan in total investment in R&D. A new Pacific order is emerging, a rebalancing of traditional powers among a host of newly dynamic Asian economies. How it shapes up is the Asia for the Asians story for the twenty-first century.

ASIA for the ASIANS

China in the Lives of Five Meiji Japanese

Introduction

On the Merits of Reading History Forward

A century and a half ago the West's ascendancy in Asia seemed all but assured as Europe's superior technology, capital, and economic dynamism fueled an expansionary surge into the Pacific. The reality of an apparently unstoppable West left Chinese and Japanese on the defensive, searching for ways to meet an alarming challenge, giving new urgency to their own longstanding questions about governance, culture, and the meaning of becoming modern. The story of their struggle with Western dominance that turned into a struggle with each other is well known: The Chinese chose reform within tradition; the Japanese embraced radical change along Western lines. Japan's successful empire building project, Western-style, hastened China's decline, and finally, a weakened China fell victim to Japanese aggression and the most destructive war in human history.

There is truth here, but the theme of tragic inevitability misses the sense of uncertainty and choice prominent at the beginning of the story. From the vantage point of the mid-nineteenth century, what we know as Japan's rise looked instead like an array of critical questions with no easy answers: how to create a new Japanese identity, how to develop a lagging economy, and how to manage a new triangular relationship, Japan-West-China, that had both political and cultural implications. Even to Japanese inclined to disparage China for its current weakness, reasons of geography and culture suggested that a productive partnership with the Chinese was an option to be taken seriously. For some, building a China connection became a passionate cause. For most, it was accepted as a rational, even humane way to further Japan's interests in a dangerous world. Asia for the Asians is about this generation, the shaping of its outlook on the world, and its commitment to the idea that Japan's experience as a late developing nation had useful lessons to offer China. The story is told from the Japanese perspective. The subtitle of the book is *China in the Lives of Five Meiji Japanese.* But as will be clear from what follows, the Chinese for a time and for similar reasons of national interest sought out Japan as a source of new technology and institutions.

Asia for the Asians consists of biographies of five Japanese who were born between 1860 and 1875; they were children of the Meiji era (1868-1912) and the momentous changes that accompanied it. Apart from Konoe Atsumaro, a prince of the highest rank and father of wartime prime minister Konoe Fumimaro, none of them is well-known now, even in Japan much less abroad. But all were prominent figures in their day. Their words carried weight in public discourse and the shaping of opinion. On the subject of China, much on the public mind, they spoke with authority. Not only were they familiar with Chinese classical traditions, standard for their generation, they also had considerable firsthand knowledge of China. Konoe Atsumaro, champion of a new Asia-oriented foreign policy, had contacts among both Chinese dissidents and progressive officials. The other four lived and worked in China for periods varying from three to twenty-five years. All went to China at China's invitation to provide advice in education, public security, and law. Interaction with China meant more to these people than mere literary acquaintance or the passing observations of an occasional traveler.

I have chosen to explore the Meiji experience of China through individual lives because I believe this is a more fruitful approach than starting with an overarching theory of some sort. Reliving a life gives full play to the uncertainties and choices facing any person or, indeed, any nation, moving forward in time, and in this way helps resist easy stereotypes and pre-defined conclusions. If done well, known outcomes fade into the background and imagined alternatives enter the realm of possibility. Listening to the voices of real people also helps illuminate the times with an immediacy so often lacking in studies focusing essentially on institutions or ideologies.

Meiji Japan is hard to grasp. It was on the one hand singularly open to outside ideas, entrepreneurial and innovative, and on the other narrowly nationalist and authoritarian. China still counted in the lives of educated Japanese though its currency was slipping; European and American ideas and systems were adopted, adapted, sometimes rejected. The five Japanese whose careers I have chosen to follow reflect the restless energy of the period. They shared a special interest in China, yet they were very different personalities with differing backgrounds and motives in going to China. Reading about China in their lives forces us at the very least to admit the possibility that coming to judgments about the modern Chinese-Japanese relationship is a more complex task than we imagined.

The big question for *Asia for the Asians* is whether partnership, the concept of East Asian community, ever had a reasonable chance of success in the environment of the times. And, if not, why not? This is a sensitive question. Not only the 1930s and 1940s but the entire period from the 1870s on has long existed under the dark cloud of the Pacific War. Chinese historians in particular reflexively start any inquiry with a backward glance through the lens of the war looking for negatives on the Japan side—flaws in the Meiji constitution, the militarization of Meiji society, a natural arrogance on the part of the Japanese—to explain the known outcome. The kind of honest look at questions of responsibility now common among historians of the war in Europe is just beginning for the war in Asia. Chinese and Japanese historians still label their joint history the "history problem."

The History of the "History Problem"

What a difference a century makes. The world is now stunned by China's rise and worried about signs of a declining America and Japan. China's own view of this great historical reversal was made with dramatic force at the 2008 Beijing Olympics where viewers worldwide were treated to a dazzling four-hour display of China's past glories and high-tech future. National pageantry was to be expected, of course. Using the Olympic stage to showcase national achievements is what host countries traditionally do. But at the hands of filmmaker Zhang Yimou, China's version of the opening ceremony was unrivalled in scale and eye-popping moments. Some fifteen thousand performers, amazingly in sync with each other and an array of virtual props celebrated the strength of China's 5,000 year-old civilization, innovative, sophisticated, and dynamic, bursting into a future of unparalleled global reach and prosperity. The Games' organizers had chosen "One World, One Dream" as the ideal to strive for in the 2008 Olympics and beyond. As the performance unfolded, with cultural highlights punctuated by fantastic fireworks, it appeared that only the Chinese had the long-proven capacity to lead the way.

This image of a China on the fast track to superpower status is part of China's new national identity. The public is optimistic about the future. When asked as part of the 2010 Pew Global Attitudes Survey "is your country heading in the right direction," 90 percent of the Chinese respondents replied yes (compared to 30 percent of Americans asked the same question). And the Chinese know that the world knows they are on the rise. At the same time, they are acutely history-conscious. They may believe that history is now on their side, but their reading of their own past has left them suspicious of the intentions of outsiders, Westerners and Japanese in particular. Strikingly absent from Zhang Yimou's celebration of the

Chinese experience were any highlights from the modern period, overshadowed as it is in Chinese minds by what they call, "the century of national humiliation (*bainian guochi*)." Referring to the years of foreign intervention and invasion beginning with the Opium Wars in the 1840s, the humiliation theme retains broad resonance in nationalist discourse, reminding Chinese to exercise vigilance in dealing with foreigners and foreigners to recognize the past suffering they visited on the Chinese. After America's 1999 bombing of the Chinese embassy in Belgrade Chinese turned out in droves to protest what they saw as a deliberate provocation, yet another U.S. attempt to bully China.[1] More routine Chinese complaints about periodic U.S. arms sales to Taiwan or terms of trade are likewise couched in the language of wounded pride linked to what happened a century and more ago. China's Olympic self-image is haunted by the ghost of grievances past.

Japan is the primary target of China's outrage over past wrongs. Nothing strikes the humiliation chord more sharply than Japan's failures, real or imagined, to acknowledge and atone for its record of aggression and atrocity in China during World War II, a war that claimed the lives of millions of Chinese. Ironically, the issue of Japan's war guilt has gained rather than lost intensity in the years since Japan's surrender in 1945. Until the seventies it remained a subdued theme for a host of reasons having to do with Chinese domestic developments and international constraints. Civil war was China's main preoccupation in the immediate postwar years. Score-settling pitted Nationalists against Communists with wartime collaborators despised by both; pursuing Japanese for war crimes was a lesser priority. Nor did the U.S. managed Tokyo Tribunal, for all its weighty proceedings, lay out in full the case for China or hold to account those most guilty among the Japanese leadership, most notably the emperor. In the American calculus, limiting the scope of retributive justice served the more important U.S. goal of ensuring Japan's support in the deepening Cold War with the Soviet Union.

Japan had no choice in its China policy in the aftermath of the communist victory in 1949. Economic and security ties with the United States bound Japan to the U.S. containment strategy of isolating the new People's Republic of China (PRC) as it struggled to harness agriculture to pay for industry and to survive the appalling excesses of the Great Leap Forward and the Cultural Revolution. But pragmatic considerations intruded. The absence of diplomatic ties notwithstanding, Communist China and capitalist Japan carried on two decades of a surprisingly robust, though often contentious trade relationship deemed in the interests of both sides. And whatever bitterness toward Japan was felt by the Chinese public, China's official line during this period mirrored the judgment of the Tokyo Tribunal: that ordinary Japanese had suffered as much as ordinary Chinese at the hands of Japanese militarists, who were the ultimate guilty party. Again, very likely for pragmatic reasons, China did not raise the sticky matter of compensation paid out in the early fifties to other of Japan's wartime enemies. In the 1972 Sino-Japanese Joint Statement concluded on the heels of Nixon's China breakthrough, China officially relinquished its claim to reparations.

What China and Japan currently call their "history problem" surfaced in a serious way only at the end of the decade when the PRC leadership, determined to pull a long stagnating economy out of poverty, moved full force ahead with a policy of re-engagement with the rest of the world. This new, normalized relationship has been increasingly complex, mutually beneficial, and often contentious. Multiple, open channels that have facilitated vastly expanded trade, technology transfer and investment—sought-after entries on the plus side of the ledger—have also invited searching public reappraisals of Japan's wartime guilt resulting in predictably sharp disagreements. The fact that U.S.-style freedom of speech in democratic Japan gives a hearing to a mix of voices from those roundly condemning Japan's actions on the one end to atrocity deniers on the other is not always well appreciated by the Chinese public. On their part, PRC leaders, though operating in a more controlled environment, have faced the tricky task of managing strong popular anti-Japanese sentiment, at times a useful negotiating tool but also a double-edged sword capable of turning against the government itself.

For the past thirty years Chinese have monitored Japanese public utterances and actions, looking for evidence of appropriate contrition or, more accurately, lack thereof, regarding Japan's conduct during the war. Japan's public school history texts have been the subject of especially close scrutiny. Changes in wording in some of the officially approved texts—calling Japan's march through China an "advance" rather than an "invasion" or downgrading atrocity figures, for example—have triggered widespread Chinese protests. Another item always on the Chinese radar screen are visits of Japanese prime ministers to the Yasukuni Shrine, memorial to some 2.5 million war dead, including fourteen convicted by the Tokyo Tribunal. Shrine visits are taken as a sop to Japan's right wing and have been met with strong Chinese objections. The language of apology is another persistent sticking point. Chinese have dismissed official Japanese apologies issued in various forms and formats over the years as insufficiently heartfelt, citing the contrast with Germany which long ago accepted the war as a national shame to be expiated in part by billions of dollars in reparations. Apology and compensation questions are at the heart of the ongoing battle on behalf of the wartime "comfort women" (*ianfu*) carried on by civil society groups in Japan as well as China and Korea.

Beginning in the 1990s, political dynamics on the China side heated up the rhetoric on the history problem. Intent on creating a new nationalist ideology supportive of current market socialist goals, China's leaders encouraged what Parks Coble has aptly called a "new remembering" of China's war of resistance against Japan. In a peculiar turnabout, this new interpretation emphasized not China's *heroic resistance* against but its *collective victimization* by the Japanese. Official estimates of Chinese wartime casualties were suddenly without warning or evidence revised upward from 9 to 35 million. The shared experience of Japanese-inflicted loss and humiliation was used to justify continued demands for retribution at the same time as it provided a rationale for common action to build a strong China that would be impervious to weakness and shame.[2]

But not only politics was at work here. The opening of archives and the work of both Japanese and Chinese scholars revealed new evidence of war crimes. Media coverage drew the larger public into new calculations of guilt and what to do about it. *The Rape of Nanking: the Forgotten Holocaust* (1997) by the journalist Iris Chang landed like a bombshell into the middle of the controversy. Though Chang's book is arguably flawed, sensational in its telling, occasionally inaccurate, and completely blind to extensive Japanese research on Nanjing, it spurred a round of exceptional new books on the subject by professional historians—Chinese, Japanese, *and* Western—which are evidence-based yet refreshingly diverse in their interpretations. Chang's book also added fuel to the Japan-bashing fire by implying that not only Japanese militarist elements and the people as a whole but also a forever-deficient Japanese national character were responsible for the war.[3]

It was in this increasingly charged atmosphere that anti-Japanese riots broke out after China's loss to a Japanese soccer team in 2004 and again in 2005 over textbook revision issues. The annual shrine visits of Prime Minister Koizumi Junichirō, in office from 2001 to 2006, also drew strong public protests resulting in the total suspension of meetings with his Chinese counterpart, President Hu Jintao. Top-level people on both sides began to view with unease the worsening climate of antagonism and its possible damaging effects on the critical economic and strategic relationship between Asia's two leading powers. A special Chinese concern was what impact it would have on the upcoming 2008 Olympics, ten years in the planning stage. Hosting Games free of political incident, including anti-Japanese demonstrations, was no trivial matter to a leadership concerned about world image.

In October 2006, within a few weeks of being elected to office, Prime Minister Abe Shinzō traveled not to the United States, routinely the first destination for a newly elected Japanese leader, but to China to meet with President Hu Jintao. It was a gesture of conciliation and even deference well appreciated by the Chinese. The atmosphere of the Abe-Hu talks was positive, constructed around the idea of containing the combustible history problem in the interest of moving ahead with the pragmatic business of managing trade, investment, energy demands, environmental issues, regional alliances—all vital areas requiring cooperation and partnership. The history problem was literally taken off the main agenda, assigned by joint agreement to a new history working group called the Japan-China History Joint Research Committee (Nit-Chū Rekishi Kyōdō Kenkyū—hereafter Japan-China History Committee). History, as Prime Minister Abe observed, would be left to the historians.[4]

Establishing bilateral history commissions is a constructive way of trying to moderate potentially explosive history issues and one with ample precedents—e.g., the Franco-German textbook commission and Japan's own joint research project with South Korea. The Japan-China project got off to a promising start. Mainstream historians were chosen to represent two national committees, each headed by a highly respected chairman, Bu Ping, director of the Chinese Academy of Social Sciences' Institute of Modern History, and Kitaoka Shin'ichi, professor of Political Science at Tokyo University. It was agreed generally that the scope of research would encompass the entire 2,000 year record of relations between the two countries, not simply the fraught history of the last century. Participants decided to take a parallel history approach, producing two interpretations of agreed topics rather than attempting any kind of common understanding or reconciliation of views. Plans were to release a final report in the summer of 2008.

Though the project started smoothly, it quickly became apparent how difficult it would be to escape the burden of politics. The two chairmen had a lot to say to the press in the early months, but strikingly it was not at all about the overall design of a study covering 2,000 years. Rather it was about a single topic: wartime responsibility. Bu Ping believed that as the basic premise for research into China and Japan's shared history, the Japanese team must adopt a "correct view of history," that is, acknowledge from the outset Japan's wrongdoing, including a pattern of aggression beginning in the Meiji period. This would be the governing idea for the entire study. Kitaoka Shin'ichi argued equally strongly in favor of developing working hypotheses, doing evidence-based research, and extending the boundaries of inquiry beyond the war era. He told a *Wall Street Journal* reporter that he wished the Chinese would "stop looking at history where relations were most awful." The parallel history approach was seen as an effective compromise, allowing for different points of emphasis on both sides.[5]

While the committees downplayed any disagreements in the working relationship over the next two years, it was clear by the summer of 2008 that how to handle the final product had itself become a contentious issue. Whether because of timing—that the release of a possibly controversial report might sour the good feeling surrounding China's highly successful Olympics—or because it was feared that the very parallelism that was agreed to might seem to give too much weight to a Japanese alternative view, the Chinese team argued against making the report public. After more than a year of negotiations the report was issued in January 2010, but without the promised chapter summaries for the post-World War II period. The Japanese conceded this point only reluctantly since it obscured from public view both Japan's entire postwar record as a uniquely peaceful nation and China's brutal politics during the Great Leap Forward and the Cultural Revolution.[6]

The *China Daily* greeted the 539-page report with the headline, "Japan admits war 'act of aggression.'" Kitaoka countered that this was nothing new, that Japanese committee members and, indeed, virtually all Japanese historians, had long ago accepted this view. He did, however, acknowledge that there was still an atrocity-denier fringe in Japan, and he tried to preempt possible objections from it by detailing Japan's wrongdoings in the Manchurian incident, Japan's fateful move in 1931 to occupy Manchuria, and its violations of the laws of war in the Nanjing Massacre of 1937-38. On some key points—for example, the death toll at Nanjing—the two sides agreed to disagree. Both Kitaoka and the Chinese chairman, Bu Ping, officially supported the idea of a follow-up project, possibly resulting in a joint history textbook. A Japanese government spokesman probably best summed up the official reaction on both sides: "History is just history. The government will work for the future."[7]

"History Is Just History"?

In an institutional sense, as a mechanism to help clear away differences over history as an impediment to future bilateral ties, the government-sponsored Japan-China History Committee has been a welcome first step. Japan's broad public acceptance of responsibility for aggression and atrocity represents progress in what will necessarily be a long process of restitution and reconciliation. The PRC's agreement to release a report that gives equal space to a Japanese perspective on sensitive topics indicates a new receptivity to moving the process forward. But these are essentially political goals. What about history in all this? What is the responsibility of the historian? Is history "just history," something to be negotiated, voted upon, and enacted like a piece of legislation?

For the serious historian intent on doing an honest job of reconstructing China and Japan's shared past the answer is obviously no. It may be good politics to encourage fixed interpretations, but good history is dynamic and demands openness to new empirical evidence and new interpretations however inconvenient that might be. In his essay, "The Past Is Another Country: Myth and Memory in Post-war Europe," the late historian Tony Judt reflected on how the immediate construction of official versions of wartime Europe led to distorted assessments of how people experienced the war, obscuring the ethnic score-settling that went on under cover of German occupation, downplaying the collaboration and complicity that made the Vichy government possible, inflating the role of resistance movements in countries like France, Norway and the Netherlands. It is only since the 1980s that professional scholars have—have *dared* to in light of convenient public acceptance of a fixed view—fully expose the 'Vichy Syndrome' and the role of what Judt calls the Nazis' "active partners in ideological collaboration" not only in France but in other European countries that counted themselves on the allied side of the conflict.[8]

In China, wartime collaboration is an even more sensitive subject, though less so than it was pre-1980 when it was thought that only the study of the Maoist past leading inevitably to the communist present was morally acceptable. Since then, the gradual release of archival materials revealing both informal and institutionalized collaboration with Japan has pushed the topic more into the forefront, particularly as researchers tap into what appears to be a vast reservoir of richly varied materials. David Barrett and Larry Shyu took a major step in bringing the Chinese collaborationist experience into public discourse in their edited conference volume, *Chinese Collaboration with Japan, 1932-1945,* published in 2001. In their introduction to the collected essays, they speak of the challenges Chinese China scholars face in trying to tackle the subject, chief among them the need to "break free from the moralistic framework in which wartime history is viewed." Breaking free, they go on to say, will prove difficult since the "moralistic interpretation of history, which holds the historian's task to be that of assigning 'praise and blame,' has its roots in 2,500 years of Confucian historiography."[9]

A willingness to buck official versions and moralistic frameworks in favor of writing empirically sound history characterizes the above-mentioned spate of studies, also in English, triggered by Iris Chang's account of the Nanjing atrocity. A notably fearless effort to do honest research on this most painful of all subjects is the volume of essays edited by Bob Tadashi Wakabayashi published in 2007. In his introduction, tellingly subtitled, "The Messiness of Historical Reality," Wakabayashi writes, "We contend that the Atrocity was a shameful violation of law and morality, but find ourselves in grudging and qualified agreement that certain intractable facts betray key points in the official Chinese narrative and in Western accounts that follow it."[10] Carefully put, but one is reminded of John Maynard

Keynes' response to a reporter who asked him why he had shifted his position on a certain issue. "When the facts change, I change my mind," he said. "What do you do, sir?"

It is the responsibility of the historian, in other words, to declare nothing off-limits in his search to understand and explain the past but rather to be willing to consider new evidence and new kinds of evidence however much it might require modifying previously held beliefs. This principle of historical openness applies as much to new evidence of Japanese atrocities in conducting gas warfare as it does to new evidence to refute the Chinese figure of 300,000 victims at Nanjing now inscribed on a stone monument in that city. Paul Cohen, in his superb study, *History in Three Keys: the Boxers as Event, Experience, and Myth,* argues in favor of dispassionate inquiry in explaining the difference between the memoir writer and the historian, the one psychologically vested in recreating past events, the other intellectually: "Although as human beings we are subject to the same spectrum of emotional needs as anyone else, in our capacity as historians our efforts to understand the past are guided by a conscious commitment (never fully realized in practice) to a socially agreed-upon and enforced standard of accuracy and truth. This commitment defines us as historians."[11]

Defining precisely what is meant by "a socially agreed-upon and enforced standard of accuracy and truth" is a tricky thing. I would prefer to think more simply of a commitment to empirically-based research or perhaps, in the China-Japan case, a willingness to examine and reevaluate the facts of the matter within the context of recognizing universal standards of morally acceptable human behavior. Any of these definitions, however, argues for expanding rather than restricting the field of vision in examining the history of the 1930s and 1940s. And, in making history more dynamic and open in this way, it necessarily challenges the official-version-approach to explaining the past that Tony Judt decries in the case of Europe and that the PRC government has used to strategic advantage in its recent relations with Japan.

The attempt to get at the truth even if it means telling "an uncomfortable story" as Judt puts it, must be the guiding principle in reassessing not only wartime and immediate pre-war history but the entire period of China's and Japan's modern relations beginning in the mid-nineteenth century. To a large extent this period, too, has been in thrall to fixed interpretations derived from what happened *later* in wartime China. This is what I call reading history backward, the tendency to look at the entire modern relationship between the two countries through the prism of World War II, a time when relations, in Professor Kitaoka's words, were "most awful." At the time of Prime Minister Abe's 2006 visit to China, Chinese Premier

Wen Jiabao interposed his welcoming comments with the remark that Japanese militarists had imposed great suffering on the Chinese people since 1894.[12]

Indeed, the history writing produced by the Japan-China Joint History Committee generally follows this "long pre-war" tradition. Particularly in the Chinese report, the overriding focus in the discussion of modern relations is on the inexorable expansion of Japanese militarism and interventionist activities in China from the 1870s on—the Meiji military modernization program, the tensions over Korea, the Sino-Japanese War, the Boxer Uprising, the Russo-Japanese War, the 1911 Revolution, the 21 Demands, all of this treading over old familiar ground in old familiar ways. Even a fourteen-page section with the promising heading, "Conflict and Cooperation," devotes only a page and a half to the cooperation theme and this only to emphasize Japan's military motives in inviting Chinese students to study in Japan and to note that Japan was but a conduit to Western knowledge in any case. The Japanese report, too, is constrained by the very topics the two teams agreed to cover: treaties, friction, wars. With the emphasis throughout on the political-military dimension, both reports not surprisingly segue easily into aggression in Manchuria in the 1930s and the march to all-out war.[13] The very framework of inquiry encourages pre-defined conclusions. Not that there is not truth in this recital of events; it is simply not the whole truth.

Nor is questioning the choice of topics meant to say by any means that such important episodes as the Russo-Japanese War and the 21 Demands do not merit further inquiry. They surely do, but from new vantage points and considering new evidence and interpretations. This reevaluative task is difficult under cover of the Japan-China History Committee where politics is an inevitable intruder. But it is not easy to dislodge settled views in any environment. Take the case of the imperialism/informal imperialism framework that came into prominence in the late 1980s with publication of W.G. Beasley's definitive study *Japanese Imperialism, 1894-1945* and the groundbreaking essays in *The Japanese Informal Empire in China, 1895-1945,* edited by Peter Duus, Ramon Myers, and Mark Peattie. By treating Japan's presence in China as an Asian variant of European-style "informal empire," these studies suggested a kind of moral (or immoral) equivalence between Japanese and Europeans in their empire-building phase in China, rebalancing the Tokyo Tribunal view that condemned the former while soft-pedaling the latter. The studies were intended to establish ever-questioning, comparative thinking as the basis for follow-up work.

And yet, though meant to be a working model only, the notion of informal imperialism as applied to Japan has, in fact, tended to constrain historians rather than embolden them to push the boundaries of inquiry and interpretation beyond the usual accepted categories. First, it lumps together under the label "imperialism," albeit the less coercive informal variety, not only military and economic ventures, but also educational and cultural exchanges, activities that in today's lexicon are more commonly referred to as instruments of "soft power." One can contest definitions, but certainly Americans today see the export of American ways of thinking and doing as a positive contribution, the product of humanitarian impulses, not evidence of expansionism or imperialism. Strictly speaking, however, this and any other form of "extending footprints," as we now like to call it, could just as well be labeled informal imperialism. Distinctions among forms of expansionism and varieties of imperialism bear thinking about in the earlier Japanese case, too. The most clearheaded assessment of Japan's prewar foreign policy in my view is Ian Nish's observation "that there was neither a single-minded and uninterrupted pursuit of expansionist goals nor was there a grand pattern of continuity in Japanese imperialism."[14]

Second, assuming a "grand pattern" based on asymmetric power as the informal imperialism model does, not only overstates the passivity of China's response to Japan, it also underrates the qualitative difference in relations between Japanese and Chinese on the one hand and Westerners and Chinese on the other. There was a cultural dimension in the former case that both sides were willing to use to national advantage. For example, thousands of Chinese students were educated in Japan after 1895, at Japan's invitation but also as part of a Chinese government policy to create a cadre of young people trained in modern systems and institutions.[15]

Third, and related to the latter point, because the subject has been *Japan's* informal empire, the role of *Chinese* actors in shaping the China-Japan relationship has been underplayed, thereby seeming to absolve the Chinese side of any measure of responsibility for the ultimate failure to achieve accommodation. In sum, it seems safe to say that since imperialism is now generally regarded as a bad thing—Niall Ferguson's argument about the beneficial effects of British imperialism notwithstanding[16]—research that starts with it as the story heading risks simply providing more grist for the well-worn tale of Japanese aggression and Chinese victimization. Again, it is not that there is not truth to the military-aggression narrative. It is simply not the whole truth.

Some recent works have reopened old case files on Japan's empire, notably the verdict on Manchukuo, Japan's colony in Manchuria. Much credit goes to the relentless research of Japanese scholar Yamamuro Shin'ichi whose 1993 publication was all but ignored until brought to light by Joshua Fogel's 2006 translation, *Manchuria under Japanese Dominion.* In Yamamuro's telling, Manchukuo is no less the brutal puppet state we thought we knew, but in fact much more than that, the product of a variety of expert analyses, public passions, misguided idealisms, and Chinese complicity. As Fogel observes, "Taken as a whole the entire era of Japanese expansion into what is now Northeast China becomes simultaneously much richer and more complex."[17] Other, subsequent studies such as those by Prasenjit Duara and Louise Young have widened the lens further, Duara in examining Manchukuo as an experiment in pan-Asian identity formation, Young in looking at the role of the Japanese media in reinforcing the pro-expansion sentiments of an already enthusiastic Japanese public.[18] Susan Townsend's biography of Yanaihara Tadao (1893-1961) published in 2001 fills out the record on Manchuria in a different way, giving a hearing to the neglected voice of a hugely influential and dogged critic of Japan's colonial policies and the war in China, an "icon of resistance to the militarist tendencies of 1930s Japan."[19] Here not only is the inquiry broadened but an accepted narrative is brought into question: the view that critical voices were non-existent in Japan of the 1920s and '30s or at least that repressive Japanese government measures rendered them so.

Reading History Forward

In writing *Asia for the Asians* I have sought to derive from real experiences rather than imposed narratives what China meant to Japanese searching for a path to modernity and a secure place internationally in the late nineteenth and early twentieth centuries. My job as historian has been to recreate the context of issues and events engaging China, Japan and the rest of the world, yet to step back to allow my five subjects to speak in their own voices and to lead their own lives as we all do with a range of outcomes apparently possible. Still, as the "knowers" of the eventual tragedy between China and Japan we are forced back to the eternal question, "could things have turned out differently?" Were technology transfer and effective collaboration between Chinese and Japanese ever viable and sustainable options? Examining these questions anew, unfettered to the extent possible by official versions and moral frameworks is what I mean by reading history forward.

Without the luxury of retrospect, the world as viewed from the vantage point of 1870s Beijing or Tokyo appears a kaleidoscope of realities. There is no overriding theme to suggest a single path forward, certainly nothing to point the way to the Japanese-led holocaust that engulfed the two peoples seventy years later. What the 1870s observer would have noted, in fact, was the striking absence of conflict in the centuries-long encounter between Chinese and Japanese. Apart from an ill-conceived Mongol campaign to invade Japan in the thirteenth century and a failed Japanese thrust into Korea/North China in the sixteenth, the record showed no major military confrontations. The chief point of contact was cultural, a one-way flow of language, philosophy, religious beliefs, art, and artifacts from China to Japan. China, not Japan, was long the dominant power in Asia, its power derived from resource self-sufficiency and superior cultural products—institutional models, books, manufactures—much in demand. You have nothing to offer us, China bluntly informed all non-Chinese, both its near neighbors and the Europeans coming to Asia for purposes of trade and evangelism beginning in the late sixteenth century. We Chinese set the rules and terms of trade.

For the Japanese, the European presence combined with Chinese assertions of cultural and economic hegemony represented a double-barreled threat, first, to Japan's security and, second, to a developing Japanese view of the world that had its own component of ethnic superiority. Japan responded in dramatic fashion in the early seventeenth century by drastically limiting outside contacts through a remarkably effective regime of travel bans and regulated trade known as the "closed country" *(sakoku)* policy. Though isolationist, Japan remained open in one important sense. Chinese and Dutch were allowed to continue their trading operations, albeit on an exclusive basis at the single port of Nagasaki, thereby enabling Japan to maintain a window on the world and the cultural and economic benefits it had to offer. On the other hand, with a single exception, government-to-government relations were entirely cut off. Only in the case of Korea did Japan carry on active diplomacy, this in an effort to countervail the power of a new dynasty, the Qing, Manchu in origins, Chinese in pretentions, now expanding into Mongolia and Tibet and claiming Korea as its satellite. Japan was very much closed, also, at the people-to-people level. Not only were "outside barbarians" unwelcome in Japan, Japanese were forbidden to travel abroad.

For a period of nearly 250 years after Japan's turn to isolationism, China and Japan were not only free of conflict, but were in a curious state of suspended relations. There were no official ties, and, apart from Chinese traders calling in at Nagasaki, only the rarest chance of interaction on an individual basis. While the trade itself—mostly Japanese metals for Chinese silks and books—benefited both sides, the arms-length quality of the relationship over such a long period led to stereotypes, positive and negative. Japanese tended to idealize the traditions of Old China, to see China as the universal high standard of human output in art, poetry, historical writing, and political and social norms. Chinese who thought about Japan at all over these years regarded it as nothing more than a nuisance country, a country of racially inferior "dwarfs," which exported pirates to raid towns on the China coast.

What finally jolted China and Japan out of the status quo into a new relationship with new rules was not a bilateral issue at all, but the crisis posed by Western expansion into the Pacific. Japanese isolationism and Chinese assertions of imperial power, effective in holding off seventeenth century Europe, were no longer workable in the nineteenth when much greater demands for market access were backed by undeniably superior military power. Fear of what appeared to be a threat of unprecedented proportions to Asia triggered a new Japanese interest in what was happening in contemporary China.

Accounts of British attacks on Chinese coastal cities from the 1840s on conditioned the Japanese response to the presence of foreign gunboats off its own coast, most alarmingly the appearance of Commodore Perry's coal-burning "black ships" in 1853. China's experience provided a lesson in the perils of military un-preparedness, the futility of trying to resist even a small country like Britain if it possessed clear technological superiority. Issues of national defense or, more simply, how to deal with foreigners, precipitated the domestic crisis over power sharing that led to the momentous societal changes of the Meiji period, a dramatic shift in course matched only by the defining events of America's postwar Occupation.

Outside pressure provided the impulse to remake Japan in both the Meiji period and the Occupation. The difference, of course, was that in the latter case, American occupiers imposed U.S. systems on a defeated Japan, a pariah in the world, whereas in the former, Japanese leaders themselves embraced changes along Western lines precisely to enable Japan to join the world and thereby avoid defeat. Three interrelated issues were of critical importance to the new Meiji leaders, each with implications for Japan's China relationship: how to restructure internally to meet the foreign threat, how to master the new rules of international engagement, and how to reposition Japan in Asia. In other words, the old isolationism was out, and acting like a Western power and engaging China as a natural collaborator were options on the table. Japanese initiatives to renew contacts with China and put the relationship on a modern footing resulted in a trade agreement in 1871, the first formal treaty between the two countries ever. Commercial and diplomatic considerations aside, Japan's deep-seated concerns about maintaining security in the new climate in Asia, drove follow-up actions to challenge the old Chinese imperium in both the Ryūkyūs and Korea.

There was a cultural counterpart to the strategic choices facing Chinese and Japanese as the West advanced into their part of Asia. People in both countries were forced to grapple with trying to reconcile traditional norms and values, no longer effective in dealing with the external world, with modern technological civilization, which worked but came in Western guise. But Japanese had to make a double adjustment. Their own traditions were strongly suffused with

China-centered elements, edited and revised over centuries, but China-based, nevertheless. Opening to the outside world put in sharp relief the need to accommodate to two cultural alternatives: a Western present with its well-tested lessons in how to survive and thrive in the wider world and a Chinese past, an eternal source of spiritual sustenance. No such dilemma faced the Chinese in their dealings with the new Meiji leaders. Japan, from the Chinese vantage point, was a country to be instructed, not emulated.

While no Japanese living in 1870s Japan could have predicted the challenges to follow, they were well aware that their country was moving in a momentous new direction and were poised to make creative adjustments. They embraced an international outlook with a speed and energy that set them apart from their Chinese neighbors. Joshua Fogel has long argued that "a full understanding of either China or Japan requires bringing the other into account."[20] I heartily agree, but would make a further claim: that from the nineteenth century on, an equally essential ingredient to our understanding of either country singly or their interactions is full knowledge of what was happening internationally, not only politically but in the broad realm of technology and ideas.

The standard Chinese account of the Meiji era bores in almost exclusively on military modernization and then projects this onto the whole canvas of Meiji activity as evidence of a society propelled forward by aggressive forces released in final virulent form in the 1930s and 1940s. Military strengthening was indeed a vital part of the reform agenda—as it was in late nineteenth century China—and its results were much applauded by Western observers at the time, particularly after Japan's victory over China in 1895. But Meiji Japan was much more than this. Stepping back and widening the lens shows a highly variegated picture of the Meiji experience as a late-developing nation. Modernization of the military along Western lines was not an isolated case but illustrative of the broader phenomenon that Eleanor Westney so convincingly demonstrates in her incisive analysis, *Imitation and Innovation: The Transfer of Western Organizational Patterns to Meiji Japan*: the conscious importation from Europe and America of a wide range of institutions that were reworked and transformed in the Japanese setting.

As Westney shows in her case studies of the postal and police systems and mass circulation newspapers, emulation invariably produced innovation. And what was true in those instances was equally so in such areas as constitutional law, women's rights and the biggest of Meiji Japan's achievements, construction from the ground up of a national system of schools. The speed and scope of this transformation had no precedent anywhere in the world. By the late 1890s Japan had become a mediator of global culture, a late developer now capable of passing on its own lessons to developed and less developed countries alike. It was this Japan with its evident innovative capacity that caught the attention of a Chinese leadership at last convinced of the wisdom of across-the-board reforms. Over the next decade and more, with Japanese encouragement and Chinese receptivity, a series of exchange programs went into high gear: 10,000 Chinese students studying in Tokyo, 1,000 Chinese officials visiting Japan on short-term study tours, and 600 Japanese advisers and teachers working in China as employees of the Chinese government.

This was a remarkable episode, both the internationalizing of a generation of Japanese and the impulse to bring China along in the development process. Yet it has been largely neglected. A notable exception is Douglas Reynolds' survey of Japan's wide-ranging contributions to a modernizing China, *China, 1898-1912: The Xinzheng Revolution and Japan,* an extension of the work of the pioneering scholars of Sino-Japanese relations Sanetō Keishū and Wang Xiangrong. But there is room for much more analytical work along the lines laid out by Westney, particularly emphasizing the linkages among Euro-American forms, themselves changing, and Japanese and Chinese innovations, the latter often reflecting the influence of Japanese models.

And not only is the transfer process itself important to understand, but so are the people behind it. In my view, research into institutions, ideologies, policies—impersonal factors—must always be validated by the "lived experience" of direct participants. What did China mean to an individual growing up in 1870s or 1880s Japan? What place did China have in his or her life at a time of competing draws to learn European languages and study in the West? How did those Japanese who went to China, not simply as travelers, but to teach or work with Chinese on institutional change, view their experience? We talk about Chinese-Japanese interactions in an abstract sense, but how did people *really* interact, and what difference did it make in their own lives, in public perceptions of China, and in Japan's all-important foreign policy goal of exerting increased influence in China relative to the other foreign powers? And the same haunting question: did cooperation appear to be a viable alternative to the conflict that followed?

These are some of the questions I have had in mind in writing *Asia for the Asians.* I have sought the answers in the lives of five individuals, all part of the new Meiji generation, all public figures who were engaged professionally and personally with China in important and enduring ways. Each chapter is a separate biography, though as I proceeded with the writing I found the subjects and their circle of friends interconnected to a degree I had not foreseen at the outset. The obvious question, of course, is why these five people and to what extent might we see them as representative of their generation? Four of the figures came to my attention in researching my book on the Chinese students in Japan (*Sowing the Seeds of Change*): Konoe Atsumaro, father of Japan's wartime prime minister, Konoe Fumimaro, and early supporter of pan-Asianist thinking; Hattori Unokichi, Tokyo University professor and adviser to Beijing University; Ariga Nagao, legal scholar and adviser to the president of China's first republic; and Kawashima Naniwa, who made China and Manchuria the focus of his entire career. Kawahara Misako, the first Japanese woman to teach in China, surfaced as an interesting person in the course of researching the others.

All five were products of the evolving Meiji school system and the array of new choices that made Meiji Japan an entrepreneurial environment in the broadest sense of the term. They were part of the new elite, a remarkably large, public service-oriented group engaged in the task of achieving modernity fast. Three of the five studied abroad. All contributed in concrete ways to China's institutional development. Konoe set the tone, putting his considerable reputation as an imperial prince behind efforts to encourage the flow of Chinese students to Japan and Japanese teachers and advisers to China. Of the four hired by the Chinese government to work in China, Hattori organized Beijing University's first teacher training program, Kawahara introduced the Japanese model of women's education, Kawashima built China's modern public security system, and Ariga broadened the thinking of China's early republicans on constitutional systems worldwide.

A key criterion for selection was a practical one: the availability of diaries, authorized biographies, and other materials written about or by the individual under consideration. Konoe left a richly detailed diary covering five years of his short but influential career in politics. Both Hattori and Kawahara left firsthand accounts of their China experiences, Hattori's of his summer in Beijing during the Boxer crisis, Kawahara's of her time in Shanghai and Karachin, written in beautiful prose. Kawashima dictated his life story to his chosen biographer and authored numerous articles and books outlining his views of China. Hattori, a prolific academic, produced works on China's philosophy and institutions and was much written about. Ariga Nagao's "diary" was the highly influential journal he founded and edited *Gaikō jihō (Revue Diplomatique)*. In it are clues to his personal life and his opinions on every foreign policy issue imaginable; he was the complete internationalist whose professional interest in China came into focus later in life at the peak of his career. Ariga also left a large body of works on international law, many of which he wrote in French. There were many other candidates on my list, equally interesting but less covered in the literature. Two that come to mind are Hirai Seijirō and Haraguchi Kaname, both graduates of Rensselaer Polytechnic Institute in the late 1870s (both on the baseball team), who were key figures in railway development in Japan and later in China as well. Japan's role as a mediator of global culture is a rich field for inquiry.

The five lives overlapped, and I have been mindful of the need to explain the larger and local contexts while minimizing repetition in the interest of moving the stories forward and making them readable. I have also tried to convey the sense of real choice that each individual faced along the way—that is, to avoid imposing too much on the material as the actual knower of outcomes. Each chapter is intended to highlight particular events and issues so that in the end, by accretion, the reader will understand not only the dynamics of the Japanese-Chinese advisory relationship per se but also the changing context in which the advisers operated. Specifically, the Konoe chapter analyzes Japan's response to its new role in Asia after 1895, the Hattori chapter puts the spotlight on the Boxer Uprising and post-Boxer reforms, the Kawahara study focuses on women's issues and the Russo-Japanese War, and the chapter on Kawashima emphasizes China's 1911 Revolution and the origins of Manchu-Mongol separatism. The Ariga chapter is a study of Japan's internationalism. Ariga participated in and exemplified the broad process in the period from the 1890s to 1915 whereby Japan opened up to world culture, joining international gatherings and acting in compliance with international law, all of which legitimated and thereby encouraged Japan's expansionist vision. Ariga advised the Chinese on constitution writing and his own government on the 21 Demands in 1915 from the vantage point of the international legal and diplomatic order that he knew so well and valued so much.

What is striking about the issues these five figures were caught up in is their contemporaneity. The East Asian community concept articulated by Konoe more than a century ago is now current, as is the Asian values debate. Should we think in universal terms or is there something different about Asia when it comes to human rights or other issues in international law? Boxer-style terrorism, violently anti-Western, is still with us, as are larger threats to foreign interests and questions as to how to deal with them. How to fight a just war avoiding citizen casualties is as unresolved now as it was when Ariga was at The Hague in 1899 and on the battlefield in the Russo-Japanese War. Manchuria is no longer a contested space, but we have in its place Afghanistan and Iraq where local interests clash and instability is regarded as a threat to the rest of the world. Certainly the issue of ethnic separatism that bedeviled Kawashima later in his career is still the subject of conflict and debate. But to frame the lives of our five figures around issues alone understates the "messiness of historical reality," as Wakabayashi calls it. At the end of the day, these stories of people whose lives were China bound in both senses of the term are human stories. People changed their minds, refined their thinking, made decisions they regretted, and had aspirations met and hopes dashed. They were typical of their generation in their dedication to public service, in their consciousness that they personally had a responsibility and a role to play in making Japan a stronger nation—but circumstances, luck, and character had a lot to do with their ultimate contributions.

Chapter I

Konoe Atsumaro and the Case for Chinese-Japanese Collaboration

"The situation in Asia is getting increasingly tense," the head of Japan's upper House told a Chinese visitor in 1898. "Today, Asia's problems are not those of Asia alone but involve the whole world. The European powers are all engaged in conflicts in Asia to further their own interests. But Asia after all belongs to the Asians. Asians alone should have the right to solve Asia's problems. Presumably it's this very notion that is the principle behind America's Monroe Doctrine. And, as a matter of fact, the task of developing a Monroe Doctrine for Asia is the responsibility of your country and mine."[1]

The spokesman for this "Asia for the Asians" vision was Konoe Atsumaro, already at thirty-five a much respected public figure who seemed destined for a long career as a shaper of national policy. Like his American contemporary, Theodore Roosevelt, Konoe exuded energy and passion, whether directed to politics, to travel, to sport or simply to recording the day's events in his diary. Well-educated, well-connected and handsome, with a curling moustache and tall, athletic build, Konoe was the consummate people-person, a natural leader. His eldest son, Fumimaro, remembered a youthful, utterly capable figure, an extrovert, intensely engaged in the politics of the day. The Konoe mansion fairly pulsated with visitors arriving for meetings from early morning till late at night, much to the excitement of the Konoe children. A painful memory after his father's death, Fumimaro said, was the house suddenly enveloped in silence.[2] Konoe's confidence, his easy assumption of leadership as both duty and right, reflected in part his privileged background, something he, too, shared with Roosevelt, however different their aristocratic credentials. For Konoe's status derived not from wealth but from imperial connections. He was a prince, head of Japan's most illustrious imperial branch family with a pedigree that reached back thirteen centuries.[3]

Konoe Atsumaro was born in Kyoto, Japan's old imperial capital, in June of 1863, ten years after Commodore Perry's U.S. fleet first appeared in Japanese waters, a month before British ships fired on Japanese coastal defenses at Kagoshima. This was a fateful moment in Japan's history, unprecedented, matched only in its repercussions by the U.S. occupation of Japan after 1945. At issue was who should govern the country at this time of unimaginable crisis and the unstoppable advance into Asia of Western powers fueled by the Industrial Revolution. Was the current governing model, a military federation deputed to rule by an age-old imperial institution, capable of mounting an effective response or was drastic restructuring required? The issue spilled beyond debating councils to trigger murderous plots and civil war. In 1868, as Atsumaro's fifth birthday approached, troops loyal to the emperor defeated supporters of the status quo, ushering in a new politics of youth, change, and central control, all under the old banner of imperial rule. In one sense a restoration of power—hence the usual term "Meiji Restoration"—it was at the same time nothing short of revolution. Its leaders installed the newly empowered Meiji emperor in a new political capital, Tokyo, swept away feudal structures, nationalized all spheres of public life, and launched the country on a modernization program that made it a world class power in forty years.

Education of a Prince

In 1870, Konoe's father moved from Kyoto to Tokyo, to serve in the relocated court offices. Seven-year-old Atsumaro stayed behind at the behest of his grandfather, Konoe Tadahiro, who insisted on remaining in Kyoto but could not bear to part with his beloved grandson. Prominent member of a prominent family, grandfather Konoe had served as tutor and close adviser to Emperor Meiji's father, the staunchly anti-foreign Kōmei. Now retired, sixty-two-year-old Konoe Tadahiro continued to be consulted on imperial matters until his death in 1898 at age ninety. Atsumaro was the center of his emotional life, the hope of the Konoe future, the more so with the loss of Konoe Tadihiro's thirty-five year-old son, Atsumaro's father, in 1873. When the Imperial Household Agency prevailed on young Atsumaro, newly invested as official head of the Konoe family, to move to Tokyo in May of 1877, grandfather's loneliness got the better of him. Within months he had set up a second residence in the new capital.[4]

The Konoe family mansion was in Kōjimachi, a wealthy part of Tokyo and the site of the palace, government buildings, and foreign legations. One contemporary foreign visitor, approaching Kōjimachi from Tokyo's recently built Shimbashi Railway Station, remembered, ". . . miles of dark, silent, barrack-like buildings, with highly ornamental gateways, and long rows of projecting windows with screens made of reeds . . . and miles of moats with lofty grass embankments or walls of massive masonry fifty feet high, with kiosk-like towers at the corners, and curious, roofed gateways, and many bridges, and acres of lotus leaves." For fourteen-year-old Atsumaro, coming from quiet, rustic Kyoto, Tokyo was less forbidding and everything exciting and different—horse-drawn buses, trains, gaslights, Western-style architecture, and foreign fads in dress. It was a city fast changing, the center of political decision making, and a new opening to the world that admitted an array of foreign visitors, including America's celebrated general and former president Ulysses S. Grant in 1879.[5]

The timing of the Konoes' move from Kyoto to Tokyo in the spring of 1877 was probably no coincidence. By mid-March government forces had turned the tide in its do-or-die battle to quash the Satsuma Rebellion, "the last civil war to be fought in Japan," as Donald Keene calls it. Impending victory swept away any lingering ambiguities about the meaning of the Restoration. Reinstating the emperor as the country's direct ruler, a point on which both sides agreed, was not to signal the bias toward native culture and rejection of foreign influence the rebels demanded. Instead, the imperial house, the very embodiment of tradition, would continue to underwrite change on the Western model. Enthusiastic embrace of Western technology—institutions, ideas, styles, whatever appeared modern—would be the clear way forward. Career prospects for the offspring of the old court aristocracy lay in Tokyo.[6]

Konoe Atsumaro arrived in the new political capital already well schooled in the Chinese classics, calligraphy, and Japanese poetry, de rigueur for the nobility and certainly for the top-tier Konoes. Grandfather Konoe, tutor to the previous emperor, had supervised little Atsumaro's training in these subjects himself. But to be well educated in the late 1870s required something more. To Atsumaro's delight, his mentors at court added English to his curriculum, enrolling him first in a private academy, then in a local public school, putting him on track to enter Tokyo University's Preparatory School, which he did in 1880. A sports enthusiast, young Konoe started training in sumō, Japan's ancient wrestling sport, an interest that became a lifelong passion.[7]

What happened next is something of a puzzle. After less than a year at Tokyo Preparatory, Konoe withdrew from classes, reportedly to recover from a persistent intestinal ailment. This may well have been the case, as witness his future health problems. But he might also have been thrown off balance by the level of competition he encountered at this feeder school for Tokyo University, attended by ambitious self-starters from all social classes. In any case, Konoe's chosen antidote to the setback, whatever its origins, was the rigor of travel, an escape to the beauty of the

Japanese countryside he barely knew. With financing provided by the emperor, he soon departed for Yokohama on the new rail line, an easy start to a rugged, rewarding journey by sedan chair, boat, and on foot crisscrossing the Osaka-Kyoto region. It was a trip with health benefits but also designed for the scion of a prominent family pegged to play a leadership role. Eight months of exploration, meeting local leaders and immersion in Konoe family history had the required restorative effect. After a final round of parties in Kyoto with his grandfather and friends, he returned to Tokyo with renewed energy for intensive study, this time with private tutors and an expressed determination to make his mark on the basis of his own abilities rather than family status.[8]

Konoe Atsumaro at twenty (Kudō Takeshige, *Konoe Atsumaro-kō*; Tokyo: Dainichisha zōban, 1938)

However tradition-minded, diligent, and dutiful Konoe was, he was also a young man of his generation. Study abroad, he decided, preferably in England or America where he could build on his English-language training, would best prepare him to contribute to a modernizing Japan. When he raised this possibility with his mentors at court, there were strong objections, particularly on the question of location. Count Iwakura Tomomi, who ten years before had led an overseas study mission that spent six months in America and four in England, worried about Konoe's exposure to popular rights theories so at variance with Japanese political values. He recommended Russia instead. Spending time in a country with a strong state authority Konoe would be less likely to return to Japan with outrageous ideas. Needless anxieties, Konoe protested, pointing out that, besides, he had prepared himself in English, not Russian.

And so there ensued an entire year of negotiations during which time Iwakura died and Konoe enlisted Itō Hirobumi to present his case to the emperor. The politically powerful Itō, the emperor's most trusted minister, was himself well traveled, one of the rare Japanese visitors to England before the Restoration and a member of the Iwakura Mission's twenty-one-month tour of Europe and America soon after. At the time Konoe approached him in 1883, Itō had just returned from a nine-month trip to Europe to study European constitutions as possible design prototypes for Japan's new constitution. Itō's intercession on Konoe's behalf produced a compromise of sorts. In 1884 Konoe was given imperial permission to study abroad for five years, not in England or America but in Austria. He would be escorted by Marquis (later Prince) Saionji Kinmochi, newly appointed minister to Austria-Hungary.

But there was still Konoe's grandfather to convince. At seventy-five, Konoe Tadahiro feared he might not survive Atsumaro's five-year absence, a fear Atsumaro shared, however certain he was that study abroad would best equip him for a life of public service. In the end his grandfather relented, persuaded that it was time for his twenty-one-year-old grandson to gain some independence. Along with his blessing, he presented Atsumaro with a fine jade piece to symbolize the pure in heart and a poem fondly noting that, though growing old, he would be there awaiting his grandson's return. When, at last, Konoe set sail for Europe, on April 19, 1885, months of negotiating behind him, he confessed to feeling forlorn even as he exulted in having won the day. The family he left behind included his grandfather, two younger brothers, and seventeen-year-old Sawako, his wife of one month.[9]

Konoe's positive feelings about the West as a place to study were counterbalanced by his negative reactions to Western colonial policies in Asia. Fresh in his mind was the dispute between France and China over rights in Annam (present-day Vietnam), the subject of headline news in Japan the previous summer. Particularly alarming to Japanese readers were reports of the crushing defeat of China's new naval force by a small French fleet in late August 1884, an event that confirmed French control over Indochina and gave Britain the go-ahead to occupy Burma. Five days out of Yokohama, Konoe's ship passed the Pescadores Islands, the small island group between Taiwan and the mainland, Chinese territory now in French hands. Visible evidence of the French presence made a strong impression on Konoe: "Seeing the French national flag here and there fluttering in the wind makes me really understand that this place has been occupied by enemy troops. Isn't it pitiful! But as the territory of our neighboring countries is gradually taken over by Westerners, can we allow ourselves to sit by and watch this firestorm on the other shore?" [10] Konoe's son, Fumimaro, suggested that, like others of his generation, his father was beginning to see the East-West problem in racial terms:

> Around 1885, when my father went abroad, the era of extreme infatuation with Europe and America had passed and something of a reaction had set in. If you look through his diary at his impressions as he crossed the Indian Ocean via Hong Kong and Singapore, he expresses deep resentment that the Chinese, Indians, and other East Asians are being oppressed by the white race.[11]

Critical as he was of the West's Asia policies, on a personal level, Konoe found his five-year stay in Europe to be a happy, productive experience. After a few months of intensive language study in Vienna, he entered law school at Bonn University. His two younger brothers soon followed. Grandfather worried, but offered no objections. Ever eager to travel, Konoe explored Germany and traveled to London and Paris. He made lasting friendships. The kindness of Professor Johann Rein and his family in Bonn prompted a thank you note from grandfather who was kept abreast of Konoe's doings through regular correspondence home. With characteristic thoughtfulness, Konoe made a point of visiting the Reins when he traveled to Germany in an official capacity in 1899. Much later, in 1919, Konoe's son, Fumimaro, in Europe for the Paris Peace Conference, made a special side trip to Bonn to see Rein's widow and his father's old digs. In 1888, Konoe transferred from Bonn to Leipzig University, which awarded him a doctor of law degree in the spring of 1890 for a thesis entitled, "Ministerial Responsibility in the Japanese Constitution." In September he returned to Japan.[12]

Konoe Atsumaro, student at Leipzig University, 1888. (Kudō Takeshige, *Konoe Atsumaro-kō;* Tokyo: Dainichisha zōban, 1938)

The Old Aristocracy in a New Public Role

Konoe at twenty-seven found himself in a unique position to assume the public policy role he eagerly sought. As a prince with impeccable imperial connections, he had access to people at the highest level of government, including the emperor and his closest advisers. The Konoes were the very standard-bearers of imperial tradition. At the same time, as the highest-ranking aristocrat ever to study abroad, the holder of a doctor of law degree from a German university, he was in tune with everything up-to-date and cosmopolitan in Meiji Japan. His hair now closely cropped and parted on one side, sporting a moustache and Western-style suit coat, he looked every bit the modern young man. Konoe's study focus, politics and law, also fit him for a public role in a country poised to introduce representative institutions. When he returned to Japan in the fall of 1890, the country's first bicameral parliament (the Diet), consisting of an elected lower House and an appointed upper House, was about to be convened under the new constitution, the first to be enacted in Asia.

Japanese Imperial Diet Building, 1890s. (George N. Curzon, *Problems of the Far East;* London: Longmans, Green and Co., 1894)

The constitution's principal author, Prime Minister Itō Hirobumi, raised some eyebrows among longtime colleagues by pushing forward young Konoe to join and then become acting head of the new upper House, the House of Peers. But to Itō it seemed a smart political move. No one knew better than he the uncertainties surrounding Japan's experiment in constitutional monarchy: how the two Houses, coequal in their legislative power, would work together, what impact parliamentary politics would have on cabinet dominance which he sought to preserve, and whether upper House members chosen at his recommendation for their talent and independence of mind would be willing to march in lock step with an Itō-directed agenda moving forward. It was in this latter sense that elevating Konoe to a leadership position made strategic sense, a career boost for Konoe in exchange for political loyalty.[13]

But if Itō thought he had a yes-man in Konoe, he was badly mistaken. To Itō's great annoyance, Konoe made it clear from the beginning that he had his own convictions about government and politics. In a speech outlining the constitutional powers of the emperor and his cabinet ministers, Konoe for the first time suggested publicly that Itō as prime minister was hiding behind the throne, so to speak, taking action in the name of the "sacred and inviolable" emperor, as the constitution put it, to avoid responsibility for unpopular political decisions. When Itō invoked the imperial will to dissolve the Diet in 1894, Konoe went so far as to accuse him of failing to understand the function of a bicameral parliament in a constitutional monarchy. His filial feelings for Itō had their limits, he said, when it came to matters of principle.

Konoe was equally forthright and consistent in his refusal to accept offers of cabinet posts or to align himself with any political group. On one occasion, he startled several senior figures trying to persuade him to join their coalition government by launching into a tirade about the current state of Japanese politics. Japan had no real political parties at all, Konoe asserted. There were only personal cliques or factions (*jintō,* he called them) that were constantly fractionalizing, torn by internal struggles for power that had little to do with public policy considerations. Neither these groups nor the cabinets that had come to be associated with them offered a clear, consistent vision of where Japan should be headed. It made no sense, in Konoe's view, to jump into such a political quagmire.[14] He felt he could be far more effective in getting his ideas across—and he had returned from Europe with strong views on Japan's political future—if he operated in an independent fashion from his base in the House of Peers.

The year 1891 was a busy one for Konoe as he began to carve out a role for himself as upper House leader. He issued opinion papers on current government rulings, organized political discussion groups, and helped revise the rules governing the association of fellow nobles known as the Peers Club. In July he was asked to serve as vice-president of a newly formed Asia research group, the Oriental Society (Tōhōkyōkai). In his personal life, too, there were new things happening: the Konoes were expecting their first child. A son, Fumimaro, was born in October. But Konoe's joy was short-lived. His wife, only twenty-three, died eight days after the child was born.

> Overwhelmed by grief at the death of my wife Sawako
> Just seeing my son's smiling face, unaware that his mother is gone, brings tears

> And I stare at the flowers in front of her coffin
> As if through their beauty I could fix in my mind the image of my departed wife.[15]

Just a year later Konoe married Sawako's younger sister, Motoko, with whom he had a daughter and three sons. Fumimaro was of school age before he was told that Motoko was not his real mother, a revelation that shocked and upset him.[16]

For Konoe, just shy of thirty, the demands of public life helped ease any lingering sorrow. He was chosen to sit on the Tokyo City Council. He founded a magazine of public commentary. He sponsored bills in the Diet to fund development of railways and ports in Hokkaidō. Unafraid of controversy, he threw himself in the middle of debates roiling the Diet in 1893 over the issue of treaty reform, revision of the "unequal" treaties imposed on Japan by the foreign powers. Joined by colleagues from both Houses of the Diet, Konoe came out strongly against the government's concessional approach to negotiations. Dismantling the treaties step by step while granting special privileges to various foreign interests along the way, Konoe argued, would do more damage to Japan's economy and sovereign status than extending the treaties in their present form. Japan could only achieve parity in foreign relations by wiping out extraterritorial jurisdiction and foreign control of tariffs without conditions. When an angry Prime Minister Itō responded to this assault on his judgment by dissolving the Diet, Konoe and friends organized a watchdog group to scrutinize the terms of a revised treaty proposed by the British government.[17]

Konoe's all-or-nothing nationalist stance on treaty reform reflected a hardening public view on an issue debated for many years. As Donald Keene says, ". . . treaty reform was of immense psychological importance to most Japanese as it would signify that Japan had been recognized as a modern nation."[18] Yet until the mid-eighties when Konoe went off to study in Europe, most still felt that the burden was on them to show Western diplomats that they deserved equal treaty status, that they were "civilized and enlightened" in institutions and in appearance, too, as they waltzed away their evenings in Western gowns and cutaways to the tunes of Johann Strauss. None other than Itō Hirobumi led the way in what seemed new and fun and good for public relations.

The problem was that however much Japan promoted openness to outside ideas—and, indeed, Meiji Japan was remarkably adaptive and innovative—it never seemed quite enough to convince the powers, most importantly Britain, to back away willingly from a system that worked to their economic advantage. By the time Konoe returned home in 1890 Japan's infatuation with the West had begun to wear thin, replaced by public impatience with lack of progress on equal status negotiations. The highly charged debates in Japan's new parliament, discussions that thoroughly aired all the complexities of treaty revision, served not only to inform the Japanese public but foreign governments as well of the limits and possibilities of any particular proposed solution. Britain finally yielded in 1894, signing an agreement that allowed Japan to regain judicial sovereignty in 1899 and full tariff autonomy in 1911.[19] The new treaty was signed in July 1894. In August Japan declared war on China, the climax of a long simmering dispute over control of the Korean peninsula. Eight months later a victorious Japan concluded a peace treaty with China. In a brief two years, 1894-95, Japan had moved from a nation whose very sovereignty was in question to a possible challenger to European and American dominance in Asia.

Konoe, Head of the House of Peers (front row third from left), pictured with fellow Diet members in1896. (Wikimedia Commons)

Konoe's performance in the parliamentary debates of the early nineties established his reputation as someone who would fight for his principles and speak his mind whatever the consequences. In fact, Konoe's elders in the House of Peers who were so impressed with his social standing and foreign education that they had overlooked his youth, now found that they had in their midst an outspoken critic of some of their own titled members. Japan's new nobility, Konoe complained, was not contributing as it should to the good of the nation. Everyone wanted the special titles and perks awarded under the 1884 Peerage Act without realizing that rank carried with it certain obligations. "The simple fact is that members of the nobility, given the wealth and high social position most of them enjoy, ought to cultivate a keen sense of morality and improve their character and conduct. They ought to take upon themselves the responsibility of constantly safeguarding the Imperial House and devote themselves wholeheartedly to the state."[20]

As Konoe saw it, specialized training was the key to developing the kind of European-style, public-spirited nobility he had in mind, people equipped with "a greater measure of creative thinking and mental discipline" than ordinary citizens who were necessarily "caught up with mundane worries about making a living."[21] Konoe made his debut as an educator in the spring of 1895 when he accepted the job of president of the Peers School (Gakushūin, forerunner of the present Gakushūin University), the elite school for sons of the nobility established a decade before the Restoration, now expanded to accommodate offspring of the new peerage. Determined to give this next generation of titled and well-to-do better preparation for their responsibilities, he put students in dormitories to improve discipline, established a college-level curriculum, and introduced a new foreign-service track to train diplomats to serve in Europe. Sociology, Western diplomatic history, law, and foreign languages were added to the curriculum, while Japanese and Chinese philosophy and literature were cut. For a school noted for producing military leaders, the emphasis on civilian service and modern subjects was something new.[22]

Equally so was Konoe's argument that diplomacy—"peaceful national defense," as he called it—should ideally be the exclusive domain of men of high rank because they alone had the financial independence to ignore the pressures of special interest politics. No matter how well educated, anyone working in government who had to depend for a living on his official salary was, in Konoe's words, "but one step from the ordinary worker. It is probably too much to expect such people to perform genuine public service."[23] One must not read too much into this single statement, a mix of idealism and elitism, but certainly Konoe's convictions about the importance of disinterested service remained dominant in his thinking throughout his own career. It was shared heartily by other Meiji leaders in other fields. Shibusawa Eiichi, pioneer industrialist, later made viscount, cast his vast accomplishments entirely in terms of service to the state and the public good.[24]

It was in April 1895, just a month after Konoe took up his post at the Peers School, that Japan signed its peace treaty with China. Konoe makes little reference in his diary to the conclusion of this popular war that gained Japan its first colony, Taiwan, along with a sizeable indemnity, and MFN (Most Favored Nation) rights in China. Granted he was busy with development of the Peers School, a project he took very seriously. But a more likely reason for his restrained reaction, a contrast to the triumphalism of many of his colleagues, is that he shared the emperor's view of the war with China: regret that Japan had gone to war with its near neighbor in the first place and hope that future ties would be stronger than ever. Viewed thus in sober terms, Konoe could see but one positive lesson to come out of the conflict. It illustrated starkly the benefits of developing a first-rate educational system. China lost, Konoe said, because its illiterate, demoralized troops were no match for Japan's highly motivated, well-trained Imperial Army. Military requirements aside, he hammered home the point that Japan's entire industrial growth program and visions of future prosperity depended on the ability of its schools to produce quality products. Funding for public education should top the national agenda. "Everyone needs to get an education, nobility and commoners alike; I see no difference at all between them," he said. At the end of 1895, Konoe sponsored a bill in the Diet to use a portion of the China indemnity to finance public primary schools. The bill, which earmarked 10 percent of the funds to provide 2,000 yen for every primary school in the country, passed easily in early 1896.[25]

Women's Education: Training "Good Wives, Wise Mothers"

As head of the House of Peers for five years Konoe had engaged in some key issues and achieved a degree of influence, but it was only in the years after the Sino-Japanese War that he began to make his mark in two critical areas, education and foreign policy. The war put education in the spotlight. The press touted Japan's victory over China, a surprise to the world, as a triumph of civilization over backwardness, confirmation that a better-trained and educated population held the advantage when it came to projecting national power. Indeed, the government's 1872 landmark decision to construct a nationwide school system from the ground up had produced some remarkable results: 75 percent of school age boys and 40 percent of girls enrolled in four years of compulsory schooling in 1893, figures comparable to those in Europe and America.[26] And Japan's comparative advantage was not simply a matter of numbers of students studying modern subjects. As Konoe and others pointed out, it was also tied to motivation. Conscious government decisions in the 1890s to redefine the purpose of a modern education, dropping the insistence on following American and French models and reemphasizing Japanese Confucian ideals, meant that youngsters were being trained to be not just good citizens but good *Japanese* citizens, loyal contributors to an emperor-centered state.

If, however, as postwar Japanese agreed, Japan was on the right track in education, there was still much left to be done both in quantitative and qualitative terms to prepare the manpower necessary to foster industrial growth. Expanding educational opportunities took on new urgency. The most pressing issue was what to do about women, half the population but still representing just a third of overall primary school enrollments and 10-15 percent at the secondary level. Only a tiny percentage of young women went on to normal school or any other higher-level training.[27]

Konoe had in effect announced his interest in getting involved in education in a hands-on way when he accepted the Peers School headship and drafted the school subsidy bill. And he, with his high visibility, energy and cosmopolitan outlook, was a natural magnet for educators with innovative ideas. In 1896 he was approached by Naruse Jinzō, an ordained Christian minister known for his progressive views on women's education, with a proposal to establish Japan's first private women's college. Naruse had spent three years in the United States studying theology and pedagogy, returning to Japan just before the war to become principal of a church-supported secondary school for women in Osaka. Naruse had caught public attention—and no doubt Konoe's—with a book published early in the year promoting women's higher education on the grounds that it was good for women and good for the nation. Konoe was immediately supportive of the college project. He conferred frequently with Naruse over the next few years, often several times a month, served on the planning committee for Japan Women's University (Nihon Joshi Daigaku) which opened in 1901, and spoke out vigorously on the need to expand educational opportunities for women.[28]

The idea of emancipating women through education did not in any sense for Konoe or for Naruse signal support for political rights for women, which was hardly surprising. Women were still excluded from the voting rolls in England and America, where electoral systems had been operating for decades; their suffragist efforts gained them the right to vote only after World War I. When Naruse talked, as he often did, about the need "to educate women as human beings, as women, and as members of the community," he made it clear that "we are not working for any so-called women's rights, but for women's consciousness of her worth and responsibilities."[29] Where a woman was worth a great deal, in his view, was in the home, as a well-educated, competent homemaker capable of guiding the next generation of citizens. Konoe agreed. He had learned from his experience at the Peers School, he said, how important the home environment was in molding the character of young students, and the principal influence in the home was the mother. He may also have been speaking as the parent of young children when he observed: "There's truth in the old saying that 'a wise mother brings up a gifted child'."[30]

Konoe and Naruse were typical spokesmen for "good wives, wise mothers" (*ryōsai kenbo)* thinking, the educational ideal then in vogue among mainstream Meiji educators. Like most buzzwords, "good wives, wise mothers" meant different things to different people and was often referred to without precise definition, the way we might now talk about "family values." But the term was based on certain common assumptions: that it was possible and desirable to establish a standard of womanhood for the new Japan, that this model woman had a productive role to play in national development, and that essential female traits—of the "good" and "wise," at least—were discipline, loyalty, and a willingness to be the backstop on the home front to men acting in the public sphere. At the time, this notion had resonance elsewhere. Theodore Roosevelt was not far off when he declared in a speech in 1901: "Throughout our history the success of the home-maker has been but another name for the up-building of the nation."[31]

As Konoe was meeting with Naruse, he was also in contact with a woman who wrote the classic text for "good wives, wise mothers," Shimoda Utako (1854-1936). Nine years Konoe's senior, Shimoda was a formidable figure: scholarly, self-assured, ambitious, not as high born as Konoe but definitely upper class. In a society freed from old constraints, Shimoda had moved easily from her position as tutor to children of the imperial family in the 1870s into elite social circles in the 1880s, becoming a regular at the fancy dress balls sponsored by Itō Hirobumi with whom she was romantically linked. In 1886, with Itō's backing, Shimoda was named dean of a new women's division of the Peers School. Her idea was to provide upper class girls with a basic, modern education as preparation for middle school where they would be expected to set a high standard of performance for the rest of female society.[32]

Running this elite school attended by imperial princesses and daughters of the rich and powerful was a prestigious job. Shimoda was promoted to senior imperial rank and paid the handsome annual salary of 1,800 yen, about twenty times that of the average teacher. Still, she felt she had more to offer. She had her sights on the much larger arena of public education where Meiji gender-inclusive policies seemed to open up limitless possibilities for female educational advancement.

But as an advocate of women's education for a new era, Shimoda was increasingly concerned that she lacked the right credentials. Her own education was almost entirely classical. She had been born twenty years too early to take advantage of the new public schools. A few lessons in French and English and exposure to foreign influences in the capital hardly equipped her to understand current world trends in school development. She took her arguments to the Imperial Household Ministry, which in 1893 obliged by allocating 6,000 yen for her to take a year-long study trip to Europe and the United States, specifically to examine Western models of education for upper-class girls. Shimoda was not the first Japanese woman to study abroad. A handful of much younger women preceded her. But she was the first to go abroad for what we would now call mid-career training. For a woman of her age (thirty-nine), social position, and professional level taking this step was unprecedented. In the end, her year abroad was extended to two, spent mostly in England, and the experience gave her the confidence to become not just a school headmistress, but a real educator, a spokesperson for a new, Japanese/Asian style of women's education.

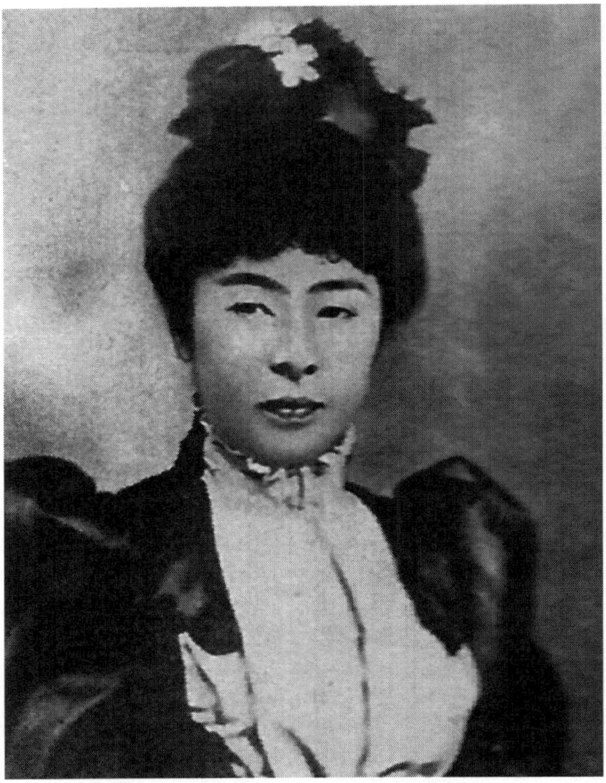

Shimoda Utako, dean of the women's division of the Peers School, 1886. (*Shimoda Utako sensei den;* Tokyo: Ko Shimoda Kōchō sensei denki hensanjo, 1943)

Among Britain's privileged classes were some of the most emancipated women—socially, economically, and politically—in the world in the 1890s. Shimoda was struck by the extent to which female opinion mattered in British politics, however much policymaking itself remained a male domain. Even the cleverest politician could not get his way on policy without taking women's interests into account, she said. British women, she added caustically, tended to look down on a country like Japan where women were regarded as servants.

What Shimoda wanted to understand, what seemed relevant to the Japanese case, was how the typical upper-class Victorian woman managed to have her independent voice yet retain a kind of traditional femininity as the mainstay of the household. What she found was that the model wife and mother was no mere ornament in the house, as Naruse put it. She was a semi-professional, a household manager responsible for everything from family finances to moral education to general health and welfare. Her education prepared her for this role by providing a standard set of skills under a new curriculum labeled domestic science or home economics. And the role was not personally limiting. At the forefront of training the next generation of youngsters to be proudly British, society viewed her as a key element in what Roosevelt called, "the up-building of the nation." "The hand that rocks the cradle moves the world," Shimoda chimed in, using a nice bit of imagery.[33]

Even if Shimoda had done nothing more than target elite women with home economics courses and textbooks as she did after her return to Japan in 1895 she would have merited a place in the history of Japanese feminism. As tame as it might seem now—and did to some in Japan by the 1910s—professionalizing a woman's work in the home was in its time and place an innovative idea. Furthermore, it had the harmonizing quality of what Eric Hobsbawm calls "the invention of tradition," because it was grounded in the old notion of domain specialization where home was the accepted focus of female concerns. In fact, however, Shimoda returned to Japan with more on her mind than home economics for Peeresses students. She had new views on the value of physical education courses, the benefits of "sound minds, sound bodies" then in vogue in the West. More important, her eyes had been opened to a fundamental benefit of general education in Western countries, the link between a trained female labor force and successful industrial development. Finally, she came away with an appreciation of how Victorian women got their points across, not by being stay-at-homes but through mobilizing women to present their views in public forums.

The Imperial Women's Association (Teikoku fujin kyōkai), which Shimoda founded in November 1898, represented a new type of organization for Meiji Japan, a female-led public interest group formed to focus attention on women's issues in education. This is not to imply that there was anything anti-establishment about it or even, strictly speaking, feminist. Quite to the contrary, at the top of the agenda was an effort to develop a modern curriculum that was both gender-specific and Japanese/Asian-specific and to extend this model to schooling for girls from lower income families. Shimoda's chief backers in getting the group going were her male friends at the very center of the power elite, including, most notably, Konoe Atsumaro and Itō

Hirobumi whose wives were both association members. In other words, though Shimoda's activist, outspoken style and consciousness-raising approach were innovative, the Imperial Women's Association was essentially pushing a mainstream modernizing agenda quite in keeping with the goals of the Meiji state.[34]

Konoe records in his diary some dozen meetings and communications with Shimoda over the next few years. On at least one occasion, he helped her resolve a personnel dispute within the Association. They met informally as well at events at the Gakushūin. Konoe was a good resource. As a member of the high nobility, he had the clout to get things done and the confidence to do so diplomatically. Moreover, while he railed against the special interest politics of politicians in the Diet, he was an enthusiastic supporter of special interest organizations outside the Diet, seeing them as instruments to both shape and respond to broader public opinion. With eligible voters, all male, at only 1.14 percent of a population of nearly 40 million, he may have had a valid point about creating a channel for public opinion, though hardly an acceptable solution to those calling for an expanded electorate.[35]

The Politics of Educational Policy

Endorsing Shimoda's brand of female activism was the easy part. When Minister of Education Saionji Kinmochi, Konoe's old friend from Austria days, announced his education plan for 1895, he stated unequivocally the government's intention to prioritize women's education. Though Lafcadio Hearn, longtime foreign resident in Japan, might have been right when he declared that the general public was not yet comfortable with the reality of women working outside the home, few doubted that as a practical matter expanding the trained female work force was a national need. Certainly those at the decision-making level in postwar Japan were quite in accord with Saionji's view that "the higher the degree of civilization, the higher the position of women is."[36]

On the other hand, Saionji's blunt message to educators and school administrators that science teaching should take precedence over morals education and foreign languages over Japanese was greeted with surprise, even dismay in some quarters. It stoked a long-simmering debate over a very fundamental issue, the purpose of a modern Japanese education. Was it, as Saionji saw it, to produce scientifically minded, independent thinkers, contributors to world knowledge who also happened to be Japanese? Or was it more narrowly nationalist to create citizens loyal to the Japanese imperial tradition who were also equipped with advanced, scientific knowledge? And who was to decide this: local education officials, teachers, foreign-trained educators, school administrators, bureaucrats in Tokyo?[37]

Although these positions were not antithetical and Konoe was new to pedagogy, his heart was with Saionji's more internationalist outlook. Certainly at the practical level he did his job to encourage unified support for the Saionji agenda when he agreed to mediate a longstanding dispute between the nation's leading teachers organizations, the All-Japan Education Association (DaiNihon Kyōiku Kai) headed by Tsuji Shinji, one of the drafters of the original 1872 plan for universal education, and the State Education Society (Kokka Kyōiku-sha) under U.S.-trained specialist in teacher education, Isawa Shūji. Both Tsuji and Isawa were highly respected, influential educators, regarded as open-minded and adaptive in their approach to teaching methodology. Both had spent their careers in and out of Ministry of Education jobs, first during the 1870s when American educators were hired to work in Japan, but also continuing into the 1880s and '90s as the foreign-hires began to leave and photographs of the emperor put up in every classroom signaled the turn toward a more tradition-centered curriculum. Tsuji and Isawa were not afraid to criticize the Ministry of Education or a particular minister and often did, but theirs was by no means an adversarial relationship with education authorities. Nor did they differ with each other on substantive grounds, which is why Isawa felt comfortable proposing that they join forces in the first place. Friction quickly developed, however, over questions of transfer of assets, annual dues, organizational structure and executive titles, and it was at this point that Konoe was brought in to try to work out a compromise.[38]

For the most part Konoe met with the two elderly educators separately and perhaps with good reason. Joint sessions were contentious with members stalking out, having to be coaxed to return to the table. With all the headaches and time it was taking, Konoe appeared to wonder why he had taken on the task of mediator. Still, the urgency of putting the combined weight of the educational establishment behind Saionji's school expansion policies was a convincing argument for them and for him. Late in December 1896 Konoe records the first meeting of the new Imperial Japan Education Association. Early in the New Year he agrees to act as interim chairman. It was rumored that he himself would become the next Minister of Education; he found this amusing.[39]

Konoe was soon to turn thirty-four. He was regarded as a rising political star. He had the obvious advantage of birth and connections, but beyond this he was well liked, known for being principled and fair-minded, an effective consensus-builder. For him personally, working with Japan's top educators, frustrating as it was in the context of the merger, was a good learning experience, an introduction to educational technology relevant to his new job as head of the Peers School. From Isawa Shūji, just back from a tour as Japan's Education Director in Taiwan, he heard about the challenges of providing a Japanese education to Japan's new colonial subjects. He discussed with Isawa the problems of oversight of Japan's Christian-affiliated schools and was introduced to some of Isawa's American colleagues such as the celebrated art historian Ernest Fenollosa. Tsuji Shinji was less prominent on Konoe's schedule; he resigned his position as head of the All-Japan Teachers Association midway through the talks. But this gave Konoe the chance to work with his replacement, the highly experienced and high-energy President of Tokyo Teachers College Kanō Jigorō.[40] Conversations with people like Kanō, Tsuji, and Isawa proved an eye-opener for Konoe, not only on pedagogical questions but on the enormous number and complexity of choices the nation faced in its efforts to develop a world-class educational system. At the same time, Konoe, like many Japanese after the Sino-Japanese War, was becoming increasingly convinced that, however incomplete, Japan's development model including Japanese adaptations of concepts of modern schooling, held greater relevance for Japan's Asian neighbors than all the pure Western alternatives available. Of all the educators in Konoe's widening circle of contacts, no one was more passionate and engaged on this point than Kanō Jigorō.

Kanō was an on-stage personality, a longtime favorite of the press, certainly known to Konoe by reputation for years before their actual meeting. As a student at Tokyo University in the early 1880s, Kanō had created a stir by creating a new—or rather a new-old since it had traditional roots—sport, Kōdōkan judo. When the Police Bureau incorporated judo into its training regimen in the mid-'80s the sport attracted broader public notice, a home-grown competitor to baseball then becoming all the rage.[41] And Kanō's personal stock went up with tales of his own physical prowess. Sounding remarkably like an eyewitness account, a press report from 1891 describes a wrestling match that had taken place a few years earlier between Kanō and a Russian passenger aboard a ship bound for Japan from Europe.

> The two men readied themselves and calmly entered the ring. The spectators, who until that very moment had been extremely noisy, quieted down as if they were watching water about to boil, their eyes transfixed, their mouths dry. At this point, both men sparred evenly. But when the conceited, arrogant Russian extended his long arms and lunged forward with the force of an enraged lion to grab the little Japanese in one motion, Kanō, with a yell, made as if to thrust him into the sea. At just the right moment, gripping the Russian's left shoulder with his left hand and twisting his body to the left, Kanō managed somehow to bear the weight of the great, fat Russian and, remarkably, to flip him over.[42]

Kanō Jigorō, founder of Kōdōkan judo, in his later role as Olympics promoter. (Yokoyama Kendō, *Kanō sensei den;* Tokyo: Oda Nobutada, 1941)

The David versus Goliath story no doubt delighted readers, particularly as it involved a Russian when Russia was viewed with growing distrust. But the punch line was yet to come. Kanō, the report went on, showed his "high principled nature" by extending a hand to the defeated challenger, helping him up, and brushing off his clothes. "The name Kanō is synonymous with the name Japan: though small in stature, both have gained a reputation for fighting spirit, nobility of soul and excellence."[43]

As a fellow wrestling enthusiast, Konoe could appreciate the sports reputation of Kanō Jigorō, who eventually achieved fame worldwide for securing for Japan and Kōdōkan judo a place in the Olympic Games. This is how Kanō is remembered now. In 1890s Japan, however, he was known not only as an enthusiastic judo promoter but more broadly as an educator who brought energy and expertise to the task of developing new schools for a new Japan. His parents had inspired him to seek a life of public service, he later explained, and he was by his own account a born teacher. "For me teaching things to people has been one of my joys." As he saw it, building a first-class education system was the single most important task of the Meiji government.[44]

When Kanō graduated from Tokyo University in 1882 with a politics and finance degree, the Ministry of Finance had expected to welcome a new recruit. Instead, he followed his heart, accepting a teaching post at the Peers School, a two-year grant to study pedagogy in Europe, then a succession of jobs as school principal. Like Isawa and Tsuji, he did advisory work for the Ministry of Education from time to time but rejected the idea of a permanent position. He much preferred classroom teaching or running a school. His dream job came up in 1893 when he was named president of Tokyo Teachers College,[45] the institution that set the standard for future teachers of Japan. It was a big job with the scope for input into all aspects of general public education, including physical education and schooling for women. Kanō taught the judo classes at the college himself. When asked by the government to help plan a nationwide system of secondary schools for girls, he consulted with Shimoda Utako, one of the big names in women's education and also one of his private students in judo.[46]

Late in 1896 as he was meeting regularly with Konoe, Kanō was in the early stages of an entirely new project. The Chinese and Japanese governments, only a year after signing their peace treaty, had agreed to launch the first-ever study-in-Japan program for Chinese students. Kanō Jigorō was put in charge. In April he had welcomed into a special three-year course he had organized at the Teachers College the first contingent of thirteen Chinese, as foreign looking a group with their queues and long gowns as any Westerners in Tokyo. Within ten years and with continued input on his part, the program had swelled to 10,000, at the time the largest study abroad program anywhere in the world.[47]

Asia for the Asians

To Konoe, hosting Chinese students was a welcome first step, but it needed to be placed within an entirely new framework of thinking about China and the rest of Asia. Writing in the January 1898 issue of the influential monthly, *The Sun* (Taiyō), he challenged the Tokyo government to articulate a new foreign policy for a new era, a policy with long-term strategic goals suited to Japan's postwar status as the most advanced country in the region. His experience in Europe, which in fact had made him what he was, had evidently left him with lingering doubts about the extent of Western good will toward Japan and the Japanese. He felt that Japan's policymakers, fixated as they were on Western alliances, were naïve in failing to appreciate the reality that East and West were on a collision course with race a central issue. "As I see it, East Asia in the future will inevitably be the stage for racial struggle. Though there may be fluctuations based on foreign policies of the moment, these will simply be temporary. East Asia is ultimately destined to face a racial struggle between the yellow and white races, in the course of which both the Chinese and the Japanese will be regarded as the bitter enemies of the white race."[48]

To prepare for this eventuality, Konoe called on the Tokyo government to disengage from its current Euro-centered foreign policy and to focus instead on forging a strategic relationship with its natural ally, China. He urged that this shift take place immediately while Japan's victory over China still reverberated in world capitals and Western expansionists were caught short as to how to respond to the "formidability of the yellow race." Once Western nations woke up to the fact that it would not be as easy to colonize East Asia as Africa and other parts of the world, they would strengthen Western bloc alliances to keep up the pressure, further sharpening East/West racial tensions. Now was the time to approach China, too, as the shock of defeat had changed some minds about the need to step up the pace of reform and turn to Japan for aid. He allowed that some in China's central government remained stubbornly wedded to an isolationist view but insisted that reform-minded provincial governors like Zhang Zhidong saw their best interests in improved ties with Japan.[49]

We must think in a hundred-year time frame, Konoe urged his fellow Japanese, and develop a corps of China experts to match the number of Europeanists now directing Japan's affairs. He worried that far from reaching out to the Chinese, Japanese were becoming as overbearing as the Europeans:

> Because of their imposing victory in the Sino-Japanese War, Japanese of late have grown increasingly arrogant and ever more extreme in their contempt for the Chinese. Japanese resident in China, in particular, take the same kind of attitude toward the Chinese as the Europeans do, it seems to me, viewing Japan as the only civilized nation in Asia, more advanced than China. In building modern systems and carrying out modern education, Japan really is ahead of China, so using civilization in this sense to guide the Chinese and establish these things is very appropriate. But solely on the basis of advanced nation status being offensively boastful and treating the Chinese with scorn and abuse serves instead to bring on ill feelings. This kind of behavior is not only unworthy of an advanced nation, but, also, how can it do anything other than seriously damage the conduct of China policy and leave a black mark on the future?[50]

Konoe was correct in reading the trend toward European collusion in extracting rights and concessions from China. The year 1898 proved to be, as one contemporary British observer put it, the "great leasing year" when Port Arthur became Russian, Qingdao German, Guangzhou Bay French, and Weihaiwei and the New Territories British. Summing up his father's Asia views some thirty years later, Fumimaro commented: "He felt that, as the European powers relentlessly pushed into Asia, Japan should guide China and, working together, secure China's territorial integrity. This is the kernel idea behind the Greater East Asia doctrine, I would say."[51]

Konoe's *Taiyō* article was more than a simple opinion piece. It was an announcement from Konoe the politician that he intended to get involved in shaping Asia policy. He was not angling for an executive appointment, however. As a man of independent means and ideas, he judged he would have greater impact if he acted outside government, unimpeded by the political deal making that attended formation of every new cabinet. Predictably, when an invitation to join the inner circle came from the new prime minister, Ōkuma Shigenobu, in June of 1898, he found polite ways to decline. He turned a deaf ear also to increasing mention in the press of his own name as an ideal—incorruptible was the image—candidate for prime minister.[52]

For someone who wanted to enlarge the scope of his influence, Konoe had the best of both worlds. He could claim the outsider's freedom of action while retaining the advantage of the ultimate insider, easy access to anyone at any level of government and elite society. The Konoe name opened doors. In the case of Naruse's college project, Shimoda's Imperial Women's Organization, and the feuding teachers unions Konoe was content to play a supporting role: endorsing the effort, acting as patron, and prodding people toward agreement. When it came to foreign policy, however, he took the lead in bringing together a disparate group of journalists, businessmen, party politicians, and members of the House of Peers who shared his conviction that Japan should redirect its attention to Asia. Many of these people had been active for years in small China/Asia research and business promotion groups. Konoe himself had served as vice-president of the Oriental Society in the early 1890s. In the postwar atmosphere of confidence about the Japan model, it was not difficult to convince these groups that it made sense to join forces to bring China into the twentieth century and open it up to Japanese investment. In July 1898 Konoe and his colleagues founded the Common Culture Society (Dōbunkai) to strengthen bilateral ties, promote greater understanding of China in Japan, and coordinate Japanese business, newspaper, and education projects in China. Konoe agreed to serve as president.[53]

The very name of the new organization indicated a shift in thinking. Previous Asia groups emphasized location—Asia, the Orient and the like. *Dōbun*, "common culture," on the other hand, was qualitative, evocative. Shorthand for "same culture/same race" (dōbun/dōshu), it gave voice to a notion increasingly appealing to postwar Japanese that a China-Japan partnership had something unique to justify it beyond the usual realpolitik. Like Winston Churchill's invocation of the "special relationship" between Britain and America, Konoe's emphasis on *dōbun* put history, language, race—civilization, in other words—at the forefront of what it took to create a successful alliance. To Konoe the same-culture approach also implied reaching out to the Chinese people more broadly, not the political leadership alone. Japanese should not ascribe to the Chinese people the faults of their corrupt politicians, he said. What Konoe was proposing, in a nutshell, was to employ what we now call "soft power" in service of promoting Asian solidarity against the West. It was an "us versus them" mentality, Asia for the Asians.[54]

The appearance of the Dōbunkai was perfectly timed. In June 1898 a powerful reform faction backed by the young Qing emperor had seized control of China's central government. Based on a blueprint long in preparation, the reformers were now moving rapidly ahead to overhaul the very foundations of China's governing system along the lines suggested by Meij Japanese models. It seemed a unique moment to strengthen bilateral relations. Prime Minister Ōkuma responded with a pledge of Japanese assistance.

In late summer, Konoe was again approached by Ōkuma people about his possible interest in an official job, this time a diplomatic posting. How would he like to be ambassador to Germany and Austria? Konoe's reaction was lukewarm. Word got back to the emperor that Konoe was reluctant to accept for family reasons. Embarrassed and annoyed, Konoe issued an emphatic denial. It was not personal matters at all, he said, but his responsibility for the Peers School reform agenda that made him hesitate.[55] But, in fact, it had been a difficult year for the Konoe family. Konoe's beloved grandfather who on his ninetieth birthday in August 1897 still had the will to struggle from his sick bed to acknowledge imperial gifts, developed serious heart problems the following March and died within a week. Konoe, at his side to the end, was heartbroken. In a message to his students at the Peers School, he made special mention of the jade piece and farewell poem his grandfather had given him on the eve of his departure for Europe. Bring a smile to the old man's face in the world beyond, Konoe urged them, by studying hard and remembering him with affection.[56]

Konoe was, in fact, interested in an overseas assignment, but on his own terms. Of course, he assured a senior official, he was willing to take the original assignment at a moment's notice should that be the emperor's wish. But to be frank, he said, what he had in mind was a broader brief than the posting to Germany, preferably, a special appointment to visit a number of countries worldwide.[57] He also wanted to make certain that after his tour abroad he could count on returning to the House of Peers and the Peers School. Polite reference to the emperor's wishes aside, Konoe made it plain that he intended to shape the assignment to his advantage no matter what delays might occur in working out the scope and financing for the trip. But by late September, events in China had taken center stage and it was clear that his departure would be postponed in any case.

China's reform movement had failed. In a sudden military coup on September 21, 1898, China's empress dowager and her conservative supporters ousted the reformers, executed those they could lay their hands on, and put the young emperor who had backed them under virtual house arrest. Reform leader Kang Youwei and his junior colleague, Liang Qichao, escaped to Japan where they hoped to gain permanent asylum. Through their Japanese contacts in the Dōbunkai, Kang and Liang appealed to Konoe for assistance. The Japanese government which, like the other foreign powers, chose to conduct business as usual in China turned to Konoe to deal with the Chinese dissidents without giving offense to the new leadership in Beijing.

By mid-October, Konoe and his Dōbunkai colleagues had developed a tentative position regarding Kang and Liang: both must be given asylum status as international law required, but Kang, who had initially sought refuge in British-held Hong Kong, would be encouraged to move on either to England or the United States. As they were discussing the specifics of the Kang/Liang case, Dōbunkai people were also trying to generate the necessary funding to pursue the commercial and cultural projects on their agenda in a meaningful way. In early November, the group merged with yet another small Asia society to form the Tō-A Dōbunkai (East Asia Common Culture Association), its membership now broad and diverse enough to attract a grant through a Foreign Ministry discretionary fund. The largest private contributor to Tō-A Dōbunkai activities was Konoe Atsumaro, the organization's new president.[58]

To describe the Tō-A Dōbunkai as a nongovernmental organization is perhaps not entirely accurate since it had definite reporting responsibilities to Japan's Foreign Ministry over the forty-six years of its operations as well as a mission to further the government's foreign policy agenda in China. On the other hand, one could say something of the same in terms of funding, overseas offices, and political aims of the current U.S.-based Asia Foundation. With respect to Chinese politics, the new East Asia group refrained from overt backing of any particular person or faction. In fact, its membership covered a broad spectrum of views on the problem of reform in China from those backing the go-slow pace of the central government to supporters of the Kang/Liang version of regime change to Japanese friends of the revolutionary Sun Yatsen. It was Konoe who urged consensus around the very general goal of helping to improve (*kaizen*) conditions in China; this is what appeared in the official platform along with a commitment to maintaining China's territorial integrity (*Shina hozen*) and noninterference in China's political affairs.[59]

Konoe Atsumaro, front row center, with Tō-A Dōbunkai colleagues, probably in Tokyo around 1900. (Wikimedia Commons)

Konoe and Kang Youwei met for the first time the evening of November 12 at Konoe's residence. There was no question in Konoe's mind how Beijing would view this meeting with China's leading dissident. Kang was a wanted man; the Chinese authorities had executed his younger brother at the end of September for his part in the reform movement. At the same time, Konoe felt it could be useful to talk with Kang. Reportedly, the situation in China was fluid and Kang might have more support among China's local officials than was immediately apparent. Some of these people were pro-Japanese. Konoe was also well aware that providing safe haven to Kang and Liang in accordance with international law would be viewed positively in the eyes of the foreign community.[60]

With a Tō-A Dōbunkai member acting as interpreter, Konoe began the meeting with a few polite inquiries about Kang's well-being, then got down to business, describing for Kang the outlines of his Asia for the Asians policy. Faced with Western territorial designs on the region, Asians must develop cooperative relationships. What did Kang think of an Asian version of America's Monroe Doctrine, Konoe asked? But Kang was more interested in domestic politics than regional defense policy. He respected Konoe's opinion, he said, but his top priority as a Chinese was how to engineer the return to power of the emperor and the reform faction, and for that task, Japanese assistance was essential. Konoe avoided the assistance issue, commenting instead that when he had first heard about the reform movement his reaction was mixed: he felt heartened that changes were in the works but worried that China was moving too fast. China should consider a gradualist approach to reform. "Our Meiji Restoration was not accomplished in the two or three years before 1868," he said. "It was a long time coming. It required perseverance and sacrifice. Compared to our Meiji reforms, I think it's quite fair to say that what's happened in China recently is just the beginning phase."[61]

Kang was not interested in the broad sweep. He countered with a detailed analysis of the September coup. Konoe, well briefed on this already, listened as long as he could stand it then interjected a pointed question about South China. If the reported unrest among local leaders in the south were to develop into a successful movement to oust the empress dowager's faction, he asked, would those same people necessarily want to see the emperor restored to power? The gist of his question, Konoe explained later in a footnote to his write-up of the meeting, was whether a republic might be one of the political alternatives. If Kang got the implication, he chose to ignore it. The emperor, he insisted, was essential to the success of any reform program and, with Japanese aid, he could regain authority. "Should this happen, we Chinese would never forget your generous help." Konoe was ready for the meeting to end. Japan could not afford to get involved without sounding out the position of the other foreign powers, he responded. But he offered to put Kang in touch with five or six other Japanese knowledgeable about China affairs.[62]

Konoe was also willing to listen to a plea on Kang's behalf from Liang Qichao in a meeting two weeks later. But the decision had already been made. As he said to two Chinese visitors to the Peers School, Sino-Japanese formal exchanges, including his own planned trip to China, would be jeopardized by Kang's continued presence in Japan. Over the next few months, Konoe worked with the Foreign Ministry to arrange for political asylum for Kang in Canada. Liang was warned to tone down his anti-Qing rhetoric, but allowed to stay in Japan. Konoe tried to keep all sides happy. In February, he even arranged for Kang and Liang to sit in on a session of the House of Peers. By mid-March Kang's departure date had been set, the Japanese legation in Vancouver alerted to his arrival, and funds from the Foreign Ministry to cover the trip passed on to him by Konoe. On March 21, Kang paid a courtesy call to Konoe to thank him for efforts on his behalf. The next day he was on a ship bound for Canada. Official China appeared satisfied. Proof of this was that the powerful governor-general Zhang Zhidong enrolled his grandson in the Peers School for the spring semester.[63]

Taking Measure of the World

On April 1, 1899, Konoe himself set sail for North America, the start of an eight-month trip around the world, his first trip abroad as head of the House of Peers and, in fact, his first time away from Japan since his student days. He had a grand sendoff. When he and his wife Motoko and eldest son Fumimaro arrived at Shimbashi station to catch the morning train to Yokohama, four or five hundred people were waiting there to say goodbye—the prime minister, the Imperial Household minister, students from the Peers School. A crowd of hundred or so joined the Konoes at Yokohama for a final round of toasts in the NYK (Nippon Yūsen Kaisha) departure lounge. Here Konoe said his farewells to Motoko and Fumimaro. Fifty of his closest friends then accompanied him on the steam launch that took him to the ship.[64]

The last time Konoe left Japan, fourteen years before, the ship had hugged the China coast making its way around South Asia through the Suez Canal to Europe. This time the route was straight across the Pacific with the first stop Hawaii, "a tiny little island," Konoe noted, but "a very important place commercially and militarily. In the future, once the Nicaragua canal is cut through and the Siberia railway completed, its value will be considerably increased."[65] Hawaii was very much on Japanese minds in the 1890s as the Americans crushed Queen Liliuokalani's "Hawaii for the Hawaiians" movement and called for annexation. Japanese may not have heard the current hit tune in Washington, "Come, Liliu-o-kalani/ Give Uncle Sam/ Your little yellow hannie . . . ," but they were well aware of the sentiments of the U.S. expansionist lobby whose biggest proponent was the assistant secretary for the Navy, Theodore Roosevelt. When the Japanese protested the annexation treaty of 1897, Roosevelt proclaimed, "The United States is not in a position which requires her to ask Japan, or any other foreign Power, what territory it shall or shall not acquire."[66]

Konoe Atsumaro at the time of his second trip abroad, 1899. (Kudō Takeshige, *Konoe Atsumaro-kō*; Tokyo: Dainichi zōban, 1938)

Western empire-building in Asia—what the Japanese termed, "Western power advancing Eastward" (*seiryoku tōzen*)—was precisely what worried Konoe. He found it particularly ominous that the United States, which had become increasingly interventionist in the Americas, now had its sights on the Pacific.

> America abandoned the Monroe Doctrine, the basic policy on which the country was founded, seized Hawaii, and has gradually expanded its power in the Pacific. British power is entrenched like a huge rock. Russia also is not

> to be underestimated. Imperial Japan alone occupies a position of advantage without realizing it and, worse still, has no power. Only tens of thousands of Japanese migrants follow along to cultivate Hawaii. I wonder which country will really be dominant in the Pacific in the future, and also, what will be the real future of this central point, Hawaii?[67]

For all of his concerns about American expansionism, Konoe did not use his U.S. trip to talk to Americans about their Asia policies. The plan was simply to see the country, and that he did on the long train ride from the West Coast across mountain and prairie to Chicago, then on to Washington, Philadelphia, New York, and Boston. All of this was accomplished in two weeks, which meant that each stopover was a mere two or three days of intensive socializing with resident Japanese, filling up on Japanese food, and seeing the city sights. In Chicago, it was the stockyards, the city library, and Marshall Fields (a scheduled meeting with reporters might have been a diversion, but Konoe, feeling ill after four days on the train, chose to cancel); in Washington, the Capitol building, the Library of Congress, and the Washington Monument; in New York City, Wall Street, Central Park, and Delmonico's Restaurant. Konoe met with the presidents of Columbia—where he had an extensive campus tour—and Harvard, but, other than that, there were no high-level meetings, and, in fact, little interaction with Americans at all. He spent more of his time with members of the Japanese community, taking a measure of the country through their eyes. Put it down to a lingering cold perhaps, but he seemed weary at the end of his trip, enervated by a freak May heat wave on the East Coast, confounded by the complexity of transport arrangements from Boston to Fall River to New York. It was probably with some relief that he boarded the White Star Line's *Majestic* bound for Liverpool on May 3, glad to find several Japanese acquaintances on the ship's passenger list, including noted international law expert, Ariga Nagao. Ariga, Konoe noted in his diary, was on his way to The Hague to attend the world's first-ever international peace conference scheduled to begin mid-May.[68]

Konoe's visit to Britain was quite a contrast to his American tour. In London he was very much a public figure and treated as the royalty he was. He had an audience with Queen Victoria, met with other royals and aristocrats, attended sessions of both houses of parliament, had talks with Britain's foreign minister, Lord Salisbury, was feted by leading academics from Oxford and Cambridge, and saw the latest hit play, "Robespierre" with renowned actress Ellen Terry. In short, he had a thoroughly good time in the month he had allotted to the visit. In an address he made to the London Japan Society, Konoe spoke of Japan's need not only to master Britain's technology, but to emulate the unshakable confidence in their superior heritage the British carried with them wherever in the world they found themselves. He very much hoped, he said, "that you British with your advanced nation status will take it upon yourselves to instruct the Japanese not only in material culture, but in the spiritual elements that are behind it."[69] Konoe might have worried about Britain's "great game" in the Pacific, but he could not conceal his admiration for a nation which taught its children the ABCs with verses like, "C is for Colonies/Rightly we boast/That of all the great nations/Great Britain has the most."[70]

After a week in France and the Netherlands, Konoe traveled to Bonn where he immediately contacted Professor Rein, his mentor and host from student days. The professor and his family greeted him warmly, treated him to lunch at home, then extended the occasion with hours of wine and conversation at a restaurant overlooking the Rhine River. Konoe's ease in German and familiarity with the setting put his visit to Germany on a personal level not possible elsewhere. His contacts included numerous German friends from the past—some of them now in high places—as well as Japanese diplomatic personnel, a few with Peers School connections. Clearly energized, Konoe spent from mid-June to mid-July dashing about from city to city, trying to fit everyone into his schedule. There were reunions with former professors and classmates, meetings with German foreign ministry officials and parliamentarians, briefings by school administrators, evenings spent with resident Japanese, all of which helped him understand the mood of the new Germany. Letters from home, coming with increasing frequency, gave immediacy to his more mundane reponsibilities. Motoko reported on the health of the children, particularly little Fumimaro who had been ill at the time of Konoe's departure. Konoe's Tō-A Dōbunkai colleagues submitted a detailed budget for his review and comment, while his temporary replacement at the Peers School provided a somewhat gloomy update on school affairs, the one bright spot being that Governor Zhang's grandson was making progress in Japanese and math.[71]

In mid-July, Konoe resumed a travel schedule which was nothing short of heroic. With Berlin as his departure point, he took a great circular route, much of it on overnight trains, to St. Petersburg, Moscow, Odessa, Bucharest, Constantinople, Athens, Naples, Rome, and, finally, Marseilles where he boarded a boat to Colombo on September 11. In Colombo, he transferred to the *Sidney*, a smaller passenger ship bound for Singapore, Saigon, and Hong Kong. By the time he reached Hong Kong on October 13, after near disaster in the monsoon-lashed South China Sea, he had visited a dozen countries. He had found out firsthand what he most wanted to know: how Japan ranked with the rest of the world.

Japanese were only kidding themselves if they thought Japan was advanced economically, he said. It was not that Japan lacked the well-trained minds required to move the industrialization process forward; even now, Japan had one of the highest literacy rates in the world. What was missing was the underpinning of economic success, a supportive ethical structure of the sort Christianity provided in Western countries. "I believe that we must create a force to instill moral values in our citizens comparable to Christianity which has played such an extraordinary role in moral education in Europe and America."[72] What impressed Konoe most about Western public education was that it taught children to be responsible, healthy citizens. He liked the emphasis on sports, the self-discipline displayed by students, and "the wonderful tendency among students to regulate each other's behavior." He wrote admiringly of Western public library systems which encouraged boys and girls, and indeed, as he noted, anyone of any age or socio-economic level, to take books home to read. A tour of the Chicago city library left him thinking, "how good it would be if in Japan, as well, pupils were not only taught in the classroom but could study on their own."[73]

In foreign relations, Konoe confirmed the current view at home that Japan's standing in European capitals had gone up since the Sino-Japanese War. The British, he reported, talked to him about the need for an alliance with Japan to maintain peace in East Asia; the French assured him that their ambitions did not extend to north China; the Germans claimed that German-Japanese relations had never been on a better track. They were all full of talk about the importance of good relations with Japan. But the real agenda here, he warned his fellow Japanese, was a desire to expand spheres of influence in East Asia. "In other words, it's nothing more than waking up to the fact that we're not to be trifled with. I don't see in it any suggestion at all of new respect for the Japanese people."[74] Where Konoe hoped to find such respect and a real congruence of interests was in China.

China Realities

In the early morning of October 13, 1899, the *Sidney*, well behind schedule but still seaworthy, sailed into Hong Kong harbor, much to the relief of Konoe's Japanese contacts who feared the ship had sunk in the waters off the South China coast. On hand to escort Konoe by steam launch from ship to shore were Hong Kong Consul Ueno, the manager of the Yokohama Specie Bank's Hong Kong branch, the head of the Guangdong office of the Tō-A Dōbunkai, and Miyazaki Torazō, political activist and supporter of China's leading revolutionary figure, Sun Yatsen. The NYK steamship company branch manager and a visiting official from

Japan's Agricultural and Commercial Ministry met Konoe at his hotel. This assorted group—a composite of Japanese interests in South China—joined Ueno at the consulate for a dinner in Konoe's honor that lasted until 11:00 PM.

After a month in which his chief diversion was observing weather conditions in the Pacific, Konoe was revitalized by an evening of "lively conversation," particularly as it had to do with his agenda of activities on this much-anticipated first visit to China. One question that needed to be resolved immediately was how Konoe should respond to requests from China's dissident groups that he meet with them during his China stay. Both Kang Youwei's reform faction and Sun Yatsen's revolutionary party had organizers posted in two safe havens within territorial China, British-controlled Hong Kong and the Shanghai International Settlement. Konoe turned down both requests. He thought there were too many political risks. He did not trust the Kang people and, though he liked what he had heard about Sun, he felt he could not, in his capacity as head of the nonpartisan Tō-A Dōbunkai, meet with one and not the other.[75]

Konoe had originally planned to include North China in his itinerary, but, because of his late arrival in Hong Kong and the great distances that had to be covered, this was scratched. The revised schedule allotted most of his five-week stay to visiting coastal cities from the Macao-Canton-Hong Kong cluster in the south to the Shanghai-Nanjing hubs in the east-central region. The exception to this coastal focus was a two-day trip up the Yangtze River to Wuhan, the most industrialized of China's interior cities (actually a tri-city formed of Wuchang, Hankou, and Hanyang) and, like the others on Konoe's list, a center of foreign commercial activity.

Konoe's world tour thus far had been essentially fact-finding. His China trip was intended to be a real working visit, a diplomatic exercise to persuade Chinese officials and businessmen that rapprochement with Japan was in their best interests. In making the right appointments to this end, he was ably assisted by Japanese consular staff and colleagues from the Tō-A Dōbunkai, which had offices in Canton, Shanghai, and Wuhan. The Tō-A Dōbunkai people in particular had a wealth of China experience. Shiraiwa Ryūhei, who coordinated Konoe's Shanghai visit, had gone to China first in the mid-1880s, then after the Sino-Japanese War joined with a Chinese partner to establish a small steamship line between Suzhou and Hankou.[76] Munakata Kotarō, Konoe's key contact in Wuhan, had been a journalist and intelligence agent in China for fifteen years and now managed a Tō-A Dōbunkai-subsidized Chinese-language newspaper in Hankou.[77] Shiraiwa, Munakata, and others served as interpreters for Konoe in high-level meetings, provided solid briefings—he was impressed by the detailed fact sheet on local factories and schools prepared for him in Wuhan—and gave him access to the extensive contacts they had developed within the Chinese official and business communities. Now that Japan had gained (as of 1896) the most-favored-nation status enjoyed by the other foreign powers in China, developing business opportunities was a real possibility.[78]

As a confirmed "people person," Konoe was in his element. In Canton, several Chinese businessmen and Japanese from the Tō-A Dōbunkai hosted a dinner for him, "a very cordial banquet" with Chinese singing girls—Konoe took note of the tunes—and liberal consumption of wine. A wonderful occasion, he said in a toast to his hosts, with such beautiful women and beautiful music. But what really made him happy was that "gentlemen from China and Japan have gotten together to host a banquet for me." He was slightly less enchanted with a banquet to introduce him to Shanghai industrialists because it was dominated by a four-and-a-half hour theatrical entertainment that made conversation impossible. But then there was a more interesting dinner for him in Shanghai hosted by the head of the Imperial Bank of China who had just returned from a business trip to Japan. This dinner was a Western coat-and-tie affair with the food an opulent mixture of regional specialties, including frog's intestines which Konoe found "rather strange." Konoe was also the guest of honor at gatherings of the Japanese community in China. He particularly enjoyed a gala occasion at the recently opened Hankou (Wuhan) consulate, which featured fireworks, games, and banzais to the Japanese emperor.[79]

At 3:30 in the morning on October 29, Konoe's steamer docked at Nanjing where he was scheduled to meet with one of China's most powerful political leaders, the governor-general of China's lower Yangtze provinces, Liu Kunyi. In this post, which one contemporary Western observer called "the richest plum in the basket of Chinese officialdom," the sixty-nine-year-old Liu was responsible not only for "thousands of miles of fat land and hundreds of wealthy cities" but also for regional foreign policy. Not only that, Liu was concurrently Commissioner of Trade for Southern Ports which meant that he had particular clout in determining China's commercial relations with the foreign powers. Reason enough for Konoe to feel optimistic as he disembarked into the chaos of the Nanjing port, still in darkness that October morning. On hand to welcome him and his party, which included both Shiraiwa and Munakata, was one of Liu's vice-governors who took them on a five-mile trip by horse carriage to the gateway of the city's massive, encircling walls now outlined clearly against the dawn sky. While Konoe rested at the official guest quarters, Shiraiwa and Munakata went to the Foreign Affairs Bureau to get the day's schedule. Governor Liu would not be available until afternoon, they were told, so the morning would be dedicated to sightseeing. Off they went, Konoe in a sedan chair, his colleagues and a Chinese interpreter on donkeys, to tour the tomb of the first Ming emperor and other monuments, some of which still bore witness to the destruction visited by the Taiping rebels thirty-five years before. After several hours of viewing temples, towers, and cityscapes, a weary Konoe was allowed time for a short nap before his historic meeting with Liu Kunyi.[80]

Powerful provincial leader Liu Kunyi at seventy engaged in fruitful talks with thirty-six-year-old Head of the House of Peers, Konoe Atsumaro, on Konoe's 1899 visit to China. (Courtesy of the Library of Congress)

The procession to the governor-general's office compound was designed to impress. Konoe and his party, dressed in formal Western suits, were taken in a convoy of sedan chairs to the huge outer gate of the compound, still bolted shut. They waited. A crowd gathered, pressing in close to stare at the foreign visitors. At the sound of a three-gun salute, the great doors swung open, shrill flutes and bugles played a cacophonous welcome, and an honor guard appeared, directing the convoy through yet another gate. Konoe's colleagues alighted and followed on foot while he alone continued by sedan chair to the final entranceway where Liu and his staff waited to show him into an elegantly-appointed meeting hall.

In both symbolism and substance, the meeting between the aging Chinese leader and thirty-six-year-old Konoe seemed designed to emphasize a new atmosphere of accord between China and Japan. In his welcoming statement, Liu said he was pleased to see the growing trend toward closer Chinese-Japanese relations and grateful for Japan's recent willingness to advise the Chinese. This was the perfect opener for Konoe. "Because I believe the relationship ought to become increasingly close," he replied, "my hope is that we might expand both public and private exchanges between citizens of the two countries." The Japanese were more and more inclined to lend China a hand, which was critical to China's future, he noted, adding that he was speaking "without the kind of calculated flattery the Europeans use." Liu happily agreed that bilateral cooperation made sense and spoke of the possibility of a Chinese-Japanese alliance. He took pains to point out that his Japan tilt was no passing phenomenon. In the great policy debate of the 1870s over whether to face down Russia in Xinjiang or Japan over the Ryūkyūs, he had argued against "offending our near neighbor, Japan, over insignificant islands like the Ryūkyūs." When Konoe proposed establishing a Tō-A Dōbunkai language and area studies institute in Nanjing, Liu, not surprisingly, offered his immediate support. The meeting was short—about an hour with half the time taken up by interpretation—in deference to Liu's ill health, but Konoe could feel a sense of concrete achievement as Liu escorted him out with a handshake and a warm farewell.[81]

The blast of a steam whistle got Konoe and Munakata up and out at 5:30 the next morning to board a Butterfield Company steamer for the two and a half day journey up the Yangtze River from Nanjing to Wuhan. Konoe marveled at the scenery. Small fishing boats plied in and out of vast reed marshes from which flocks of geese suddenly rose skyward. Rock islands jutted up precipitously from the water, now turbulent with currents that impeded progress upstream. Then great Boyang Lake opened up on the Yangtze's south bank, its blue expanse a contrast to the mud-colored river. The panorama before him as the steamer moved upriver turned his thoughts to Chinese poetry and descriptions he had read in Chinese classical accounts of travel inland.

But when Konoe arrived in Wuhan, the tri-city with an estimated two million inhabitants, it was strictly business—a meeting with another titan of Chinese politics, governor-general of Hubei and Hunan provinces, Zhang Zhidong. In his Hunan-Hubei post for eight years now, the sixty-two-year-old Zhang was working to transform the tri-city into an industrial center of the middle Yangtze with iron-works, coal mines, arsenals, cotton mills, and water and rail links to the rest of the country. His driving interest in economic development made him eager for advanced technology, both the machines and the systems that trained people to produce them. Japan as a source of technology and a model of successful, gradual reform looked increasingly attractive to Zhang in the years after the 1895 war. His was the strongest voice within the central government advocating study abroad for Chinese, particularly, for reasons of cost-effectiveness, study in Japan. His own grandson was under Konoe's wing at the Peers School.[82]

As in Nanjing, Konoe's meetings in Wuhan were carefully staged. Due to a national holiday on November 2, one of Zhang's staff people explained, Zhang would see Konoe on November 1, the day of his arrival, but not until mid-afternoon since Zhang had scheduled previous appointments with British and American officials. If there was a slight intended, Konoe chose to ignore it. At 1:00 PM. Zhang sent a steam launch to transport the Konoe party, a dignified group in Western morning coats, across river to his Wuchang office. A Chinese honor guard, smartly dressed in khaki, waited at the dock to escort them by sedan chair to the governor-general. Zhang, like Liu Kunyi, showed Konoe and his party the courtesy of greeting them outside his office before inviting them into the formal meeting room. The talks and the dinner that followed seemed to go well. Zhang politely urged Konoe to stay longer in Wuhan, thanked him for looking after his grandson, and echoed Liu's words on the growing improvement in Chinese-Japanese relations. But something of the glow was taken off the occasion later that evening as the Japanese visitors returned to their lodgings. Konoe wrote of the incident:

> Along the way, a gang of about twenty or thirty carrying paper lanterns of various sizes approached, and as they got nearer held out their hands insistently begging for money. Though Oka Kōjirō handed over some money, they continued to beg and it seemed as if none of them would yield. Suddenly someone threw a rock at us. Segawa, our consular representative, picked up the rock, went into the crowd and gave them a tongue-lashing. Gradually they drew back. Because of these stupid people, our feeling about the governor-general's goodwill has diminished somewhat.[83]

Over the next two days Konoe visited the iron works and munitions factories at Hanyang, climbed the surrounding hills to see the tri-city sprawled out amid the snaking river, and had a constant round of meetings and social events. He lunched with Chinese officials, had dinner with the Japanese consul and his European counterparts, met with Edwin Conger, the American minister to China, and was the guest of honor at parties given by the fifty or so Japanese now part of the foreign resident community. The morning of the fourth, Konoe set off by steam launch to Wuchang to watch Zhang's German-trained troops conduct military exercises. This was followed by a tour of the Lianghu Academy, one of Zhang's Westernized schools. What did he think, Zhang asked, when they met later that day? Konoe had understood from Zhang's German military adviser that aside from the 1,000-man elite corps, the Hunan troops were a pretty substandard lot, but he managed to be mildly complimentary while noting that he did not have the military credentials to really judge. On the question of the academy, Konoe was too direct a person to offer praise when in fact he had found the science and math curriculum poor, surprisingly so, he thought, considering this was one of the best of China's modern schools. Instead, he turned the question into an opportunity to comment on the potential for Japanese assistance to China's educational development. "In the long run it's a good thing for you to send students from China to Japan and to hire Japanese teachers to teach in China; most effective of all, however, is for people involved in education in China to go to Japan themselves to observe educational practices."[84] Zhang, whose own policy statements on education cited the usefulness of the Japan model, expressed his delighted approval.

But then the conversation took an ominous turn. The Japanese government's recent decision to deport Kang Youwei was a positive development for Chinese-Japanese friendship, Zhang said. Konoe corrected him. "It was not the Japanese government but some of us private individuals who advised Kang to leave. Our government won't do something like expelling political offenders from other countries, which is contrary to the rules of international law."[85] Then perhaps you private individuals would also like to encourage Liang Qichao to quit Japan, Zhang shot back. Konoe parried this with a little lecture as to why it made no sense to oust Liang. He was young, scholarly, and had agreed to tone down his rhetoric in his Tokyo publication, *Public Opinion*. Zhang was becoming annoyed. Like the other Chinese dissidents, Liang was committed to overthrowing the state, he said. Talk of restoring the emperor to power was a convenient subterfuge. What worried him was that a lot of young Chinese now studying in Japan were being taken in by what they read in *Public Opinion*. "If you think by getting rid of Liang, you'll suppress *Public Opinion*," Konoe responded sharply, "you're greatly mistaken. There are more than one or two people in Liang's group in Japan; even if he goes, I want you to know that it still won't change things one iota."[86]

Konoe tried to shift away from the Kang/Liang issue. "What about Sun Yatsen?" he asked, expecting to hear some kind of analysis of the potential threat from the revolutionary group. Instead, Zhang shrugged the question off with "a small-time thug, not worth bothering with" and continued to press his case for Liang's ouster from Japan. Konoe was thoroughly dismayed at the unpleasant turn in a conversation that had started on a high note of Chinese-Japanese cooperation. He tried to salvage things by introducing an entirely new topic, the economic development potential of Hunan and Hubei. But Zhang was unresponsive, clearly signaling that the meeting was over. Konoe left feeling "very disappointed."[87]

Governor-general of Hunan and Hubei Zhang Zhidong at the time of Konoe's testy meeting with him in Wuhan in 1899. (Samuel I. Woodbridge, translator, *China's Only Hope*; Edinburgh and London: Oliphant, Anderson & Ferrier, 1901)

The afternoon ended with visits to two more of Zhang's "modern" schools where Konoe was briefed by some Japanese Zhang had hired to teach language and general studies courses. Then it was on to dinner at the famed Yellow Crane

Pavilion in the hills above the city. In keeping with what had been a frustrating day, the Konoe party arrived well after sunset, too late to enjoy the spectacular view of the Yangtze River. By morning Konoe was once again on the steamer making his way down river to Nanjing and Shanghai for more talks and banqueting with Chinese and Japanese businessmen. On November 18, he boarded a ship bound for Japan. On November 25—at precisely 11:38 AM, he noted—he arrived at Tokyo's Shimbashi train station where Motoko, Fumimaro, and other family, friends, and dignitaries were waiting to welcome him home.[88]

Though Konoe had read and thought about China since childhood, his first China trip was an eye-opener nonetheless. As he told a Tō-A Dōbunkai audience shortly after his return to Tokyo, he was struck as he traveled through China by the country's sheer physical size, the abundance of its natural resources, and its hardworking people. On China's leadership, he came away with ambivalent feelings: though people like Liu Kunyi and Zhang Zhidong were sharply critical of Western bullying and domestic political corruption, they seemed incapable of coming up with decisive proposals to address China's underlying problems. Finally, he stressed that Japan stood to benefit from at last achieving parity with the West in commercial rights in China. The Japanese government simply needed to reinforce the legal gains by financing infrastructure improvements in the Japanese "concessions," Japan's newly leased areas within treaty port cities like Wuhan. Above all, he believed that Japan must take a long view in establishing economic links with China.

> To be specific, in my estimation, now is not the time when a country limited in land area like Japan can establish its national base completely on agriculture. From now on, we must actively encourage industry. This by no means requires seeking distant markets in Europe and America. We have a large country like China nearby. China will not only be a good customer of ours as an outlet for manufactured goods, but we will find opportunities to obtain raw materials from that country. The fact that Japanese to date have failed in the China trade is really due to their not being well informed about conditions in China. On this point, I believe it is essential that Japanese increasingly work to develop China-related educational projects.[89]

Projects Ventured, Progress Deferred

Konoe was in his usual high energy mode from the moment he stepped off the train in Tokyo. He dropped in on a Diet meeting on his way home from Shimbashi station and filled the days to follow with appointments, press interviews, and talks to groups about his world tour. China was at the top of his agenda. On December 2, he and his Tō-A Dōbunkai colleagues worked over a draft plan to establish the Japanese-funded school in Nanjing agreed to in principle by Governor-general Liu Kunyi in October. On December 3 and 5, Konoe attended meetings to finalize the Tō-A Dōbunkai request for budgetary support for 1900. The version sent to the Foreign Ministry on December 10 called for a 100 percent increase over 1899 and included subsidies for existing schools and newspapers in China, and funds to develop the Nanjing school, a school in Tokyo for Chinese students, and projects in Korea. On the twelfth, Konoe argued his case for the funding increase—to no avail ultimately—in separate meetings with the foreign minister and finance minister. In mid-January 1900, Konoe heard from colleagues in China that Liu had enthusiastically endorsed final plans for the Nanjing school. A few days later Konoe received a personal note from Liu praising Tō-A Dōbunkai efforts to build Chinese-Korean-Japanese unity and enclosing a photograph from Konoe's recent trip.[90]

In mid-March Konoe gave a newspaper interview at his home in Kōjimachi. Speaking in an elegant reception hall dominated by a bronze statue of his grandfather, Konoe entertained questions on three topics: corruption in the House of Peers (he vowed to continue to fight it), his political aspirations (he was not interested in heading a political party), and his involvement in East Asian affairs (a topic he addressed by describing the work of the Tō-A Dōbunkai). The organization's China projects, he said, were beginning to have a positive impact. With the support of influential people in both China and Japan, schools like the one about to open in Nanjing were prospering and could count among their students, sons of important Chinese officials. Tō-A Dōbunkai-subsidized newspapers in China were likewise doing well, with circulation figures now around four to five thousand. He pointed out also that Tō-A Dōbunkai field personnel were helping to keep Tokyo well informed on what was happening in China.

Konoe ended the interview with some comments on Governor-general Zhang Zhidong's grandson who for the past year had been a student at the Peers School. Konoe placed great weight on developing personal contacts with China's top leadership, and he clearly regarded young Zhang's presence in Japan as proof positive of an improved climate in Chinese-Japanese relations. The young man's reaction to having his academic record publicly aired can only be imagined, but Konoe, as always, spoke his mind. The lad performed well in his language courses in the recent exam period, Konoe told his interviewer, but was still lacking in basic math skills. With extra tutoring, he was expected to be able to join the regular students next year.[91]

However, as spring turned to summer the forward movement in Chinese-Japanese relations slowed. Tō-A Dōbunkai reports from China described a country that seemed headed for political collapse. In North China, isolated peasant attacks on Christian missionaries were developing into an epidemic of anti-foreignism spreading violence northward to China's capital. Japanese observers, like other foreigners on the scene, had few hard facts on the Boxers as the anti-foreign fanatics were called, and could only speculate on the size of a force that seemed to emerge from, then melt back into, the general population. A question in everyone's mind was whether China's central government would bring out its troops to protect foreigners against Chinese or if the foreigners would need to call on their own armies to stop the violence.[92] The answer seemed to come on June 21 with the government's declaration of war on the powers. Attacks were launched on the diplomatic compounds in Beijing where foreigners (including Japanese) were trapped, virtual hostages of the government. As unclear as the fate of the foreign community as summer began were the ultimate intentions of southeastern provincial authorities Liu Kunyi (Nanjing), Zhang Zhidong (Wuhan), and their senior colleague, Li Hongzhang (Canton), all of whom opposed the decision for war.

In statements to the press at the end of June, Konoe argued that any Japanese military action in China should be limited to protecting foreign nationals and restoring peace in Beijing. He believed that declaring war on China as some were suggesting in retaliation for the June 11 murder of a Japanese diplomat by Chinese troops would be an overreaction. It was not at all clear, he said, that China's notoriously undisciplined soldiers had acted on orders from the central government in targeting the diplomat. If not, severing diplomatic relations would be too drastic a response. It would disrupt Japanese trade and the whole network of official and private relationships the Tō-A Dōbunkai had worked to construct in South China. "The present disturbance in North China alone has dealt a serious blow to our textile and other enterprises. Should disaster overtake South China as well, it would have an even more alarming impact on our national economy."[93] No country's interests would be served by the breakup of China, Konoe felt, because the place was basically ungovernable by outsiders. "In my opinion, occupying a single point as the Germans have in Jiaozhouwan and the British in Weihaiwei [both in Shandong Province] is an exception. To penetrate deeply into the interior of China to oust Chinese officials and to control the area with foreign officials actually would be difficult no matter what foreign power is involved. The fact that it's not feasible is made clear now by the rise of people like the Boxers."[94]

Konoe believed that Japan should operate on two levels in China. In South China, Japan should continue to build on its contacts with provincial leaders. As he told an aide to Zhang Zhidong in early July, he hoped that Zhang, Liu Kunyi, and Li Hongzhang, united as they were in opposition to the current war policies of the central government, would form a joint working arrangement. The Tō-A Dōbunkai would willingly act as facilitator. In North China, Konoe recommended that Japan act in concert with Britain, the United States, and Germany to handle post-crisis settlement terms and political reform. Within the scope of this new alliance, Japan would have responsibility for checking Russia's advance southward into the Korea/Manchuria region.[95]

On August 14, 1900, an international force of about twenty thousand, about 40 percent of them Japanese, marched into Beijing to bring an end to the world's first hostage crisis. The empress dowager, the emperor, and dozens of top officials fled 700 miles west to Xi'an, leaving a political vacuum in the capital. Konoe worried that the Western powers would use the joint peacekeeping mission as a pretext to keep permanent occupying forces in China, thus expanding their already-established spheres of influence at Japan's expense. There were unsettling signs, too, that Japan's budding special relationship with influential Chinese was in jeopardy. Konoe was greatly annoyed when word came from Zhang Zhidong just two days after the siege ended that he wanted to remove his grandson from school in Japan. Zhang was reportedly concerned about being viewed as too pro-Japanese.

Konoe believed that Japan should make a dramatic gesture to assure leaders like Zhang who were destined to be major actors in post-Boxer politics that its overriding interest was in maintaining an independent China and peace and security in Asia. On August 31, Konoe went to the prime minister to urge him to withdraw Japanese troops from China, unilaterally if necessary, in hopes of encouraging the other powers to do the same. Such action, he felt, would demonstrate good faith to the Chinese and check the ambitions of Russia and Germany which were, in his view, the most worrisome of the current players in China. The prime minister acknowledged the soundness of Konoe's position, but equivocated, unwilling to take action that might offend the international community. As Konoe feared, Russia continued to move troops south into Manchuria, the homeland of China's ruling Qing dynasty.[96]

Konoe was not to be put off by what he considered excessive timidity on the prime minister's part. He immediately turned to his contacts in the Diet, the press, academia, and the Tō-A Dōbunkai with an appeal for joint action to pressure the cabinet into formally opposing Russia's troop buildup in Manchuria. By the end of September, he had mobilized about a hundred influential figures to form the Kokumin Dōmeikai (People's League), a political advocacy group whose slogans were "maintain the integrity of China" (*Shina hozen*) and "safeguard Korea"

(*Chōsen yōgo*). The ultimate goal of the group's campaign against Russian expansion was peace, not war, Konoe insisted. People who accused the People's League of being pro-war were completely off base. War might prove unavoidable for Japan at some point, he acknowledged, but, in that case, it would be for reasons totally understood by any of the other foreign powers with interests in China. Nor was the group anti-Russian in a racial sense. The idea was not to promote a Japan-China-Korea alliance of Asians against Caucasians. "I must say that if people persist in labeling the People's League as favoring a white exclusion policy, this indeed would be counterproductive; it would arouse the suspicions of the whites and would be a mistake in long-term planning."[97]

Throughout the fall and spring, the People's League under Konoe's leadership carried on an active campaign of public speeches, newspaper articles, and appeals to individual cabinet members to build up support for its views on North Asian security. Konoe, who had recently voted with the lower House to deny the government the right to suspend politically offensive publications, was particularly adept at using the press. In China, the People's League played to mixed reviews. Governor-general Li Hongzhang, sobered by decades-long experience managing foreign crises, voiced skepticism to a Japanese visitor that the League's "maintain the integrity of China" slogan would actually translate into Japanese government action on China's behalf. But Konoe has clout, his Japanese visitor protested. Besides, he added expansively, the group has strong support in the Diet and the sympathies of all 30 million Japanese. If the cabinet does not follow public opinion, it will be replaced with one that supports an independent China as key to East Asian peace.[98]

As the People's League campaign heated up, Konoe was forced to deal with a new problem—his health. He appeared robust. In fact his doctors had for some time advised him to lose weight, which given his habit of irregular meals and late night meetings he found difficult to do. But, beginning in September 1900, he developed a persistent, painful cough that refused to respond to treatment. In November he had surgery to remove an abscess from his throat. At a League meeting on December 20, Konoe apologized for his raspy voice and offered a briefer than usual speech.[99]

New Initiatives: Training Chinese Men, Mobilizing Japanese Women

Within a month Konoe seemed to have recovered his old energy. His calendar was once again crowded with meetings on the People's League action plan, on the Tō-A Dōbunkai budget, on construction of Naruse's women's college, on staffing problems at Shimoda's Imperial Women's Association. There were reasons to feel more optimistic about the issue uppermost in his mind: improving Japan's relations with China. After six months of political uncertainty, the goals the Tō-A Dōbunkai wanted to achieve suddenly appeared more achievable. In January 1901, the Empress Dowager and her advisers, viewing the grim scene of foreign-occupied Beijing from their refuge in Xi'an, issued a statement of intent to introduce a full package of reforms. As the details were worked out over the next few months, it became clear that partnership with Japan was to take center stage in a program that emphasized above all the need for wholesale import of institutional patterns from abroad. The drivers of the program known as the New Policies (*xinzheng*) were none other than Zhang Zhidong and Liu Kunyi, already on board with the idea of expanded Japan exchanges when they met with Konoe the year before.

When reform-minded pragmatists like Zhang and Liu chose to establish a national school system after the Japanese model in the post-Boxer years, cost-effectiveness not friendship was their primary motivation. It was cheaper to send study missions and students to Japan to observe and be trained in modern schools than to ship them off to Europe or America. Likewise, Japanese teachers in China, while highly paid relative to those at home, commanded lower salaries than their Western counterparts. Choosing Japan as an alternative source of outside expertise was also politically smart. It made educational restructuring more palatable to the anti-Western element within the Chinese leadership, people who had encouraged the Boxers and now feared European and American dominance of the reform process. Aside from saving money and mollifying conservatives, there was a fundamental ideological reason for turning to Japan in the vital matter of educational reform. Japanese educational philosophy fit the Chinese mindset, particularly in its emphasis on moral education and on creating national standards to unite the citizenry behind the state.

As China's New Policies took hold, the Chinese-Japanese relationship entered a new phase of constructive collaboration marked by unprecedented numbers of student-teacher exchanges. China's leaders were no longer waiting to be wooed by the Japanese, but were actively seeking Japanese assistance. The number of Chinese students in Japan, some three hundred in 1901 rose to about one thousand in 1903. Japanese employed by the Chinese government, probably no more than twenty in 1901, climbed to around one hundred and fifty in 1903. Chinese officials on study tours to Japan became a regular feature of government-to-government relations; some twelve hundred spent a month or more in Japan in the years 1898-1911, most in the field of education, most holders of top positions in China.

The Konoe and Shimoda imprint was on many of the small new initiatives that added up to this significant transfer of knowledge, Konoe on the boards of a new business school for Chinese and a language training center, Shimoda translating her home economics texts into Chinese and publicizing the benefits of Japan study for Chinese women. As one Meiji commentator remarked, the names Konoe Atsumaro and Shimoda Utako were linked in the public mind as Japan's chief China development advocates. Visiting Chinese educators put them at the top of the list of people they hoped to see along with Kanō Jigorō, who had worked with Chinese students, trying to accommodate to their special needs, since 1896. By 1901 when the New Policies were issued, Kanō had graduated one small group under Teachers College auspices and was making plans to build a large, new facility entirely for Chinese, scheduled to open in January 1902. From the Foreign Ministry's standpoint the project represented a plus for Japan's image in China. Suddenly funds were available to finance a four-month China tour for Kanō the following summer. For him personally the trip was a chance to better understand the background of the incoming students and to explain directly and specifically to Zhang Zhidong and Liu Kunyi the advantages of the Japanese pedagogical model.[100]

Konoe had gotten to know Kanō when trying to sort out the teachers' union dispute, but they met only occasionally thereafter. Though they overlapped in their interest in hosting Chinese students, they were on different paths. Kanō was involved at the level of curriculum development, school administration, teaching methodology. While Konoe had his own bailiwick in education as head of the Peers School, which had admitted a few Chinese students, he was chiefly a policy advocate, working to advance a whole range of Tō-A Dōbunkai development projects which included newspapers and commercial ventures as well as educational exchanges. His efforts here as well as his single-issue advocacy of a hard line against Russia and, in fact, his patronage of various mass organizations were all to the end of building public support for a new relationship with China and Korea based on Japan as defender of Asian interests and source of modern knowledge and expertise.

Konoe was part of the emperor's inner circle, head of the House of Peers, at ease in the company of Queen Victoria, but he was in no way an aloof aristocrat. To the contrary, part of his effectiveness was his genial way of including in his endeavors people of diverse, sometimes unconventional backgrounds, women as well as men. Nowhere was this better illustrated than in his friendship with a powerhouse of a woman with a Meiji rags to riches story named Okumura Ioko. Okumura who always relished her role as a thorn in the side of powerful officials claimed that the only politician who ever liked her was Prince Konoe. He evidently did. He met with her often beginning in 1895, and when she organized the Patriotic Women's Organization in February 1901 to provide aid to Japanese veterans of the Boxer expedition, Konoe and his wife Motoko were on the list of supporters.

While the Konoe-Okumura connection is personally revealing about Konoe's general broadmindedness, it also points to a larger truth about Meiji political life usually overlooked, that upward mobility was clearly possible in Meiji Japan for the smart and aggressive from any income group, even if they were women. Okumura was born in Nagasaki in 1845. Her father was the head priest of a small Buddhist temple. Married at twenty-two and widowed three years later, she seemed headed on a downward spiral after a disastrous second marriage in 1872, this time to a low-ranking samurai from Mito who had fled to Kyushu to escape punishment for acts of terrorism against the new government. As three children came along and the couple struggled to make ends meet, Okumura hired herself out to local families as a wet nurse and seamstress, all the while trying to prop up her husband in a small business peddling tea and sundries. But the poor ex-samurai had no stomach for business and simply loafed the days away, squandering what little money he took in. Finally in 1887, the longsuffering Okumura loaded up a cart with her children and belongings and left her hapless spouse for the port city of Karatsu where new opportunities were opening up in the food vending business. She quickly made a small fortune, enough to provide financial backing to a candidate running for the lower house of the Diet in Japan's first election in 1890. He won, and Okumura emerged as a fierce campaigner on local development issues, taking the case of open port status for Karatsu directly to Tokyo politicians—and winning. So much for regulations barring women from politics.

Okumura got to know Konoe after the Sino-Japanese War. Now in her early fifties and financially secure, she returned to her roots with a decision to do missionary work in Korea under the auspices of the great temple of the Buddhist True Pure Land (Jōdo Shinshū) sect, the Eastern Honganji in Kyoto. Prince Konoe was the temple's official patron. Okumura spent 1895-1896 in Korea. To help the local population she organized a vocational school for Korean women and training in Japan for men. As a person with a natural bent for business, she also scouted out prospects in the silk and tea industries and reported to political leaders at home, including Konoe, on general economic and political conditions in the country.

It was Konoe who encouraged Okumura to follow up with a missionary assignment to south China in 1899. By this time her reputation was well established. Several prominent people sent farewell messages, including Shimoda Utako, who provided a happy *waka*, "Plant the seeds of Japan's sincerity in China's fields, you daughter of Yamato." It was a nice antidote to the more somber note of the Honganji head priest who said something to the effect of go ahead and die, your reputation will be enhanced (literally, "Even if the sandalwood withers, an aroma is left behind").[101]

Okumura spent January to June 1899 in China, leaving just as Boxer terrorism was engulfing the north. She returned in October 1900, two months after the international force had marched into Beijing to crush the uprising. She was horrified by the devastation, ruined crops and villages, decaying bodies she witnessed on the trip to the capital from the Tianjin port. It angered her that Japanese women were living in comfort back home, protected from all of this, oblivious to both the suffering of Chinese women and the hardships faced by Japanese soldiers serving with the Beijing occupation force. She believed that women had a public role to play in general and, in particular, in times of national crisis. To remain uninvolved, "handicapped" like Chinese women, she said, was a waste of national resources.[102]

Okumura's China experience was the genesis of her women's volunteer group, the Women's Patriotic Association, which took formal shape with Konoe's and Shimoda's endorsement the following February. The organization was a characteristic piece of Meiji progressive conservatism. While Okumura herself—opinionated, outspoken, unfazed by rank—was hardly the submissive Japanese woman, she was nevertheless mainstream in her approach. What she was demanding for women was not equal rights with men but greater responsibility in the life of the Meiji state. It was the kind of role that Shimoda applauded in British women and Konoe highlighted when he spoke of the centrality of educated, "wise" women in producing the next generation of citizens. In a more immediate sense, Konoe was also well aware that Okumura's new group represented a potential bloc of support—all-important female opinion—for the Asia-first goals of the People's League organized just months before.

Saving China

In June 1901, Konoe met with Japan's new prime minister Katsura Tarō to discuss the League's latest position paper on China/Korea policy. The key points were that Japan must step up the pressure on Russia to end its occupation of Manchuria and insist on a regional open door policy that would pave the way for Japanese railway construction. In mid-July, Konoe left on a six-week trip to North China, the Russian Far East, and Korea to assess the situation himself.[103]

On July 17, Konoe's ship closed in on Shandong Province and passed by the British leased area of Weihaiwei before heading into Bo Hai Bay. At 10:15 the next morning, the ship anchored in the waters off Dagu, the port city on the Hai River south of Tianjin. As a launch carried passengers to shore, Konoe for the first time saw evidence that Japan had come up in the rankings of the powers.

> Approaching Dagu by steam launch, we soon had a commanding view of the forts. The fort on the left bank at the mouth of the Hai River, extremely important strategically, was captured by our army. The fort on the right bank is occupied by the Russian army and the others by the British, Americans, Germans, and French. And not only the forts. The whole territory—the landing places, of course, and also villages, fields and salt flats—are under occupation. In particular, what's called the Yuleiying Dock in East Dagu was seized by the Russians early on and they continue to hold it. Under such circumstances, the flags of the various nations are flying intermingled—it's really a strange and wonderful sight.[104]

The Japanese had established as much of a presence in the occupied cities as any of the other foreigners, Konoe found. In Tianjin, officers with Japan's military garrison took Konoe on a tour of the local field hospital, the naval barracks, and the headquarters of the Japanese second battalion. He met with local representatives of the NYK Steamship Company, the Yokohama Specie Bank, and Mitsui Trading. Traveling to Beijing by rail a few days later, he was greeted by a full contingent of high-ranking Japanese navy and army officers along with diplomatic personnel. He toured China's new Japanese-style police academy and got a briefing on post-Boxer conditions from its director, Tō-A Dōbunkai member Kawashima Naniwa, who was a close personal friend of one of the Manchu nobles, Prince Su. Meetings were interspersed with sightseeing—excursions to the Summer Palace and the Forbidden City and visits to churches and city walls damaged during the Boxer siege. Evenings involved the usual sequence of banquets and performances, the latter Manchu martial arts.[105]

But for all the activity it generated, Konoe's visit to China's capital lacked the excitement and ceremony of his trip to South China's cities two years before. For one thing, with the empress dowager, emperor, and top court advisers still in Xi'an (they did not return to Beijing until January 1902), there were fewer high-level people to see. Konoe did have appointments with Governor-general Li Hongzhang and Prince Qing, China's negotiators in the Boxer settlement talks, but recorded little of their conversations. Since Li was known to be pro-Russian, the meeting may have been unproductive. Konoe had more to say about Prince Su, who at first glance struck him as oddly diffident. "Because he is excessively polite, he lacks the commanding presence of royalty," Konoe observed. But when Konoe, in his forthright way, told the Prince that China ought to reform its civil service examination system, he was startled by the Prince's insightful reply.

> That's really good advice but the exam system is a long-established practice and, while its abuses have been recognized before now, reform has been impossible. This method of selecting civil servants is extremely unworkable in the present context. However, we owe to its existence the fact that we Manchus, a minority group from China's border areas, control this large and diverse country and have been able to maintain this position over several hundred years. At present, if it weren't for relations with foreign countries, quite likely this system of selecting officials on the basis of exam performance would still be the very best means to hold people's ambitions in check. At a time when we must compete with today's world powers, yesterday's sharp sword has become an instrument of our own destruction. Today we must reform the exam system, do away with the foolish eight-legged essay, implement a recruitment system based on modern science, and greatly increase ways to promote talented men.[106]

After eight days in Beijing, Konoe took the train back to Tianjin then traveled on the northern coastal rail line to Tanggu and Shanhaiguan, the gateway to Manchuria. North China put Konoe in an uncharacteristic somber mood that summer of 1901. He found the looting of the palaces in Beijing, which most foreign troops engaged in—the Japanese were reportedly the least of the offenders—appalling. In his view, the royal residences should be respected even in the absence of the monarchs. The dreary mud flats and mud-brick village dwellings between Tangu and Tianjin elicited no poetic images of China's past as had the trip up the Yangtze to Wuhan. What stuck in his mind were the unsanitary conditions, the unsafe drinking water, and the ever-present flies. "The number one bothersome thing in these parts is the flies. It's bad enough that when you swat them they don't go away, but when the dishes of food are put out there are some inside that one can't see. The Chinese are nonchalant. Without brushing away a black swarm of flies, they eat around them. Sometimes when you're talking a fly flies into your mouth."[107] He was bothered by the general rundown appearance of public buildings, which he attributed to a Chinese underdeveloped sense of public responsibility.

> If I had to say why it is that private homes are splendid while government compounds are dirty and shabby, it's that the official residences are not privately owned. Because it's considered foolish to spend money on renovations and the like, expenses earmarked for upkeep by the government are put into the pockets of officials as is, and no more repairs are made. Buildings are left the way they are to the point of ruin. Actually, this is self-interest carried to the extreme. It's wrong to say that the Chinese people are dirty. The fact that they seem so is that they're unconcerned about public things. Whatever lies outside their own personal interests, they turn their backs on. It's this way on

> the roads and rivers. Because inattentiveness is the order of the day, the situation has totally run wild. This is the end result of acting out of self-interest, but it seems that the Chinese are not yet aware of the fact that "what benefits the other fellow, benefits me."[108]

Konoe saw some hope in the fact that in money matters the Chinese were capable of thinking in terms of mutual benefit. He echoed the opinion of other foreigners that "in their credit dealings in commercial transactions, the Chinese are very advanced . . . probably the best in the world . . . Since one would expect this principle to extend to other things, with some guidance in their case, development of public spirit is probably possible." To avoid sounding arrogant in his judgement of the Chinese, Konoe added a comment on how generally "untrustworthy" Japanese businessmen were in their operations in North China. "The moment a market opens," he said, "they immediately put out shoddy goods, resulting in a loss of trust in an instant."[109]

Konoe's August travel schedule was rugged. On August 1, after a twelve-hour trip by rail on the Tianjin-Shanhaiguan line, he journeyed on horseback to a Japanese military encampment where he spent the night. Two days later in a driving rain he made his way back to the coast. A small launch was waiting to take him out over raging seas to a Japanese warship bound for the Chinese city of Yingkou in South Manchuria. There he met with members of the Japanese business community to hear their views on trade prospects and the current Manchurian crisis. August 9-15 he traveled to Lushun and Dalian, port cities in the part of south Manchuria Russia had leased from China three years before, for talks with Russian officials, including the governor of the territory. From there he headed north by boat to Korea for an audience with the king and meetings with resident Japanese. On August 27 Konoe set sail for Japan. In early September he was back in Tokyo well prepared to rejoin the Manchuria issue.[110]

Konoe employed two tactics in his campaign to redirect Japan's China policy. First, he made use of his personal contacts with Governors-general Liu Kunyi and Zhang Zhidong. He assured them that the Japanese public—that is, the People's League—supported their opposition to Russian moves to expand mining and railway projects and build up troop strength in Manchuria. He urged them, in the interests of stability in the North China/Manchuria area, to encourage the court's early return to Beijing. Both leaders responded positively. Liu, in particular, wrote in a personal vein, praising Konoe's efforts to promote Chinese-Japanese solidarity and welcoming his pledge to help resolve the issue of Russian encroachment in Manchuria. Once the empress dowager and emperor returned to Beijing, Konoe in the name of the People's League was quick to send a congratulatory telegram. Konoe followed up on this with a memorandum to the central and provincial authorities advising them on reform policies, particularly in the area of education. Second, Konoe used the media to pressure the Japanese government to adopt a hard line on Russia. In taking this stance, he found himself once again in his career at odds with his former mentor, senior governmental adviser Itō Hirobumi, who favored yielding control of Manchuria to Russia in exchange for Russian recognition of Japan's paramount position in Korea. It was a contentious issue within Japan's top leadership. Itō ultimately lost out to an anti-Russia, pro-British faction, much to Konoe's satisfaction. In January, the same month the Chinese monarchs returned to Beijing, Japan signed the Anglo-Japanese Alliance. The Alliance, Konoe declared, was the basis for maintaining China's integrity, safeguarding Korea, resolving the Manchuria problem, and keeping the peace in Asia. It was, he believed, a natural partnership.

> Although I don't doubt that this is actually a great change in international relations, still, if you look at how it came into being, it must be termed a natural outcome of the diplomatic position of the two countries. Japan's paramount position in East Asia is already widely recognized. Britain's commercial prosperity and naval strength in East Asia are also unmatched by the other foreign powers. Now, accordingly, we see these two great forces coming together. It's like the unsurpassable strength of adding wings to a tiger.[111]

Alliance with a Western power was palatable to Konoe as long as it was an equal partnership.

Bowing to international pressure, in April 1902 the Russians agreed to a phased evacuation of Manchuria. Their mission achieved, People's League members terminated their activities. Konoe turned to other pursuits, including a grueling, month-long trip to Hokkaidō in August. In October he published a detailed analysis of progress made in Hokkaidō port and railway construction over the previous ten years.[112] That same month, on his way from the Peers School to his Diet office, Konoe was in a carriage accident. He was only slightly hurt so he went on to his meeting as scheduled. But for weeks afterward he was bothered by unusual discomfort in his right shoulder. The following January he developed chest pain that was diagnosed as pleurisy. After several months of bed rest, he felt fit enough to resume an active schedule.

In April 1903 Russia failed to honor the second pullout date as required by the agreement signed the year before. Worse still, employing tough tactics, Russia demanded that China recognize Russia's special interests in Manchuria as a precondition for withdrawal. Konoe and his colleagues immediately revived the People's League and its campaign of public pressure. At the end of May, seven prominent university law professors added their voices to the effort, forcing meetings with the prime minister and foreign minister. The press was delighted, and the issue got front-page coverage. Konoe himself, however, suffered a setback. In June he was operated on to remove another abscess from his throat. On July 30, pale and tired-looking, he called on the prime minister to present a People's League position paper on the Manchurian crisis. He finished his presentation and returned to his office where, as his staff looked on in alarm, he suddenly began coughing up large amounts of blood. A nurse was called, but Konoe assured everyone it was nothing serious, merely the strain of rushing around too much that day.[113]

Konoe Atsumaro (on white horse) on a trip to review development progress in Hokkaidō, August 1902. Six months later, Konoe's health took a turn for the worse. (Konoe Atsumaro, *Hokkaidō shiken*; Tokyo: Akaishi Teizō, 1902)

A message from Konoe calling for the total expulsion of Russian troops from Manchuria was read to the August 9 meeting of a successor group to the People's League called the Tairo Dōshikai (Anti-Russia Comrades' Society). Konoe was too ill to attend. A newspaper article on September 10 described Konoe's illness as actinomycosis, a chronic infectious disease that attacked the jaw and throat then gradually spread to the lungs and other internal organs. German medical researchers had identified the disease, the article noted, but it was virtually unknown in Japan.

Konoe Atsumaro with his wife and children, including Konoe Fumimaro, far left, 1903. At the time the photograph was taken, Konoe was in brief remission from actinomycosis, the infectious disease that took his life on New Year's Day, 1904. (Kudō Takeshige, *Konoe Atsumaro-kō*; Tokyo: Dainichisha zōban, 1938)

On September 14 Konoe entered Tokyo University Hospital for surgical removal of abscesses that had erupted all over his body. This seemed to provide some relief. But in October his condition worsened. He had surgery to remove an abscess from his lung. By the end of the month, he was racked by fevers, splitting headaches, and constant coughing. He was in intense pain from infected lesions. His weight dropped from 190 to 140 pounds. With the prognosis grim, he resigned from the presidency of the House of Peers. Still, he struggled to welcome visitors with his usual good humor. Above all, he wanted to hear news of the Russo-Japanese negotiations that had dragged on since August with no breakthrough in sight. His biggest concern was that to avoid conflict, the government would capitulate to Russia and agree to some kind of Manchuria-Korea exchange. In late December Konoe endured an agonizing carriage ride back home. Nothing more could be done.[114]

Early in the morning of January 1, 1904, thirteen-year-old Fumimaro and one of his younger brothers went into the sick room with New Year's greetings for their father. In intense pain and breathing with difficulty Konoe had left his bed and was sitting formally dressed ready to pay his respects to the emperor. Within minutes after they left, he died of cardiac arrest. He was forty years old. January 6 in the late afternoon, as the setting sun yielded to the bitter cold, he was buried in Tokyo's Enmeiin cemetery. The trees swayed and moaned in the strong north wind, as if sharing the mourners' grief.[115]

News of Konoe's death came as a shock to Beijing's leaders who saw him as a young, vigorous friend of China. In an unprecedented honor for a foreigner, they invited the Japanese community to hold a memorial service for Konoe at the Yonghegong Lama Temple. Built by the Yongzheng emperor in the early eighteenth century it was—and is—one of the most beautiful, profoundly serene places of worship in the entire city. Gathered there for the service was a cross-section of the Beijing elite, from Manchu princes and top Chinese officials to foreign diplomats, officers with the international peacekeeping force, foreign newspaper correspondents, and virtually every resident Japanese.[116]

A month after Konoe's death, Japan broke off negotiations with Russia and launched a surprise attack on the Russian fleet at Port Arthur. By March of 1905, after the loss of 80,000 Japanese lives, Japan had secured Port Arthur and pushed the Russians north of Mukden (present day Shenyang in China's Liaoning Province.) What finally precipitated peace talks between the war-weary belligerents was Japan's total defeat of the Russian navy in the Japan Sea at the end of May. The victory of a small Asian country over one of the Western powers took the world by surprise. President Theodore Roosevelt called it, ". . . the greatest phenomenon the world has ever seen." When the telegraphed reports came in, he recounted, "I grew so excited that I myself became almost like a Japanese, and I could not attend to official duties. I spent the whole day talking with visitors about the Battle of the Japan Sea, for I believed that this naval battle decided the fate of the Japanese Empire."[117] With Roosevelt acting as intermediary, Russia and Japan signed a peace treaty in Portsmouth, New Hampshire in September of 1905. The treaty reaffirmed Chinese sovereignty over the whole of Manchuria, transferred to Japan Russia's lease in South Manchuria, and recognized Japan's special position in Korea. Japan had now achieved parity with the other foreign powers on the Asian mainland.

Chinese saw Japan's victory over Russia as an Asian triumph. In the year after the war, thousands of Chinese students flocked to Tokyo to learn the lessons of Japan's success. Chinese central and provincial authorities increased their requests for Japanese advisory services in education, finance, technical areas, and law. China's constitutional movement was given a boost: Japan's victory over Russia seemed proof positive of the superiority of constitutional government over autocratic rule. By 1907, the Qing leadership had decided to adopt the model of the Meiji Constitution with its notion of the "sacred and inviolable" emperor at the center of political power. Even after the Chinese imperial system ended with revolution in 1911, the most patriotic of China's new leaders still looked to the possible benefits of partnership with Japan. In a symbolic gesture of support for pan-Asianism, Sun

Yatsen, father of Republican China, paid his respects at Konoe's grave in 1913.[118]

Konoe's son, Fumimaro, became Japan's prime minister in June of 1937, just a month before the clash between Japanese and Chinese troops near Beijing brought the tensions of the thirties to a crisis point. For Japan, the issue was protecting its long-term strategic and economic interests in North China and Manchuria against a threat from the Soviet Union. China's Chiang Kaishek, claiming a national mandate after two decades of civil disorder, refused to retreat further in the face of Japanese moves to create autonomous, pro-Japanese regimes in the region. Fumimaro tried but failed to negotiate his way out of crisis. Japan's invading army moved south to Shanghai, Nanjing, and Canton. In 1938, the Konoe government announced a Japanese version of the Monroe Doctrine called the New Order in East Asia; three years later, it was extended to the whole of Asia in the form of the Greater East Asia Co-Prosperity Sphere. These new doctrines sounded old Asia for the Asians themes. But the reality behind the rhetoric was quite different from Konoe Atsumaro's vision of Japan as a cultural force and commercial partner assisting China and the rest of Asia in their struggle against Western aggression. It was, instead, a Japanese-led holocaust loosed upon fellow Asians and Westerners alike.

Chapter II

Hattori Unokichi: Lessons from Beijing

A memorial service for Prince Konoe was held at Beijing's Yonghegong Temple soon after his funeral in Tokyo on January 6, 1904. The service was a large affair, attended by a who's who of Chinese officialdom and the Western press and diplomatic corps along with virtually everyone in the resident Japanese community. China's decision to host the event at Yonghegong, one of Beijing's most important religious establishments, was both a tribute to Konoe and a reminder of the scale and continuity of Qing power. An emperor's palace converted to a Buddhist lamasery in the 1740s, Yonghegong housed as many as seven hundred monks in an assemblage of ever more ornate halls stretching a quarter of a mile on a north-south axis to the very edge of the massive city wall.

Guests filing into the temple forecourt for the Konoe service were greeted by the loud drone of hundreds of monks reciting the sutras, an invitation to reverence accented by the aroma of incense wafting in clouds from great stone incense-burners. The sense of awe the temple inspired came also from its immediate visual impression: horizontal space dominated by a spread-out complex of red-painted structures, two to three stories high, topped by heavy, yellow-tile roofs that defied their weight by curving gracefully skyward. Large blue tablets hung over the entranceways to the main halls, announcing in gold lettering "yonghegong," "eternal peace hall" in four languages—Chinese, Manchu, Tibetan, and Mongol—a salute to the ethnic integration policy of the Qing imperial house. Inside the halls, dimly lit with candles and heavy with incense, were rich displays of Tibetan Buddhist reliquaries, including a fifty-foot statue of the Maitreya Buddha. That Konoe was the first foreigner ever to be memorialized in such a sacred place held multiple messages, personal and political, not least, in the eyes of the Japanese guests, China's endorsement of Konoe's vision of bilateral cooperation.[1]

No formal guest list exists for the Konoe ceremony, but certainly among the Japanese attending that winter's day in 1904 was a senior academic on the faculty of Beijing University named Hattori Unokichi. Hattori was on his second China tour. He had traveled first to Beijing in 1899 on a year-long research grant provided by Japan's Ministry of Education. The fact that he was nearly killed as Boxers terrorized the city in the summer of 1900 did not deter him from accepting a second assignment two years later, this time as a Chinese government contractor hired to establish a teacher-training unit at the new university. Hattori was well qualified for the post. A Tokyo University graduate with overseas study credentials, a Confucian scholar who knew the real China, he had also taught for three years at Tokyo Teachers College under the direction of its president, Kanō Jigorō.

Konoe Atsumaro had led the way in pursuing soft-power diplomacy with China in his talks with Chinese leaders in 1899 and in his decision to put prestige and personal funds behind Tō-A Dōbunkai-sponsored exchange programs. Within this new shift-toward-Asia policy context, Kanō with equal zeal worked at the operational level to expand facilities for Chinese youth wishing to study in Japan. By the time seven of an original group of thirteen students had completed Kanō's special three-year course of study in 1899, another hundred Chinese were enrolled in schools in Tokyo, and Kanō had plans in the works to establish a school exclusively to handle the expected upsurge in Chinese demand. His Kōbun Institute opened in January 1902. In mid-July Kanō left for China. This was his first trip, a tour not only of Beijing but of five east and central China provinces. Like Konoe three years earlier, he met with the venerable Zhang Zhidong and Liu Kunyi, but not to argue the merits of educational exchange. This was accepted policy by now, endorsed with enthusiasm by the Chinese leadership in the atmosphere of post-Boxer reform.[2]

Kanō was greeted and treated as a foreign expert. His own key purpose was to design the best possible program for his Kōbun students, enabling them to learn Japanese quickly and to overcome deficiencies in math and science. His conversations with his Chinese hosts focused on the nitty-gritty of pedagogy, curriculum content, textbook acquisition, the value of teaching ethics and, of course, his beloved judo. He was confident and passionate in manner, even in his talks with people like Zhang, clearly his senior in every respect. When Zhang argued the case for corporal punishment in the schools—"When it comes to bad boys, if you don't make a point of beating them as a warning, they will become incorrigible and you can't expect progress in their education"—Kanō had a ready reply: "If you take a number of measures such as restricting the students' idle time, or planning their after school hours and keeping them on school grounds, or laying down the law with their fathers and elder brothers, you don't have to resort to the whip. Quite to the contrary, these methods can get excellent results."[3]

The other side of the China exchange story on Kanō's mind was the matter of Japanese experts working in China. In 1902 there were about one hundred and fifty of them, a seven-fold increase from the year before. That the Chinese were hiring Japanese for all manner of technical advice and teaching posts was a welcome development to people like Konoe and Kanō. But there was the question of quality control, something that worried Kanō. "It's rumored," he wrote about the Japan-hires,

> that many of them are people without financial assets or education who cannot find suitable employment in Japan and therefore drift to China to find their way in life. We very much hope this is not the case. What we hope is that people of substance, learning, and established reputation will go in great numbers to China, will assist the Chinese in a spirit of friendly relations, and will launch sound projects . . . Those people with know-how and experience who are now being hired by China should go there not solely with thoughts of their own profit, but sincerely committed to planning for China's benefit.[4]

Kanō's ideal candidate, in other words, should be well educated, high-minded, and financially secure enough that accepting a position in China would not be based on salary considerations alone. It was just the profile of his former colleague at the Teachers College, Hattori Unokichi, who had arrived on his second China tour in early September 1902, midway in Kanō's visit. Over the years, the College continued to be a recruiting ground for contract personnel; about 10 percent of the estimated six-hundred Japanese educators in China in 1909 were either graduates or former faculty members.[5]

A China Scholar for a New Age

Hattori's fatalistic attitude toward his encounter with the Boxers had deep psychological roots. He had barely survived infancy. He was born on April 30, 1867, the third son of a low-ranking samurai family living in Nihonmatsu, a small castle town about 250 miles north of Edo, the shogun's capital. Hattori's mother died a year later. Sympathetic to the pain this sudden loss inflicted on the family, his father's brother and wife took over the care of little Unokichi. In the context of the turbulent political times this proved a lucky break for the small child. Six months after the restoration of imperial rule in early 1868, the new central government launched a campaign to stamp out pockets of resistance in the northern feudal domains that included Nihonmatsu. Hattori senior, samurai by rank if not by practice, was pressed into service with the rebel forces fighting to preserve the old ideals of feudal confederation. As it turned out he was on the wrong side of history. He was gunned down by the modern-equipped imperial troops in a skirmish below the Nihonmatsu castle walls in August 1868.[6]

Just a year and a half old, Unokichi had lost both parents. The Hattori family home was torched by invading forces along with the Nihonmatsu castle itself. Followers of the local feudal lord began to flee Nihonmatsu for the safety of the Yonezawa domain twenty miles to the west. Hattori's uncle and aunt, infant nephew in tow, joined the frightened refugees crowding along the narrow mountain roads. But Hattori's aunt, ill with exhaustion, soon realized she lacked the stamina to make the long trek. Instead she decided to seek refuge with little Unokichi in a village a few miles from the embattled town, leaving her husband to escort his employer as duty required.

For the next few months aunt and nephew lived a precarious existence as Meiji soldiers made daily sweeps through farm households searching for people connected with the resistance. Hattori's aunt disguised herself in the baggy clothes of a farm laborer. Whenever soldiers appeared she followed the lead of the other women and prostrated herself before them, never averting her eyes. She escaped detection, but there were other worries during the months of hiding out. Little Unokichi, a frail infant to begin with, developed a serious eye infection, a clear case for the village doctor. But calling in an outsider carried the risk of being found out, so she applied home remedies instead, leaving Hattori with impaired vision in one eye. As Hattori pointed out later, he was too young at the time to remember the details of the Hattori escape story, part of the family lore oft-recited by his aunt and uncle. But his vision problems were a permanent reminder of his early brush with death.[7]

There was no stigma attached to the Hattori name despite its association with the resistance. To the contrary, in the popular mind following one's lord even—or especially—unto death in a lost cause was thought an act of heroism. On the other hand, once civil unrest in the northeast was quashed in 1869 and the feudal domains formally abolished two years later, the question for uncle Hattori as for samurai of all ranks was how to make a living under the new Meiji regime. His former lord was reduced to being a minor governor of uncertain prospects and summoned to live in Tokyo, the new Edo. Moves were afoot to cut the old hereditary samurai stipends, essential for keeping low-ranking families like the Hattoris financially viable. It would have been possible under the new, less restrictive social rules for uncle Hattori to strike out on his own. Instead, conservative and old-fashioned as he was, he chose to do what he did best, act as loyal retainer. In 1873 he followed the governor to Tokyo to serve as manager of the governor's Tokyo residence.[8]

Unokichi was six when his aunt and uncle, now his adoptive parents, relocated to Tokyo. To the foreign eye, the new Meiji capital, though a city of a million inhabitants, looked like "a series of villages, with bits of green and open spaces and inclosed grounds breaking up the continuity of the town."[9] But the contrast with the country castle town of Nihonmatsu was immense and even (or especially) a small child would have been awed by the bustling department stores, the horse-drawn buses, the rickshaws, and the new train that ran from Shinagawa to Yokohama. For this particular young child, a victim of loss and turmoil, Tokyo meant stability and security at last.

The move to Tokyo also meant access to the best education Japan had to offer, traditional or modern. Unokichi started his schooling at a private Chinese studies (*Kangaku*) academy (*juku,* currently the term for cram schools) just as he would have had he remained in Nihonmatsu. The government had intended an immediate phase-out of these Edo-era private academies to accompany its new policy, announced with breathtaking confidence in 1872, to establish from the ground up a nationwide system of public schools. But demand for the new education exceeded institutional capacity and since the traditional academies continued to be popular with ex-samurai families like the Hattoris, the government was content to allow them to continue to operate, albeit under close Ministry of Education supervision. It was only some twenty years later that they died a natural death, unable to compete with a modern curriculum as the route to success. In the early 1870s when Hattori started school, Chinese studies academies were a flourishing business. Teaching jobs in the new capital attracted some of Japan's top China scholars. Quality control and curriculum standardization were maintained by the Ministry. Tradition-minded parents like uncle Hattori could be assured that their sons were getting the highest quality training in the Confucian classics and Chinese historical texts.[10]

The next step in Hattori's school career was more problematic. In 1876 the government opened a new public school in the Azabu-Roppongi area where the Hattoris lived. It was an integrated school, the children of commoners and ex-samurai in class together. When a tofu seller visiting the Hattori house opined that young Unokichi ought to enroll, uncle Hattori was furious. How could his son mingle with sons of tradesmen? But he relented, and the nine-year-old boy, bright and talented, became an eager young scholar. Good exam results allowed him to complete the six-year primary program in four years. Topping this off with an extra year of training at a private academy not only in Chinese studies but in

English and math served to secure him a place in a two-year public middle school in Tokyo's Kanda Ward in 1881. That year a major fire swept through Kanda, destroying scores of old wooden buildings and disrupting business in Kanda's famous produce market and likely Hattori's school year as well. Reconstruction was quick, however, and the area took on a new look. Within a few years it was becoming known as much for its new private law schools as for its concentration of fruit and vegetable vendors. [11]

Like many of his generation, Hattori emerged from his middle school years with some exposure to so-called Western subjects combined with a solid foundation in the language and ethics of Chinese classical texts. Opportunities existed to study both streams in the late seventies early eighties, though trends were on the downswing for Chinese studies. In the public schools math, science, physical education and Japanese language were crowding out China while private schools accommodated to demands for up-to-date training by offering a combined Chinese-Western program or special tutoring in Western subjects only. By the mid-1890s a downgraded China was taught as a mere subunit in a course entitled "oriental history," which included Japan and much of the rest of the world east of Europe.[12]

Whatever the challenge, Hattori was a conscientious student, capable of straddling with ease the traditional subjects that his uncle favored along with the foreign-language training required of students aspiring to a university education. In 1883, he was admitted to Tokyo University's elite Preparatory School (renamed Tokyo First Higher School in 1886). Four years later he reached the pinnacle of a good Meiji education, gaining admission to the nation's sole university, where he enrolled in the Philosophy Department in the Faculty of Arts and Letters.

Tokyo University—officially, as of 1886, Tokyo Imperial University—was just a decade old when Hattori entered in 1887. The government's intention in creating a university out of several previously existing professional colleges was to produce a leadership corps trained at a world-class level. Foreign instructors predominated in the early days, conducting classes in English, French, or German. They were gradually replaced over the decade with overseas-trained Japanese, but the heavy emphasis on language proficiency as the gateway to new knowledge continued as did its essential place on the university entrance exam.

Hattori was well prepared. He had had the advantage all along of family support for educational attainment in general. He was lucky, too, that his old-school uncle quickly adjusted to the reality that getting ahead in the Japan of the eighties required a foreign set of skills. But success was not guaranteed. True, the 1872 Education law was based on the radical idea that education should be open to all, regardless of social rank or even gender. But given budgetary realities, this meant only four years of schooling in Hattori's day. Beyond this, still in the spirit of the new law, access depended on ability not socioeconomic status, setting off fierce competition among the talented and ambitious no matter what their family backgrounds. Hattori no doubt had a head start, but he had to perform at every step of the way to demonstrate that he merited one of the few seats at Tokyo Prep and the state-funded university at the apex of the nation's new school system. His fellow students, 450 of them in 1887, were Japan's best and brightest. Still, old habits persisted; even in the eighties students were tagged as commoners (*heimin*) or descendants of samurai (*shizoku*) in the published lists of university graduates.[13]

But if Tokyo University was born in a moment of optimism about the benefits of openness to a Western-style education, by the end of its first decade it was embroiled in a larger social controversy over whether Westernization was becoming counterproductive, impeding formation of a *Japanese* national identity deemed essential for Japan's modernizing success. At the heart of the matter was the entire educational edifice still under construction. There was no disagreement among Meiji leaders that the ultimate purpose of education was to produce citizens capable of contributing to the nation's economic strength and rising place in the world. The question was how to get there: which of the foreign pedagogical methods to employ, how much to emphasize Japanese values and heritage relative to "universal" science and math skills, what should be the funding priorities in new schools establishment, and who should direct educational policy, the Imperial Household Ministry, the Ministry of Education, local committees, professors at Tokyo Imperial University? These were never settled matters as witness Konoe's foray into contentious debates between teachers unions in the mid-1890s. But in the late 1880s, just as Hattori was transitioning from Tokyo Prep to the university, the Ministry of Education under Mori Arinori took a decisive step in the direction of asserting control and nationalizing the system in the name of emperor-centered goals. Tokyo University became Tokyo *Imperial* University. At the operational level, a series of measures were issued to regulate student conduct, modify the curriculum, and link education explicitly to public service.

Hattori's generation was the first to feel the effect of Mori's tightening measures. In his first year at university, Hattori recalled years later, authorities suddenly made it mandatory that students take a course in military-style exercises. Mori's idea here was to shape up lazy college students. Kanō Jigorō had the same idea in promoting judo classes in the schools. What stuck in Hattori's mind, however, was what a waste of time this was, at least at the university level. To fit the model of the army recruit, he and his classmates were abruptly ordered to discard their loose fitting kimonos and report to class in Western-style military uniforms, complete with high collars, caps, and leather shoes. Unwilling or unable to comply with the new dress code, students protested and were exempted from the requirement which nevertheless continued to be rigorously enforced in the teachers colleges and secondary schools.

The other Mori measure that had an impact on the Hattori era student was the adjustment in foreign versus Japanese in course content and teaching staff. In Hattori's last year at Tokyo Prep, the premier institution for foreign-language learning, the study of Japanese (*kokugo*, the national language) was added as a required course. At the university, Mori turned his critical eye on the foreign teaching faculty, questioning whether allowing them to lecture in foreign languages to Japanese students at a Japanese university fit the image of a truly sovereign nation. This, Hattori noted wryly, was coming from someone, himself British-educated, who had earlier proposed that to modernize rapidly Japan should adopt English as the exclusive language of instruction throughout the school system. In his later recollections Hattori reports that four Germans, one Englishman, and nine Japanese taught the fifteen or so students in the philosophy program. Presumably with this kind of teacher-student ratio, he knew his instructors well, though he does not elaborate. One faculty member he definitely had a close relationship with was the eminent China scholar Shimada Jūrei (1838-1898) soon to be his father-in-law. As Joshua Fogel has pointed out, Shimada was one of a number of influential Meiji-era Sinologists dedicated to promoting a revitalized *Kangaku*, certain as they were of its continued relevance in an age of Westernization.[14]

Graduation from Tokyo University meant entré to top civil service positions, either within the bureaucracy itself or in academia, and the promise of prestige, a relatively high salary, and a chance to influence social policy. In fact, a Tokyo University education was so highly regarded that its graduates were exempted from taking the civil service exam to qualify for government posts.[15] Hattori was not sure what he wanted to do when he graduated in 1890, but on the advice of his faculty advisers he accepted a job in the Ministry of Education's prestigious Bureau of Professional Affairs. Within a matter of months he realized he was not cut out to be a bureaucrat, required to play politics to get ahead. At the first opportunity, he left the Ministry to take a job as an English teacher and head of general instruction at Kyoto's Third Higher School. When the school was closed in 1894 he moved up in the ranks, joining the teaching staff at Kanō Jigorō's Teachers College in Tokyo, where he spent three productive years helping to implement a school expansion program. In 1897, a new Minister of Education sought his services as an adviser; it was common practice at the time for the Ministry to rotate Tokyo University graduates in and out of Ministry positions. Reluctant as Hattori was to reenter the bureaucracy, he felt obligated to accept. The new minister, concurrently president of Tokyo University, was not only Hattori's mentor but a personal friend and the official go-between in his marriage in 1891 to Shimada Shigeko, daughter of his favorite Chinese studies professor, Shimada Jūrei. Hattori may have found networking distasteful, but with these kinds of connections he seemed on his way to a promising career.[16]

In 1899, Hattori received one of the Ministry of Education's sought-after study abroad assignments, in his case a year in China followed by three in Germany. Germany was a study destination favored by many Meiji intellectuals and political figures. Konoe, we will recall, received his doctor of law degree from the University of Leipzig. Prefacing this with a China tour was unusual but fit Hattori's strong China background and the Ministry's growing interest in taking a lead role in China's educational reform. It dovetailed as well with the agenda of leading China scholars like Shimada and Shigeno Yasutsugu who had been arguing for years that Japanese needed to improve their communication skills in Chinese. The only way to modernize the field of Sinology was to talk with the big names in Qing scholarship firsthand, in their own language. Hattori was an ideal candidate to represent Japan's next generation of China scholars. A year's stay would enable him to develop fluency in the spoken language, pursue China research, and make contacts with China's scholars and officials. He would be on track to become a broad-based China expert, equipped not only to teach and publish but to help expand student-teacher exchange programs between China and Japan. Six months before his departure for China in October of 1899, Hattori received another plum promotion, an appointment as assistant professor at Tokyo University.[17] Though his official title as he set off for China was the humble *ryūgakusei* (overseas student), possibly in deference to his Chinese hosts,[18] his status within Japan's educational hierarchy was assured.

Encountering the Real China

Hattori had studied China his entire school career. He had a thorough knowledge of Chinese philosophy, history, and traditional institutions. In his father-in-law's early days in China scholarship, the Tokugawa travel ban to China was still in force, limiting face-to-face contacts and making the field a more bookish pursuit. The ban had been lifted in early Meiji, and Hattori had the happy prospect of adding the real China to the China he had imagined from long study. But as was the case for many Japanese China scholars traveling to China for the first time, encountering the real thing proved a rude awakening. "You've really arrived at a terrible time," the Japanese minister informed Hattori in his initial briefing in Beijing.

"Prominent Chinese are avoiding contacts with foreigners. I can introduce you to people and you can probably meet with them, but chances are they'll be annoyed and in the end you won't be able to make close contacts. This is truly a bad time."[19]

The atmosphere in the capital following Kang Youwei's failed reform movement the year before was tense and uncertain. The conservatives back in power regarded things foreign, progressive, modern, the wellspring of the reform agenda, as a danger to the state. Bureaucrats were told to observe the dress code, read only the official news, and limit their outside contacts.[20] The Japanese were not above suspicion, despite their "same culture, same race" (*dōbun, dōshu*) rhetoric and their commitment to joint efforts to expand study in Japan for Chinese students. After all, Japan was providing political asylum to Kang and Liang Qichao, two of the people who had tried to oust the current government. No less a public figure than Konoe Atsumaro had defended their political right to be there. The Chinese were wary, as Hattori found out at his first official banquet. While China's top leaders—from Governor-general Li Hongzhang (signer of the 1895 peace treaty with Japan) to ministers of the Grand Council—did him the courtesy of attending, conversation was nothing more than polite and superficial. Hattori got no further in the days to follow. Chinese scholars he contacted made excuses not to meet with him, either out of genuine antipathy to foreigners or simply fearful of being labeled pro-foreign. He was clearly disappointed: "In their offices they were too busy with public matters, at home too many family affairs—no time for meetings."[21]

Being snubbed by anti-foreign officials was a setback. But a far more serious problem was emerging for Hattori and the other foreign residents of Beijing in early 1900: that was the growing threat to their personal safety coming from an anti-foreign element at the lower end of the social scale, the Boxers. A fanatical cult of impoverished peasants enraged by the special rights enjoyed by Christian missionaries and their converts, the Boxers, or, more literally, the Righteous Harmonious Fists, had been on the rampage in northwest Shandong for a year, attacking Christians and vandalizing property. In the spring of 1900 the movement gathered force, broke out of Shandong, and became indiscriminately and ferociously anti-foreign. Gangs of ragtag Boxers, with their angry rhetoric "support the government, exterminate the foreigners," began to infiltrate the Beijing-Tianjin area. Their drift into the Beijing labor market, Hattori realized later, probably explained the sudden proliferation of rickshaw drivers working the streets in the six months after his arrival.[22] At the time, however, foreigners in the city generally ignored such warning signs. Few read the pulse of China with the accuracy of Sir Robert Hart, who wrote in 1892: "Chinese blood has been well cooled by the training its brain has had the last twenty centuries, but I think it quite possible that one of these days despair may find expression in the wildest rage, and that we foreigners will one and all be wiped out in Peking."[23]

The "summer's madness" as foreigners called the Boxer rampage in China's capital started with small incidents of intimidation. One day in early summer, Hattori and two other grantees—one of them Kano Naoki, professor at Kyoto University—hired a cart for a day's excursion outside Beijing's city walls. On their way home they stopped to eat at a local inn near the main gate. As they lingered in conversation after their meal, they suddenly became aware of two tough-looking Chinese observing them with angry looks. Abruptly, one of them approached their table, shoving a clenched fist in their faces. "This fist will break what's hard and crush what's strong and isn't afraid of anything in the world. Destroying this table and dishes would be mere child's play." Hattori and his companions hastily departed. But the sense of being targeted was palpable. On the cart ride through the maze of narrow lanes back to their lodgings, an unseen assailant pelted them with roof tiles. No one was injured, but it was a clear indication of the deteriorating security in the city.[24]

By early June the Boxers growing bolder appeared everywhere. Hattori out on his nightly walk stumbled across a group practicing calisthenics and military drills. Outside his lodgings he could hear Boxers, unafraid, chanting "crush the foreigners." A Chinese friend from China's Foreign Office visited him at great personal risk and urged him to flee to the safety of Tianjin in Chinese disguise, complete with false queue. Hattori gently refused, pointing out to his agitated friend that even if the disguise worked, his Chinese was not fluent enough to get him by and he would surely be killed. Besides it would hardly do to abandon his fellow Japanese.[25]

The most painful lesson Hattori learned after eight months in China was that there was no special category of Asian friends in the eyes of most Chinese; he was as much a *yangren* (foreigner) as any Westerner—and foreigners were generally disliked. For Hattori, whose mission was to facilitate closer Chinese-Japanese cooperation, this was a source of considerable frustration. Western observers in Beijing at the time, trying to explain to their home publics "Why they hate us," focused on the reactionary politics of the current Manchu power-holders bent on using Boxer cult fanaticism to strike at foreign interests. Hattori addressed this point too in the preface to his diary account of the events that riveted world attention on Beijing during the summer of 1900. But his interpretation of the origins of Chinese antiforeign sentiment, one of the few authoritative analyses available to a Japanese audience seeking answers, went far beyond that to look at the broader historical context. The current phenomenon, he argued, reflected deep-seated, long-standing cultural attitudes, a systemic mind-set about foreign versus Chinese that was both an impediment to progress and difficult to overcome.

Chinese hostility to Christians did not erupt suddenly in the late nineteenth century, Hattori told his readers. It had been a festering problem from the early days of Catholic missionary work in China more than 200 years before. At the time these first contacts took place, China was in a period of dynastic change. The most pressing task for the new Qing rulers was to consolidate control over a society which, as Hattori described it, was in moral and political decline, cut adrift from the unifying principles of traditional Confucian ideology. China's gentry lived by privilege and exploitation. They studied the Confucian classics not for their intrinsic worth as a guide to humanist values but because knowledge was power: a Confucian schooling was the ticket to success in the examination halls and official careers to follow. "Though they often recited the Classics," Hattori wrote of China's elite, "they failed to provide a moral example personally and their behavior sank to an ever lower standard . . ."

At the other end of the scale, China's masses, increasingly blocked from upward mobility, had become so demoralized that they pursued only their narrow self-interests without giving a thought to larger state concerns. The Qing solution to this crisis in values was to develop a Qing "mass line," so to speak—Hattori's exact words were ***kokumin shisō no tōitsu***—based on traditional Confucian precepts and popularized through public lectures held monthly nationwide. As he put it in terms Meiji Japanese would understand, it was an effort "to standardize public morals and forge a link between the court and the people."[26]

In the eyes of the Qing leaders, Catholic missionary work appeared a potential threat to this attempt at indoctrination. Edicts were broadcast warning people, "to renounce false doctrines in order to honor orthodox teachings."[27] Taken by the book, "false doctrines" included Buddhist and Taoist-related sects, but in practice, Hattori wrote, these sects were viewed with some tolerance. Only Christianity was consistently proscribed. At the same time, he noted, citing an early Qing source, the state made a careful distinction between religion and technology: "Western preaching about their god is wrong. But because these Westerners understand calendrical sciences, the state makes use of them. You all should be aware of this." Though such statements had lost their literal force by the late nineteenth century, Hattori explained, their net effect was to instill a negative image of Christianity in the minds of ordinary Chinese.[28]

But more than thought control was at issue in Chinese opposition to Christianity in Hattori's view. The Christian mindset was in certain fundamental ways incompatible with Chinese teachings and social practices. Christianity, he said, focused on spiritual happiness in the hereafter and on the search for ultimate truth.

Chinese ancestor worship was oriented to the here and now, to achieving happiness in a material sense; placating the spirits of the dead was meant to ensure the well-being of the living. As Hattori put it in a clear note of sympathy with the missionary position, the Chinese with their profit-driven mentality were utterly incapable of understanding the Christian missionaries whose work in China was motivated by idealism rather than personal gain. Particularly perplexing to the Chinese was that the missionaries were directing their efforts to China's poor whose lives were so vastly different from their own. Wealthy Chinese felt an obligation toward the poor in their midst, Hattori acknowledged, but, in his view, self-interest was at work here too. Contributing to local welfare programs was simply a way to enhance the prestige, power, and material status of the donors.

Given their own materialistic orientation, Hattori wrote, the Chinese could only conclude that the missionaries' investments in schools, hospitals, and orphanages were a cover for some form of exploitation. "When the Chinese who do not understand doing favors for others without recompense see the missionaries striving to raise large sums for hospital construction, to provide free medical care, and to support foster care for infants, they inevitably find it suspect."[29] The way the missionaries operated, holding secret meetings, treating men and women as equals, only heightened Chinese distrust. Rumors spread of missionary atrocities: that they abused infants abandoned to their care, even murdered some to use their organs in drug manufacture. That such rumors as these could gain easy currency, Hattori argued, was evidence of the scientific backwardness of the Chinese, a deficiency that he attributed to intellectual arrogance.

> What must be taken as the principal shortcoming of the Chinese these days is their lack of scientific knowledge and the almost complete absence of modern industry, which is the product of applied science. Nevertheless, the majority of scholars, because of their reluctance to defer to anyone else, because, with their unformed intellects, they have not developed the power to reason deductively from disparate data, and because they take the narrow-minded view that nothing other than what focuses on human affairs like ethics and politics can be called scholarship, satisfy themselves that science in the Western sense all originates from China (in the *Book of Changes* and Mo Zi's works, for example). Without bothering to investigate, ordinary people consider things like steam engines, steamships, and the telegraph to be like toys. They don't direct their attention further to such things as structure and function. With this kind of mindset, the Chinese thus blindly take themselves as the measure of all things; they are unaware of *my* weaknesses and *his* strengths. The concept of taking the self as insufficient and trying to learn from others is weak.[30]

Whatever specific grievances Chinese had against Christian missionaries, in other words, were reinforced by a kind of knee-jerk negative reaction toward foreigners in general. This attitude, Hattori explained, was not simply the result of the recent Chinese versus Western experience but a product of centuries of interacting with people the Chinese considered their cultural inferiors, the ethnically distinct groups on China's borders they collectively referred to as barbarians. By the Qing period, this Chinese-barbarian frame of reference had habituated the Chinese to think that they were self-sufficient and needed nothing from the outside world. Not only that, what originally were comparisons of culture had hardened into racial stereotyping whereby physical appearance was taken as an index of inner worth. Racial prejudice, Hattori said, clouded the Chinese judgment of Europeans who, despite their demonstrated technological superiority, were relegated to the same category as the lowly border peoples. Hattori did acknowledge in passing that many foreigners likewise considered the Chinese unenlightened, barbaric and godless, but he clearly felt that the burden of misperception lay with the Chinese and that, at the very least, their "you need us more than we need you" attitude was self-defeating in the modern context.

After eight months as a China watcher, Hattori also well understood that the foreign-Christian issue was as much about power as ideology or emotion. At the grass-roots level, he told his readers, missionary efforts to convert the masses represented a challenge to the entrenched local elites whose authority depended on community acceptance of a Confucian moral order. Within the central government, the question of how to deal with foreigners, linked as it was to important trade and security concerns, fueled factional infighting among shifting coalitions of Han Chinese, Manchus, liberals, and conservatives.

Jockeying for power in an atmosphere in which Han Chinese-liberal was associated with foreign culture, Manchu conservative elements began to manipulate Boxer anti-foreign fanaticism to their own ends. As Hattori made clear, this decision was to some extent taken by default. In the absence of a centrally administered police system, the central government had no other option but to rely on local leaders to maintain public security. Besides, the Boxers first appeared in the guise of a local defense group, the very kind of militia operation the government was encouraging as a means to keep order. But even after facts on the ground proved this false, Hattori explained, Qing hard-liners in control at the top saw political advantage in the groundswell of popular anti-foreign sentiment stirred up by the Boxers, so they publicly issued orders to suppress the group, which they had no firm intention of implementing. Only Yuan Shikai in his capacity of governor of Shandong used his crack troops to rout the Boxers, but they regrouped and by early 1900 had extended their activities to the Beijing-Tianjin area. Because foreigners in Beijing were unaware of the relationship between the central government and the Boxers, they tended to underestimate the real danger signaled by the growing number of incidents of Boxer harassment.[31] Meanwhile, Hattori wrote, the arrival in late May of a contingent of about four hundred foreign troops from eight nations including Japan gave foreign residents a renewed sense of security. [32]

Boxer gangs roam the streets of Tianjin (Courtesy of the Library of Congress)

Siege of the Legations

This did not last long. In his first diary entry, dated June 4, Hattori wrote:

> At daybreak, there was an urgent message that the Boxers had destroyed the rail line in the vicinity of Huang Village, again cutting off transport between Beijing and Tianjin. Communications, both rail and telegraph, between Beijing and Baoding remain damaged as they have been for the past few days and have not yet started operating. Although, because of this, the situation in that area is totally unknown, reportedly the Boxers have victimized many of

the local foreign residents. It's rumored that the American church received a report saying that the bodies of two foreigners wrapped in matting were found floating in the Daqing River. People are once again very alarmed.[33]

Heightened alarm prompted urgent messages to warships anchored in Tianjin harbor requesting additional troops to guard the legations. The Japanese, whose protective force numbered only twenty-four sailors and a single officer, hoped to add another fifty. Foreign diplomats, called together by British Minister Sir Claude MacDonald, drew up plans in case of Chinese attack. The Qing court responded to the escalating violence with mild assurances that while both native Christians and Boxers were "children of the state," fanatic fringe elements that had infiltrated the Boxer group would be treated as rebels.[34]

In his diary entry for June 8, Hattori reported that about thirty Japanese in Beijing had volunteered their services to help the small military contingent guard the Japanese legation. It was a mixed group of civilian professionals: legation diplomats, journalists, photographers, technicians with the Beijing Electric Light Company, a couple of Japanese language teachers, and several *ryūgakusei* (overseas students), including himself and Kano Naoki. The volunteers and the twenty-five-man naval force were under the command of Colonel Shiba Gorō. In a contemporary photograph of the combined group, Hattori, glasses off, looks tense, uncomfortable and professorial in suit, tie and, derby hat.[35]

Japanese volunteers during the siege of the legations, summer 1900. Hattori is in the second row from the front, second from the right. (Hattori Unokichi, *Pekin rōjō nikki;* Tokyo: 1926)

Over the next ten days Hattori's diary records a rapidly deteriorating situation in Beijing. Boxers brazenly paraded the streets, knives drawn. Rumors spread that the government was in the grip of anti-foreign elements. Troops from China's far west, the Gansu cavalry of General Dong Fuxiang, could be seen amassing outside the city walls; they had been called in by the government but whether to protect or attack the foreign community was unclear. On the hopeful side, word got through on the tenth that an allied force of about two thousand under Admiral Edward Seymour was on its way from Tianjin. The rail lines, it was assumed, had been quickly repaired.

On the afternoon of June 11, First Secretary Sugiyama Akira accompanied by a single Chinese servant set out from the legation to the Beijing railway station to greet the Japanese troops supposedly on their way. To the alarm of Hattori and others waiting at the legation the servant came running back in a panic only minutes later. Chinese soldiers from the Gansu unit had halted Sugiyama's carriage at the Yongding Gate and forcibly dragged him away. Reports soon followed describing Sugiyama's savage murder. As Hattori saw it, this was a message to foreigners about what they might expect at the hands of the notoriously brutal Gansu troops. Equally troubling to him was the sense that the Boxers were not the only enemy. Neither the provincial forces nor the central government could be trusted. That night the Japanese volunteers were called to the legation and cautioned to be on guard. Warnings of an impending attack by Chinese soldiers and Boxers made everyone jittery.[36]

The Chinese government issued a statement that deplored Sugiyama's murder and offered assurances that those responsible would be apprehended. But given the government's performance thus far, Hattori wrote, there seemed little reason to expect curbs on Boxer activities.[37] In the week following the murder, with still no sign of Seymour's relief force, Beijing erupted in mob violence. Hattori records a jumble of harrowing scenes. At night, from the sanctuary of the Japanese legation, he describes a city ablaze with fires set by the Boxers, the leaping flames and bright moon illuminating the maze of walled streets and winged tile roofs as if by daylight. Churches, clinics, bookstores, schools, homes of Chinese Christian converts—anything touched by the foreigner's hand—were put to the torch. Whole families burned to death. From all directions came distant screams for help. Converts who managed to flee to the legation told of looting, burning, and women and children brutalized.[38]

Meanwhile, the government was sending mixed signals on its policy toward the Boxers. When out-of-control fires spread to Beijing's banking quarter and money exchange shops were going up in flames, the government issued a statement calling for protection of property. American diplomats were informed that government troops were being ordered to put a stop to Boxer violence that had gotten out of hand. At the same time, rumors were afloat that Boxer leaders had met with the empress dowager herself and that the Boxers were in effect a kind of government-controlled militia. Foreigners suspected the worst. While the government had some concern about the recent spate of violence, Hattori concluded, it was both openly and covertly backing the Boxer cause.[39]

To add to the growing fear in the foreign community, word filtered through from Tianjin that Seymour's combined force had run into Boxer resistance in its advance north from Tianjin to Beijing and was facing severe shortages of supplies. What Hattori and the others in Beijing found out only weeks later was that to secure access to Tianjin from the south, thus protecting Seymour's rear position, the foreign powers had seized the coastal forts below Tianjin. In response, the government on June 19 issued an ultimatum to each of the foreign ministers that all foreign nationals leave Beijing in 24 hours. The ministers countered with a request for a meeting with Foreign Office officials the next morning to discuss extension of the time limit, transportation arrangements, and assurances of safe conduct. At the end of a day spent anxiously tracking fires raging in various parts of the city, foreigners were told the grim news of the government's ultimatum. It took every effort to keep up a courageous front, Hattori wrote, as the extent of Chinese hostility and the precariousness of the foreign position became abundantly clear. Even if the Chinese government agreed to provide a military escort, would this be enough to protect foreigners in the face of angry Chinese crowds? Could some four hundred foreign sailors and a few volunteer units guarantee the safe passage to Tianjin of hundreds of elderly people, women, and children? The feeling of panic increased when it was learned that senior diplomats disagreed on the very question of security guarantees. Some felt it was suicidal to quit the relative safety of Beijing.[40]

On June 20 Hattori describes what world opinion greeted with even greater outrage than Sugiyama's murder. On his way to a morning meeting with the Foreign Office, the German minister was shot and killed by a Chinese soldier. The crisis entered a new phase. All women, children, and elderly were rushed into the large British legation. Able-bodied young men stayed at their various legations, preparing to defend the area against attack. Sometime after three o'clock, just as the 24-hour time limit expired, Chinese soldiers started firing. Austrian and British forces returned fire. On the twenty-first the government issued a formal declaration of war against the powers, citing a history of foreign aggression that justified the current wave of popular opposition. The siege of the legations had begun.

What was known as the legation quarter was a 200-acre area extending east from Tiananmen Square to Wangfujing Street and south to the massive Tartar Wall, now the location of the Chairman Mao Memorial Hall and the Museum of Chinese Revolutionary History. This was the site of eleven foreign missions, a number of important government offices, Prince Su's estate which itself occupied about ten acres, and scattered among the more prominent compounds, many low wooden houses of ordinary Chinese. It was not, in other words, an exclusive foreign enclave but was intermixed with the Chinese community. Crowded into eight of the legations and Prince Su's estate as the siege began were about 475 foreign civilians, 400 marine guards, and 3,000 Chinese Christians. This small group in a hostile city of a million was extremely vulnerable to attack. From the 60-foot-high Tartar Wall the Chinese had a commanding view of the entire area. The legation quarter itself was not in 1900 the fortified camp of walled enclosures it was to become a few years later, nor were the people caught there militarily prepared to counter an all-out assault. They were in effect hostages of the Chinese government. They lived with the day-to-day reality that they could be wiped out in a moment at the whim of that government; a widely distributed report appearing in the London *Daily Mail* in early July entitled "Peking Massacre" claimed that such a tragedy had in fact occurred.[41]

Beijing, legation quarter, British, Russian (on left), Japanese (on right). (Courtesy of the Library of Congress).

Prince Su (Shanqi), 1866-1922. Prince Su's villa, known to foreigners at the Suwangfu or simply "fu," was used by Japanese volunteers as a defense post during the siege. Original caption cites Su as a man of "distinguished bravery" who "gave palace and provisions to besieged Legations." (Courtesy of the Library of Congress)

In an unimaginable turnabout, Hattori Unokichi, China scholar and university professor found himself on sentry duty the first night of the siege. He remembered standing in the pitch dark shaking with fear as he listened to the intermittent crackle of rifle fire coming from some indeterminate direction. After weeks of constant bombardment, serving as a volunteer under Colonel Shiba became routine, but there were a number of close calls. Relaying messages between legations one night, Hattori was within inches of having his head blown off as an artillery shell crashed into the wall behind him. Thoughts of his mortality brought a longing for home. He thought of his wife, waiting for him in Osaka, and of his adoptive mother, now in her final years, and their narrow escape from death in 1868. As Hattori recalled later, "I followed the cycle of days and nights, just resigning myself to fate in all matters, conscious that tomorrow I could be among my dead and injured friends. Facing danger countless times, in the end I simply lived out my life, and my belief in fate became ever more profound."[42]

Hattori was appalled by the destruction around him. For weeks before the siege, fires had raged in the Chinese quarters as the Boxers torched the dwellings of Christian converts. Of Beijing's four Catholic cathedrals three had been gutted. With the government's June 21 declaration of war, the fourth became, like the legations, a refuge for converts and foreigners struggling to survive Chinese attack. On June 23 Chinese forces set fire to the Hanlin Academy, China's premier scholarly institution, housing a great library of Chinese books, documents, and manuscripts dating back hundreds of years. The idea behind this self-inflicted wound was, in the view of London *Times* reporter G.E. Morrison, "to be revenged upon foreigners." The Hanlin Academy and the British legation were on abutting lots, separated by a low wall. It was expected that the steady north winds blowing that day would spread the conflagration to the British compound, creating havoc in the foreign community. Hattori and other Japanese volunteers rushed to the aid of British marines, who broke into the Academy grounds to stop the blaze. By nightfall it was under control. Most of the library was reduced to ashes, though Hattori and others managed to salvage a few smoldering books by throwing them into an adjoining pond. Hattori himself retrieved several priceless volumes from the great Ming dynasty encyclopedia, the *Yong-lo Dadian*, but handed them over to the British minister in response to an order that all such works be collected for eventual return to the Chinese government. When he revisited the Hanlin Academy in 1902, Hattori reported that the volumes he had passed on to the British were nowhere to be found.[43]

As the siege settled into routine, Hattori reflected on the irony of Japan's role in the crisis. "I would call it a very strange turn of events," he wrote on June 24, "that our non-Christian nation has been sucked into the center of a disturbance in which Christianity is the issue, and that we have found ourselves the protectors of Christian converts and also relying on them for help." Of the approximately three thousand converts, a mix of Protestants and Catholics, crowded into the legation quarter, some two thousand were housed in Prince Su's compound under Colonel Shiba's command. During the first heavy bombardments by Chinese troops, Hattori recalled, the Chinese converts fell to their knees and prayed loudly, but as after a few days of relentless attack, they directed their energies instead to help the sixty Japanese defenders fight fires and build barricades.[44]

Day after day, as summer temperatures in Beijing reached record highs—"like sitting on a cauldron"—the shelling continued. Hattori's diary entries were variations on a theme.

> June 29, morning. Extremely heavy enemy attack on Prince Su's compound and the French legation. Artillery shifted aim to the northeast side of the compound; furious bombardment. At about 1:00 PM they smashed part of the outer wall, then set fire to the main shrine. As the flames rose, the sounds of bugles and terrifying howls started up outside and we thought that at any minute they would probably break through. But actually it was a bluff; they were trying to intimidate us.[45]

Almost daily the morning brought furious shelling followed by silence and then, at any time into the night, another fusillade would begin, often punctuated by nature's fury of thunder and pounding rain.

For the defenders, as Hattori described the scene, day and night blurred into an endless struggle to strengthen battered barricades and pick off advancing Boxers and Chinese soldiers. An occasional sortie was made into nearby streets to try to silence Chinese shelling at its source. By the end of the first week of July, relentless attacks on Su's compound had worn down the small Japanese force. Casualties were high. Three Japanese were wounded on July 6, including the head of the volunteer unit who died a few hours later; another five were wounded in an early morning Chinese assault on July 9. Colonel Shiba, worried about maintaining the forward defense point, sent for British reinforcements.[46] News of the outside world was gleaned from paid informants, often enemy soldiers, sometimes converts who at great personal risk carried messages between the legations and foreign representatives in Tianjin. Rumors were rife: that the Chinese government wanted to put an end to the fighting, that the allied relief force was nearing Beijing, that on July 15 a combined force of Boxers and Chinese troops were planning an all-out assault and mass slaughter of foreigners. Day to day the legation defenders lived with the awful knowledge that the Chinese government could apply superior force at any point and annihilate them all, probably with the brutality shown Sugiyama. That such an order was never given was evidence of divided council among decision makers as to the wisdom of allying with the populist Boxer movement to make war on all the powers at once. The biggest gap was with the governors of China's southern provinces who refused outright to endorse the court's June 21 declaration of war.

Suddenly on July 17, the government announced a cease-fire. Incessant rifle fire, Hattori wrote, was replaced with unnerving silence. Characteristic of this bizarre little war, enemy soldiers now appeared at the gates of the legations selling watermelons, vegetables, and eggs to the very people they had been trying to kill a few days before. Additional food was sent courtesy of the empress dowager herself. This was like manna from heaven to the legation defenders who were subsisting mainly on rice gruel garnished with an occasional piece of horse or donkey meat from those creatures unfortunate enough to have been caught in the siege. The animals sent to slaughter, Hattori recalled sadly, were so starved that they stood dully immobile as bullets whacked into the walls around them. Along with acting as food vendors, the now friendly Chinese soldiers were a source of new rumors: that Dong Fuxiang's cavalry was still in the city, troops from Shanxi were about to arrive, a Boxer force of two thousand was readying for an attack on the North Cathedral. More important, the cease-fire allowed legation messengers to sneak in with news from Tianjin. Tianjin had been occupied on July 14. A Japanese force of 3-4,000 men had arrived on June 29; another 5,000 bound for Tianjin had departed from Hiroshima on July 8. The delay of Japanese reinforcements had been a sore point with the other foreigners. Now, said Hattori, "the Westerners are overjoyed and suddenly showering us with compliments."[47]

The cease-fire was the occasion for a flurry of communiqués between the legation diplomats and the Chinese Foreign Office. In some, the Chinese took a conciliatory tone, suggesting that the foreigners consider releasing the converts from the hot, overcrowded legations and working out some modus operandi for their own withdrawal from Beijing. The foreign diplomats were skeptical: Why had the government initially refused to extend the time limit and negotiate a way out of the crisis? Each side accused the other of bad faith and claimed its own actions were in self-defense. As these maneuvers were going on at the diplomatic level, teams of foreigners and converts were busy repairing defense works under the curious stares of idle Chinese soldiers.[48]

The reprieve was short-lived. At the end of July the government launched a campaign of intimidation, if not as lethal as before, equally nerve wracking, in Hattori's view, due to its unpredictability. Harmless explosions from firecrackers were followed by dangerous shelling and rocket attacks, and then long intervals of silence. Often gunfire could be heard several miles away, in the direction of the North Cathedral. During these weeks of wearing down tactics, the Foreign Office continued to press its proposal that the legation occupants agree to withdraw under escort and announced that the venerable Li Hongzhang had been appointed minister plenipotentiary, raising hopes that peace talks were in the offing. Items in the official *Peking Gazette*, smuggled into the legations, pointed to a nasty power struggle within the central government. Hattori was greatly saddened by the announced execution of two top Qing government officials, both of them anti-war advocates whom he knew personally. Reports from Chinese scouts for the legations told of the steady advance of the allied relief force, which was inflicting heavy casualties on the Chinese. From the Japanese commander came word that the force expected to reach Beijing on August 13 or 14.[49]

At two in the morning of August 14, the sound of distant guns could be heard in the east announcing the imminent arrival of the allied troops. In his final diary entry, dated the fourteenth, Hattori wrote:

> Yesterday, taking advantage of a break in the hail of enemy bullets, Kimura and others raised our Japanese flag to the very top of the highest tree in front of our headquarters. The sight of our flag mirrored in the rising sun this morning filled me with inexpressible joy. From dawn the booming of guns grew increasingly intense with each passing hour. At around 10:00 AM, there seemed to be a marked increase in the number of guns firing and a fierce bombardment began in the vicinity of the Qihua Gate. Meanwhile the enemy directed relentless rifle fire at the various legations from the city walls and from the other side of Prince Su's compound.

At around three in the afternoon, the British marched in by the Water Gate; by evening the Americans, Russians, and Japanese, all encountering fierce resistance, had reached the legation quarter. The siege was over. [50]

Allied troops entering through the Water Gate in the Tartar Wall to relieve the siege of the Legations. (Courtesy of the Library of Congress)

Hattori's joy and relief were indescribable. Liberated after sixty-three days of gripping fear and uncertainty about whether he would see home and family again, he felt "like a fish restored to water after gasping in a dry rut." He had an emotional reunion with friends who were officers in the Japanese relief force. Writing about the event some years later, Hattori confessed to a feeling of pride at the performance of the Japanese marine guards and volunteers charged with defending Prince Su's compound, the part of the legation quarter most vulnerable to attack. There were only sixty of them, marines and volunteers together, a much smaller unit than the other national contingents and poorly armed. Yet, as Hattori told his Japanese readers, they bore up under the worst fighting and had the highest casualty rate. Lest he be regarded as unduly boastful, he was quick to point out that the Japanese contribution was sympathetically acknowledged by a number of foreigners, including the London *Times* correspondent, G.E. Morrison and the British minister to China who, in his report to the allied commander, gave half the credit for successful defense operations to the Japanese. In fact, Hattori very much understated the reaction of the foreign press, which was positively extravagant in its praise of Japan's performance, if slightly condescending in its constant reference to "the plucky little Japanese." The style of patronizing compliment was captured well by the old American missionary W.A.P. Martin, himself caught in the siege, who reported to the *New York Times*, "The rescue was the work of Christendom, aided by Japan, which deserves to be admitted into that honored brotherhood."[51]

When Hattori left Beijing to return to Japan in September 1900, the empress dowager and her entourage had fled the city and order was being imposed by thousands of foreign troops. Hattori had been in China nearly a year. During that time, he had little opportunity to solidify professional contacts with Chinese and work out arrangements for Japanese assistance to educational development. In fact, Hattori probably learned more about the workings of China's foreign community—and that the Chinese viewed Japan as part of that foreign community—than he did about Chinese bureaucratic networks. And, after a year witnessing China in the grip of reactionary politics, he came away evidently proud that Japan was not China with its narrow-minded mentality, that Japan was fast becoming recognized as world-class. What left a lasting impression on him was the disaster the Chinese had brought upon themselves by their violent anti-foreignism. In the forefront of his mind as he left Beijing were images of the legation quarter in ruins, of unimaginable brutalities the Boxers had visited upon their fellow Chinese, of wounded and dying legation defenders. From corroborating accounts, it is clear that the scenes Hattori witnessed were even more horrifying than what he chose to reproduce in his diary. Summing up his Boxer experience, he wrote: "Making a show of anti-foreign thought is dangerous for East Asia as a whole. Japan must guide the Chinese so they don't make this mistake in the future."[52]

Japanese soldiers guarding the gutted ruins of Prince Su's compound. (Hattori Unokichi, *Pekin rōjō nikki*; Tokyo: 1926)

Back to Beijing: Advising on Post-Boxer Reform

Hattori was in Japan less than three months—time enough to arrange for publication of his Boxer account which came out in October—when he was packing his bags once again. Having spent an unusual year in China, he was now eligible for the second portion of his grant, three years in Germany where he expected to study not only German philosophy but German scholarship on China. By early 1901 he had enrolled in a German-language course at Leipzig University, Konoe's alma mater. The scorching heat, violence, and ruins of Beijing had begun to recede in his mind, replaced with the gray chill of a German winter, the order and solid structures of a modern city. In 1902 Hattori transferred to the University of Berlin where he audited classes taught by well-known German China scholars and copied rare documents from the university's China collection.

But the real China was soon on the horizon again, interrupting his stay in Germany midway. In June, he received a cable from Japan's Ministry of Education asking if he were interested in heading a new teacher-training division at Beijing

University. He replied in the affirmative and started the month-long trip back to Tokyo via Paris, London, Southampton, New York, and Seattle, arriving in mid-August. As Hattori traveled the world, Foreign Minister Komura and Minister to China Uchida were busy resolving a last minute glitch. The Chinese authorities, who had initiated the request for a qualified Japanese to fill the advisory position, wanted assurances that they were getting a full professor. Hattori, the candidate recommended by the Ministry of Education, was only an assistant professor and a relatively new assistant professor at that. A promotion was quickly in the works. By the time he arrived home, Hattori, aged thirty-five, had been elevated to the rank of doctor/full professor at Tokyo University. In early September 1902, accompanied by his wife Shigeko, he departed for Beijing, his home for the next six years.[53]

Except for the choking dust and the uncommon blue of the sky on a clear fall day, Beijing presented a different scene to the arriving traveler from what Hattori encountered three years before. It was a city diminished, ruins from the siege still much visible, though reconstruction had begun and canals were being filled in, roads extended, a foundation laid for a new Catholic cathedral. The temples, imperial halls, and other landmarks for which the city was famous were still closed to visitors. Curio shops and porcelain stores had little to offer collectors of antiques. The enormous seventeenth century astronomical instruments standing atop the old observatory were gone, looted by the Germans.

Above all, Beijing was a city under foreign occupation. Along the Tartar wall, its finest towers destroyed, foreigners were busy constructing defensive works to prevent Chinese troops from firing down on enemies below. The legation quarter, site of the siege-drama, was crawling with foreign troops, the Germans a particularly noisy presence with their constant practice drills and bugle blowing. Everywhere walls were going up to keep out the Chinese now forbidden to wander through streets newly named Boulevard d'Italie and Thomaun Strasse. Prince Su's compound where some thirty Japanese were killed or wounded had become the new legation grounds of the Japanese, Italians, and British, heavily garrisoned with guards. Beijing's Legation quarter was fast developing into an exclusive foreign enclave, "a mere Ghetto shut off from the rest of the world and knowing but little of what is going on in China."[54]

Build-up of security at the legations and an increased foreign troop presence in China were sanctioned by terms of the Boxer Protocol (September 1901) which also required punishment of court officials found guilty of war crimes and imposed a $330 million indemnity on China. But repercussions from the Boxer events reached beyond these punitive actions. The two years Hattori was in Germany marked a fundamental course reversal in China's domestic politics, back to the reform agenda of 1898 with a new twist. In January of 1901, the empress dowager and her advisers, their backs to the wall, issued a statement from their place of refuge in Xi'an endorsing fundamental institutional reform based on Western models. By July, Zhang Zhidong and Liu Kunyi, powerful regional leaders who had opposed war with the powers, had translated this general endorsement into a series of concrete proposals that the court approved a few months later. The centerpiece of what became known as the New Policies (*xinzheng*) was the government's educational development program which authorized establishment of a nationwide system of schools, changes in the civil service examination system, and study in Japan.

Street scene in Beijing, 1902. (Courtesy of the Library of Congress)

All of this was in the works, then, when the Boxer Protocol was signed in September, and the way was paved for the return of the empress dowager to Beijing in January of 1902. Foreigners were now back in the dowager's good graces. They, on their part, found support for old leaders embarked on New Policies to be the best way to preserve their commercial interests in China. The field of foreign competitors now included Japan. All observers of the contemporary scene remarked on Japan's rise to regional power in the post-Boxer world. The very month the dowager returned to the capital, the British and Japanese signed a treaty of alliance. As Hattori quite correctly observed, Anglo-Japanese cooperation during the siege helped smooth the way for the new accord. Indeed, while the Boxer episode decidedly improved Japan's international image, it seriously damaged China's in the eyes of Europeans, Americans, and Japanese.[55]

In a formal ceremony on October 9, 1902, Hattori signed a contract with China's Ministry of Education to head the teacher-training division *(shifan guan)* at newly established Beijing University. A Japanese colleague, Kyoto University professor Iwaya Magozō, shared the honors of the day with his appointment as head professor of the university's public administration division (*shixue guan*).[56] To Hattori, the respectful welcome given the new Japanese faculty must have been especially gratifying. Vivid in his mind was the university in shambles two years before, one of its top administrators executed as a foreign sympathizer, its buildings and equipment vandalized by Russian and German forces in the aftermath of the Boxer siege.[57] The China scene had now shifted and foreigners were being asked once again to play an advisory role in China's higher education.

Chinese Minister of Education and university president Zhang Baixi could take justifiable pride in affixing his name to the contracts with Hattori and Iwaya on October 9 and with seven additional foreign teaching staff—three Japanese and four Westerners—a few days later.[58] That university development was so quickly back on track was testimony to Zhang's considerable bureaucratic skills in working out a university design with broad political acceptance within government.

This was no small feat. Since 1896, when the first official proposal for a national university was made (by a vice-president of the Board of Punishments who was also Liang Qichao's brother-in-law), the university issue had been a flash point of controversy over the timing and direction of educational change generally. While most within government agreed in principle that some kind of overhaul of China's school system was required to meet the demands of a modern state, how to do this without cultural capitulation, in other words, how to accommodate advanced science and technology *within* Chinese culture, was the subject of continuous debate. Supporters of the university proposal argued that a balance could be achieved by introducing so-called Western subjects as a supplement to core courses in Chinese philosophy and ethics, making Western teachers subordinate to their Chinese counterparts, and selecting students on the basis of their mastery of classical scholarship.

Even the most passionate proponents of educational reform were concerned that the new system should retain distinctively Chinese characteristics. In making his case for the need to develop higher-level teacher education, Liang Qichao warned against the inefficiencies of an over dependence on Western teachers in Chinese schools. He cited the Japanese practice of limiting the tenure of foreign-hires as a model of how to do it right. The balanced approach taken by Liang and others notwithstanding, conservative politicians saw creating a national university as an assault on both Chinese culture and their own political power, a threat to the exam system's monopoly on preparing people for government service. They tried to put the brakes on higher education projects, citing, with justification, problems of financing.[59]

But as the reform movement gathered momentum in the summer of 1898, the university proposal was looked at with renewed interest. Liang Qichao drafted a lengthy document, "Planning the Structure of a National [lit. capital] University," that referenced the Japanese school system and discussed in detail curriculum requirements, faculty selection, entrance requirements, and the all important question of how to finance the new institution. In Liang's conception, the university was to be a model of integrating Chinese and Western learning in programs designed to train civil servants and produce teachers to man China's new schools.

Such was the consensus achieved on the university issue that a version of Liang's plan went forward even after the September coup eclipsed the reform faction and most of the other items on its agenda. By December, a mansion and grounds of one of the Manchu princes had been converted into a campus for the new university. The inaugural ceremony was held there on the thirty-first, an observance of Confucian rites attended by government officials, 380 students ranging in age from sixteen to forty, and twenty-five Chinese and foreign faculty members. Of the eighteen Chinese teachers, most had studied in Europe or the United States; eight reportedly were Christians. Leading the foreign faculty in the ritual bows before Confucius that December day was their head professor (*zong jiaoxi*)—in fact, he liked to be referred to as Beijing University's first president—the American missionary W.A.P. Martin, a vigorous man of seventy who had worked in China for forty-seven years. Another well-known figure on the foreign faculty was F. Huberty James, a British missionary with twenty years of China service. Nishigōri Sōzaburō, the sole Japanese on the roster, was listed as professor of Japanese language.[60]

Beijing University in its opening semester in the spring of 1899 was more the equivalent of a cadre training school than a real university. Most students were mid-level officials who enjoyed higher social status than their teachers. The curriculum consisted of refresher courses on the Chinese classics supplemented by foreign-language training. By the fall semester, additional courses were offered in politics, math, and science, but still, the foreign community considered the program quite substandard, undeserving of the name "university." In the spring of 1900, Beijing University development fell victim to the Boxer turmoil and classes were suspended altogether. On June 20, as the siege of the legations began, Professor James, "an awfully decent sort," was decapitated by the Boxers. Head professor W.A.P. Martin, his fifty years of educational work in China apparently for naught, spent the summer under bombardment in the British legation while Nishigōri joined Hattori and other young Japanese in a desperate defense of the beleaguered foreign group.[61]

Zhang Baixi, appointed Minister of Education upon the court's return to Beijing in January 1902, was charged with the enormous task of translating the Zhang/Liu proposals into a concrete plan for a national school system capped by an imperial university. His approach was both bold and bureaucratically savvy. The Zhang Baixi model for primary and secondary schools departed from earlier schemes by placing more emphasis on educating the general public rather than training future bureaucrats. Drawing upon ideas earlier rejected as too radical, his plan for the university provided for a preparatory course with science and humanities divisions and an accelerated course which had two priority streams, an upgraded cadre training division and the entirely new division of teacher education. In structuring and staffing the university, Zhang invited Japanese influence. He persuaded classical scholar and ardent modernist Wu Rulun to accept the post of dean, then underwrote Wu's much-publicized, three-month study tour of educational facilities in Japan. He abruptly dismissed W.A.P. Martin and other Westerners on the original Beijing University faculty and hired nine new professors, five of them Japanese, including Hattori and Iwaya.[62]

Zhang's moves were smart politics. Starting with a new roster of teachers made it more likely that Zhang as new minister could control the direction of educational development. Getting rid of Martin, the veteran missionary, and bringing in professionally trained Japanese (remember that the government wanted assurances that Hattori had a doctorate) made educational restructuring more palatable to politicians with anti-Western views, who were fearful of European and American dominance in the post-Boxer reforms. When Zhang needed someone to teach English literature and law, he hired Edmund Backhouse (later Sir Edmund), age twenty-nine, over the venerable Martin. The quirky Backhouse had much to recommend him—he was a superb linguist, known as the best translator of Chinese documents in Beijing—but but surely one of his key qualifications was that he was *not* a missionary.[63]

Beijing University students and teachers in 1902, just as Hattori and four other Japanese arrived to join the faculty. (Courtesy of the Library of Congress)

There were other reasons for hiring Japanese than the desire to blunt Western, particularly missionary, influence. Most important, the Japanese had recent experience in dealing, apparently successfully, with the same dilemma facing the Chinese: how to integrate Asian values and Western technology in building a system of schools from the ground up. As discussed in the previous chapter, the benefit of learning from Japan was increasingly touted by Chinese who had visited Japan as students or on official missions. Already by 1902 such people represented a kind of educational lobby favoring closer ties with Japan. Equally significant for a Chinese government burdened with Boxer reparations payments, hiring Japanese teachers and advisers made financial sense. Salaries and transportation costs were lower than for their European and American counterparts. Finally, prominent Japanese from Konoe Atsumaro to Kanō Jigorō to Foreign Minister Komura Jutarō were pressing the Chinese to choose Japanese over Westerners to fill the high visibility, potentially influential teaching positions at China's new university.[64] Japanese arguments, for a time, won out.

Precisely what Hattori and his colleagues were being hired to do in their jobs at the new university was nowhere laid out on paper. For all the fanfare accompanying the contract signing, the actual document was a thin three pages devoted almost entirely to financial arrangements, salary, housing allowance, travel subsidy, sick leave, and remedies in case of early termination of the contract. Both Hattori and Iwaya had agreed to three years of teaching and advisory work for a salary of about 600 taels or 400-yen equivalent per month, probably 50 percent higher than their salaries at Tokyo and Kyoto universities.[65] Apart from financial terms and conditions, the contract had little to say, except to note that while the advisers were permitted to make proposals on departmental matters, the ultimate decision-making power rested with China's Minister of Education.[66] There was nothing in the contract in the way of a job description or scope of work, nor does Hattori report meeting with Chinese educators to discuss the specifics of his assignment. By Hattori's own account, Minister Zhang Baixi and his staff, who "knew nothing whatever about the new education," were content to let Hattori and his assistant set the agenda for teacher training. This meant some weeks of intensive work, beginning immediately after Hattori's arrival in early September 1902, to organize the curriculum, equip classrooms, laboratories and dormitories, to purchase books and lab specimens, and to devise a school entrance exam. By October 17, 130 students had been selected as the first entrants to Beijing University's teacher education division.[67]

More than two decades later, Fan Yuanlian, president of what had grown into Beijing National Normal University, welcomed Hattori back to the campus with these words of praise: "In the future, when someone writing the history of education in China recounts the origins of teacher education, the first page must certainly begin by citing the dedicated service of Dr. Hattori."[68] From his place at the banquet table, Hattori must have enjoyed this public tribute to his pioneering role, particularly coming from Fan, who had worked with him as translator/assistant eighteen years before. Both knew well what the rest in the audience could only have guessed: that Hattori's "dedicated service" in those early days included dealing with constant bureaucratic hassles, a factor that caused Hattori to leave China after his six years' stay in a mood of some frustration.

To some extent the government's vague contract terms invited problems. In the absence of job specifics, Hattori chose to define his role in the broadest terms, positioning himself as a university-wide educational planner, not simply the man in charge of teacher training. He wanted to expand university curricula and quickly train Chinese to assume teaching duties, replacing foreign personnel as had happened in Japan. "To make the present university into a future comprehensive university, the pivotal problem is selection of teaching personnel. Teachers responsible for at least the fundamental courses must be Chinese or the institution has no value as a Chinese university and there can be no hope for real development."[69] To hasten the development process Hattori proposed selecting promising students from the university's teacher education and public administration divisions and sending them to Japan to be trained in specified subject areas. Education Minister Zhang Baixi took some convincing, but eventually agreed to a pilot program.

On the Japan side, Hattori got the support of Education Minister Kikuchi and Tokyo University president Yamakawa. One of Zhang's last acts in his short tenure as top education official was to give the thirty successful candidates a formal send-off at the Beijing train station. It was an auspicious beginning, but the program soon foundered due to management inexperience on both sides. Some students changed the course of study they were charged to pursue, others simply quit altogether and went home. "Regrettably," Hattori observed some years later, "our plan to develop a cadre of teachers at Beijing University didn't have the anticipated result."[70]

By the fall of 1904, Hattori was feeling frustrated in his dealings with the Chinese bureaucracy. No matter how many reform documents are on the books, he wrote in an article for the magazine *Taiyō*, nothing will change until new people are appointed to key positions. It is not enough to train people; they must be utilized. Though the Japanese had urged top officials like Zhang Zhidong to open up appointments to people with a modern education, not much headway was being made: "There are almost no returned students from Japan whose knowledge is adequately made use of."[71] Hattori was pessimistic about the immediate prospects of bringing new people into government. Even if Zhang Zhidong and Yuan Shikai joined forces—an unlikely scenario anyway, in Hattori's view—to press for personnel upgrading they would be hamstrung in their efforts by central government hard-liners who saw the newly trained younger generation as a potential political threat. Still, as Hattori saw it, the empress dowager, "taught a hard lesson" by the Boxer events, might turn out to be a better transitional figure in a reform era than her young nephew, the emperor.

> As the Empress Dowager comes up on her [seventieth] birthday this year, it is rumored that she might transfer the reins of government to the emperor. But, in our considered opinion, it would be better if she kept power in her own hands as in the past. Though one hears that the present emperor is an extremely wise man, failing to foresee that the Kang Youwei movement would trigger the reaction it did [i.e., a conservative coup] cannot be called too smart. Furthermore, if he did anticipate a reaction, he should have devised a counter strategy; in not doing so, he deserves to be called someone too easily influenced by others. Since the reform policy will backfire if it is carried out so aggressively that it produces a reaction, it is probably advisable for the moment, until reforms are more firmly in place, that the empress retains power.[72]

While China's bureaucracy had him stymied, Hattori had better luck building the teacher education program. With the entrance of the second class in 1903, total enrollment topped 300. Teachers were recruited to offer new courses, mostly in the sciences. Soon thirteen Japanese were on the education division faculty roster, seven of them teaching on a full-time basis. In addition, Hattori had an able staff of Chinese teaching assistants chosen from students recently returned from study in Japan. Fluent in Japanese, these talented young men served as translators and interpreters for Hattori and the other newly arrived Japanese professors who were burdened with the enormous task of preparing course materials from scratch and who needed help in particular with the variants of colloquial Chinese. Hattori's long friendship with Fan Yuanlian, later Education Minister (from 1912 to 1913, 1916 to 1917, and 1920 to 1921) and president of Beijing Normal, dated from 1906 when Fan spent six months working as Hattori's teaching assistant.[73]

Hattori had a heavy workload. In addition to designing the entire four-year teacher training program and supervising staff, he had to prepare all the teaching materials for his own courses in education, psychology, and logic. Communication was always a problem, not only rendering Japanese into Chinese but conveying the meaning of new terminology. It was not easy to get his points across, Hattori complained, when students did not know the difference between *kaisha*, the Japanese character combination for "business firm" and the characters in reverse order, *shakai,* meaning "society." Discussion of new concepts sometimes had embarrassing consequences. Hattori recalled an incident that occurred when Governor-general Zhang Zhidong decided to make a surprise visit to one of Hattori's psychology classes. The topic was the function of memory, and Hattori was in the midst of explaining to the group that as people aged their memory of events from childhood grew sharper but their recall ability for recent events was apt to be fuzzy. The eminent governor-general, who was around seventy at the time, took this as a personal insult, stomped angrily out of the room, and threatened to strike the course from the curriculum. Reportedly, the only thing that held him back was his reluctance to offend a foreigner.[74]

By his own admission, Hattori kept a tight rein on his teaching staff and so avoided the kind of academic infighting and, at the extreme, drunken brawls that tarnished the reputation of some of his Japanese colleagues working in other parts of China. By his account, relations with Chinese students were good. Many, after all, were in their thirties and high-caliber classical scholars in their own right, a quality that their Japanese professors, themselves products of *Kangaku* training, could not fail to appreciate. Initially, these status-conscious students were treated with some deference. When they and their teachers dined together, the students took the seats of honor, a practice that was discontinued when Zhang Baixi's replacement took over. Hattori and his colleagues showed their own concern for rank by insisting on being conveyed to class in the red carriages reserved for mid-level Chinese officials. Despite some sensitivity on the issue of relative status, Japanese teachers were well regarded by their students. Students in these years tended to be pro-Japanese. In the much publicized demonstrations at Beijing University in May 1903, students condemned Russia for aggression in Manchuria, but called for strengthening China's ties with Britain and Japan.[75]

In a matter of a few years Hattori had managed to secure a lead role for Japan in directing the teacher education program at the new, all-male Beijing University. He felt confident enough in his position to approach his high-level Chinese contacts on an issue far more likely to raise their conservative hackles—women's education. In this he was urged on behind the scenes by his wife Shigeko who believed strongly in the need to expand the educational horizons of Chinese women. She had all the qualities of a credible advocate. Not only was she the product of the new Meiji schooling and a close friend of the highly placed Shimoda Utako, she was properly credentialed as the daughter of a prominent China scholar and personally an attractive model of old-fashioned femininity. No sooner had Shigeko arrived in Beijing than she became the spark behind a women's discussion group on education. Her enthusiasm about Japan study opportunities soon convinced at least one firebrand Chinese feminist to strike out on her own for Tokyo to study teacher training at Shimoda's Practical Arts School.

But senior Chinese officials were unreceptive to the idea of including girls in their plans to establish public education nationwide. In part they failed to understand the argument for changing a system that gave males a monopoly on schooling, the tried and true route to power and wealth. Far better, it seemed, to perpetuate the traditional view that "a woman's lack of ability is her virtue." In part also, as Prince Gong, one of the few people sympathetic to the proposal, explained to Hattori, it would be politically risky for even a high ranking official such as himself to advance a major reform idea without first knowing the empress dowager's mind. On the other hand, he suggested artfully, a foreigner like Hattori could take such a step. Should the proposal backfire, he could claim he was unfamiliar with the ways of Chinese politics.

With Prince Gong's encouragement, Hattori wrote directly to the empress dowager, suggesting that she meet with Shimoda Utako to talk about broad, new policies to promote women's education in China. Shimoda was the perfect choice. She had connections at the highest level in Japan's imperial government, and her home economics textbooks had already been given a stamp of approval by Chinese educators. Shigeko, Shimoda's former student and well-schooled in classical Chinese, was an ideal choice for interpreter at what was meant to be an historic meeting. Shigeko began to work on her spoken Chinese. But things worked slowly in the Chinese bureaucracy. When the empress dowager died in 1908 details of the agreed meeting with Shimoda had yet to be worked out.

But if the total reform idea failed to gain traction, the empress dowager even in 1905 was willing to consider at least a token step in the direction of schooling for girls. In the fall of that year with the backing of the Hattoris, Beijing's first officially sponsored girls' school opened its doors to about thirty students, all members of the imperial family. The number soon increased to seventy. Shigeko was in charge of the day-to-day running of the school. Two teachers were hired from Japan, the rest recruited from among Japanese wives in Beijing.[76]

A year later, in the fall of 1906 when Hattori's contract was up for annual review, the Hattoris had less reason for optimism about the headway they were making in helping to modernize China's education using the Japanese model. No doubt the government was committed to reform—the tradition-bound civil service exam was phased out entirely in 1905 as planned—but there were too many turf battles and philosophic differences within the bureaucracy to make it a smooth process. Even Zhang Zhidong, whose policies got the reform project going, showed a healthy degree of skepticism when it came to the realities of foreign pedagogical methods and course content, as witness his encounters with Kanō Jigorō and Hattori. As in Japan and anywhere else in the world, how teachers were trained and in what went to the heart of the critical matter of creating a national citizenry.

Outsiders were not privy to the details of controversies within the educational establishment, but there were clear indicators of important administrative changes likely to affect Hattori's position. Zhang Baixi, who had worked well with Japanese staff in his dual capacity as Beijing University president and overall supervisor of education, was suddenly reassigned. The university and ministry posts were made separate appointments, thus creating an additional layer of bureaucracy in educational decision making. To further blur the lines of control from Hattori's standpoint, the government indicated its intention to detach the teacher training division from Beijing University and make it a separate teachers' college.[77]

Japan's Ministry of Education, probably on Hattori's advice, sought to capitalize on the new developments by proposing that Hattori be confirmed in the position he had aspired to all along, educational adviser writ large rather than the more narrowly defined director of teacher training. It seemed a reasonable time to make such a case. In 1906, the year after Japan's victory in the war with Russia, Chinese-Japanese exchanges were at an all-time high. Nearly 10,000 Chinese students were in Japan. China had hired some 550 Japanese teachers and advisers to work in China. Returned students from Japan were becoming prominent in China's public life. On the Beijing University faculty alone, eight of the thirty-seven Chinese teachers were returned students from Japan. China's provincial heads were routinely sending education officials on study tours to Japan. A 1905 list of directors of the newly created "education promotion offices" in three Zhili prefectures shows ten of the twenty-eight with Japan experience. Hoping to find favor within China's Japan faction, Japanese consul Hayashi Gonsuke took the Hattori proposal to Yan Xiu who, following his own Japan tour in 1905, had been made director of education promotion offices nationwide.

Yan diplomatically but firmly refused the Japanese request. He greatly admired Hattori personally and professionally and acknowledged his distinguished services to China's education, Yan reportedly told Hayashi. But there was concern within China's Ministry of Education about exceeding the terms of Hattori's original contract, which assigned him to a single institution. Hayashi concluded that it would be counterproductive to continue to press Yan on the matter. It was clear to him that the ministry's reluctance to broaden Hattori's brief related to a recent upsurge in rights-recovery activity in China that made the government wary of anything that looked like foreign intervention.[78]

If Hattori was frustrated in his attempt to expand his advisory role, he could take satisfaction in the progress made in producing new teachers, 106 in the first graduating class in 1907, another 206 in 1908. "Now that you've graduated, this is your alma mater *(muxiao),*" Hattori told the class of 1907, introducing a new term into the Chinese lexicon.[79] With their names now on the Beijing University alumni roster the new graduates returned to their home provinces to serve as teachers and administrators as required in exchange for their four-year subsidized education.

For a brief time in 1908 it seemed that Hattori and his Chinese friends might yet win their bid for an expanded Japanese role in teacher education. In May the government finally made it official that a teachers college would be established independent of Beijing University. Fan Yuanlian, Hattori's colleague and now an assistant professor at the Beijing College of Law and Administration was nominated to head the new school. With Fan's blessing, Japanese teachers from the old teacher education division were asked to extend their contracts to serve as his core teaching staff. But, as in the case of W.A.P. Martin eight years earlier, the government suddenly withdrew support for foreign teachers, claiming a shortage of funds to pay their salaries. Fan quit. Hattori and six teachers returned to Japan in January 1909. Though Hattori's skills had been well used, the Chinese government was in a mood to curb foreign influence. The teachers college opened, but with purely Chinese administrators and faculty and a curriculum that devoted more hours to moral education than ever before. Regulations were issued to prohibit students from engaging in politics.[80]

The China Problem

Japanese newspapers speculated that the real reason for the departure of Hattori and his colleagues was that they had lost out to the Europeans and Americans in the competition for influence over the Chinese government. Not so, claimed Japan's Foreign Ministry, noting that other foreigners had also been dismissed from the staff of Beijing University. Budgetary problems and the fact that there were not enough qualified applicants to justify a large outlay on foreign teachers were what caused the Chinese government to shift to a scaled down version of the original plan. However, in an article appearing in *Chūō Kōron* shortly after his return to Japan, Hattori himself suggested that competition among foreigners for Chinese hearts and minds played a role in the dismissal of the Japanese. We have become mere bystanders, he warned, as the Europeans and Americans build schools all over China and aggressively promote sales of educational materials and equipment. Western efforts have the advantage of multiple sources of financing: churches, foundations, governments, supplemented in some cases, he claimed, by subsidies from the Qing government. For Japan to compete with the Yale-in-China types of projects, the Japanese government must be prepared to make a significant financial commitment, perhaps as a starter, to establish a first-class college, Japanese-staffed, in the Beijing area. Hattori's message, clear enough to *Chūō Kōron* readers, was that the teachers college might have served this purpose had the Japanese government acted in timely fashion to finance salaries of Japanese faculty.[81]

Already by February 1909, just a month after his return to Japan, Hattori had made the shift from teaching Chinese youth the rudiments of psychology and logic to lecturing Tokyo University students on Chinese philosophy, history, and literature.[82] Hattori was now in his early forties. He had on his résumé a decade of China experience, not simply as an academic, an observer of the China scene, but as a participant in China's post-Boxer reform experiment. He represented a new breed of Japanese China expert. His research and teaching about China's past were grounded in his firsthand knowledge of the real, working China just as his everyday, sometimes frustrating, encounters with Chinese bureaucrats had been tempered by his deep interest in Chinese culture. The Chinese acknowledged Hattori's contribution to China's educational development by awarding him an honorary doctorate in October.[83]

But Hattori returned home with feelings of ambivalence about China's long-term development prospects. On the one hand, he felt that there was real momentum for reform within the Chinese government, a commitment that went beyond the efforts of the most vocal reform advocates. Whatever faction was in power,

Hattori expected the government to stick to its announced nine-year timetable for introducing a constitution. On the other hand, he felt it was hugely ambitious to expect to draft a constitution, issue parliamentary laws, hold an election, convene a national assembly, change institutions at both the central and local levels, and raise literacy to 20 percent, all by 1917. From the vantage point of 1909, he saw only Manchuria's new governor demonstrating the kind of leadership that would ensure success.[84]

What was slowing down the process of change, Hattori believed, was a fundamental Chinese close-mindedness to outside ideas, a smug certainty that anything worthy in human culture had a made-in-China label. He had made this point earlier in his analysis of the Boxers and was to return to it again and again in his writings on China after 1909. It was not that the Chinese were incapable of the kind of complete change that would qualify them as "modern," he stressed. As he noted in an article written in the 1920s, since its revolution in 1911 China had recorded some remarkable shifts in social attitudes, particularly toward women, who were now freed from bound feet and other forms of male oppression. But he continued to feel that Chinese close-mindedness, or, at its worst, a deeply ingrained, inherently racist anti-foreignism, crippled the Chinese intellectually and cut them off from institutional and technical innovations in other parts of the world. Because the ancient philosopher Mo Zi was credited with developing physics, the Chinese discounted Western advances in the field. Because the characters *xian* and *fa* appeared in early Chinese texts, the Chinese assumed that the idea of a "constitution," now coined as *xianfa,* was a Chinese invention and thus thought there was little to learn from foreign constitutional models. In his reading of China's history, Hattori observed wryly, he had found no evidence to suggest that anything remotely like a modern constitution was ever in use in ancient China.[85]

But Hattori saw it as more than a problem of mindset. Even Chinese who supported reform in the best of faith faced enormous obstacles in communication. Hattori cited the example of the new Chinese criminal code drafted at the central government level with Japanese advisory help and distributed to local offices in 1906. Enforcing the code was difficult, not because those in charge were unwilling, but because they were confused by Japanese versions of Western legal terms adopted in the absence of Chinese equivalents. For example, the Japanese had coined the term ***karishutsugoku,*** literally "temporarily out of jail," for the English "release on bail." The problem was that the character read "***kari***" and meaning "temporary" in Japanese, more commonly meant "false" or "fake" in Chinese, so the new concept as understood by Chinese local enforcement officers carried the sense of "unauthorized release from jail," quite different from what was intended.

If local officials were in the dark about these new legal terms, Hattori wondered, how could ordinary people be expected to understand them?[86]

The use of Japanese terminology and idioms was increasing, Hattori pointed out, not only because Japanese advisers were a significant presence in China in many fields, but because hundreds of Chinese students educated in Japan were now taking up posts in new government agencies, new schools, and new businesses. This common language based on Japanese neologisms had the potential to solidify Chinese and Japanese cultural ties. But Hattori questioned the extent to which the Chinese really understood the new concepts being introduced and the lessons they could learn from Japan's development experience. After all, he said, referring to language barriers among China's provinces, "The Chinese don't even understand each other, much less have a true view of Japan."[87]

China's failure to understand the real Japan was a regret Hattori voiced again and again. He was especially concerned about the younger generation studying in Japan. Chinese students must stop viewing Japan, he said, "from the second story of a lodging house," as nothing more than a handy source of Western technology. They needed to examine Japanese society from within, asking what unique factors accounted for Japan's successful growth path. The Japanese had a responsibility here, too, he said, to ensure that Chinese youth were well treated and got more from their Japan experience than a love of Japanese pop culture. Hattori was critical as well of some of his Japanese compatriots working in China, describing them as insular and arrogant. The result was a growing distrust of Japan among Chinese, an attitude he was made painfully aware of during his long stay in China. Hattori felt such distrust was generally unwarranted. In his university lectures for 1914, published two years later as *China Studies* (Shina kenkyū), he dismissed Chinese fears that Japan's recent troop mobilization and arms buildup were preparatory to an invasion of China. These were simply general security measures, he insisted. That the Chinese would feel so suspicious only showed how little they understood the Japanese national character.[88]

While promoting Chinese-Japanese understanding remained high on Hattori's agenda, his experience working in China made him doubt the possibility of developing truly close relationships at a personal level.

> I lived for a fairly long time in China and came into contact with all sorts of people, but at a certain point I couldn't help but feel there were obstacles to proceeding further. If those barriers could be broken, it would be great but it isn't easy. One can talk about developing intimate ties, but I feel that in reality it's difficult to do. If there are common interests involved, that's something else.

> Other than that, I think real friendships are problematic. On this point, I must confess, I originally saw things this way: insofar as relations between countries must essentially be people-to-people not just government-to-government, I thought, as a first step, wouldn't it be good if there was more intermarriage between Chinese and Japanese. This, I learned later, was the way Prince Konoe also viewed things. I felt this way when I first got to China, but now I am strongly opposed: I believe intermarriage is a thoroughly bad idea. I've gotten to the point that when a Japanese woman says "I plan to marry a Chinese," I feel I'd like to put an absolute stop to it. The reason for this is that, while so far there have been rather few of these marriages, when it does happen, the wives are generally abandoned.

As Hattori saw it, the crux of the marriage problem between the Chinese and other nationalities, including the Japanese, was that the Chinese had no compunction about entering into numerous liaisons without making any legal distinction between wives and mistresses. So in what context could Chinese and Japanese realistically interact? Hattori asked himself. "I think the only viable relationships are those based on joint interests."[89]

As Hattori readied *China Studies* for the press, he was also making plans to travel to the United States. The Harvard Club of Cambridge had selected Hattori Unokichi—China expert, noted Confucian scholar—to lecture at Harvard University during the academic year 1915-16. Like his predecessor, Japanese Buddhist scholar Anesaki Masaharu, Hattori was given the title Professor of Japanese Literature and Life. Like Anesaki also, Hattori deposited a collection of books in his field at Harvard's Widener Library. Odd for someone recruited for a visiting professorship in an entirely new environment though, Hattori had virtually nothing to say about his U.S. experience. He only noted—as did Harvard's comptroller, the man responsible for advancing him $375 in travel expenses—that he returned to Japan a few classes short of completing the spring semester. We know from correspondence between Harvard President Lowell and Tokyo University that Hattori was not Harvard's first choice. Perhaps Harvard was not his either. He may have made the trip simply to fulfill an obligation to his university. Hattori was known as an excellent linguist, conversant in English, French, German, and Chinese. But quite possibly he found that that his spoken English after twenty-five years of disuse was not up to the demands of lecturing to classes of seventy-five and more and giving public lectures which were, according to the Philosophy Department which sponsored them, "largely attended."[90]

It may have been a taxing two semesters. Yet Hattori's classes on "Confucian Ethics and Japanese Life" provided a new forum for his argument that it was in present-day Japan that Confucius' original teachings were achieving new operative value, providing the underpinning to economic success and political strength. Japanese were getting back to Confucian fundamentals—the ideals of humanity, responsibility, and dedication to learning—which in their Chinese context had ossified into Confucianism, nice-sounding rhetoric to turn attention away from corruption and disorder. The Chinese talk a lot about the teachings of Confucius and Mencius, Hattori said again and again, but how they behave is dictated entirely by calculations of personal gain. In the modern world, Japan, not China, was the exemplar of the best in Asian values.[91]

The image of China unable to govern itself was strong in Hattori's mind, indelibly fixed there after the trauma of the Boxer siege. Equally strong was his belief that China could overcome such disorder by revitalizing its own cultural ideals. China could, as Japan had, organize modern governance structures around the core Confucian principles, which, after all, were grounded in notions of order and stability. Hattori saw no incompatibility between modern life—or life itself—and Confucian practice. The social rituals and patterns of human interaction that found expression in China's ancient texts were alive and relevant now and should be the starting point for understanding China past and present. Hattori did not fall into theorizing in trying to teach China to scores of Tokyo University students. His students always found him refreshingly down-to-earth, a sociologist in his approach, whether lecturing on the *Analects* or the works of the Daoists or "China's Ancient Rituals and the Life of the People."[92] In this he was unique, even among his forward-looking colleagues such as Kano Naoki. Kano had been part of the siege-drama and had traveled in China. But Hattori's experience was different. He had worked in China. His real-world engagement in institution building had forced him to confront the realities of manners and morals and bureaucratic hassles, giving immediacy to his efforts to synthesize this with what he knew about China's past.

For Hattori, Japan as Asian neighbor had a moral, human obligation to try to set things right in China. The starting point was cultural, the kind of soft-power approach Konoe Atsumaro would have approved. As Akira Iriye points out, the extent to which cultural connections—rather than economic or political—dominated the Sino-Japanese relationship in the 1920s and even into the thirties is often underestimated. Ironically, the major binational cultural initiative of the 1920s was a legacy of the Boxer disaster. In 1923, Japan, taking the U.S. lead, stipulated that the unpaid portion of the Boxer indemnity be used for China cultural projects. Hattori was one of a handful of senior academics selected by the government to oversee project preparation.[93]

It was in connection with this preparatory phase that Hattori made a trip to China in 1924, his first visit since his departure in 1909. He traveled from Shanghai to Nanjing, Hangzhou, Jinan, and other cities on his way to Beijing. As Hattori recalled it, he was welcomed everywhere by his former students at Beijing University, most of whom were now in high positions. "We reminisced about the old days and talked of the future—it was an extremely happy time." During twenty days spent in Beijing, Hattori worked with his Chinese counterparts, including Beijing University president Jiang Monlin, on plans to establish a social science research center and a library using remitted Boxer funds.[94] His schedule included the banquet at Beijing Normal University mentioned earlier, presided over by his old friend, now university president, Fan Yuanlian. While Fan had cordial words for Hattori and his contributions to teacher education, there was an edge to his remarks on Japan's handling of the Boxer funds. He hoped that Hattori was right when he said that Japan's cultural activities in China transcended politics and had the enthusiastic support of the Japanese people. But he warned that some of Japan's actions at the operational level left the Chinese feeling uneasy:

> While in an intellectual sense cultural activities transcend politics, since the China Cultural Affairs Bureau has been set up within Japan's Foreign Office and the budget for project expenditures also must pass through the Japanese Diet every year, it looks on the face of it as if cultural activities are entirely Japanese internal affairs, much at odds with the aim of transcending politics. The Japanese naturally see it differently, but from the standpoint of the Chinese this is a matter that must be addressed. We now face many bilateral problems that require prompt solution, and these problems really have a considerable impact on the sentiments between the two countries. Cultural activities ought to be ongoing, not short-term. The Chinese population is large and you can't expect that the average person will understand the spirit behind these activities. If they look at how the projects are administered and conclude that they are purely Japanese affairs, they will criticize those of us involved, saying we should not participate. Once this kind of misunderstanding actually occurs, isn't it very difficult to explain away?[95]

Indeed, there was considerable Chinese opposition to the proposed cultural program. To many Chinese intellectuals, Japan's insistence on total control of funds sounded suspiciously like cultural imperialism, not a commitment to bilateral cooperation. In 1925, despite such objections, the Chinese government authorized formation of a binational advisory group called the East Asia Cultural Activities Committee to finalize plans for a social science institute in Beijing and a joint research institute in the natural sciences to be located in Shanghai. In the summer of 1925, Hattori traveled to China as one of the Japanese delegates to the committee, which also included Kano Naoki. A second working session of the joint group was held in Tokyo in the fall of 1926. New tensions arose, this time within the Chinese delegation between the younger members who, as former students in Japan, knew the language and felt at ease in a Japanese setting and the older members who spoke only Chinese. On a return visit to Beijing in 1927 it took all of Hattori's persuasive powers to keep the fractious committee together and move forward with project planning.[96]

Hattori Unokichi (on left) poses with fellow scholar and former Legation volunteer Kano Naoki in front of the monument in Beijing commemorating the Boxer siege, 1925. (Hattori Unokichi, Pekin rōjō nikki; Tokyo: 1926)

Hattori was at the peak of his career and influence at this point in the mid-1920s, but under pressure as well. His reputation was on the line in the matter of the bilateral program with China. At Tokyo University he kept up a demanding schedule of teaching and publication. In 1923 Korea became part of his brief when he was recruited to serve on a design and planning committee for a new university in Seoul. In 1925, concurrent with his other assignments, he was appointed president of Seoul University. He resigned after eighteen months when it became apparent that the constant travel required was taking a toll on his health. It would have been a taxing schedule for anyone, but in Hattori's case symptoms of Parkinson's disease were beginning to become evident, making walking difficult. Within a few years he lost the use of his right arm; his eyesight, a problem from infancy, worsened. Still, he continued to work actively at the university, dictating letters and lectures where necessary. Rarely were any revisions required, his students recalled.[97]

Hattori's personal engagement with China followed the path of his failing health. In the spring of 1928, Chiang Kaishek's Nationalist forces, in a major offensive to reunify the country, swept north into Shandong Province, threatening the city of Jinan. Fearing for the safety of Japanese civilians in Jinan, the Japanese government rushed troops to the area. Skirmishes broke out. Though the crisis was contained when both sides withdrew, Chinese were outraged at Japan's intervention. Chinese members of the East Asia Cultural Activities Committee resigned from the group in protest, bringing several years of work on joint projects to an abrupt end. Hattori was deeply disappointed at the collapse of his efforts. Yet he faulted not his Japanese compatriots for their aggressive acts but his Chinese colleagues on the committee for their failure to separate politics and culture. The problem, he said, was that Chinese intellectuals, unlike their Japanese counterparts, were beholden to political interests. Their views changed with every shift in power at the top.

> We were concerned that it would get to the point that cultural activities, which should be above politics and economics, would be politically influenced. And that's just what happened in 1928 when we dispatched troops to Shandong. The Chinese members of the East Asian Cultural Activities Committee announced a general walkout and severed relations with the committee. As a result, the activities of the Beijing and Shanghai research institutes inevitably came to a sudden halt. With this, our Foreign Ministry notified us that it would provisionally provide financial backing to East Asian cultural institutes that thirty of us China researchers were planning to set up in Japan.[98]

From our present-day vantage point, knowing of the conflict to come, Hattori's complaint that his Chinese colleagues ought to have put culture above politics strikes us as naïve or detached from reality. Could he not understand their protest as an act of patriotism? But to Hattori in 1928 looking back on the sweep of China's history he knew so well—Boxer terrorism, revolutionary upheaval, a decade of warlord violence—giving up the benefits of a joint cultural endeavor in the name of loyalty to the political power-holder of the moment seemed shortsighted at the very least. And it was frustrating personally. Building cultural bridges had been the focus of his forty-year engagement with China. He was not political. Only rarely had he commented on current politics or political figures either Chinese or Japanese. His passions were teaching, historical research on China and textual analysis of the Chinese classics. At the same time, he was not of his father-in-law's generation of intellectuals who were inclined to show deference to the scholarship coming out of a newly opened China. Hattori and his fellow academics working in the 1910s and 1920s were confident in their new, Japanese interpretation of Confucian fundamentals. The old *Kangaku,* Chinese studies, had become *Tōyōgaku,* East Asian studies. Abandoned by their Chinese colleagues in 1928, Hattori and the other Japanese researchers accepted the best available alternative, using Foreign Ministry funds to establish Japan-based study institutes.

At Tokyo University, Hattori helped organize a China/East Asia research center, the Tōhō Bunka Gakuin, predecessor of the present Tōyō Bunka Kenkyūjo. Kano Naoki set up a similar center at Kyoto University. In 1933, after the Japanese installed the last Manchu emperor as head of state in Manchuria, Hattori lent his name and support to a Chinese-inspired binational organization called the Manzhouguo Cultural Association, which sponsored joint Chinese-Japanese research projects in Qing and Mongol history. In one of his last publications, *The Essentials of East Asian Logic* (Tōyō ronri kōyō), he commented that the study of Confucian thought was alive and well in the new state. In China proper, by contrast, the teachings of Confucius had been eclipsed by Sun Yatsen's Western-inspired Three People's Principles; only in Japan were people making the principles of Confucius the abiding ideals in their daily lives.[99]

Hattori had been China bound in a metaphorical and real sense his entire life. His contributions to China's institutional development had been publicly acknowledged by his friends at Beijing Normal. But in the final analysis where he made a real difference was not in making Japan better understood by the Chinese, but in helping to create a new field of China studies in Japan and Japanese-occupied Manchuria. It was primarily his Japanese students and the Japanese public who felt the impact of his views on China, his frustrations, hopes, certainty that cultural cooperation was the ultimate answer to passing tensions in the realm of politics.

Whatever disappointments Hattori felt in his final encounter with China and the Chinese, he chose to minimize them. When in 1936 he prepared an autobiographical account to append to a volume of essays in honor of his seventieth birthday, he gave little space to his Boxer ordeal and highlighted his 1924 trip to China as a series of happy reunions with Chinese friends. Sadly, by the time Hattori died just three years later, in 1939, power politics had taken precedence over culture, and Japan and China were engaged in all-out war.

Chapter III

Meiji Japan's "New Woman" on Mission in China: Kawahara Misako in Shanghai and Karachin

Time has a way of papering over disappointments, but as he left Beijing in 1909, his six years' service fresh in his mind, Dr. Hattori could not be blamed entirely for feeling that China had let him down. The whole premise of his 1902 China assignment had been that China needed him. This was not only his personal conclusion after witnessing the Boxer madness. It also seemed to be the view of senior Chinese officials who recruited him at a handsome salary to assist in educational reform and institution building. To the Chinese leadership, trying to manage a recovery program as Westerners pillaged Beijing and thousands of Russian troops moved into Manchuria, the Japanese looked like potentially useful friends. Commenting on China's shift to a pro-Japan policy after 1900, a contemporary Western observer noted cynically, "The despised wo jen, or dwarfs, of former years had become an intelligent and excellent people."[1]

A China open to Japanese influence was attractive to a variety of Japanese experts in this period, some mere opportunists, but most, like Hattori, looking for both professional satisfaction and the chance to contribute to improved Sino-Japanese ties. The year 1902 when Dr. and Mrs. Hattori started their China tour marked the take-off point of what might now be termed a Japanese assistance program. From approximately 150 in 1902, the number of Japanese advisers in China had risen to about 550 by the time Hattori left in 1909. While the mix changed markedly after the 1911 Revolution, until that time about 70 percent on the list were teachers and educational administrators, the rest were technical experts in finance, law, and railway development. Almost all were men, hired to work with male counterparts on projects in which the primary beneficiaries were men. Hattori pushed the issue of women's education, but this was out of personal conviction shared by his wife, Shigeko, not part of his official job description.[2]

China's plan to create a modern national school system, issued in 1901 as part of the reform agenda, was entirely silent on the subject of public schooling for girls. In fact, one of the authors of the new plan, Governor-general Zhang Zhidong, reportedly dismissed it as a thoroughly bad idea. He thought girls ought to be trained at home and then only minimally in those subjects directly relevant to their future role as wives and mothers—basic reading and writing and the traditional arts.[3] In the absence of central government support, the only study opportunities for girls other than Zhang's narrowly conceived form of home schooling were foreign missionary schools, study abroad, or local Chinese initiatives. None of these amounted to much. A mere 500 girls were enrolled in missionary schools and overseas programs in 1904. Chinese-run schools had been set up here and there after 1900 with the backing of local planners and private funds, but here too the numbers enrolled were only in the hundreds.

Zhang was traditional but never inflexible, however. Public education for women was finally given a boost after 1907 when the government issued regulations requiring all local areas to establish girls' primary schools and teacher training institutions. Still, overall, girls continued to lag far behind boys whose opportunities were rapidly expanding. Less than 5 percent of the estimated 2.8 million students enrolled in Chinese schools in 1912 were girls.[4]

One of the key problems in organizing girls' schools whether private or public was finding suitable teachers. Since there were no Chinese women with teacher-training degrees and young men had to be be excluded on propriety grounds, the choice came down to professionally qualified Chinese men, preferably over fifty, and Japanese women. China's interest in hiring female graduates of Japan's recently established teacher-training colleges is understandable enough, particularly since the salaries the graduates commanded were relatively low (though higher than what they would have received in Japan), and they were conversant to some degree in Chinese.[5] Less clear is what motivated these young women, first, to take up teaching, a new profession for women in Japan, and second, to accept teaching posts in China where working conditions were difficult and the notion of an independent career woman was nonexistent.

"Little Shimoda"

On August 28, 1902, just a week before the Hattoris left for Beijing, Kawahara Misako arrived with her luggage at the dock at Yokohama in time for the 10:00 AM boarding of the Shanghai-bound *Kobe-maru*. It was one of those oppressively hot days, she wrote, "when even the morning glories lacing the bamboo fence drooped early and the chirring of the cicadas sounded loudly from the trees." She was touched that despite the awful heat and humidity so many friends had come to see her off. They stood in a cluster, the young ladies holding hands, seemingly at a loss for words now that the actual time for leave-taking had come. Suddenly it was ten o'clock and dazed by excitement and anxiety, Kawahara was conscious only of hasty good-byes, then watching from the deck as the ship moved out to sea. "The shore quickly receded, the figures of my dear friends grew faint, and soon I could not see even the flash of white handkerchiefs. Now we were in the vicinity of Hommaki and there were only scattered fishing boats. I was overwhelmed with the emotion of parting and stood for some time on the deck. Then, as a sea breeze blew into the sleeves of my travel dress, I had the slight sensation of awakening from a dream and went into my cabin."[6]

It proved to be a rough passage to China. Four days into the trip, as the ship pitched and rolled in the high seas, Kawahara felt her resolution slipping away, replaced by dread and longing for her father, teacher, and friends. How sad they will be, she thought tearfully, when they hear that the ship went down. But she quickly rallied. A life jacket would keep her afloat, she told herself, and even if she drowned, what could she do about it anyway. When the ship steamed into the calm waters of the great Yangtze, approaching Shanghai, her spirits revived. "At the point the China mainland majestically drew near, I felt a sudden return of optimism."[7]

It was the realization of a childhood dream. Born in 1875 in Matsumoto City, Nagano Prefecture, Misako had learned about China at the knees of her father, a China scholar whose family had been in the business of *Kangaku* schooling for generations. But Misako's early knowledge of China was not purely academic. As the Hattoris found true in Tokyo, the best of the traditional academies were alive and well and accommodating to the fact that China was now an actual destination, not simply a literary creation. When Misako's father and his friends talked as they did incessantly about the "China problem," they were not referring to the old, idealized China as the epitome of culture but the more sober reality of a country mired in poverty and backwardness. And the visitors to the Kawahara household were not just fellow scholars, but people who had firsthand China experience. The Kawaharas were particularly close to the family of Captain (later General) Fukushima Yasumasa, a Matsumoto native whose China connection dated from his service as military attaché in Beijing in the early 1880s. Kawashima Naniwa, another China expert in the Matsumoto group, went to China first in 1886 to work as an interpreter. Fifteen years later in the wake of the Boxer Uprising the Chinese government hired him to organize training for a new public security force.[8]

Little Misako was a bright, perceptive child with a winning manner and tomboyish energy when it came to games and sports. In fact, she was so obviously talented that her parents and relatives could not suppress an occasional, "If only she were a boy." Sensitive to the tone of regret in comments admiringly offered, Misako silently vowed to make her parents proud by accomplishing whatever a son might have done. Her determination stayed with her. But her early carefree days ended with the death of her mother in 1889. Grief created a special bond between the fourteen-year-old Misako and her father, a widower still in his thirties. Misako was deeply touched by her father's decision to delay remarriage for some years to spare her the burden of a stepmother. Her devotion to him showed in her growing commitment to what he valued most, a good education and an interest in China, past and present. With his encouragement, she set her sights on getting the best schooling available to women in 1890s Japan. She hoped that somehow, thus prepared, China would figure in her future.[9]

Educational opportunities for women were still limited twenty years after the government's landmark decision to establish public schools nationwide for girls as well as boys. But in striking contrast to China where it took until 1907, Japan's central government was behind the idea from 1872, and the trend was decidedly upward. Female primary enrollments, though much lower than for boys early on, steadily increased to 41 percent of the school-age population in 1893 to 87 percent in 1903 and 95 percent in 1910, by which time compulsory education had been set at six rather than four years. Female literacy, estimated at 15 percent in 1868, was nearly universal forty years later. Girls' high schools expanded at a slower rate for women than for men, but expanded nevertheless, from twenty-eight schools enrolling about 3,000 women in 1893 to eight enrolling 21,500 in 1903. Western scholars writing from the present vantage point tend to decry the inadequacies on the female side of the ledger. Comparisons made perhaps more fairly in terms of the times show gains comparable to those in late nineteenth century Europe and the United States. The startling fact in both the West and Japan was that schooling for girls was now the accepted norm.

Newly educated Japanese women were fit for new occupations, some, like teaching, previously confined to men, others, in the telephone and telegraph business, for example, representing new technology and easily feminized. Already in the 1880s there had emerged a small group of what might be termed female opinion leaders, well-educated women like Shimoda Utako who were taking on public, professional roles as educators, teachers, and leaders of civic groups. Press coverage of women's activities and issues increased, as did the importance of the press itself. In 1870 Japan had one daily newspaper. By 1904 the number of papers had increased to around 375 with an estimated 200,000 subscribers in Tokyo alone. [10] A significant percentage of the public could now read about new schools for women, women's charitable organizations, equal rights for women, questions of proper dress and hairstyles, and gossip about prominent women, their family affairs, and professional squabbles. Meiji women, as the phrase goes, had "become visible."

In 1891, Kawahara Misako, aged sixteen, entered the women's division of Nagano Normal School. There were at the time only forty-seven teacher training institutions nationwide enrolling about 5,500 male students and probably 500 women. Whether male or female, this was a small, select group. Nagano Prefecture's school attendance rates were notably high beginning in the 1870s, which likely accounts for the fact that it supported one of the nation's few available teacher-training programs for women. Graduates were expected to spend their careers teaching in one of Nagano's new primary schools. Misako had higher aims. With her father's permission she took the national entrance examination to the recently-opened Women's Teachers College in Tokyo, a spin-off of the prestigious men's college most often associated with Kanō Jigorō, who was president from 1893 to 1897 and again from 1901 to 1920. In the 1890s these two institutions were Japan's only national-level teachers colleges. For young ambitious Meiji women a teaching career was one sure route to financial and social independence, and the Tokyo program was the best available. As one applicant—who was not lucky enough to be admitted—recalled of the first graduating class: "To us they were magnificent, heavenly beings, dressed in Western-style uniforms, with a dignity and refinement that left us speechless."[11]

When the exam results were announced for 1895, Misako was elated to learn that she was one of about of about thirty women to win admission to the class of 1896. But what began in triumph ended badly. She had a demanding schedule of classes including pedagogy (U.S.-based teaching methods), English, mathematics, biology, psychology, gymnastics, and the arts. As she recalled later, she was naturally competitive and inclined to overwork with the result that within a few months she fell ill with what was diagnosed as pleurisy. Given the length of her eventual recovery period, perhaps it was tuberculosis. To give her the proper long-term care, her doctors insisted she leave school and return home to Nagano. She was devastated by the prospect of disappointing her father and losing her government scholarship, but her protests were to no avail.[12]

In 1899, her health much improved, Misako accepted a teaching position at the Nagano High School for Girls, one of the independent girls' high schools established by the Ministry of Education's order of that year. But the new teacher, Ms. Kawahara, was soon restless. She wanted to turn her vague China interest into some useful reality. "Little Shimoda" her fellow teachers called her teasingly, noting how often she talked about China and how much in her strong features and confident bearing she resembled Shimoda Utako, progressive educator and China sympathizer, whose picture had been in the Nagano newspapers. When Kawahara read that Shimoda would visit Matsumoto City sometime in August 1900, she was determined to try to meet her. It was a bold move for a young woman of relatively modest family to propose a meeting with Shimoda Utako, a nationally known figure twenty years her senior, but with her father's approval, she arranged the proper introduction through the Nagano school principal. Shimoda said yes.[13]

Shimoda Utako, Kawahara's role model, in 1902. (*Shimoda Utako sensei den*; Tokyo: Ko Shimoda Kōchō sensei denki hensanjo, 1943)

Shimoda was certainly enough of a celebrity to merit a photograph in the local papers. Her name was long familiar to any reader of the Meiji press. Since being widowed at thirty, Shimoda had embarked on an independent life that brought her increasingly into public view. Socially she was part of the 1880s smart set, young members of the Meiji power elite who set store in appearing cosmopolitan, up-to-date. She took lessons to learn Western dance steps, a must for those attending government-sponsored balls where Japanese women "got up" in Western corsets and gowns, their male partners in tailcoats, waltzed the evening away to the tunes of Johann Strauss.[14] As everyone knew, the hidden agenda behind the fun at the Rokumeikan, the new hall designed by a British architect, was to impress Western diplomats that Japanese, too, were "civilized and enlightened," worthy of equal treaty status. A mark of enlightenment or not, the craze for social dancing sanctioned a degree of public interaction between men and women unprecedented in Japan. There was ample room for scandal. Rumors of an affair between Shimoda and a big supporter of the Rokumeikan social events, Itō Hirobumi, Japan's first prime minister and a married man, surfaced first in the mid-1880s and continued to provide grist for the gossip mill for some years. In the late nineties, she, not he, was publicly raked over the coals for unseemly behavior in a series of newspaper articles which provided entertainment but did nothing to curb her independence. She had many admirers. An article on women writers appearing in *Tōhoku shinbun* in 1897 cited Shimoda as one of the Meiji talents capable of reviving the glory days when women like Murasaki Shikibu of *Tale of Genji* fame dominated the literary world.[15]

For the reading public in the eighties and nineties reports on beautiful Shimoda the natural talent with unconventional ways added some zest to the daily news. But it was her advocacy of a new education for the new Japanese woman that caught the attention of more serious readers of the press. The fact that such articles began to appear was not because the press suddenly became more responsible, but because Shimoda herself began to control her own media image, as we would now put it, to advance a certain set of goals. Just as Konoe Atsumaro issued a call for a new Asia-centered foreign policy in the pages of *The Sun* (Taiyō), Shimoda on her return from England used the magazine to reintroduce herself to the Japanese public as a foreign-trained educator, not simply a teacher at a private school for upper-class girls. Similarly, relying on the media to get out the message—and this was a fast-expanding venue—was at the top of her mind as she drew up plans for the Imperial Women's Association (IWA), the public interest group she launched with Konoe's help at the end of 1898.

As IWA head, Shimoda began a round of contemporary-sounding professional activities, public speaking, networking, lobbying, fund-raising, all of which drew press attention to herself and her message. She encouraged each prefecture to organize its own IWA affiliate. Boosting the efforts of the Nagano group is what took her to the Kawaharas' hometown in the summer of 1900. Shimoda had two key items on the much-publicized IWA agenda, one to convince the public of the need for a distinctive Japanese/Asian-style curriculum for women, the other to broaden access to schooling to include women of lower income groups. While Shimoda acknowledged that women had made major advances over the past twenty years, she argued that in the mood of reformist zeal, Western educational models had been introduced too quickly and uncritically. The result was a "disconnect" between what women learned in school and the reality of their everyday lives. It was like dressing Japanese women in foreign clothes, she said—not a good fit.

The issue of curriculum relevance, in Shimoda's mind, was particularly serious when it came to girls from lower income groups whose parents could ill afford the cost in time and money of letting them attend school in the first place. It is striking to hear the classically educated Shimoda, head of an elite school, voicing concern over the quality of education for ordinary Japanese. But two years abroad, particularly the time spent in London where Fabians and other social activists were much in the news, made her more conscious of the link between popular education and economic development. Japan's economic future, Shimoda pointed out, was critically dependent on the availability of a well-educated female labor force capable of handling new jobs as telephone and telegraph operators, shop girls, nurses, factory workers. Japan's image was also at stake. Lacking adequate skills training and moral guidance, many women from lower-income groups had turned to prostitution, a practice so widespread that it did serious harm to Japan's reputation abroad. She reported how shocked her European friends were that Japanese upper-class women showed so little concern for these members of their own sex so much in need of assistance and training in legitimate occupations. Just six months after founding the IWA, Shimoda had started two small schools in Tokyo, the Women's Practical Arts School (Jissen Jogakkō) and the Industrial Arts School (Joshi Kōgei Gakkō). By the end of the year the IWA had published the first issue of an affiliated magazine, *Japanese Women* (Nihon fujin), one of about twenty women's magazines then available in Tokyo.[16]

Shimoda had returned from England a strong proponent of a new discipline, home economics, which she taught at both the upper-class school, the Peeresses School, and to girls from ordinary families at the Practical Arts School. From our present vantage point it is a stretch to see the female half of the world liberated through home economics, but at the time professionalizing a woman's role in the home was a novel concept, even in Victorian England. It was an acceptable one, too, because in both England and Japan it was presented as a means for women to achieve personal independence at the same time as contributing to the betterment of society as a whole. This is the simple meaning captured in the term "good wives, wise mothers" (*ryōsai kenbo)* associated with Shimoda and Naruse Jinzō, the first generation of "progressive" educators pushing expanded schooling for women.

What Shimoda had to say on the theory and practice of home economics in a Japanese setting was widely broadcast. She lectured and wrote textbooks. The best of her early lectures were included in a volume called simply *Home Economics* (Kaseigaku), published in 1902. The message was traditional in presenting men as breadwinners, active in the public sphere, women as faithful helpmates and homemakers, specially endowed with abilities in cooking, sewing, cleaning, and raising small children. It was conservative, too, in reinforcing the underlying message of the Imperial Rescript on Education (1890) that the purpose of education was to produce obedient, loyal citizens. Well-ordered families are the foundation of a well-ordered state, said Shimoda, sounding like a Confucian primer. But *Home Economics* departed from the expected script in according women a major, explicit role in running the family. The implication was that women as household managers were performing a job different from but equal to the jobs men were doing in the public sector. There were practical skills involved, a standard to be achieved, which Shimoda carefully outlined in sections entitled, "household economy," "hygiene," "food and drink" and the like. The typical woman who emerges from the pages of *Home Economics* is not the meek doormat of *The Greater Learning for Women* (Onna Daigaku) but strong and decisive, very much involved in her children's lives, supervising their choice of friends, activities, selecting their schools, monitoring their schoolwork. She was the Japanese equivalent of the model Victorian woman.[17]

Shimoda's message that Japanese women should be educated to be independent, modern yet still Japanese in their ethical and lifestyle choices had broad public appeal. Konoe Atsumaro had readily signed on as an IWA supporter. It made sense to him to get female public opinion behind his Asia for the Asians argument that as an adapter of modern systems Japan had something unique to offer the rest of the region. Shimoda was quick to try to join the Konoe initiative on China exchange programs, which were showing some results already in 1900 on the men's side chiefly through the efforts of her fellow educator and occasional judo teacher, Kanō Jigorō. Her idea was to start a training program for Chinese women at her just-opened Practical Arts School. As a classical scholar Shimoda was well-versed in Chinese literary texts, but now in anticipation of working with Chinese women she began lessons in spoken

Chinese. Her tutor was one of Kanō Jigorō's students at the Tokyo Teachers College, a talented young man who was making a name for himself as a translator. He and Shimoda began to collaborate on translation projects, including translations of Shimoda's books on "good wives, wise mothers" for publication in Tokyo and Shanghai. What began as a push from the Japan side became a pull as visiting Chinese educators sought out Shimoda's advice on women's education. "Good wives, wise mothers" resonated well in the conservative Chinese context.[18]

One can imagine that "Little Shimoda," as Kawahara was called, approached the meeting with the real Shimoda with considerable excitement. Her father, too, had evidently given his approval without reservations. He had been consistently supportive of his daughter's aspirations and meeting with someone as highly educated and China-connected as Shimoda fit with his own interest in reconciling China scholarship with contemporary concerns. He clearly supported his daughter's desire for independence as a woman, this too perhaps an indicator of the new kinds of family dynamics possible in the Meiji context. Misako was twenty-five in 1900 and apparently under no pressure to marry. She was becoming what Shimoda was in fact, a Meiji "new woman." However, Mr. Kawahara may not have understood at this point how much Shimoda's lifestyle as a single woman appealed to his daughter. Ironically, major spokeswoman for "good wives, wise mothers" though she was, Shimoda in fact was neither. She was a widow without children, a financially independent career woman not only prominent in public life but also a ready target of gossipy press articles.

Mission to Shanghai

There was a political side to Shimoda's China contacts that the Kawaharas could not have known about. The young Teachers College graduate who provided Shimoda daily Chinese lessons was a leading figure among Chinese student dissidents in Japan. As Shimoda was scheduling her IWA fundraising trip north to Nagano in the summer of 1900, he was laying plans with his fellow activists to stage a coup against China's empress dowager. Shimoda was also acquainted with some of the major Japanese backers of exiled Chinese revolutionary Sun Yatsen, including Inukai Ki—with whom she had a rather testy exchange during his brief tenure as education minister in 1900—and Kiyofuji Kōshichirō, whose sister was an active member of the IWA. When the decision was made to go to Nagano, Ms. Kiyofuji arranged a private meeting between Shimoda and Sun who was in the area and wanted to talk about fundraising. By some accounts, Sun came up with the bizarre proposal that Shimoda convince the Chinese government to contribute funds to educating Chinese women in Japan, then secretly divert the money to Sun's revolutionary cause. If the revolution succeeded, Japan's reward would be a free hand in Manchuria. Whether such a proposal was actually made is impossible to corroborate, though it sounds like the Manchuria deals Sun was willing to make a few years later. Proof that the Shimoda-Sun meeting actually took place, however, exists in the form of a friendly exchange of poems between the two written on both sides of a Japanese fan.[19]

On this same trip, in Nagano, Shimoda met Kawahara Misako. Shimoda was much impressed with the young high-school teacher so eager to talk about China. She seemed a model of Japan's "new woman." A product of Japan's new schools, in a profession which until recently had been male-dominated, Kawahara at twenty-five was not contemplating the usual path of marriage and family but wanted to pursue a career. She was unconventional but still mainstream. She was not rebelling against her family or demanding equal rights with men. Emotionally and intellectually, in fact, she was living out the values her father placed on duty, hard work, a good education, and a concern for the "China problem." To Shimoda, Kawahara's positive feelings about China made her seem especially interesting. In the eyes of many Japanese after the war, the Chinese were not worth bothering about. A month after the Nagano meeting, when Shimoda was asked to recommend someone to teach in a new girls' division at a school for Chinese residents of Yokohama, she immediately telegraphed Kawahara. By the end of September 1900, Kawahara had resigned from her high school job and moved to Yokohama, eager to take up the new challenge.[20]

Teaching the daughters of Chinese businessmen in Yokohama proved to be a harder job than Kawahara had imagined. She was dismayed by how little she understood of her students' background, customs, and outlook on life. To improve communication, she began to study spoken Chinese with the school's head teacher, a Beijing native. In the classroom, she tried to maintain reasonable academic standards without being too exacting. On a personal level, she did her utmost to be consistently patient, kind, and sensitive to the difficulties her students faced living in a foreign environment. But no matter how hard she tried over the year and a half at Yokohama, she found the girls "most often unappreciative and hostile."[21] She told herself not to take this personally. As she saw it, their hostility stemmed from the anti-Chinese prejudice they so often encountered in postwar Japan. Still, she found the atmosphere in the classroom dispiriting and from a practical standpoint an obstacle to effective teaching and to establishing the kind of rapport with her students that would contribute to Sino-Japanese friendship.

Over the long months of getting nowhere in Yokohama, Kawahara began to entertain a larger ambition, to take her teaching skills to China. She expected she might be better received in a totally Chinese setting and that by working with Chinese women she might also influence male attitudes and contribute to the larger goal of "promoting national development and peace among human beings."[22] Her experience at the Yokohama school was good preparation. She now understood both the reality of teaching foreign students and the gaps in her own knowledge of Chinese ways of thinking and behaving. She had improved her spoken Chinese. And, she had begun to study French, believing that to undertake international work, "I must get to the point where I feel confident dealing with Westerners." Hers was a rational, well-thought-out plan, but as she recalled later she wondered if she were being presumptuous in harboring such ambitions. Indeed, while it was common enough at the turn of the century for Japanese women to go to Europe or the United States to study, it was unprecedented for a Japanese woman to go to China to teach.[23]

But the timing was right. China's current policy favored hiring Japanese teachers and advisers, and Shimoda, Kawahara's new sponsor, had in place a good network of China contacts. In 1902 Shimoda received a letter from a Shanghai educator who had just established a private school for women run entirely by Chinese. To keep the teaching staff fully Asian yet introduce outside expertise, he was seeking recommendations for a qualified Japanese female teacher. Shimoda searched her roster of possible candidates focusing not simply on pedagogic skills but on strength of character, commitment, and the ability to persevere. She selected Kawahara, who promptly asked her father's permission. He needed little convincing to approve the assignment, though for good form's sake, he traveled to Tokyo to speak directly with Shimoda. Overjoyed to be chosen, Kawahara was brought back to earth by the sober tone of Shimoda's farewell, "As the first woman teacher from Japan, you must put forth your best effort or it will reflect badly on all Japanese women."[24] Suddenly it was August 28, 1902, and Kawahara was on a ship bound for China.

Her new school, the Women's Academy of Fundamental Learning (Wuben Nüxuetang), was located in what foreigners called native Shanghai to distinguish it from *their* Shanghai, the foreign settlements, where Westerners and Japanese worked the deals that made the city the commercial and trading hub of all of East Asia. "London on the Yellow Sea," one Western observer called Shanghai, "a splendid example of what British energy, wealth, and organizational power can accomplish."[25] That she had come to a vibrant, cosmopolitan city was also Kawahara's impression as she rode in the Japanese consul's carriage along the Bund, the wide waterfront avenue, past grand hotels, banks, and office buildings to the block of diplomatic missions. She had heard, she said with evident excitement, "that there was no better example of modern culture than this, even in Europe and America, the acknowledged centers of culture!"[26]

When she set foot in the crowded native city, hidden from foreign view behind high encircling walls, the scene was appallingly different:

> A flower garden and a garbage heap run alongside each other with the north wall a border between them. The incongruity of twentieth century modern culture and fifteenth century barbarism adjoining each other, separated by the width of a single wall, must be seen to be believed . . . There are people passing through those narrow streets carrying buckets of garbage and sewage. It's virtually impossible to walk along without brushing your clothing against them. Also, there are piles of accumulated garbage here and there, swarming with flies. When people approach, the flies suddenly fly off in all directions and the stench is overpowering. One can put up with the stench, but seeing the agony of ill and half-dead people lying at the sides of the road is not for the fainthearted. In such circumstances, epidemics spread during the summer months. It's said the death count is several hundred every day![27]

Fear of disease and a general distaste for the sight of squalor meant that "with the exception of one or two foreigners who had ventured in for a short time for some essential reason, absolutely no one had lived or spent any time in the inner city in twenty years. Hardly surprising, then, when I was told that it was completely unprecedented for a foreign woman to live in the native city."[28] Still, when it came to her personal decision as to where to live, she felt she had no choice. If she were to get to know her students and understand their needs, she was duty bound to share board and room with them at the school.

The student body assembled in September 1902 would have been a challenge for any teacher. There were forty-five women, some little girls of nine or ten, others in their thirties who, as Kawahara put it, wobbled around on their previously bound feet like beginning skaters on the ice. Most students lived in the school dormitory. A few were "commuters" who traveled to and from school daily in sedan chairs. It was a gabble of dialects, confusing not only to Kawahara but also to the women themselves. All of them had come with the encouragement of husbands and parents, but with somewhat ill-defined goals and academic preparation that defied categorization. Strictly speaking, Kawahara noted, there should have been forty-five different curricula. As it was, she and her eight Chinese male colleagues, all part-timers, geared classes to the equivalent of Japanese primary school. Kawahara was responsible for teaching Japanese language and literature, music, math, and drawing.[29]

Shanghai as it looked when Kawahara arrived in 1902. (Courtesy of the Library of Congress)

Like a present-day Peace Corps volunteer, Kawahara was committed both to "getting inside" Chinese society and to opening up the world to China using the vehicle of language teaching. She also felt tremendous pressure to perform well in her role as the first Japanese female teacher in China; Shimoda Utako's don't-fail-us message was always at the forefront of her mind. But adjustment to her new environment was a challenge. She was probably the only foreign woman living in the native city, not to speak of being the only woman and the only Japanese on the academy teaching staff. All around her were people speaking the unfamiliar dialects of the Shanghai region. Yet getting away from the school for so much as a casual stroll was unthinkable. If the squalor of the streets were not enough of a disincentive, she knew that as a foreign woman walking alone she would be the object of rough stares or, worse still, mistaken for a prostitute. What a relief it was, then, to escape every weekend by rickshaw to Consul Odagiri's residence for a Japanese-style bath and a chance to relax with a Japanese family.[30]

In October, a month after the start of classes, an obviously discouraged Kawahara got a much-needed psychological boost.

> The autumn wind whistled in the window of my room away from home and, feeling unbearable homesickness, I turned to my desk to write a letter to a friend in Tokyo. Just then, unexpectedly, a note from Consul Odagiri arrived. I opened it hurriedly, wondering what it was about. It said that tomorrow Professor Kanō Jigorō would be inspecting Shanghai schools, so I should drop everything to see him. I was so happy to get the news! In my mind's eye I could already picture the professor's kindly face.[31]

Kanō Jigorō (Yokoyama Kendō, Kanō sensei den, Tokyo: Oda Nobutada, 1941)

Kanō was on his three-month tour of China for talks on educational reform with leading provincial authorities Zhang Zhidong and Liu Kunyi. It was his first trip to Shanghai, and like Kawahara he felt less at home than he had expected.

> Until I got to Shanghai, I didn't have the feeling that China was different from Japan. However, when I saw the curious architecture of the Chinese houses, I thought, aah, it's just this different look that we call "foreign." Really, the houses are strange. I would like to show such interesting things to my close friends in Japan. And then when I went out into the streets, I felt something beyond strange. Being in the midst of the dirty houses, streets and lifestyle of the Chinese, even the rich, I was struck by the feeling that I wanted to study Chinese society. When I went to Hong Kong, at first I thought the British had done well to fortify the harbor. And then, when I met Suzuki and heard the circumstances of the war between the British and the Chinese, once again I felt I wanted—though not the fashion in research—to try to find sociological answers to why the productive Chinese were defeated in conflict with the British.[32]

Kanō knew Shimoda well and it was likely she who encouraged him to see how Kawahara was managing after a month in China. Her students did well by her, regaling their distinguished visitor with polite greetings and songs in Japanese. Professor Kanō was pleasantly surprised, she reported happily, by the students' proficiency in Japanese so early in the school year.[33]

Kawahara was further inspired a few weeks later by a visit to a Shanghai school for poor girls run by French nuns. What struck her above all was the missionaries' steadfast commitment to their work. "It's reported that some of them have lived in China for about twenty years. I was deeply impressed with their courage and devotion. It was as if they thought that nothing short of staying on knowing they would be buried in a foreign country would ensure the success of their educational ventures."[34] The Westerners she met seemed to offer a yardstick by which she could measure herself. On a cold, blustery December day, she made her way to an imposing home on the outskirts of Shanghai to give the first of a series of Japanese lessons to an American lady, Ms. Dewey, who planned to stop in Japan for a month on her way back to Boston. "How wonderful, how spunky" it was of Ms. Dewey to tackle a new language simply to make her trip more meaningful. Conversation practice apparently focused on their common view of life in Shanghai. At their final lesson a few months later, Ms. Dewey said in her newly acquired Japanese: "The Chinese city is very dirty. I walked there holding my nose. I'm worried about you. Take care. Let's meet in America in three or four years. Goodbye."[35]

In her work at the Wuben academy, Kawahara from the start was more effective as teacher and mentor than she had been in Yokohama. For one thing—and this was a key contrast to the Yokohama school—the students' enthusiasm cheered her along when she ran into obstacles in getting her point across using a combination of Japanese and the Beijing dialect she had studied the year before. She was a lively, energetic teacher, but also strict. Based on her own training, she believed that learning good discipline was itself part of the education process. She was determined that classes should begin and end by the bell. "And I was convinced that this policy of respect for rules would bring beneficial results in other aspects of their lives."[36]

Music was a favorite subject. Students came in after school hours for further instruction, singing with great gusto and laughter. In addition to teaching them popular Japanese tunes, Kawahara set to music a number of verses then making the rounds among Shanghai Chinese, adding phonetic marks to indicate pronunciation of characters. This was music with a message. One Chinese song, entitled "Encouraging Study," contains the following lines:

> Black slaves and the red race are both done for.
> Only our yellow race is sleeping, unaware.
> And the East Asian continent will sink into oblivion . . .
> Follow Japan nearby and Europe and America far away.
> World civilization will open up step-by-step.
> Put forth an effort, young people.
> You must make the most of yourselves.
> The time is at hand; it won't come again.[37]

Along with music, foreign languages, particularly the spoken version, came easily to the students; within six months they had achieved basic fluency in Japanese. Their aptitude, Kawahara realized, was largely a question of attitude, an unselfconscious desire to communicate whatever they had learned, regardless of correct pronunciation or grammar. The woman in charge of the dormitory always greeted Kawahara with a cheerful, "Isn't it a beautiful day today!" in Japanese and no one would have guessed that she only knew three Japanese sentences. Kawahara took this lesson to heart as she worked to master the Shanghai dialect.[38]

The academy dormitory functioned like a big, happy family. The students were up at 6:00 AM to fix their hair, the younger ones in braids, the older ones in chignons stiffened with pomade. They looked to teacher Kawahara, a foreigner in their midst, as an arbiter of style. When a few strands of hair escaped her abundant chignon giving the effect of sideburns, they took it to be mod and tried it themselves the next day. More momentous was the matter of feet. In Kawahara's company, the women said they envied her for having "big feet," probably a just characterization relative to their own feet that had been so painfully bound to three-inch size. Even unbound now to meet school admission requirements, their feet remained tiny. But Kawahara noticed that when they met someone on the street with normal feet, they pointed and laughed. The women's loud banter, their easy mockery not only of outsiders but each other, made Kawahara uncomfortable, until she concluded that it was generally meant in fun. This general noisiness extended through four o'clock tea and after dinner when the students sang to the accompaniment of an organ, then turned to their studies, the older ones reading aloud as the younger ones fell asleep over their books.[39]

After a few months of living in the dorm, Kawahara began to revise some of her preconceived notions of Chinese women as unsociable stay-at-homes restricted by their bound feet, unlettered, uncultured, and lacking in ideas. The usual "conservative" and "submissive" labels did not seem to fit her young friends, who had left their homes for a new experience and were remarkably open to new ideas and confident in expressing their own. In fact, Kawahara noted, they were far better than the average Japanese woman in letting others know what they thought.

But broader exposure to the life of women in Shanghai caused her once again to rethink her views. Most upper-class Chinese women, some of her students among them, seemed irresponsible, undisciplined, and self-indulgent to a degree that made her impatient. Far from caring about national issues, they were indifferent even to family concerns like how to manage a household and educate children. Their sole interest was in making themselves decorative playthings like the heroines of the cheap novels they had read since childhood. As Kawahara understood the workings of the upper-class family, resort to cosmetic appeal and an outward display of submissiveness were female strategies for power in a system in which men were allowed multiple wives. Whatever power such women achieved came at a heavy cost:

> Fettered by their bound feet, upper-class women of the Chinese race can't even take a step on their own. They are deprived of good health and any kind of outside recreation. Unwholesome and unhappy, in a state of perpetual melancholy, they live out their lives to the end. Though there are many pitiful cases in the world, isn't the lot of Chinese women the worst?[40]

The issue of bound feet left Kawahara with ambivalent feelings toward the very group—Chinese women—she most wanted to assist. She genuinely liked her forty-five students and appreciated the courage of their decision to unbind their feet in order to attend the new school. But she found even some of them and certainly Chinese females as a general rule entirely too tolerant of the custom of footbinding. For Kawahara, a single woman intent on competing in a man's world, it was no doubt a struggle to empathize fully with women in thrall to a male sexual fetish for three-inch feet, women who willingly deformed themselves for the sake of arranging a "good" marriage. She had more in common with the French nuns and Ms. Dewey, independent women working and traveling abroad. Still, however wretched she found the lives of Chinese women, Kawahara recognized their dominant influence within the family and concluded that "in the effort to educate Chinese, I believe the best policy is to start with women."[41]

Possibly because she felt helpless to make inroads against a centuries-old custom, Kawahara did not address footbinding directly with her students. She was more forthcoming when it came to health and sanitation, another area where Chinese practices appalled her. How could upper-class Chinese, she wondered, so well groomed in appearance and long in contact with Europeans and Americans, tolerate such indescribable filth? Her Japanese lady friends realized what she meant when they ventured in for a tour of the academy. "Although they were pleased by the students' academic progress," Kawahara wrote, "they appeared totally discomfited by the dirtiness of the native city."[42] Kawahara could hardly deal with the larger environment, but in the school setting she mounted her own little campaign:

> As the senior-level students became more proficient in Japanese, I put more of a focus on hygiene and got them to wash their underclothes more often. Because of this, each one of them made cleanliness a priority and became neatly dressed. In addition to progress in hygiene awareness, they eliminated traces of bad manners like blowing their noses during meals.[43]

Kawahara's insistence on discipline and deportment apparently did nothing to dampen the students' enthusiasm for the academy program. Enrollments for the spring semester of 1903 were up from forty-five to one hundred, three-quarters of them dormitory students. By the end of the school year, Kawahara could cite progress on the part of her students, but the real beneficiary of the academy's first year, she concluded, was herself. "Really, the experience of this single year did more to encourage me and to strengthen my abilities than the previous ten or more."[44]

It is all too easy to read into Kawahara's actions the policy aims of Shimoda, who thought in broad terms, terms Konoe would understand, about the need to expand Japan's presence in China, to be competitive with the West in winning the hearts and minds of the Chinese. But in fact Kawahara was working on a smaller canvas. She was much more the good Peace Corps volunteer, motivated by an interest in getting to know another culture, the excitement of transmitting new knowledge to people who seemed in need, and to some extent, the sheer love of adventure. What she shared with the Konoes, Shimodas, Hattoris, and Kanōs of the Meiji world was a personal belief in public service however defined.

Mission to Karachin

In the summer of 1903, Consul Odagiri contacted Kawahara about a new assignment, one that would prove to be even more of a test of her skills and stamina than teaching in Shanghai's native city. On the face of it the new job was straightforward enough: to set up the first school for girls in one of the Mongol counties—known then, and now, still, as *qi* or "banners"—about 250 miles north of Beijing. However, since there were at the time few schools for girls in Beijing and none north of the Great Wall, the assignment was unusual and, as Kawahara found out, required more than experience in education.

In the spring of 1903, the head of Karachin County—known as the "prince" of Karachin—made an unpublicized trip to Japan, principally to visit the Osaka Exhibition, a show highlighting Japan's industrial and social progress in the thirty-five years since the Meiji Restoration.[45] Very likely he also met with Kanō Jigorō and Shimoda Utako, who were typically on the programs of visiting Chinese. Certainly the prince was well briefed on educational matters because when he returned home, inspired to improve life in Karachin, education was at the top of his agenda, particularly that totally unknown phenomenon, schooling for girls. In Japan, he had no doubt learned, primary school enrollment ratios had recently shot up to a remarkable 96 percent for boys and 87 percent for girls, figures comparable to those in England and the United States. Stopping in Beijing en route to Karachin, the prince talked with Consul Uchida about the possibility of Japanese assistance in establishing the first girls' school in the Karachin county seat.[46]

There was another topic of conversation between the prince and his Japanese contacts: that was the growing crisis over Russia's troop presence in Manchuria, whose southern capital, Mukden (present-day Shenyang), lay about 200 miles east of Karachin. In April of 1902, Russia had given in to international pressures and agreed to a phased withdrawal of the nearly 100,000 troops it had brought into this region of China after the Boxer Uprising. A year later, just prior to the prince's visit to Japan, Russia reneged on the agreement, instead demanding new concessions from China as a precondition for further force reductions. As the Chinese government sought the support of the international community, Chinese students in Beijing and Tokyo organized public demonstrations to protest Russian aggression and to urge their own government to respond militarily. The Japanese, too, reacted with public outrage. The continued buildup of Russian strength in Manchuria, people were convinced, would jeopardize Japanese interests in Korea and by extension the security of Japan. Japanese newspapers talked of possible war. Konoe Atsumaro, hospitalized with only a few months left to live, used his remaining strength to direct a public campaign to pressure the government into demanding full Russian compliance with the evacuation agreement.[47]

Sometime during the summer of 1903, as the governments of Japan and Russia traded proposals and counterproposals defining their special interests in China (Manchuria) and Korea, the pro-Japanese prince of Karachin quietly invited several Japanese military officers to visit his county as observers, presumably to track the activities of Russian troops in the region. A post was set up at a local school, known somewhat too grandly as a "military preparatory school," where the officers stayed until January 1904, a month before the outbreak of the Russo-Japanese War. At some point during the summer, also, Consul Uchida conceived the idea of providing the prince the educational adviser he had requested, installing the adviser in Karachin, with the prince's approval, and making the adviser a contact point for Japanese intelligence operations. Though one of the smaller of the hundred or so Mongol/Manchu counties, Karachin's strategic importance loomed large because of its proximity to the Russian-controlled Chinese Eastern Railway.[48]

Kawahara seemed the ideal candidate for the dual position of teacher and Russia watcher. She spoke Chinese, had two years of experience teaching Chinese women, and had lived in China for a year in somewhat difficult circumstances. Professional qualifications aside, being a woman was itself a distinct advantage. Her presence within the protective walls of the king's compound, the prime listening post for regional information, seemed fitting and proper, not likely to raise questions from Karachin's predominantly pro-Russian officials.

But there was one important person who had to be consulted before Kawahara's contract could be finalized: Kawahara's father. He did not hesitate. This was the era when not only in Japan, but in Europe and America as well, hearts were stirred by accounts of patriotism and national mission. Sounding like Theodore Roosevelt sending his sons off to war, Mr. Kawahara gave his enthusiastic blessing to the Karachin venture. Promoting ties with the Mongolian people was a worthy cause, he wrote his daughter, a neglected part of the larger effort to build Chinese-Japanese friendship. It was her patriotic duty to accept, he said, reminding her of the story of Mulan, the Chinese woman who, 2,000 years before, had joined the army disguised as a man to help China resist the invading Huns. But certain as he was that she must do the right thing he worried about her personal safety. She was his treasured only child. Along with words of encouragement, he sent his daughter a dagger that he urged her to keep on her person at all times.[49]

Kawahara was in high spirits on the day of her departure from Shanghai, November 22, 1903. A recent side trip to Nanjing had whetted her appetite for the "real China" by contrast to "Europeanized" Shanghai. She was impressed, too, with the contribution Japanese were making to education in Nanjing; Japanese were head teachers in five of ten major schools in the city. The only discomfiting thing about the Shanghai-Beijing journey was getting there—another sea voyage. The first class accommodations Japanese enjoyed along with the Western passengers did not make up for stormy weather and Kawahara's fear of sailing. But as the sole Japanese woman on board, she felt it a point of honor to join the Westerners strolling casually on deck. As she described it with her usual good humor:[50]

> Since I realized from my first sea voyage last year that it was useless to fret about stormy seas, I got up my courage now. Thinking to myself that it was a national disgrace for a woman from Japan, a maritime country, to be afraid of waves that were just so high, I walked on the deck with them. In the end, egged on by the Western women, I had a try at a walking race on the deck, which was pitching and rolling excessively. I won hands down and was happy.[51]

Kawahara's two weeks in Beijing put a stamp of reality on her mission to Karachin. Suddenly the issue of schooling for girls was in the background. On her schedule instead were intelligence briefings with legation officials, including Consul Uchida, Military Attaché Aoki, and Kawashima Naniwa, Beijing's public security adviser and an old friend of her father's. She met with the brother of the princess of Karachin, the Manchu Prince Su who was fiercely opposed to Russian occupation of the Manchu homeland. Everyone talked about war as a virtual certainty. The romance of travel to the hinterlands now seemed a deadly serious responsibility. Kawahara felt an awful sense of dread. Uchida's attempts to reassure her were scant comfort. She would travel to Karachin under military escort, he told her, to guard against bandit attack. Once there, if she found herself in danger, she could contact the legation by telegram from Jehol (present-day Chengde) and they would come to her immediate rescue. Jehol, she thought with a sinking feeling, was about 75 miles from Karachin, which was 250 miles from Beijing. Even if her rescuers came at a gallop, they would hardly reach her in time. Personal safety aside, Kawahara worried about whether she was capable of performing well. Only her father's words encouraging her to forget herself and focus instead on service to her country had the required calming effect.[52]

At two in the afternoon on December 13, Kawahara and her small send-off party gathered at Beijing's Dongzhi Gate, exodus to points northeast. In addition to Consul and Mrs. Uchida, the Kawashimas and Hattori Shigeko were there. The departing group consisted of Kawahara, two Japanese soldiers, three Mongol escorts sent out from Karachin, and an odd assortment of conveyances and donkeys, stolid creatures apparently impervious to the bitter chill. Kawahara was borne along in some privacy, if not comfort, in an enclosed sedan chair whose poles were attached to the backs of donkeys fore and aft. The send-off party stood somberly as this little caravan jolted off into the winter landscape, becoming a speck in the distance. Kawahara herself was too tense to feel sad.

It was a nine-day trip to Karachin. From the windows of her sedan chair, Kawahara watched as the rugged mountains looming up beyond the barren plains imperceptibly drew closer with each plodding step of the donkeys. Dust storms gave way to snow. Beyond the Great Wall, the rutted road to Jehol provided spectacular scenes of forested mountains and rivers below. The temperatures grew colder. It was ever harder to leave in the chill darkness each morning, ever more inviting to arrive at the next night's lodgings to sleep over the heated *kang,* despite the dirt, insects, and unappetizing looking food served on grimy dishes. Fortunately, Kawahara had brought her own canned goods.

Kawahara set off on her nine day journey from Beijing to Karachin in December 1903 in this type of mule-drawn conveyance. (B.L. Putnam Weale, *The Re-shaping of the Far East*; London: MacMillan and Company, 1905)

The group reached the outskirts of Karachin City on the afternoon of December 21. The two soldiers immediately went to report to their superior at the military school, leaving Kawahara alone to face a welcoming party of about fifty Mongols, most of whom, she found on inquiry, had never seen a Japanese before, much less a Japanese woman. Escorted through the gates to the king's compound, she was numb with worry. How could she manage this critical first meeting with the prince and princess without an interpreter, she wondered? But she found her Chinese quite adequate to converse with the unassuming young rulers of Karachin. Dinner was an easy affair. The prince jokingly apologized for not serving *sashimi*. He talked about his visit to the Osaka Exhibition and his special interest in women's education. In the dining hall on prominent display, a surprised Kawahara noticed a photograph of teachers and students she knew from the Tokyo Teachers College. Might she come to take an occasional look if she felt homesick, she asked. The prince urged her to do so. He liked this young teacher from Japan, so confident in her knowledge and hardy enough to have survived the rugged trip from Beijing besides.[53]

Kawahara went to bed that night ready to drop from sheer exhaustion. But she was so cold in her unheated chamber in a Mongolian winter that she was unable to sleep at all. She awoke the next morning with a pounding headache and had to struggle to make it through her scheduled meetings with the princess on plans to open the girls' school. The following day, "suddenly I couldn't stand it any longer and spent the whole day in bed. As if they found this newly arrived foreigner frightening, the maids fluttered about nervously, so that they were of no use at all. I was indescribably annoyed and depressed. That evening I had a visit from Captain Itō from the military preparatory school. It was more reassuring than a visit from a famous doctor!"[54]

On December 28, just a week after her arrival, Ms. Kawahara, the new "head teacher," was a star attraction at the opening ceremony of the Proper Training Girls' School (Yuzheng Nüxuetang). She was asked to address the assembled crowd of 200 Mongol notables and their ladies, but as befitting a newcomer she made only a few polite remarks, this time in Japanese, which was then rendered into Chinese and Mongolian. The princess, who saw the occasion as a chance to publicize women's education, took a more provocative approach. "Men and women are born equal," she declared to her startled listeners. The problem was that Chinese society operated under the misguided belief that women were better off not developing their natural abilities. Denied the educational opportunities open to men, women were left functionally inferior, even in matters of household management. If Mongolia—and here the princess specified Mongolia, not China—were to keep pace with other countries, women must become literate and competent in handling family affairs and the instruction of their children. The princess's argument linking women's education not with personal fulfillment but with the larger social benefits was precisely the point of Shimoda Utako's "good wives, wise mothers" (*ryōsai kenbo*) message. The prince had carried back from his Japan visit the current buzzword in education. In the context of Karachin in 1903, "good wives, wise mothers" was a liberating concept.[55]

Kawahara (center) with the Prince and Princess of Karachin. (Kawahara Misako, *Mōko miyage;* Tokyo: Jitsugyō no Nipponsha, 1909)

For Karachin, Kawahara quickly found out, was a remarkably backward place, a startling contrast to foreign Shanghai. "I was amazed by what I saw and heard. The thought crossed my mind that it wasn't clear which was more surprising from a Japanese perspective, advanced civilization or a rough, primitive existence."[56] In Karachin, too, she became aware of a lurking ethnic question, the relative status of Mongols and Han Chinese. Of the population of about 450,000 occupying an area the size of Connecticut, only 10 percent were Mongols. Ninety percent were Chinese who, in successive in-migrations over two centuries, had pushed the Mongol minority into the western part of the county around Karachin City. The prevailing culture in Karachin was Han Chinese, unfortunately so, in the view of Kawahara who liked the Mongols' simple life style if not the stultifying effects of their Tibetan-based religion. In the past the Mongols shared ethnic roots with the Japanese, Kawahara noted, adding, "It's indeed a shame that it's gotten to the point that they've really become a dispirited race living under Chinese oppression."[57] Politically, on the other hand, the Mongols held the top positions in local government by virtue of their connections through marriage—the princess was Prince Su's younger sister—with another ethnic minority, the Manchus, who, through an ingenious system of checks and balances, had ruled the whole of China since 1644.

Introducing women's education in a minority culture steeped in superstition was no easy task. People were deeply suspicious. When the princess hired a carpenter to make school desks and benches, rumors immediately circulated that his real plan was to construct cages which foreigners would use to ship Karachin girls out of the county, perhaps even to Japan. In Japan, some said, the girls would be killed and their bones used in soap production or maybe their eyes might be removed to insert in photographs. The prince and princess were mortified by this display of ignorance on the part of their people, but Kawahara took it in stride. She pointed out that sixty years before the Japanese had shown the same kind of fear and distrust when the government established new local schools with a foreign-style curriculum. Confident that the benefits of schooling would become obvious, she was not at all downhearted when just twenty-four girls, mostly teenage daughters of the Karachin elite, were enrolled on opening day. To overcome objections fathers might have about the costs associated with schooling their daughters, the prince and princess subsidized books and materials, lunch, and carriage transport to and from school. The princess's support was more personal: she attended classes along with the youngsters, in part to expand her own knowledge, in part to function as teacher's aide. With this kind of encouragement, enrollment quickly rose to sixty.[58]

Kawahara taught Japanese language, drawing, singing, knitting, home economics, mathematics and physical education. Two other teachers, one Mongol, the other

Chinese, handled history, geography, and language studies in Mongolian and Chinese. There were two levels of classes to accommodate the wide age range, which ran from seven to twenty-three. Working with these young women was an immense challenge. They were barely literate, unfamiliar with math concepts, and unused to classroom discipline. Surprising even to Kawahara was the extent of their—and their parents'—ignorance of the world outside the Karachin grasslands. Only China, along with a few countries to the West and Japan to the east, loomed up large on their conceptual map. Not surprisingly, they lacked any sense of Asian identity. If asked, "Are you Asian?" the Karachin native would reply, "No, I'm Chinese."[59]

Kawahara Misako (upper left), the Prince of Karachin (center), and the Princess (upper right) with some of the students at the Karachin school, 1904-1905. (Kawahara Misako, *Mōko miyage*; Tokyo: Jitsugyō no Nipponsha, 1909)

Whatever limitations they had conceptually, the girls made up for in their lively enthusiasm for learning. They responded well to Kawahara's pragmatic, learn-by-doing approach to teaching. She delighted especially in their rapid progress in Japanese. In a trilingual setting, language practice was an exercise in patience. Kawahara first said a phrase in Japanese, then repeated it in Chinese. The princess then translated the Chinese into Mongolian. This tedious process was livened by the cheerful good humor of the princess and Kawahara, and the lessons proceeded amid much laughter. The focus was on everyday Japanese with core vocabulary related to family, food, school, and polite greetings. Occasionally, however, after practicing the proverbial "this is my pen," the class was asked to repeat something startling like "this is his gun battery."[60] The latter was no joke. In early February 1904, about a month after school began, war broke out between Japan and Russia. Kawahara evidently felt it important to introduce some "awareness training" to the Karachin locals who, she reported, were quite ignorant of the conflict occurring only a few hundred miles away.[61]

But the war was very much on Kawahara's mind. Her Karachin assignment included intelligence gathering for the Japanese legation in Beijing; the outbreak of war made the task more critical and more dangerous. Her work involved classifying communications from the Manchuria war zone and sending on the most urgent to Beijing by special courier. She also reported what she heard via the Karachin rumor mill. Even her students were a source of information. Word of mouth, she concluded, was faster than the telegraph system. Karachin's predominantly pro-Russian officials suspected her activities and were not happy about her presence in the prince's residence. They only refrained from criticizing her publicly because she was a respected educational adviser, much liked by the princess. Still, their hostility was palpable, and Kawahara was not overreacting when she worried about being poisoned or stabbed in the night. She prepared herself for this grim prospect by making sure her belongings were in order, her clothes always clean, and her lesson plans complete. She had also thought through the other awful possibility: that the Russian army might suddenly overrun Karachin. She had a pistol ready to fend off Russian attackers and, as a last resort, her father's dagger to use as a suicide weapon.[62]

On February 28, as the late afternoon sun gave way to a darkening sky, Kawahara sat in lonely reverie at the window of her room watching the crows buffeted about by an icy wind. Suddenly a houseboy appeared with a message from a young man named Waki Kōzō, who had just arrived in Karachin. Twenty-four-year old Waki was the son of one of Kawahara's early mentors, the principal of the Nagano Normal School, which she had attended ten years before. Waki had come to China in 1902 after a period of schooling in Taiwan. Kawahara had met him briefly in Tianjin as she was passing through on her way to Beijing in early December. Shortly after, with war imminent, Waki and about fifty others were recruited by the Japanese legation in Beijing to conduct hit-and-run raids against the Russian army in Manchuria. Waki was a member of a twelve-man squad charged with blowing up bridges and tunnels on the Chinese Eastern Railway northwest of Harbin. Success would mean major disruption of Russian troop and supply flows to the front. What lent urgency to the commando mission was a message Kawahara had sent to the Beijing legation in mid-February: "Russia is clearly mounting an aggressive invasion of Mongolia."[63] Waki and his companions, disguised as Chinese merchants to avoid detection by Russian intelligence agents, departed Beijing on February 21, making their way on horseback through ice, snow, and bone-chilling cold some 250 miles to Karachin.

Over the next few days, both the prince of Karachin and Kawahara briefed the twelve commandos on local conditions and possible routes north toward Chichihar. The prince provided them with fresh horses, rations, new disguises as lamaist monks, and a yurt where they could practice their hit-and-run operations. These activities were carried on as discretely as possible so as not to raise an alarm from the strong pro-Russian element in the Karachin leadership.

Kawahara's support was not only logistical. She was like a sister—a spunky, cheerful sister in a family of boys—serving the young men tea and cakes, chattering about familiar Japanese things, listening to their concerns, and assuring them she would write to their families. To the commandos, well aware that the Manchurian winter might kill them off if the Russians did not, the feminine touch was comforting. At least one member of the group, a handsome thirty-year-old bachelor named Oki Teisuke, was reportedly so smitten with Kawahara that he declared his intention to ask for her hand in marriage on his return to Japan. Given Oki's fitful career path, his proposal might not have appealed to Kawahara's father. After a brief period studying English at Waseda in the mid-1890s, Oki had worked translating Japanese legal codes for the Chinese reformer Kang Youwei, a job cut short with the failure of Kang's coup attempt in 1898. In 1901 Oki went to Beijing to teach at a Japanese-run school for Chinese then switched to another school the following year. Unattached and restless, Oki was a natural recruit for the commando operation.[64]

When the time came for the mission's departure from Karachin, Kawahara helped the men re-pack their gear, adding as parting gifts medicines, soap, and other items from her own supplies. Only the soap was turned down with a joking remark at Chinese expense: "If we scrub with this, we'll peel off our intentional Chinese disguise—far better to stay dirty as we are."[65] The princess's farewell party for the group the evening of March 2 was a jolly affair until thoughts turned to what everyone knew was a desperate venture. Choked with tears, Kawahara could only manage to say that she would pray for their safe return. Waki, the junior member of the squad, was outside her window before dawn, needing reassurance that she would contact his father if he failed to get out alive. Long after the twelve figures faded into the dark beyond the city wall, Kawahara stared into the distance at the threatening sky and snowflakes swirling in the wind.[66]

The trip northwest was a nightmare. Day after day men and horses stumbled on through the desolate Mongolian steppe in a seemingly endless snowstorm. There were no signs of human habitation, no sheep, no wild horses, only deep snow that completely covered the dried dung needed to fuel an evening fire. Everyone kept saying, "tomorrow it will clear," but instead the blizzard continued. Military maps and compass readings were useless. After a week, the group found temporary shelter in a temple, but time was of the essence and it was necessary to push on into the deepening winter. By mid-March, with food supplies running low, the exhausted men decided to divide into two subgroups, hoping that at least one might succeed in hitting targets on the Chinese Eastern Railway. The plan was to launch coordinated attacks the first week of April.

Waki and Oki were part of a six-man squad whose senior member was forty-year-old Yokogawa Seizō. Yokogawa's career included five years as a journalist, part of it covering the Sino-Japanese War, three years of independent study in the United States, and two years with a Japanese emigration company in Hawaii. At the end of 1901 Yokogawa accompanied Consul Uchida to his new post in Beijing, where he proceeded to study Chinese, then, on assignment for his newspaper the following summer, to travel to Mongolia. At Hairar station on the Chinese Eastern Railway, he was arrested by the Russians and jailed in Harbin for a month, after which he filed his story and started off on a similar reconnaissance trip to Sichuan. Yokogawa was tough, smart, and highly experienced, an ideal person to lead a daring mission.[67]

By early April, the Yokogawa-led squad was in the vicinity of Chichihar, looking for an opportunity for a quick strike against one of the rail bridges. But the Russian army had been alerted that Japanese commando groups were infiltrating the area, and General Aleksei Kuropatkin had posted additional infantry and mounted troops to protect the rail lines. The Japanese could do nothing but wait and watch. On April 12 a Cossack patrol caught sight of two pitched tents on the snow swept plain and, riding closer, encountered what appeared to be two Mongol monks. The Cossacks could not speak Mongolian, but something about the situation struck them as suspicious so they took the two men to the local Russian military base for questioning. The two "monks" were Oki and Yokogawa; the rest of the squad, including Waki, was out on reconnaissance and managed to escape capture. Presented with powder and fuses the Cossacks later found in the tents, Oki and Yokogawa finally confessed—Yokogawa, strangely enough, in English—to being agents for the Japanese military.

In a curious twist in a war in which Russians and Japanese were slaughtering each other by the thousands, Oki and Yokogawa were not summarily executed as enemy agents. Instead, they were transported to the central Russian command at Harbin—over the very rail line they had hoped to destroy—for a military trial, which was covered in detail by Reuters and other foreign press agencies. By all accounts, the two prisoners were treated with surprising humanity. Their captors supplied them with tobacco and liquor as they left for Harbin where they found their cell furnished with a Manchurian stove. On April 20, after the expected death sentence was pronounced, the judge allowed their request to pay their respects to the emperor, which they did with resounding *banzais*. The local Russian commander was reportedly touched by the prisoners' resolute behavior and asked for a reduction in sentence. General Kuropatkin refused. He thought he knew the Japanese character. Even if the court were lenient, he said, the two would take their own lives because their mission had failed. Generosity instead came from the Japanese prisoners. In a final unique gesture, Yokogawa, who was a Christian, donated the money in his possession to the Russian Red Cross.

Death by firing squad was set for April 21. At daybreak, in samurai fashion, Oki asked that they be allowed a final bath. Yokogawa requested a priest to administer the last rites. The two were then taken by cart to the execution ground where a crowd of locals and a few foreign journalists had gathered to stare as graves were dug and stakes pounded into the still frozen soil. A photograph of the event shows the Russian soldiers in the foreground ready to fire and, against a hillock about fifty feet away, the two Japanese, still in Mongol dress, bound to tall stakes. Yokogawa was blindfolded. Oki had refused the blindfold, preferring to watch till the moment of death.[68]

Kawahara probably heard about the executions in early May from reports relayed to her from Japan. Her feelings can only be imagined. The fate of Waki and his three companions was still unconfirmed; she continued to write to Waki's family. Only some months later did she learn that he and the others, mistaken for Mongol merchants—their disguise in this case was an unwanted success—were brutally murdered in a routine robbery attempt. From March when the commando group left Karachin to September (1904), Kawahara communicated to Japanese headquarters whatever information she could glean about Russian troop movements in the west Manchuria area. She also maintained contact with the commando squad that had split off from Waki, Oki, and Yokogawa in mid-March. This group had no more success with bridge-wrecking operations than the first, but at least managed to survive the winter and evade capture by the Russians.[69]

Kawahara carried a heavy burden during these long months of the war, juggling her activities as intelligence operative with her duties at school, which ran from 10:00 AM to 4:00 PM, five days a week with a half day on Saturday. In addition, she provided the prince and princess with special tutoring in Japanese. The results were heartening. Her students were now proficient enough to translate orally and in written form passages from Japanese to Chinese and vice versa, no mean feat since Mongolian, not Chinese, was their first language. Some showed particular talent—the princess's seventeen-year-old daughter was a notable example—leading Kawahara to think they would benefit from a period of study in Japan.[70]

The young women were making progress, but Kawahara sensed that their fathers and brothers remained unconvinced that women's education was a good thing. In the summer of 1904, to get some positive publicity, Kawahara organized a turn-of-the-century equivalent of "back to school night." Known in Japan at the time as a school "garden party," this was an occasion when parents would visit the school to listen to musical performances, see their children's artwork on display, and talk with teachers. The 300 people who attended this first-ever event in Karachin seemed to approve, Kawahara felt. She was also pleased to learn that they found her unexpectedly approachable, not at all the odious figure they had imagined. Held two or three times a month, these garden parties became a local attraction; 700 attended the program in August 1905.[71]

Kawahara could not have made the school project a success without the help of the princess whose idea it was and who was involved in every detail from the beginning. How this young woman wedded to life in the remote grasslands developed a passion for women's education is not at all clear. But passionate she was, about this and about the broader issue of modernizing Karachin. As Kawahara put it, "The princess very much loved progress and civilization and considered conservatism and backwardness disgraceful. She thought she must introduce the modern culture of advanced nations in order to improve the well-being of her people."[72] The princess's pro-Japanese leanings are easier to explain. She came by them naturally as the younger sister of the Manchu Prince Su, who looked to Japan to rescue the Manchu homeland from the Russians. "Strong-minded by nature," as Kawahara called her, the princess almost certainly influenced her husband's decision to hire a teacher from Japan in the first place.

Given their shared interests, Kawahara and the princess were disposed to work well together from the outset. But theirs became more than just a working relationship. After months of daily interaction, the two young women, both around thirty, developed a deep attachment based on mutual admiration. Each was a role model for the other. In the princess's eyes, Kawahara represented everything she aspired to: to be highly educated, knowledgeable of the world, up-to-date. Kawahara valued the princess's emotional warmth, independent spirit, and enthusiasm for life.

> The princess was a genuine free spirit with an abundantly cheerful disposition. Her usual form of exercise was to take her horse at a gallop over the countryside. Every day she went to the girls' school to learn along with the students. But, though she was very smart, she was obsessed with the fear that she was intellectually deficient. The princess, whose progress would probably have been remarkable had she had unbiased and honest advice, was also an emotionally deep and sympathetic person. Once she trusted you, she would treat you like a fellow countryman; I was treated almost like a real sister. Also, she cared for the two children of the prince's concubines as if they were her own. There were warm relations within the family, not the dreary, unemotional interaction of South China families.[73]

Kawahara liked the easy sociability of Mongol women. For one thing, she no doubt found it a relief to be with women who did not bind their feet, that crippling process so universal in Shanghai that her own normal feet excited comment. Rural Karachin with its vast, empty plains was also a welcome contrast to the crowds and pollution of Shanghai's native city. Kawahara was more independent than she had ever been in her life. Beginning in the fall of 1904, dressed in loose fitting Mongol style, she frequently joined the princess for horseback rides into the grasslands, a liberating experience for someone who started out a tomboy. In her work, too, Kawahara was on her own. As the legation's contact in Karachin, she alone had to evaluate, classify, and distribute whatever information seemed relevant to the war effort. When the commando squad made its briefing and supply stop, she was part of the team—of men. At the school, she was the highly regarded foreign expert whose words were heeded, advice taken. She even ventured beyond the education realm in her advisory role. After one of her rides with the princess, Kawahara suggested that the Karachin rulers consider a long-term development program for the region that would include extension of agricultural land and reforestation. When the prince showed an interest in Japanese assistance along these lines, she urged the legation in Beijing to hire consultants. Two Japanese soil and agriculture experts arrived in Karachin in June 1905 to carry out a six-month survey.[74]

At the end of 1904, the princess wrote to Shimoda Utako requesting an extension of Kawahara's contract. She praised Kawahara "for coming so far to teach under hardship conditions"[75] and emphasized that, while progress to date had been better than expected, the future success of the enterprise depended on Kawahara's continued services. The extension was granted through the good offices of Consul Uchida, but school was interrupted in mid-December when the prince and princess with a large entourage including Kawahara embarked on the long trek to Beijing. Kawahara described it as a routine visit, simply a high-level delegation paying respects to the Qing court. But December was hardly the best time to travel in such a harsh climate. Most likely the decision to leave Karachin was a response to what was happening on the war front. Though Japan had been victorious at Liaoyang in September and Shaho in October, losses were enormous—20,000 casualties at the Battle of Shaho alone—and it seemed doubtful that the country could continue to sustain such a costly effort. If the war shifted to Russia's advantage, the pro-Japanese prince and princess would be in a precarious position.[76]

When Kawahara departed from Karachin on December 13, she feared she might never return.

> About sixty sweet little girls accompanied us the three-and-a-half miles from the Prince's residence to Shangwanfang Village. At that point, we stopped the horses, got down from the sedan chairs, and said our farewells. Without a note being sung, the girls' faces reflected Wang Wei's sad song about leaving old friends behind. The notes of the plaintive melody came to mind, and, as I looked off in the distance, it seemed as if even the mountains over there regretted my leaving and the willows along the road were tugging at my sleeves. How my heart ached! My pupils surrounded me on all sides, clinging to my sleeves, clutching at my pockets, all of them choked with tears, some sobbing. When I said good-bye, they let go of my sleeves and tearfully said, "Teacher, please come back soon." I only nodded. My heart was too full to utter a word.[77]

The caravan of 150 people, 250 horses and ten carts laden with gifts for the Qing court moved slowly across the snowy plain, arriving in Beijing on January 2, 1905. Kawahara was at the legation by 4:00 PM, overjoyed to be speaking Japanese to her heart's content.[78]

Over the next few months, senior colleagues and friends urged Kawahara to return to Japan for a much-deserved rest, but she refused to consider the idea. There was still much to be done to get the school running smoothly and, besides, the princess and those "sweet little girls" were counting on her to go back. How Kawahara occupied her days in Beijing waiting out the war is not entirely clear. She probably continued to tutor the Karachin ruling family in Japanese. After the strain of the past nine months, she no doubt also welcomed the chance to socialize with Japanese friends—Mrs. Uchida and Mrs. Kawashima from the legation, and Dr. Hattori's wife, Hattori Shigeko. On at least one occasion, Kawahara hosted a meeting between the Hattoris and the prince and princess and their daughters, presumably to discuss women's education. In the obligatory photograph of the occasion, the ladies were at center stage, Kawahara sitting tall with the bold demeanor of a samurai. Dr. Hattori in his trademark derby hat had placed himself discretely off to one side.[79]

Kawahara Misako (front row, third from right) posing with the Prince (third from left) and Princess (fifth from right) of Karachin on their official visit to Beijing in early 1905. Mrs. Hattori is seated between the prince and princess with Hattori in the front row far left. (Kawahara, *Mōko migage*, 1909)

When it came to women's issues, the Hattoris had their own interesting experiences to relate. While Dr. Hattori was primarily responsible for directing the teacher-training division at the new, all-male university, from the beginning of his stay in China—the Hattoris arrived in September 1902, just a week after Kawahara—he had also taken a personal interest in promoting education for Chinese women. In this he was urged on by his wife, who, like Kawahara, was the daughter of a China scholar, a product of the new Meiji schooling for girls, and close friend of Shimoda Utako. Shigeko had no sooner arrived in Beijing than she became the spark behind a discussion group made up of upper class, forward thinking Chinese women, among them radical activist Qiu Jin. Qiu Jin who wore her radicalism on her sleeve so to speak, dressing in men's clothing, deriding Confucius for putting down women, and calling for revolution in China, seemed quite a contrast to the dignified Shigeko, supporter of mainstream Meiji values. But after a series of conversations, it was the more conservative Shigeko who prevailed, persuading Qiu Jin to go to Japan in 1904 to study teacher training at Shimoda Utako's Women's Practical Arts School. Three years later, back in China, Qiu Jin was executed by the Qing authorities for her part in a planned uprising in Zhejiang Province.

By early 1905 when the Hattoris had a chance to compare notes with Kawahara, their plans for the fall opening of a small school for women of the imperial family were well under way. No doubt Kawahara provided useful input on what challenges there might be in trying to teach these women, what techniques worked and did not work in language training and in introducing the rudiments of math and home economics to students with little knowledge of life beyond the palace walls. They likely talked also about the Hattori's efforts to get the Japanese involved in women's education at the policy level, using a meeting between the Empress Dowager and Shimoda as an opening wedge. This initiative was currently bogged down in bureaucratic politics from the China side and eventually came to nothing.[80]

Kawahara returned to her work at the Proper Training Girls School in Karachin sometime in the spring of 1905. However, this time her father was not entirely happy with the idea and increasingly wrote entreating her to come home. By December, she convinced herself she was at a good stopping point. Peace talks between Japan and Russia had been concluded, so her services as intelligence agent were no longer needed. In her role as educational adviser and general goodwill ambassador, she was reasonably satisfied that she had accomplished her mission. She had introduced Japanese style schooling to Karachin. She had the full confidence of the prince and princess—"Teacher, please become a Mongolian,"[81] the princess urged her—and her students had become very attached to her. Even ordinary folk in Karachin treated her as one of them. But after three years in an underdeveloped country, she felt out of touch. It was time to go home, not for good, but for one or two years as an intellectual refresher after which she would return better equipped professionally and with renewed zest for work. Dr. Hattori offered to help find a replacement. The princess agreed that three of the school's top students, a thirteen year old and two fifteen year olds, would accompany Kawahara back to Japan for a period of overseas study.[82]

On January 24, 1906, Kawahara and her send-off party were at the Beijing railway station, waiting amid the hubbub of Chinese vendors and mostly European travelers for the afternoon train to Tianjin. Mrs. Hattori, Mrs. Uchida, and Mrs. Kawashima were there. Prince Su, too high ranking to appear in person, paid Kawahara a compliment by sending a representative from his office. In an unprecedented show of respect for a foreigner, both the prince and princess appeared, the princess, warmhearted soul that she was, quite overcome now that the departure hour neared. Promise us you will come back, she begged Kawahara, and promptly burst into tears.[83]

Kawahara's young charges, used only to horse carts and desert travel, were awestruck by the speed of the train, as mountains, trees, and rivers flashed by on the route to Tianjin. "Are you lonely," Kawahara asked them later that evening as they prepared for bed in their Tianjin lodging house. "Teacher's here, why should we be lonely,"[84] one replied with an endearing trust that touched Kawahara's heart. Their first sight of the ocean expanse likewise left them wide-eyed, but in their innocence again, they boarded the steamer without any apparent unease. Only Kawahara found her nerves on edge at the prospect of a sea voyage. In her bunk the first night, she pulled the covers over her head, hoping to blot out the sensation of the ship rocking in what seemed to be a rough crossing. She had to laugh at herself in the morning when she found that the ship was still anchored in the harbor. On February 7, they reached Nagasaki. Kawahara had been away from Japan for three and a half years. It seemed to her like a decade.[85]

Mr. and Mrs. Ichinomiya, 1906. (Kawahara Misako, *Mōko miyage*; Tokyo: Jitsugyō no Nipponsha, 1909)

Kawahara was now almost thirty-one, in 1906 a spinster by anyone's reckoning. Still, she relished her independence and fully expected to keep her promise to the princess to return to Karachin. But her father and close friends, including the Fukushimas and Shimoda Utako, had different ideas. No doubt they were proud of her work in China. Her intelligence activities would soon win her an imperial award, the first ever given to a woman for military service. But they may have been concerned when her celebrity status drew press coverage of the sort in a *Nihon Shimbun* article of May 22, 1906, entitled "Ms. Kawahara Misako, Oki Teisuke's Sweetheart." It was time she got married. A matchmaker went into action, Ms. Kawahara's objections were overcome, and a fine candidate was accepted, Ichinomiya Suzutarō, assistant manager of the New York branch of the Yokohama Specie Bank. They were married in August. What pained Kawahara was how to tell the princess that her destination was not Karachin but New York City. Her father conveyed her regrets through the legation in Beijing. The prince and princess formally expressed their gratitude for her services and hopes that at some time in the future she would come back to Karachin.

It was a time of sad partings for Kawahara, saddest of all from her father, who died only a matter of months after arranging the Ichinomiya marriage. Kawahara, who had just barely arrived in New York, managed to return home in time to nurse him during the final stages of his illness. She stayed in Japan until late summer 1907, using the time to recover her own health and to prepare her China diary for publication; it was issued as *Remembrances of Mongolia* (Mōko miyage) in 1909.[86]

Following in Kawahara's Footsteps

When Kawahara left China, the Prince of Karachin contacted Hattori Unokichi about finding a replacement. Hattori and his wife knew all the particulars of the job directly through Kawahara. In February 1906, Hattori wrote to his friend Dr. Shiratori Kurakichi, the leading Sinologist at Tokyo University, requesting his help in identifying a husband and wife team with the right qualifications for the Karachin post. Apparently a married couple was thought preferable to a single woman who might not be up to the rigors of the job or who might succumb to marriage as Kawahara had done. Shiratori immediately proposed the idea to anthropology professor Torii Ryūzō. He and Torii were working closely together at the time to develop a new Asian studies program combining research in the natural and social sciences with work in the humanities. Torii and his wife, Kimiko did not mull over the offer for long. In March, just a month after hearing from Hattori, Kimiko had deposited her child with her mother and was on her way to Karachin, like

Kawahara, traveling on her own. Professor Torii finished a manuscript he was writing on the Miao tribes of southwest China and joined her in April. Kimiko taught Kawahara's former students, building on the good training they had in Japanese. Torii was also given the title of educational adviser; he developed textbooks in Mongolian at the request of the prince. Husband and wife and new baby traveled extensively throughout Mongolia, studying regional languages and customs and investigating archaeological sites.[87]

In the spring of 1906 when Torii Kimiko arrived in Karachin, there were probably no more than ten Japanese women teaching in China, some wives of resident Japanese, others hired from Japan through the network of Japanese China experts. Invariably there was some kind of connection to Shimoda. She had a good reputation among Chinese educators, particularly because she stood for an acceptably conservative brand of education that highlighted the importance of family values, moral training, and public service. While the Chinese central government in 1906 had yet to endorse schooling for girls as national policy, there was no escaping the issue. A system to provide universal public education for boys was already in the works and many local leaders were on their own initiative setting up girls' schools as well. Kawahara's Shanghai school was a case in point. As mentioned earlier, even Zhang Zhidong was beginning to give way, conceding that a program to train teachers was a necessary accompaniment to his plan to establish regional kindergartens. In 1904 he hired a woman from Japan, Tono Michie, to oversee teacher training and kindergarten development on the Japanese model.[88] It was just three years later, probably with this as an example, that the central government acted to underwrite nationally what was happening in piecemeal fashion locally and approved a set of regulations requiring establishment of girls' primary and normal schools. The rationale offered to justify what in fact was a landmark decision sounded properly conservative: China needed to produce "good wives and wise mothers."[89]

The shift in official Chinese thinking about Japan after Japan's victory over Russia in 1905 was having a clear impact on attitudes toward women's education. Women too, as the Japanese example had shown, must be brought into the national strengthening process for there to be any hope of long-term success. The mindset was changing but there was still a big gap between acceptance of a goal and bringing girls' schooling into reality: the lack of trained teachers. Since very few Chinese women had teaching qualifications and it was unthinkable that young men should teach young girls, there was an increased demand for Japanese women teachers. Availability was not a problem. Once it became known in Japan that there were relatively high paying jobs in China for Japanese teachers, many young women were eager to go. The problem was quality control. Schools which relied on Chinese students in Japan to do their recruiting, for example, often found that they had hired people who were not only unqualified but totally unsuited to teaching.[90]

To try to minimize such mistakes, the Chinese and Japanese governments followed the same contracting process used to recruit Japanese male teachers and advisers then working in China. This entailed routing a Chinese request for assistance through one of the Japanese consular offices in China to the Japanese Foreign Ministry, which would pass it on to the Japanese Education Ministry. The Education Ministry would then contact appropriate schools in Japan to work out the details of candidate selection and terms and conditions of the assignment. It appears that everything was negotiable; approvals had to be obtained from all agencies along the line, both in Japan and in China. The final product was a written contract specifying salary, travel expenses, allowances for board and room, and hours per week of teaching. The Chinese preferred to write short-term (one to two years) rather than long-term contracts, then grant extensions as deemed appropriate. The contracting process was not necessarily a bureaucratic nightmare. Remember that Hattori Unokichi was in Germany in June 1902 when he was contacted about an advisory job in China. By early September he was on his way to Beijing.[91]

Japanese teachers, women as well as men, made much higher salaries in China than they did at home. The Chinese hired a seventeen-year-old woman in 1906 to teach at a new weaving and dyeing school for 60 yen per month, easily three times what she had received in Japan. Reportedly she traveled to China with Mrs. Hattori who apparently was in Japan on home leave.[92] Kawahara did not mention what she was paid, but based on her age, educational background and experience, 75-100 yen was not unreasonable. Salaries for men were much higher still, ranging from 125 yen per month for a young language teacher to 270 to 400 for experienced experts like Hattori Unokichi and Kawashima Naniwa.[93] In addition to salary, contracts included the cost of round trip travel and housing allowances. The idealistic, Peace Corps mentality might have been paramount in Kawahara's thinking, but for many, the humdrum matter of salary and benefits was probably a major consideration in their decision to accept a job in China.

It is difficult to determine the precise number of Japanese women working in China over the 1902-1912 decade, that is, from the time Kawahara went as Japan's first teacher to the end of the Meiji era. For one thing, many were accompanying spouses hired locally (like Hattori Shigeko) and therefore not counted in official Foreign Ministry records. Wang Xiangrong in his 1991 study of Japanese hired by the Qing government has compiled a list—the best to date—that includes at least some of the local hires along with contract teachers. He arrives at a figure of forty-seven women teaching at kindergartens, primary schools, and teacher training schools in a dozen provinces. Most are listed by name only; a scant fifteen are further identified by a line of background information. All of the latter appear to be secondary or normal school graduates. At least three were college trained, one at an American institution.[94]

Wang Xiangrong's list does not include dates of China service for women, but we know from other evidence that some of them spent significant periods of time in China. Kawahara taught at two different schools in three-and-a-half years. Hattori Shigeko was engaged in tutoring or educational development in some fashion from the time of her arrival in 1902. She managed her elite girls' school from 1905 to 1909 when she and her husband returned to Japan. Another one of Shimoda's recommendations, Kimura Yoshiko, went to China in 1904 to teach at a new school for the children of one of the Manchu princes in Beijing. She was there until 1909 when she developed acute peritonitis and died.[95] In 1907, the Usami sisters, Shigeno and Naoko, accepted teaching jobs at the Guangdong Women's Normal School. Shigeno returned to Japan in 1910, but her sister remained at the school until 1916. The latter was unusual. Most of the women teachers, and men as well, returned home at the time the 1911 Revolution. According to Wang Xiangrong, only sixty-three Japanese teachers and educational advisers were in China in 1912 compared to 424 in 1909. By this time, Chinese returned students were available to fill some of the positions.[96]

Assessing the impact of Japan on China's educational development is an enormous topic, one requiring a book-length study.[97] But even the evidence from the experiences of the Hattoris and Kawahara suggests three points worth considering. First, though few in number, teachers hired from Japan, male and female, had the potential to make a significant contribution because they were operating in a relatively receptive environment. Politics could intrude as happened in the case of Hattori. But Chinese educators as the new century opened had given the nod to the Japanese educational model. With its emphasis on centralized control of schools, standardized textbooks, moral training and the like, it seemed compatible with the traditional Chinese emphasis on ideological uniformity. In its incorporation of modern methodologies and content—the kind of thing Hattori offered in his psychology classes—it fit the perceived need to complete in a new world arena. The job of Japanese teachers was to implement, not always an easy task but easier than selling the idea in the first place. Furthermore, the fact that China's leaders had in place an active policy of seeking institutional and technical assistance from Japan and were managing the relationship effectively suggests a broader possibility:

that constructive collaboration was a workable notion. In the last decade of the Qing era China was not an entirely helpless victim of foreign intrusion.

Second, in the case of women's education, Shimoda had an important role to play in shaping Chinese public attitudes and policies. Shimoda actively promoted translation of Japanese works on education into Chinese, and her name became well known among Chinese educators. How widely distributed these works were and what public commentary they elicited are questions that need to be further explored as does the extent of her influence on Chinese women students in Japan and Chinese officials on study tours. We know, for instance, that Wu Rulun, chancellor of the new Beijing University, visited Shimoda's schools in 1902 and told an IWA audience that China should emulate Japan in women's education. We know that Yan Xiu, who visited the Practical Arts School in 1904 (on his second study tour to Japan), the following year took a top post in China's Education Ministry overseeing education promotion offices nationwide.[98] These people had clout; the question is how did they translate what they saw in Japan into public policy, in this case on the sensitive issue of women's education?

A third point worth emphasizing is that Japanese contract teachers were coming in on the ground floor of institutional development and therefore really functioned more as advisers than simply classroom teachers. And in a country that counted only 391 girls' schools nationwide in 1907, a mere fifty Japanese women teachers could exercise an outsized influence.[99] When Tono Michie arrived in China in 1904, her job was not to teach in an existing system, but to help organize kindergartens after the Japanese model. Presumably she and others started the curriculum from scratch. This was certainly true in Kawahara's case in both Shanghai and Karachin. Even in her work at the primary school level this meant introducing the standard set of Japanese courses for women in home economics, music and drawing, science, math, vocational skills, and physical education. Also important was instruction in the Japanese language, regarded by both sides as the means to open Chinese minds to the wealth of advanced knowledge available in Japan. When Kawahara returned to Japan in 1906, she took three students from Karachin with her to study at Shimoda's Practical Arts School. When they returned to Karachin after seven years, at least one of them took up a career as a Japanese-language teacher. What needs to be documented is the extent to which schools like the one in Karachin had a demonstration effect, setting a pattern in curriculum, teaching methods, and the like for other new schools developed in the same locality.

Karachin Apart in Time and Space

The year 1906 was the start of a new chapter. China and Ms. Kawahara faded out and the scene shifted to New York where the new Mrs. Ichinomiya assumed the role of accompanying spouse. She approached what must have been a difficult transition with her usual cheerfulness. "Japanese were truly happy," she later recalled of her first months in America, "because it was just after the Russo-Japanese War and Americans welcomed us with heartfelt friendliness as if it would have been closed-minded not to make friends with Japanese."[100] Kawahara soon developed a reputation as a gracious, outgoing hostess, at ease with Americans and successful in promoting American understanding of Japan through teas, luncheons, and briefings for U.S. businessmen and tourists headed for Japan. In the small Japanese community in New York, she was known as the kind Mrs. Ichinomiya who sent over miso shiru, rice gruel and pickled plums to homesick Japanese students suffering the ill effects of American food.

As Kawahara played the good Japanese wife in New York, her three young students from Karachin toiled away at Shimoda Utako's Women's Practical Arts School in Tokyo. During their seven years' absence, politics in Karachin had become even murkier than before. Revolution in 1911 had ousted the Manchus, patrons of Karachin's rulers. As Manchu power crumbled, Russia and Japan, recent combatants in a brutal war in Manchuria, joined hands to conclude a series of bilateral treaties defining their expanded interests there and in parts of Mongolia. For daily coverage of these events and the subsequent furor over Japan's 21 Demands on China (1915), Kawahara had to rely on the pages of the *New York Times*. She lived for fifteen years in the United States before deciding to return to Japan in early 1922 to take care of her seriously ill father-in-law. "I feel a great sense of relief," he reported happily to family and friends, "now that Misako has come home to us."[101]

Kawahara's career ended when she married in 1906. But her published diary account of her China experiences, *Remembrances of Mongolia,* kept her name before the public, first as a model of the new independent woman and second as a China expert. In the 1910s with the help of the media, the Japanese public had grown used to hearing about Japanese women working on China projects, whether it was Shimoda promoting study abroad for Chinese women or Kawahara Misako, Hattori Shigeko, and Torii Kimiko teaching in China. Since many of the women who worked in China continued to write or teach once they returned to Japan, their China experiences tended to take on extended life. Hamada Matsuko who taught at Guangdong Normal with the Usami sisters, took a job at Shimoda's Practical

Arts School once she left China in 1908.[102] Tono Michie, the woman recruited to advise Zhang Zhidong on kindergarten development, was named principal of a new women's school in Tokyo in 1909. Torii Kimiko wrote extensively about China's ethnic minorities. A book she co-authored with her husband entitled, *Investigating Manchuria and Mongolia Again* (Man-Mō o futatabi saguru) was published in 1932.

In the final analysis, the work of these women whose careers for a time intersected with China may have had its greatest impact not on the Chinese, but on the Japanese public. What they wrote and said exposed the "China problem" in its everyday reality—poverty, backwardness, instability—reinforcing the view that it was Japan's moral and political responsibility to be part of the solution. Their direct involvement in Chinese women's education, on the other hand, lasted little more than a decade. True, Chinese educators continued to draw inspiration from the Japanese educational model well into the Republican period, but actual people-to-people contacts diminished after 1911 as the Chinese turned more to the United States and Europe for study abroad opportunities and advisory help. Besides, it was increasingly possible for the Chinese to stay home and get a reasonable education and to staff new schools with returned students from Japan.

When the number of Chinese women at the Practical Arts School dwindled away in the years after 1911, Shimoda made no particular effort to reverse the trend. She may have grown weary of the politically volatile, often anti-Japanese, Chinese students in Japan or found the new bureaucrats in China difficult to deal with—or they with her. In any event, she put her still considerable energies into expanding curriculum and facilities at the Practical Arts School while continuing to churn out appropriate texts on morals, manners, and marriage. In 1920, at the age of sixty-six, she took over as chairman of the Patriotic Women's Association, the group founded in 1901 by Konoe's friend Okumura Ioko to encourage the female half of the population to play a public role in support of Japan's Asian ventures of a military kind. Over the next few years, the unstoppable Shimoda crisscrossed the country trying to boost support for PWA educational and service affiliates. By 1927 membership was up 40 percent to about 1.4 million.[103]

Kawahara was once more in the public eye in the 1930s as Japan moved to consolidate control in Manchuria. Following the army-instigated Manchurian incident in 1931, Japan backed creation of a separate state in Manchuria—Manchukuo in popular parlance—under the nominal leadership of the last Manchu emperor, Henry Puyi. In 1933, territory to the west, including Karachin County with its large Mongol population, was annexed to the new state. As Louise Young so dramatically demonstrates, whatever reservations Japanese may have had about military adventurism in 1931 were entirely swept away by the mid-thirties in a wave of public enthusiasm for Japan's Manchukuo nation-building experiment. The engine of "go-fast imperialism" was no longer the military alone but the public at large from the media to intellectuals to ordinary folk, all convinced that Japan's ideals and national security interests were tied up in the success of the mainland venture.[104] Backing Japan even or especially in the face of international criticism seemed the only choice for a loyal Japanese citizen. In 1935 *Women's Weekly* (Shūkan Fujo Shimbun), a magazine which supported progressive causes such as women's voting rights and co-education, contacted Kawahara about publishing a special issue highlighting her patriotic service in Karachin during the Russo-Japanese War. She agreed to the project, but with some reluctance. She wanted to set the record straight. She had gone to China to teach, not to gather intelligence. Besides, she insisted, what she had done for the war effort was no more than what anyone else would have done under the same circumstances.

> It was my good fortune that under my father's guiding hand I came to believe that my mission in life was to be involved in women's education in China. Then along came that critical event, the Russo-Japanese War, and quite by chance I was put to work carrying out an important responsibility, one I was really unsuited for. My response was just to use my poor brain as best I could; there was nothing more to it than simply pushing my limited abilities to the utmost.[105]

In 1939 Kawahara was visited at her Tokyo home by one of the students who had accompanied her from Karachin to Japan in 1906. They had not seen each other in more than thirty years. Karachin was greatly changed, Kawahara was told. There were motor cars and buses; Jehol could be reached in a day. There was telephone service, the postal system worked, security was maintained by the Manchukuo military, and rural people were no longer living in extreme poverty. Life was better for most. On the other hand, the princess, the figure Kawahara remembered galloping over the Mongol plain, was now in Beijing, suffering from poor health, her hearing gone and eyesight dim. But she still thought fondly of Kawahara and Japan she was told.[106] What was left unsaid as Kawahara and her visitor talked about changes from the old days was that Japan was now engaged in full-scale war in China, its armies pushing south to Shanghai, Nanjing, and Wuhan.

In 1942 Kawahara received an official invitation to attend ceremonies commemorating the tenth anniversary of the new state of Manchukuo. It would have been an opportunity to revisit Karachin after thirty-five years, but she was too ill to make the trip. To mark the occasion, there was talk of establishing commemorative works in her honor, a Kawahara memorial hall, perhaps, or a sculpture of herself. A publisher in Osaka engaged her to help prepare a new edition of *Remembrances of Mongolia*. In an introduction to this revised work, issued in 1943, Kawahara took pains to point out that she was not the heroine the press had made her out to be in recent years. Calling her a "spy" or "secret agent" was an exaggeration, she said, because in fact she had not infiltrated enemy lines to get information, but had lived openly in the prince's residence, her activities fully sanctioned by the ruling family. Besides, her military work ended for all intents and purposes sometime during the summer of 1904, whereas she continued her teaching duties for another year. She emphasized the same point she had made earlier in the *Women's Weekly* article: if there were any long-term significance to her Karachin role, it was in the field of education. And clearly, like a good Peace Corps volunteer, she found satisfaction in small signs that her teaching had made a difference.

> To put it candidly, Chinese women's education was my main job. Because this was something I myself wanted to do, I felt confident and eager to be involved. Not only that, as the little girls sang songs from the standard Japanese songbook and became proficient in speaking Japanese, I naturally felt increasing affection for them and more and more enthusiastic about my work.[107]

Kawahara viewed China with a mixture of nostalgia and regret in the final few years before her death in 1945 at age seventy. The excitement she had felt approaching China's shore for the first time with the high aim of "promoting national development and peace among human beings" was but a remnant in a kaleidoscope of faded memories. In fact, already long ago Kawahara's China had become not Shanghai, which for all her positive spirit she found impossible to deal with, but Mōko, Mongolia, a place of such need where progress seemed measurable. Her 1909 publication was *Remembrances of Mongolia,* not "remembrances of China," though the entire first part was a recounting of her China aspirations.

What Kawahara heard about Karachin in the 1930s was that things were better under Japanese occupation. In this sense, she had no problem agreeing to requests from the press intent on boosting sales as well as patriotism to turn the spotlight once again on her Karachin mission. She was only bothered by her new billing as "secret agent"—more likely to draw readership than "school teacher," after all—which she quite sincerely sought to downplay. Kawahara had regrets, and it is tempting to read into them sadness over the larger China war and the shattering of the Manchukuo dream. What Kawahara expressed, however, was regret of a more personal kind. She had let the princess down by failing to return to Karachin. This continued to trouble her. Apart from the betrayal of friendship, all of her career hopes had been wrapped up in the Karachin school project. She had even dreamed of taking her father to Karachin to show him the results of her efforts.[108] She went no further than this. But it is easy to imagine the reveries of an elderly woman, a Meiji new woman, turning to paths not taken. What if she had returned to Karachin to continue her work in women's education? It would have been an independent life, a satisfying public role; she might have built a full career in education like her mentor Shimoda Utako. Instead, her sense of duty, to her father most of all, that all-important factor in her choice of China and education in the first place, had drawn her ultimately back into the more conventional path of marriage. In 1943 Kawahara heard from a recent visitor to Karachin that the inner garden at the prince's old palace was completely changed after forty years, untended, its owners long gone. But the sweet-scented *nadeshiko* (fringed pinks) she had planted years before from seeds sent from Japan were still growing in profusion, she was told, thriving in the soil of the *Mōko* (Mongolia) she once knew. The thought brought tears to her eyes.[109]

Chapter IV

Kawashima Naniwa: Japan/Myself as Number One

At first glance, the two figures in the century-old photograph might be taken for twins. The eye is caught by their look-alike costumes: dome shaped Mandarin hats, Chinese imperial robes, waist length jade necklaces, and boots of soft leather. Each face with its dark mustache stares at the camera with the same expression, relaxed and confident. Both men are seated, posed identically with feet planted firmly apart, one arm resting on a small table between them, their sleeves nearly touching a vase of spring narcissus. Complete symmetry is broken only by one significant detail, the embroidered design on their robes. The man on the right displays imperial insignia on each shoulder, a privilege reserved to Qing princes; his companion wears the two stars of a high-level Chinese bureaucrat.[1] But this evident difference in rank is hardly as startling as what is revealed by the names at the bottom of the photograph: only the higher-ranking figure is Chinese. He is Prince Su, brother of Kawahara's confidant, the Princess of Karachin, and sought-after contact of Japanese senior leaders like Prince Konoe. The other man is Japanese, Kawashima Naniwa, a military interpreter with the post-Boxer peacekeeping mission appointed in 1901 to head China's first police academy.

What is the meaning behind the pose for the camera? What does the photograph commemorate? Is the look-alike image intentional, meant to tell us something about the Chinese-Japanese relationship? How is it that a Japanese commoner is on apparently familiar terms with a member of China's imperial inner circle? One can safely say, of course, that the two men would never have been captured for all time looking like brothers had it not been for the violent shakeup of the Chinese world as the century turned: the Boxer Uprising, the occupation of Beijing by an international military force, and China's eleventh-hour adoption of wholesale reform. As we have seen in the case of Hattori and Kawahara, Chinese in their post-Boxer recovery mode were newly receptive to Japanese contacts. Ties with the West came at too high a political cost. Kawashima's presence in Prince Su's parlor, in other words, was in part a case of being the right nationality at the right time. But it was more than mere chance. For Kawashima, China was not a sudden fascination. His interest was long-standing and deeply-felt, an emotional as well as intellectual attraction in which his very sense of self-worth was bound up with convictions about Japan's capacity for leadership in China and the rest of Asia.

Kawashima Naniwa and Prince Su (Aida Tsutomu, *Kawashima Naniwa Ō*; Tokyo: Bunsuikaku, 1936)

To China in Defiance

Kawashima Naniwa was born in 1865 in Matsumoto City, Nagano Prefecture, birthplace also of Kawahara Misako and Fukushima Yasumasa who would later figure in Kawashima's network of China contacts. The Kawaharas and Fukushimas were among Matsumoto's first families. Long prominent in the area's intellectual and political life, they managed the transition into the freewheeling Meiji period with their status intact. Kawashima's father, on the other hand, was a middle-ranking samurai who, like many of his class, failed to thrive in the new entrepreneurial atmosphere after 1868. A recurring theme in Kawashima's account of his past is the sinking fortunes of his family, which was left increasingly dependent on the kindness of relatives.

In 1875, in pursuit of the better life, Kawashima senior moved the family to Tokyo where he got a job as a clerk in the Ochanomizu Teachers Training School for Women. He enrolled his eldest child, ten-year-old Naniwa, in the attached demonstration school. By Kawashima's own account—and one he relished telling—he was at this stage a physically weak, oversensitive child, the natural prey of playground bullies. "I was a high strung boy with a constitution like a piece of glass ready to shatter at the slightest jarring."[2] Thoroughly intimidated by his new surroundings and rough schoolmates, young Naniwa regularly played truant, wandering the grounds of the Kanda Shrine where he shared his lunch with the pigeons before returning home at the end of the day. What saved his school career was an accidental brush with Christianity. One of his schoolmates whose father was a missionary invited him to services at the Nikolai Seminary (precursor of the grand Nikolai Cathedral under construction from 1884 to 1891) just opposite the Ochanomizu School. As the Russian priest, an imposing figure in full beard, thundered on about sin and an all-knowing God, Naniwa feared that he could "run but not hide" as the phrase goes—that his truancy would go neither undetected nor unpunished—and he ran home crying to his mother.[3]

What motivated Kawashima in later life to confess, indeed to highlight, his childhood frailties was precisely the fact that he overcame them; the clear message of his recollections was that will and discipline could turn the weakest into the strongest, losers into winners. As he told his major biographer, he sensed his own potential by early adolescence and became intensely competitive, determined to be a leader. Long the victim of schoolyard abuse, he began to fight back no matter how outmatched by his opponents. With teenage zeal he devised for himself a program of physical and mental toughening: plunging into icy streams, trekking mountain paths alone, seeking self-control through Zen. The new Naniwa was stronger and tougher, though in the view of at least one close friend, less appealing: the bullied had now become the bully.[4]

As a fifteen-year-old obsessed with becoming number one, Kawashima was intrigued by talk of a new Asia-first group whose message seemed to project his own feelings onto a larger screen. This was the Revive Asia Society (Kō-A Kai), a political discussion group founded in 1880 as the joint endeavor of a handful of Japanese politicians and intellectuals and Chinese diplomats with the Tokyo legation. While it is conceivable that young Kawashima read about the group in the newspapers, more likely he was informed firsthand by two of his closest friends, Miyajima Daihachi and Shigeno Shōichirō, whose fathers, prominent China scholars Miyajima Seiichirō and Shigeno Yasutsugu, were founding members.[5]

Establishment of the Revive Asia Society marked the start of the Asia lobby that became an important factor in foreign policy decision making in the late 1890s under the leadership of Konoe Atsumaro and the East Asia Common Culture Association (Tō-A Dōbunkai). What made the small Revive Asia Society worthy of news coverage was that its members, well-known public figures, were calling for a redirection of foreign policy to emphasize the importance of Japan's China ties as a critical counterweight to the threat of Western imperialism. Not only that, with input from academic heavyweights like Shigeno, advocate of "practical Sinology,"[6] strategic arguments for closer ties were buttressed by arguments on cultural and historical grounds—that is, that shared language, values, racial origin provided a sound basis for a strong alliance. The pro-China bias in "revive Asia" thinking struck a discordant note in 1880 when most members of Japan's elite were still partying Western style at the Rokumeikan. Yet it drew public attention precisely because a number of Asia Society members, far from being insular in their outlook, knew firsthand the West Japan was dealing with: One had lived in Europe for a year in the late 1860s, three were members of the Iwakura mission which toured the globe in the early 1870s, and still another had just returned from eight years of study in England. Shigeno Yasutsugu, history professor at Tokyo University, had not studied abroad, but was thoroughly versed in Western historiography and incorporated Western as well as Chinese approaches to history writing in his own research work.[7]

Giving practical expression to its Asia-first principles, the society organized a Chinese-language school in Tokyo with an initial enrollment of about one hundred students. The idea was to better integrate the teaching of classical, written Chinese with training in the spoken language so that Chinese, like English or French, would have real-world applications.[8] Innovative as this approach was, the school failed to attract and retain students who were drawn instead to the opportunities open to graduates trained in European languages. In 1882 the Ministry of Education transferred the few students still enrolled at the Revive Asia School into a special China course at the Tokyo Foreign Language School.[9]

For Kawashima, a teenager struggling to surmount feelings of inferiority, the "revive Asia" message had an appeal that went beyond the logic of arguments for China alliance. He could feel Japan's pain as the victim of Western bullying. He could project onto the image of a revitalized Asia under Japanese leadership his own vague hopes to accomplish something great, to gain recognition as a commanding figure in public life. Personalizing "revive Asia," Kawashima began to exhibit the defiant anti-Western, China-centered outlook that stayed with him always. When a relative who had connections at the Tokyo Foreign Language School urged him to study a European language, a prerequisite for university admission, he rudely rejected the idea, bringing on an angry confrontation. Kawashima eventually had his way, entering the school's less-prestigious China Department in 1882, aged seventeen. When he found that English was required for China study majors, he insisted that he would have a fine career without knowing even the A of the ABCs. He petitioned school authorities to abolish the course.

As a student at the Foreign Language School, Kawashima happily immersed himself in Chinese classical texts, priding himself on his ability to recite from memory long passages from Ssu-ma Qian's *Records of the Historian* (Shiji). But he had no intention of becoming an academic like his friend and classmate Miyajima Daihachi who went on to do classical studies in China in the late 1880s. His goal was to qualify as a China expert in the real world, so to speak, after the fashion of another classmate, Odagiri Masunosuke, who was to apply his Chinese-language training to a career in the diplomatic service. It was Consul Odagiri and family who provided a weekend refuge for Kawahara Misako during her year at the girls' academy in Shanghai in 1902.

For all the apparent talent at the Foreign Language School—perhaps the best-known graduate was the writer and translator of Russian literature, Futabatei Shimei—the students reportedly were a rowdy bunch, no one more so than Kawashima who had the reputation of being brash and opinionated besides. As one of the tough guys who strutted around with the sleeves of his kimono rolled up to his armpits, Kawashima was so belligerent in promoting his anti-Western nationalism that school authorities threw up their hands, declaring him unmanageable.[10] He was threatened with expulsion on more than one occasion, but action was never taken since his marks were consistently high. Behind the bravado and display of rebelliousness lay anxiety and perhaps resentment as well. Miyajima's father might be a noted scholar in comfortable circumstances, but Kawashima's own—as he presented him—was a loser, once a clerk, now a failed businessman unable to cover Kawashima's school fees. Again, Kawashima was saved by his academic abilities: his examination scores were high enough to qualify him for a state scholarship.

In 1885, in an effort to consolidate resources, the Education Minister decided to discontinue the Tokyo Foreign Language School as a separate institution. Departments of English, French and German, languages required for admission to Tokyo University, were now formally incorporated into the Tokyo Preparatory School program. The non-university-track languages, Chinese, Korean and Russian, were made part of the core curriculum of the Tokyo Business School. One might have expected Kawashima, who had just performed brilliantly in his final exams in Chinese, to have jumped at the chance to acquire a degree in business, virtually assuring him of a position with a China-based company like Mitsui Bussan. Certainly this was the course recommended by the business school director who brought Kawashima's father and uncle into the picture to press the point. But Kawashima would have none of it. The business track did not interest him. Nor was he willing to consider another possible option, becoming a student at the Military Academy. He liked military studies, but a career in the army, he said, would be like serving time in prison. Instead, he decided to head for China. He admitted that he had no clear idea what he wanted to do there, but he was determined to go straightaway.[11]

What we know about this turning point in Kawashima's life is based on anecdotes supplied by Kawashima himself and thus has something of the flavor of heroic destiny at work. At a practical level, one suspects that family members were more than a little upset by his decision, so curtly delivered, to quit his education for an uncertain future in China. His father's finances were in bad shape, and Kawashima, still in school at twenty, was probably the recipient of more assistance from relatives than he acknowledged. No doubt the extended family expected him to get a steady job as soon as possible to contribute to the welfare of his parents and siblings. In a revealing passage, Kawashima tells how he begged his unhappy mother to bear with him, assuring her that after a few years in China he would have the resources to help out in a major way.[12]

It was not money but some undefined heroic ideal that motivated Kawashima in his China quest. But once he withdrew from school in March of 1886, money was again at issue simply because he could not support himself. He turned first for help to his Nagano connection, Fukushima Yasumasa, at that time a captain employed by the Army General Staff Office. Fukushima gave him funds to tide him over until he could convince his uncle to advance him enough money to cover the ship's fare and other travel expenses. In September 1886, Kawashima set sail from

Yokohama on a boat bound for Shanghai. It should have been a triumphant moment. But judging from the poem he wrote on departure, his gamble on success in China left him feeling lonely and depressed:

> The setting sun sinks into the darkness of the Genkainada Sea
> Evening clouds drift in, obscuring Kyushu
> A darkening haze hangs ominously over East Asia
> As our small boat, vulnerable, alone, makes its way through surging waves.[13]

Reaching the China he had so long wanted to visit apparently did nothing to lift the weight of depression. There is no hint in Kawashima's account of Kawahara's breathless excitement at her first glimpse of the China coastline or Hattori's eagerness to make contact with members of China's intellectual elite. What caught Kawashima's attention—and this had nothing to do with China—was the evident second-class status of Japanese residents of Shanghai relative to Westerners, a disparity that so annoyed him that he was ready to move on immediately to Tianjin where he had the promise of a job.[14] On arrival in Tianjin, Kawashima immediately picked a fight with his potential employer with the result that he was out of work before he even started. His classmate Odagiri who was in China on a Foreign Ministry study grant advanced him some funds along with the suggestion that he book passage back to Shanghai. There was no smooth sailing here either. Traveling on a slow freighter south, Kawashima contracted malaria and nearly died. His luck finally turned when he landed a job with a Shanghai-based Japanese naval officer assigned to investigate China's coastal defense works. The story goes that Kawashima was so reckless in his pursuit of information that his superiors feared the Chinese would catch on, but he was also smart, fluent enough in Chinese that he could pass as a native, and his services were continued.[15]

Several hundred Japanese lived in Shanghai in the mid-1880s, a few of them diplomats, students, and representatives of established firms but most employed by small businesses selling a range of goods and services from pharmaceuticals to printing.[16] Joining one of the new ventures would have seemed a logical choice for Kawashima. For example, the Rakuzendō, a profitable pharmacy that shared its market research with the army, was hiring dozens of people who fit Kawashima's profile: early twenties, trained not only in written but spoken Chinese, driven by the goal of competing with the West in the China market. Kawashima differed from the Rakuzendō group in his evident desire to steer clear of business and to work independently as a freelance contractor with the Japanese military.

In his personal relationships, too, Kawashima at the outset chose to go his own way in Shanghai, spending most of his free time with his old school chum Shigeno

Shōichirō, an attractive (more beautiful than a woman, some said), bookish fellow, son of the prominent historian. The friendship caused a great deal of resentment among the Shanghai bachelor set, particularly those from southern Japan who felt that as a northerner Kawashima had no right to claim intimacy with Shigeno, whose family was originally from Kagoshima. Kawashima's contemptuous response to such carping raised tempers to a dangerous level. For a time he found it prudent to venture out only if he had with him a cane that held a concealed sword. Eventually, Kawashima tells us, he made peace with those disposed to dump him into the Huangpu River, becoming a regular at their sake and sumō wrestling parties. Still, he never joined the group clustered around the most celebrated of the young Japanese in China, Arao Sei, a Military Academy graduate who had arrived in Shanghai in 1886, shortly before Kawashima. "When I met Arao in Shanghai," Kawashima said, recalling the encounter fifty years later, "I was struck by the sense that he ingratiated himself with people to get his way; I found this a bit off-putting and we never developed a close rapport."[17]

Personal style aside, what Kawashima chose to highlight about Arao from the 1880s was how wrong Arao turned out to be on a key foreign policy question of the day, namely, the long-term impact of Russia's trans-Asia railway building program on the security of north China. Arao, as Kawashima remembered it, thought that northwest China (present-day Xinjiang) would bear the brunt of expanding Russian power. He, on the other hand, took the less popular, but ultimately correct—of course—position that Russia had its sights on China's northeast (Manchuria and Mongolia) and Korea.[18]

The elderly Kawashima may be forgiven for trying to validate his later, long commitment to Manchuria/Mongolia separatism by suggesting special insights early on. But he told only a piece of the Arao story. The Arao Kawashima met in Shanghai was very much a soldier-turned-entrepreneur with a sense of purpose more clearly articulated than his own. Arao's was a broad vision of Japan's continental policy, one that put expansion of Japanese trade and business with China on a level with developing political/military contacts and intelligence sources. When he sent out his young associates from the Rakuzendō central and branch pharmacies to various remote parts of China—not simply the northwest—to scout out local conditions, it was with this dual purpose in mind.[19] One suspects that Kawashima's decision in 1889 to try to match these efforts with his own walk from Shanghai to Manchuria had as much to do with the desire of a twenty-four-year old to do something different as with a different position on Japan's China policy.

The trek was a fiasco. Kawashima was only able to persuade Shigeno and one other friend, a Nagano contact, to join him. No one else, he complained, had the ability to think long-term. In northern Jiangsu, about a week into the trip, Kawashima was suddenly racked with an attack of malaria and his friends could see no other course but to transport him, feverish and weak, by canal and coastal ferries back to Shanghai. Shigeno returned to Japan and was promptly dispatched by his distinguished father to study in France, far out of Kawashima's orbit. Kawashima, seriously ill and out of funds, also decided to go home to gather his resources for another day.

What he found in Tokyo was a more desperate family situation than he had imagined. His parents and ten siblings were in such a struggle for survival that they often went for two or three days at a time without anything to eat. Curiously enough, the same Kawashima who supplies rich anecdotal material on his life prior to his return to Tokyo in early 1889 is rather reticent on how he spent the period 1889-1895. He does mention that he was under great stress, plagued by financial worries, disheartened that all-consuming family responsibilities left no time to pursue personal ambitions. Eventually the strain of it all—he may have suffered a nervous breakdown—drove him to retreat into Zen studies and the solace of self-discipline.[20] How the Kawashima family fared remains a mystery. Nor does Kawashima elaborate on what sorts of jobs he took on to contribute to the household finances, a sign perhaps that the work was too menial to bear mention.

Kawashima's early years in China ended in frustration, not with the Chinese, but with his Japanese colleagues who failed to warm to his Manchuria views and with himself for his inability to overcome adversity and stand out as number one. Bad luck and Kawashima's abrasive personality were part of the problem. Also, resisting wiser heads, he had gone to China without clear direction, driven only by the Revive Asia Society-inspired thought that he wanted somehow to counteract Western influence in Asia. In the vagueness of his goals and his expectation that China itself would provide answers, however, he was no different from most of the other young Japanese gathered in Shanghai. In the scholarly literature on the period these people are labeled adventurers, drifters, or rōnin, giving them a kind of romantic, underworld quality, though in fact most were, like Kawashima, simply youthful freelancers who turned up in China later on in professional positions as businessmen, journalists, and school administrators. Experience in China in the 1880s represented for these young men a kind of informal apprenticeship program, a chance to add skills in spoken Chinese to classical knowledge taught in contemporary Japanese schools and to learn something about the real China, the Chinese countryside. Certainly Kawashima's occasional work as observer and reporter for the Japanese military proved useful to him later.

In the Right Place at the Right Time with the Right Skills

For Kawashima, the outbreak of war with China in the summer of 1894 ended a painful period of inaction on the larger stage. Now his language skills were at a premium. Whatever his family obligations, there was no question where duty lay in a time of national crisis, and he quickly signed up as a contract interpreter with the army's second division. By January he was on a military transport bound for Shandong Province, where Japan was engaged in a major land and sea offensive against the port of Weihaiwei.[21] Of Kawashima's brief wartime experience his major biographer says only that he served at the front, witness to the fierce fighting that led to China's crushing defeat. Very likely his job was to interrogate captured Chinese prisoners. Whatever the assignment, he saw firsthand what the home audience viewed through the lens of illustrators and printmakers, who depicted Japanese soldiers as tall, commanding, with European features, the Chinese as cowering rabble, pigtailed, crude, ugly, another species entirely.[22] Whether Kawashima shared the new, anti-Chinese sentiment encouraged by wartime art is nowhere recorded.

But certainly the outcome of the Sino-Japanese War, a war no one outside Japan expected Japan to win, decisively altered the course of his life. Under the terms of the peace agreement signed in April 1895, Japan gained most-favored-nation status in China and more—direct colonial control over Taiwan and the Pescadores. In October Kawashima was dispatched to Taiwan as an interpreter with Japan's occupying force. He caught the attention of the commanding general (the famous General Nogi Maresuke who committed suicide on the death of the Meiji emperor in 1912) at a rowdy victory party where, after consuming a great amount of liquor, he questioned the general's worthiness to wear the imperial Medal of Honor. Whether it was that Kawashima operated outside the military hierarchy or that his China expertise made his services essential or that his lack of deference to rank had an appealing quality to it, the general appeared amused rather than angered by this startling rudeness. Far from cashiering Kawashima, he increased the scope of his responsibility.

Posted to the southern part of the island where anti-Japanese resistance remained strong, Kawashima was given broad authority to broker peace deals with local leaders, a task he managed with considerable success, relying on his fluency in various Chinese dialects. Soon he was asked to take on another tough assignment involving the local population: organizing a crackdown on Taiwan's drug trade. To his title of interpreter he could now add that of supervisor, opium suppression unit. His language skills were beginning to open doors to positions of administrative authority.[23]

In terms of proficiency in spoken and written Chinese and years of field experience, Kawashima in 1895 was "ahead of the curve." The Foreign Ministry's program to boost expertise in critical languages, including Chinese, began only in 1894 and then on a very small scale. The army did not organize its effort to train China experts until after the Russo-Japanese War.[24] One of Konoe's pet projects, the East Asia Common Culture Association's school in China, produced graduates with the kind of practical area studies training Kawashima had, but this was after 1900. In other words, in the period immediately following the Sino-Japanese War when there was a rapid rise in demand for China expertise, Kawashima was one of the few qualified people available.

The same set of factors that stimulated demand for the Kawashima type of China expert—an increase in Chinese-Japanese contacts from the 1870s on and particularly after the war when Japan gained new commercial rights in China—pushed Japanese Sinologists into the real world arena as well. Hattori Unokichi, who combined a career in traditional China studies with an advisory role in China's educational development, was typical of the new breed. More than personal choice was involved here. Japan's new national-level institutions played a direct part in encouraging young China specialists like Hattori to engage in current public policy issues. The Ministry of Education sponsored Hattori's first visit to China in 1900; the Foreign Ministry helped arrange his contract for advisory services with the Chinese government two years later.[25]

For Kawashima, tying his fortunes to General Nogi, war hero named governor-general of Taiwan in the fall of 1896, would seem to have assured him a bright future, perhaps in the colonial service. Yet after only a year on Nogi's staff, Kawashima announced his intention to quit his post and return to Japan. He was fed up, he said, with the bureaucrats assigned to the Taiwan colonial government, their factional infighting, their ties to Tokyo politicians intent on micromanaging the island's governance, all of which, in his view, undercut General Nogi's effectiveness as the colony's chief administrator. He hardly needed to state his other obvious conclusion: that in such an environment, his own chances for advancement were slim. General Nogi tried to dissuade him from leaving but to no effect. You ought to resign also, Kawashima told him.[26]

In the fall of 1897, confident of his career prospects in the new postwar environment, Kawashima returned to Tokyo. He immediately landed jobs teaching Chinese language and literature at two schools: the Military Academy, Japan's West Point equivalent, and Kanō Jigorō's Tokyo Teachers College. Kawashima was in elite company. In 1894 Kanō had hired young Tokyo University graduate Hattori Unokichi to teach logic and psychology at the school. Hattori left for a brief assignment with the Ministry of Education in 1897, the year Kawashima joined the faculty as a lecturer in Chinese literature.[27]

Given Kawashima's restless nature, the passion of his anti-Western, pro-Asia views, and his remarkable fluency in Chinese, he would have found his way back to China eventually in some capacity whatever the flow of political events. But the Boxer crisis in 1900 speeded up the timetable. As Japan put together a force to join an allied operation against Beijing, Kawashima's China expertise was once again in urgent demand. A request for his services as interpreter arrived from the office of his old Nagano contact, Fukushima Yasumasa, now the highly regarded General Fukushima, commander of the 8,000-man Japanese contingent that represented about 40 percent of all troops participating in the allied effort. Kawashima's initial response was a flat refusal. He had been treated badly by the army on his last assignment, he said. Personal intervention on Fukushima's part and appeals to Kawashima's patriotism eventually worked and Kawashima agreed to sign on once again. On June 26 he disembarked at the north China port of Dagu, just in time to take part in the allied attack on Boxer-held Tianjin in mid-July, and two weeks later to join the final push north to Beijing.[28] For the second time in five years, Kawashima was facing the Chinese as the enemy, this time on the side of the Westerners he despised.

After two weeks of battling remnants of the Chinese army on the route from Tianjin, allied troops, about 20,000 strong, entered Beijing the morning of August 14 and freed foreigners trapped in the legations, including an immensely relieved Hattori Unokichi. In his diary, Hattori mentions greeting Fukushima and other old friends attached to the Japanese contingent, very likely including Kawashima, his recent colleague at Tokyo Teachers College. Hattori returned to Tokyo a few weeks later. Kawashima stayed on in Beijing as part of the international peacekeeping mission, his China expertise deemed essential by Japanese army headquarters. His talents as an interpreter and negotiator quickly earned him the confidence of the Japanese in the military high command and the Chinese slated to run the new post-Boxer government. At last, at age thirty-five, he was achieving recognition as a China hand, albeit still as a kind of freelancer, a maverick who was relatively unhampered by ties to Japan's bureaucratic structures. Over the next fifteen years, most of it as a China resident, Kawashima organized his professional life around a single goal: to expand Japan's influence in China—and his own—by capitalizing on the pro-Japanese sentiments of the reform wing of the Manchu leadership.

Occupation of Beijing in mid-August 1900 triggered a period of "splendid looting," in the words of a British student interpreter, revenge by the allies for a summer of Chinese atrocities visited upon Chinese Christian converts and foreigners trapped in the legations and the Beitang Cathedral.[29] Contemporary British and American accounts assign blame to all nationalities for the general plunder of palaces and shops. Russians and Germans are usually cited for the worst excesses, Japanese for the greatest restraint. Only days after the allied march into Beijing, Kawashima distinguished himself on the side of restraint in action to secure the Forbidden City where reportedly 2,000 Manchu soldiers and civilians were left stranded after the empress dowager and her entourage fled to Xi'an. According to Japanese versions of the event, German arguments for use of force were about to win the day over Japan's case for caution when Kawashima volunteered to try his hand at negotiating a surrender instead. The assignment took some courage in a city where violence reigned. Whether it was a real test of Kawashima's language or negotiating skills is difficult to say. One must assume that surrender was the hapless Manchus only course. But certainly the outcome, takeover of the immense, seemingly impregnable imperial complex without bloodshed or destruction of Manchu property was a public relations coup for the Japanese. And Kawashima got high marks for his mediating role both from the Japanese command and from the Manchu leadership waiting out the crisis in Xi'an.[30]

In the early days of the occupation, the allies divided Beijing into sectors, each run by a different national force, each charged with ridding the city of suspected Boxers and restoring order.[31] For Japan the role of occupier meant proving its administrative capabilities for the first time before an international audience, a role made all the more prominent by the fact that, as the biggest contributor of troops to the allied effort, Japan was given the largest area to govern. The first chief of the Japanese sector's Military Police Office was a fifteen-year veteran of service in China, the legation's military attaché Colonel Shiba Gorō, the same Colonel Shiba who had won rave reviews from Westerners for his heroism during the siege of the legations. Painfully aware of the internal security failures that had allowed Boxer terrorism to spread in the first place, Colonel Shiba not only used Japanese soldiers for police work, but also began selecting a few Chinese from the old Beijing gendarmerie for training in modern street patrol methods. The gendarmerie, the body nominally if not effectively responsible for order in the five districts of Beijing, had at its disposal a reported force of 20,000 men.

Kawashima, currently in charge of the security detail at the palace grounds, was brought in to instruct and supervise the gendarmerie recruits. Shiba ran a tight ship. The police force was well disciplined, and the streets became safe. Seeing an end to months of violence and terror, Chinese residents talked with awe about Shiba's accomplishments. Foreigners were impressed as well. In a dispatch of October 1900, a British journalist who was with Shiba during the siege, described the Japanese zone as "the best policed and the most tranquil," adding that with improved security, businesses were beginning to reopen.[32]

But some in Japanese army headquarters felt that Shiba was getting too much credit for this success, credit that properly belonged to his superiors, and within a few months he was sent back to his old post as military attaché. Still, when it became clear that the quality of police work was suffering under his successor, Shiba did not hesitate to intervene, proposing to General Fukushima and others that Kawashima be permanently attached to the Military Police Office. Headquarters balked at losing Kawashima's services, so a compromise was reached: he would remain an army interpreter but take on the new job of military police administrator.

As Shiba had anticipated, Kawashima immediately launched a major shakeup of the police office, firing corrupt staff, hiring top-quality replacements, and generating new sources of funding to upgrade the program of training officers attached to the Beijing gendarmerie. In January 1901, forty Chinese recruits completed an intensive, three-month course in police methods and another fifty were brought in for training. As the police office regained its reputation for honesty and efficiency, Kawashima began to receive the same adulation from Beijing residents as Shiba. But Kawashima was more politically savvy than Shiba or at least had learned a lesson from Shiba's experience. He deflected compliments. Credit was due army headquarters, he said; he was just carrying out orders.[33]

Training employees of the Beijing gendarmerie was a logical first step in the process of bringing the city run riot back to normal. There were longer-term implications as well. Working within a Chinese government agency on the vital task of creating a modern public security system had the potential to give Japan the kind of commanding influence over China that the British had enjoyed for fifty years through their control of the Chinese Maritime Customs Service. Kawashima was well aware of the opportunity that presented itself. In the atmosphere of intense rivalry among the allied occupiers for influence in post-Boxer China, he moved ahead rapidly to capitalize on Japan's entré to key people in the Beijing gendarmerie. By the time the second batch of Chinese trainees had completed their course in April 1901, Kawashima had gotten the approval of General Fukushima and others in the high command to fund a permanent unit for police officer training. With the help of gendarmerie officials, Kawashima selected 340 of the agency's most promising employees to enter the new program. He drew his teaching staff from the Japanese community in China, both military personnel and civilians who had police and legal expertise as well as proficiency in spoken Chinese.

For all his careful deference to his superiors in army headquarters, Kawashima was making a reputation for himself both in police training and as manager of the day-to-day police work of the sector occupation office. In June, as the allies prepared to return Beijing to Chinese control, the Manchu Prince Qing, who along with senior statesman Li Hongzhang was the court's liaison on transition affairs, requested that Kawashima be seconded to the Chinese government to direct a new Beijing Police Affairs Bureau. What Prince Qing had in mind was a police agency organized on the Japanese model and run by Chinese with Japanese advisory help. This clear bias in favor of Japan was greeted by vigorous objections from the other powers—the Germans, French, and Russians, in particular—already wrangling with each other over what peace conditions to present to the Chinese side. Shortly before the September seventh signing of the Boxer protocol, Kawashima resigned from his new post.[34]

Though removed from direct police enforcement activities, Kawashima continued to be centrally involved in police training. Already in June of 1901 as part of the transition, the Chinese government had established the Beijing Police Academy (Pekin Keimu Gakudō) to replace the training unit financed by the Japanese army now about to depart the capital. Kawashima was asked to stay on to run the new school. The well-known writer Futabatei Shimei, who worked for a time at the school, profiled Kawashima in a letter to a friend in 1902:

> After leaving school, he experienced serious setbacks and suffered the full gamut of tragedies in human life. An ordinary person might have lost his moral compass or spiraled downward into hopeless despair. But with a mental toughness and resolution derived from his Zen training, he was totally undeterred in pursuit of his ideals. As luck would have it, the Sino-Japanese War came along providing him the opportunity to become an army interpreter and make full use of his talents. The Chinese even more than the Japanese have absolute confidence in him. In particular, his connection with Prince Qing has been key to his advancement. In a sudden boost to his career, he received a request for services from the Chinese government. As director of the Beijing Police Academy he has complete authority over all aspects of school management. In Beijing at this moment, he is the second most prominent figure after the Japanese Minister, General Yamane. From what I have seen firsthand, he is one extraordinary character.[35]

Futabatei, whose opinion of Kawashima soured after six months on the academy staff, was on the mark when he said that Kawashima had complete control. As the price for securing Kawashima's services, Prince Qing had acceded to Minister Komura's request that Kawashima be given a free hand to make budgetary decisions, hire teachers and staff, develop curricula, and determine the placement and promotion of Chinese academy graduates. Futabatei was also correct in pointing out that the job was a major step up in Kawashima's career. The former army interpreter now had the title of adviser to the Chinese government, the job of Police Academy director, a precedent-setting (for a foreigner) second rank within the Chinese bureaucracy, and a handsome salary, probably twice what he made at Tokyo Teachers College.[36] Most important, he was in a position where he could influence formation of a critical agency of the Chinese government. It was the kind of opportunity Kawashima had been dreaming of for years.

By the end of 1901 Kawashima had hired six Japanese teachers and staff, in the next year another seven. Many were, like himself, interpreters with the army. Others were from police agencies and military preparatory schools in Japan. Monthly salaries ranged from 60 to 250 taels (equivalent to 40 to 170 yen using 1901 exchange rates). Contracts were mostly for two to three years with an option to renew. The relatively high salaries he could offer enabled Kawashima to hire well-qualified people. The prospect of 170 yen per month was enough to convince Futabatei Shimei, who was barely scraping by in Harbin, to accept the low-status job of academy administrator. None of the Japanese hires came close to equaling Kawashima's terms, a 270 yen monthly salary and five-year contract. His responsibilities were also considerable. With Chinese assistant teachers and interpreters added in, Kawashima managed about thirty-five people. The academy provided short-term training, three to nine month courses in city ordinances, street patrol methods, fire fighting, and prison management. At any one time, about 300 students were enrolled; reportedly there were many more applicants than slots available. Beginning in 1902, promising students were selected for one-year training programs in Japan.[37]

The citizens of Beijing liked what they saw of the newly minted police. However, the effort to create a new force had its critics, particularly among bureaucrats running the gendarmerie who feared for their jobs as the police system was revamped under Kawashima's direction. Kawashima was well aware of the uncertainty that the new parallel structure presented. From the very beginning of his tenure as academy director in the summer of 1901, he tried to smooth the way by intensive networking and lobbying among people who counted in gendarmerie affairs. One of his co-opting tactics was to invite top officials who were part of the old force structure to lecture at the academy on Chinese laws and regulations.

Kawashima's fluent Chinese, both spoken and written, and consequent access within the Chinese bureaucracy were assets not available to most foreigners, and these enabled him to act quickly to blunt attempts to undercut his role. When he heard through back channels in late 1901 that critics were circulating a memo proposing a halt to the police reform program, he got the head of China's post-Boxer Reconstruction Office to draft an immediate counter argument to take to the Grand Council for a final opinion. That document mentioned Kawashima by name, citing the important work the academy was doing to train police officers capable of maintaining order in the capital. The document went further, urging the government to establish a new central authority responsible for both public security and public works. Foreigners, the writer quite correctly pointed out, were constantly ridiculing the awful condition of Beijing's streets.

As this document, which reflected Kawashima's input, worked its way up to the Grand Council, Kawashima in his own name sent a separate note to Prince Qing strongly supporting establishment of a national police force under a police affairs bureau. Every major country in the world has a police system, Kawashima argued. Just as the military functioned to protect and defend the nation against competing foreign interests, the police existed to keep internal order and maintain domestic peace. What was needed in China just now, he said, was to overhaul the gendarmerie and set the foundation for a centralized police agency to preside over a structure of local offices at the province, county, and town levels.[38]

The outcome of this skirmish in the turf battle over the Qing reform agenda was Grand Council approval in 1902 of a new Ministry of Public Works and Police, which was placed under the stewardship of a young Manchu, Prince Su. Prince Su (personal name, Shanqi) was one of only ten "princes of the blood," who by virtue of their imperial pedigree were at the top of the Qing aristocracy. A convivial sort, given to boisterous parties, open and generous-hearted with his friends, thirty-five-year-old Prince Su was known as a progressive among court nobles. He had endorsed Kang Youwei's reform agenda in 1898. Apparently a combination of high rank, relative youth, and good contacts allowed him to escape censure when the conservative court faction seized power again. His reputation within the foreign community was good. One longtime American resident described him as "a man of strong character, widely versed in foreign affairs," who tried, to no avail, to dissuade the empress dowager from supporting the Boxers' war on foreigners.[39]

The Boxer crisis wreaked havoc on Prince Su's comfortable existence as a hereditary prince. His was the lavish villa foreigners called the Suwangfu or simply "fu" commandeered ("rented") by Colonel Shiba as a defense post during the siege of the legations. From inside the large compound Shiba, Hattori, and the rest of the Japanese contingent answered Boxer gunfire, at one point desperately shoring up shattered walls with piles of silk brocade from the prince's private storehouse. As Prince Konoe noted on his visit to Beijing in the summer of 1901, the fu was a gutted ruin after the siege. Not only did Prince Su suffer loss of property and treasure, he was for the first time in his life in physical danger as he fled the city mid-August with the empress dowager and her entourage, a court noble in peasant disguise, uncertain of his next meal. Midway through this terrifying journey to Xi'an, Prince Su was ordered to accompany the elderly Prince Qing back to Beijing on another mission fraught with uncertainty, negotiating a settlement with the foreign powers.[40]

Witnessing the settlement process, too, was a chilling reminder of Manchu vulnerability. High on the allied agenda, along with the size of the indemnity China must pay, was the question of punishing the guilty. When the final peace terms were issued, three Manchu princes found their names on the allied list of China's topmost officials sentenced to exile, imprisonment, or death. As Prince Su assessed the scene of the legation quarter strewn with rubble and charred remains and foreign occupiers dictating terms to the Chinese government in exile, he knew that what hung in the balance was the survival of his generation of Manchu leaders. And survival required new, flexible tactics to deal with the international community so intent, as one Western observer put it, on "keeping the Chinese down, very far down!"[41]

Prince Konoe sensed the pragmatic politician in Prince Su when he spoke with him in July of 1901 on the subject of reforming China's civil service examination system, the thousand-year-old system of standardized tests used to recruit officials for all levels of government. Su politely pointed out to his guest that until now this state-controlled, performance-based recruitment method had served the Manchus well, enabling them as a minority group to stay in power for 250 years. But he readily agreed that in the present context of international competition both the standards and the mechanism for recruiting China's public servants should be drastically revised.

As Prince Su waited in Beijing for the return of the Court, the empress dowager, still in Xi'an, appointed him to the lucrative post of Beijing tax collector. The Court's intention was to help him recover some of his lost wealth and he did just that, quickly establishing another mansion in the city for his wives and numerous children. At the same time, to align himself with the new politics of change, he made a point of introducing collection standards and improving staff discipline in the notoriously corrupt tax office. In January 1902 the Court returned to Beijing. It was a few months later that Prince Su secured the potentially more influential, if not financially rewarding, appointment as head of the new Ministry of Public Works and Police. He made news immediately when he initiated construction of a telephone system and issued city traffic ordinances, including a measure to replace the lumbering two-wheeled Chinese carts with faster moving Western carriages. People remarked on his hands-on style. It was reported that he prowled the streets of Beijing incognito to observe the performance of new police academy graduates, making his identity known only when he himself was arrested for loitering. More important than this image-making effort, Prince Su established a new organizational structure for the police force in the Beijing region, including head offices, stations, and sub-stations after the fashion of Meiji Japan.[42]

Kawashima as ministry adviser was in the picture from the very beginning. Very likely Prince Qing arranged the match: his junior colleague Prince Su to head the new agency and Kawashima to provide technical guidance. Prince Qing, after all, would have given Kawashima himself the agency job had it not been for objections from the Europeans and Americans. In the summer of 1902, Prince Su asked Kawashima to accompany his newly appointed police commissioner, General Yu Lang, son of an imperial prince, on a month-long trip to Japan to study police training and operations. Again, Prince Qing's hand was probably at work here, both in the appointment of someone in the imperial inner circle and in the tilt toward Japan. Prince Konoe entertained Yu Lang with Kawashima in tow as interpreter, at the Peers Club on July 14, a couple of weeks after their arrival. Konoe had met both Yu Lang and Kawashima on his trip to China the previous July. Konoe hosted Yu Lang on two other occasions during his month-long stay, his attentiveness no doubt a response to a special request from Prince Su directed through the Japanese diplomatic representative in Shanghai.[43]

Prince Qing, the court's principal deal maker at this juncture,[44] may have had a hand in getting Prince Su and Kawashima together but each quickly realized how useful the contact could be. Prince Su by inclination and recent experience was ready to play an activist role in institutional reform. Establishing a new agency in the vital area of public security by wresting control from the Beijing gendarmerie seemed a promising route to personal power. In the area of police reform, it made sense to consult the Japanese. The Japanese-occupied sector had a reputation for order. Kawashima was a known quantity: a fluent Chinese speaker, an experienced administrator, Prince Qing's selection to head the new police academy. Kawashima on his part had been pushing for a position of influence since his arrival in Beijing as witness his abortive appointment as head of a new police agency even before the withdrawal of the international forces. Whatever his colleagues might have felt about his sudden star power, no one was likely to stop him. His personal and professional ambitions were fully in accord with Japanese military and diplomatic efforts to expand Japanese interests in China to a level enjoyed by the Europeans and Americans.

Being sought after by a Manchu aristocrat, direct descendant of the founder of the Qing dynasty, someone with a bright future in the post-Boxer government, was heady stuff for Kawashima. And Prince Su played to Kawashima's considerable ego. When Kawashima expressed sympathy to Su for his reduced living circumstances, the prince replied that China had brought the Boxer troubles on itself and that friendship with Japanese like Kawashima was welcome compensation for the loss of his villa. When Kawashima laid out his ideas on police reform, Prince Su wholeheartedly embraced them. Only on tactics did Su think he knew better. Frustrated in his efforts to shape a new ministry out of the old gendarmerie, known for its corruption and ineptitude, Su concluded that the old structure should be abolished outright rather than gradually absorbed. Against Kawashima's advice, he drafted a memo to this effect and sent it directly to the empress dowager. As Kawashima feared, the memo was taken for what it was, an assault on the reform strategy of court conservatives. Prince Su was fired. "Congratulations," Kawashima told the startled prince when informed of his dismissal. The experience was a good lesson in tactics, a chance to test the depth of reformist sentiment, Kawashima said, adding that, in his view, the prince would not fail again.[45]

Prince Su's successor at the ministry was another reform-minded Manchu official named Natong. Like Su, Natong understood the critical importance of police reform to post-Boxer state-building efforts. Also like Su, he had good Japan connections. In May 1901, as vice president of the Board of Revenue and Population, he had made a trip to Japan to study Japanese financial institutions and the police system. The following September, he was the court's choice to head a formal mission of apology to the Japanese for the murder of the diplomat Sugiyama and other Boxer crimes against Japanese citizens in Beijing. Prince Konoe met with Natong at the Imperial Hotel in Tokyo; he had been introduced to Natong at meetings with Prince Qing, Li Hongzhang and others in Beijing the previous July.[46]

The transition from Prince Su to Natong at the Ministry of Public Works and Police Affairs in no way diminished the influence of Kawashima and the Japanese on the police modernization program. Under Kawashima's direction, the police academy was a fast expanding operation. New courses were added, the curriculum was lengthened, and study in Japan became a regular option for the academy's top students. Starting with a batch of twenty sent to Japan in 1902, the overseas students enrolled in a yearlong course at Kanō Jigorō's Kōbun Institute followed by training at the Tokyo Police and Prison School. In just the first five years after its founding in 1901, the academy graduated an estimated 3,000 students, the elite core of a new police system.

Beyond the academy's own output, the school had a demonstration effect on the development of police training elsewhere in China. Shortly after he was posted to Zhili in 1901, Governor Yuan Shikai met with Kawashima and the Japanese military attaché in Beijing to discuss ways to build up a new regional police force which, unlike the local militia, would be primarily loyal to him and his law and order goals. Yuan liked what he heard and sent one of his deputies to invite Kawashima to Baoding for further talks. Within ten days, Kawashima had charted out a model for Zhili police training and operations. To get the training under way, he arranged to transfer to Baoding two Japanese instructors from the Beijing academy and to hire one from the Tokyo Metropolitan Police Office. These actions marked the start of the Baoding and Tianjin police academies. On the strength of these efforts Yuan was also able to persuade the court to issue an order calling on all provinces to initiate police reform on the Zhili model. In the period 1903-1910, about twenty Japanese teachers and advisers worked in seven provinces to develop police training institutions. [47]

Graduation ceremony at the Beijing Police Academy with Kawashima Naniwa presiding, front center, in military uniform, ca 1902. (*Tō-A senkaku shishi kiden*; Tokyo: Bunsuikaku, 1936)

Japanese assistance to police reform provided a considerable boost to the centralizing or state-building thrust of the late Qing reformers. By around 1907 all police work was handled through a vertical structure of local and provincial offices culminating in a single Department of Police Administration (Jingzheng si). In somewhat sobering testimony to its effectiveness, some twenty years later, Chiang Kaishek made this department the locus of the Nationalist government's secret police.[48]

Kawashima's own contribution to putting in place the elements of a modern police system was enormous, particularly in the early years of his twelve-year tenure as government adviser when he had the ear of members of Qing inner councils.

Given the terms of reference and access we know he enjoyed, he was probably not exaggerating when, many years later, he summed up his role in this way:

> For a time, I had administrative authority over part of the Chinese government. I managed the hiring, firing, and promotions of thousands of subordinates. I assisted high-ranking officials in the government and worked with Chinese colleagues at my own level. In all cases, I tried to adapt to Chinese practices and customs, to assume an attitude of ready acceptance of the other culture. At all levels of society, publicly and privately, I achieved the close contacts of an insider. From the Chinese side also, the view of me as a foreigner nearly faded away, so they treated me as if they felt that I was one of their own.[49]

As interesting as Kawashima's rendering of his job description is the importance he attached to acculturating and the success he felt he had achieved in this regard. No Western adviser would either have wanted or presumed to believe that the Chinese viewed him as anything other than a foreigner. There is some arrogance here—that Kawashima understood the Chinese better than any of his countrymen not to speak of Westerners—but some truth as well because he did in fact have extraordinary access within the Chinese bureaucracy. It was the kind of access Hattori hoped to gain at the Ministry of Education but was denied, though he, too, spoke of having close relations with his Chinese colleagues.

Hattori's path to China and what he hoped to do when he got there differed markedly from the motivating factors in Kawashima's case. Hattori regarded his China assignment primarily as a professional opportunity, a chance on the one hand to deepen his understanding of Chinese philosophy, on the other, to transmit to the Chinese Japanese lessons in educational development. Though he was obviously aware of the political benefit of maintaining close ties with well-placed Chinese, he saw his activities as essentially "cultural." In fact, when tensions between China and Japan heightened in the late twenties, he faulted his Chinese counterparts for allowing politics to impede progress on joint cultural projects. By contrast, Kawashima's China involvement—professional, personal, political—was total, intense, and lasted his lifetime. He was director of the police academy, government adviser, and political activist with all his passion to enhance his own rank and Japan's bound up with the fortunes of his closest high-level contact, Prince Su.

Possibilities and Limits of Friendship

The interdependency, indeed, apparent intimacy, that developed between Kawashima and Prince Su was based not only on a mutual interest in Japanese-assisted police reform, but also on a joint concern about the growing Russian troop presence in northeast China. Kawashima must have felt vindicated. He had been correct in the 1880s when he predicted that Russia's Trans-Siberian railway project, begun in 1891, would ultimately mean trouble in Manchuria. The first hint of a regional face-off between Japan and Russia came in the aftermath of the Sino-Japanese War when Russia teamed up with Germany and France to force victorious Japan to give up a key territorial concession from China, control over the southern tip of Manchuria (the Liaodong Peninsula). Russia followed up by convincing China to allow construction of a Trans-Siberian extension line, to be called the Chinese Eastern Railway, across Manchuria to Vladivostok. In 1898, in another Sino-Russian accord designed to steal the march on Japan in Manchuria, Russia got a 25-year lease to Liaodong, including Port Arthur and the nearby city of Dalian, and the right to build a 650-mile north-south rail line, the South Manchurian Railway (SMR).

During the Boxer crisis, Russia used the new rail lines for the rapid transfer of as many as 100,000 troops into Manchuria. Clashes occurred with both Boxer militants and Manchu forces. The Allied victory in the summer of 1900 did nothing to stem the surge of Russian troops into the region. Troop levels stood at over 200,000 a year later.[50] Military intervention on this unprecedented scale added an ominous new dimension to years of foreign concession grabbing in China. External interference in China's economic life may have been an established fact by 1900, but China was still a sovereign country. Now the huge Russian troop deployment on Chinese soil raised the possibility of outright colonization of the very territory denied Japan five years before. Politicians in both Beijing and Tokyo expressed concern but reacted cautiously at first, hoping to defuse the growing crisis through appeals to the international community. The tactic seemed to be working when in April of 1902 Russia agreed to a phased withdrawal beginning in the fall. The following spring, however, Russia issued new demands as conditions for compliance, and tensions mounted.

While throughout the standoff China and Japan at the diplomatic level showed restraint in their dealings with the Russians, strong anti-Russia elements on both sides called for a tougher response. Within the Chinese leadership, the main hard liners were Manchus rather than Han, people like Prince Su and Prince Qing who owned large tracts of land in Manchuria certain to be lost in the event of a Russian takeover.[51] On the Japan side, small but vocal factions within the military and foreign ministry called for a no-compromise stance, arguing that a Russian-occupied Manchuria would threaten the integrity of Korea and, by extension, Japan's own security. Echoing this same view from outside government, Prince Konoe literally to his dying breath sought to mobilize public opinion against any kind of *ManKan kōkan* (exchanging Manchuria for Korea) solution, urging Japan to settle for nothing less than total evacuation of Russian troops. The campaign tapped into growing public anger against Russia. In the end, heightened pro-war sentiment gave Japan's government the leeway to opt for a military solution when negotiations bogged down. In China, that part of the public informed on the issue tended to be pro-Japanese. China's youth, students in Tokyo, Shanghai and Beijing, protested Russia's action in print and public meetings. In an ironic twist, the students' initial display of nationalist, anti-Russia sentiment turned into sharp attacks on the Chinese government—and the Manchus in particular—for its weak response to Russian aggression.[52]

As diplomatic memoranda moved slowly between Tokyo and Moscow, Russians and Japanese in Beijing were busy spying on each other and trying to influence Chinese decision makers through bribery or persuasion. Japanese with pro-war views found a natural gathering place at the Beijing Police Academy whose director, Kawashima Naniwa, was long on record as a hawk on the issue of Russia's advance into northeast Asia. One of the plusses of the academy job for Futabatei Shimei, who argued for war on the grounds that it would "freshen the oppressive air of our society and time," was Kawashima's assurance that he would be working with people who shared his hard line position on Manchuria.[53]

Not surprisingly, when the legation's assistant military attaché needed someone to recruit volunteers for undercover work in Manchuria, he turned to Kawashima. This was a tricky assignment for Kawashima. He was a direct hire of the Chinese government, which sought to remain neutral in the Russo-Japanese crisis, so maintaining strict secrecy was imperative. At the same time, there was no shortage of young men in the expatriate community eager to join any operation that aimed to damage Russian interests. The academy, which was outfitted with stables and equipment storage areas used in police training, was an ideal staging ground. By the spring of 1903, Kawashima and his legation friends had organized a fifty-man unit charged with slowing the Russian buildup in Manchuria through bomb attacks on bridges and tunnels along Russian-owned railway lines.[54]

The Russians may have been kept in the dark about the operation, but evidence suggests that the strongly anti-Russian Prince Su was well aware of what was going on. He made a point of introducing Kawashima to his brother-in-law, the Mongol Prince of Karachin, another Russia hater, who was only too happy to give the commando unit safe passage through the county he administered north of Beijing. Sometime in the spring of 1903, Kawashima accompanied the Prince of Karachin on an unpublicized trip to Japan. The prince was taken on a tour of the Osaka Exhibition, contacted the gravely ill Prince Konoe, and probably met with educators Kanō Jigorō and Shimoda Utako. It was shortly after the prince's return to China that summer that Kawahara Misako was recruited by Kawashima to help with intelligence work in Karachin and to assist in developing schooling for women, an area of particular interest to both the prince's wife and her brother, Prince Su.[55]

Kawashima returned to Beijing after a few months in Japan to find the Police Academy in an uproar, not over the growing Russo-Japanese crisis but over the more mundane matter of school management. Before leaving, Kawashima had named Futabatei Shimei the academy's acting director. Futabatei took a hands-off, casual approach to supervising the teaching staff, particularly in their after hours' pursuits, a style with definite appeal to some of the academy's rakish young bachelors who chafed against the authoritarian Kawashima. At the same time, there were others, mostly the older, married group, who objected to what they saw as a breakdown in discipline, hence the division of staff into two warring factions waiting to greet Kawashima on his return. Futabatei insisted on taking responsibility for the imbroglio, resigning after only six months on the job. Sorry to lose someone of Futabatei's caliber and reputation, Kawashima sought to downplay his disagreement with his former classmate. Differences were bound to occur, he said, given Futabatei's liberal approach and tolerant nature and his own concern for law and order. Futabatei thought that there was more to it than this, that Kawashima was typical of Japan's China studies people who tended to view the world hierarchically, always conscious of rank and status, of who was fit to make decisions and who was not. This aristocratic mindset, Futabatei said, made it difficult for Kawashima to work with people like himself whose Western training made them more democratic leaning in manner and outlook.[56]

This was an odd distinction to make on Futabatei's part since as youths at the Foreign Language School he and Kawashima would seem to have been quite alike. Both were known for their rebelliousness and uncompromising stands on principle, both were well grounded in China studies, both depended on families fallen on hard times financially, and neither graduated from the school, choosing instead to chase ideals, in Kawashima's case a China career, in Futabatei's a life in literature. By the time they met in China in 1902, however, Futabatei had given up his dream of becoming a professional writer. Instead, in order to earn a living, he had accepted various government and newspaper reporting jobs, confining his writing and translation of Russian literature to after hours.[57]

By contrast, Kawashima, who had conquered the feelings of self-doubt that burdened Futabatei, seemed close to achieving his goal of becoming an actor of some importance in the drama of Japan's expanding influence on the continent.[58] What gave luster to his résumé apart from his position of director of the Police Academy was his close personal connection with Prince Su, imperial prince of the first rank, heir to vast imperial estates in the northeast, holder of top bureaucratic posts in the Qing government. Su had all the marks of a winner in any future Qing political lineup. Still relatively young—forty-two in 1905—he had long been associated with what had become the ascendant trend in Qing domestic policy, a program of national reforms including abolition of the civil service exam system, expansion of popular education, and plans to make China a constitutional monarchy. Moreover, his was not mere endorsement of reform but hands-on involvement in such areas as police modernization, resource development in the northeast, and establishment of new schools for the Manchu elite, both men and women.[59] For Kawashima, gaining entre at the Prince Su level of power was a real coup. Futabatei found out quickly, to his evident dismay, that the rank-conscious, "aristocratic-minded" Kawashima was a master at cultivating people in high places while playing the moralizing autocrat in his relations with staff at the academy.

Prince Su had his own game to play, namely, securing his assets in Manchuria with Japanese support. In this, Kawashima, as he no doubt made clear to Su, was a useful person to know. He had good contacts at the Japanese legation and close ties to top military leaders including General Fukushima and General Nogi, heroes of the Russo-Japanese War. Japan's victory relieved China of its immediate fear that Russia would absorb the whole of Manchuria, but raised new uncertainties about Japan's intentions. "One danger removed can only mean the substitution of another whilst China is so weak," a Western journalist wrote at the war's end, "and therefore, no matter what happens, the Court will be passing miserable for a number of years to come."[60] By the terms of the American-brokered Portsmouth Treaty in 1905, Japan acquired Russia's special rights in southern Manchuria, specifically, the lease to the Liaodong Peninsula and ownership of the South Manchuria Railway (SMR), a transfer ratified by the Chinese government the same year. In the spring of 1906, the Japanese prime minister met with anxious Chinese officials in Mukden to talk about Japan's plans for managing its new economic assets. Over the coming months, as the details of SMR administration were being worked out in Tokyo, it was clear that Kawashima could be a potentially valuable source of advance information.[61]

When Prince Su paid Kawashima the compliment of a surprise visit to his Beijing home in the winter of 1906, Japan's intentions in Manchuria were undoubtedly very much on his mind. The two men had long had a friendly working relationship. But Kawashima, man of poor background, unused to drop-in visits from royalty, was thoroughly nonplussed when the prince burst in on his bedchamber in the early morning, claiming that he just happened to be out enjoying a ride in the snow and decided to call. As Kawashima later recalled—an account central to Kawashima lore—the prince in fact had an agenda, which was to talk up the importance of personal ties in creating a special Chinese-Japanese relationship, a relationship essential not only to China's security but to stability in the East Asian region.

According to Kawashima, in order to put teeth into the rhetoric about Chinese-Japanese friendship, Prince Su proposed that he and Kawashima pledge to be "sworn brothers" (gikyōdai), a not unusual profession of fraternity in the world of Manchu/Chinese/Mongol male friendships at the time. Kawashima predictably protested that differences in rank made this impossible. Su was a top-tier prince of the great Qing dynasty, while he was a mere commoner. Prince Su countered that what counted was not rank but nobility of character, which Kawashima possessed aplenty. In Kawashima's telling, the two soon parted, agreed on brotherhood and overcome by emotion. The parting scene has an erotic quality to it: their hands touch, trembling, and Prince Su suddenly exits leaving Kawashima in stunned silence listening to the crunch of hooves in the newly fallen snow.[62]

One of Prince Su's sons, in an interview in the 1960s, scoffed at Kawashima's account, arguing that a member of the imperial family did not become anyone's sworn brother without following certain formal procedures, and no proof existed that such had taken place. But there is evidence to corroborate, if not the emotionally charged scene described by Kawashima, the sense that he conveys of an unusually close relationship between prince and commoner, Manchu and Japanese. This is the photograph of the two men in Qing court robes. Whether the Su-Kawashima photography session was part of an actual sworn brotherhood ceremony is a question. Kawashima offers no comment. Still, the photograph makes the element of sameness in everything from dress to demeanor so prominent that it projects the kind of commitment and common purpose associated with the brotherhood arrangement and, by extension, the notion of partnership in Chinese-Japanese relations.[63]

For Kawashima, having visual proof of Prince Su's friendship and esteem no doubt helped keep his reputation intact within the Japanese community as a person of influence at the highest levels of the Chinese government. The reality was that the Chinese used his skills but held his considerable ambitions in check, increasingly so in the five-year period before the outbreak of revolution in 1911. Prince Su, who had his own political minefields to navigate, could provide only so much cover. The first hint that Kawashima had run into obstacles came as early as 1906 when, to placate Chinese "rights recovery" activists—mostly returned students from Japan—the central government took measures to curb Kawashima's authority at the Police Academy. Half of the ten-man Japanese teaching staff was sent home and replaced with Chinese, and the school was put under the administrative control of the Ministry of Civil Affairs. Kawashima was still the highly paid director—in fact his salary was increased by half—but he was no longer on a five-year contract personally arranged by Prince Qing. After Prince Su became Civil Affairs Minister in 1907, he acted to compensate for the downgrading of Kawashima's authority in one sphere by raising his status in another, naming him ministry adviser in 1909.[64]

While on the payroll of the Chinese government, Kawashima spent much of his time in the years after the Russo-Japanese War serving his own government as interpreter and facilitator in negotiations with China over railway construction projects in southern Manchuria. His ability to play tough with the Chinese, pressuring them into an accord on An-Feng rail line development, won him a special citation from the Japanese emperor in 1909. Kawashima's contribution was part of a major Japanese initiative to extend concessions acquired at Portsmouth to the whole of southern Manchuria. This involved not only dealing with the Chinese whose territory it was, but also beating back challenges from Russia, a continued presence in Outer Mongolia and northern Manchuria, and the United States, which was trying to gain entry to the Manchuria market through both public and private channels. Japan was successful on both counts, fending off U.S. proposals for joint venture activity and "neutralizing" railway development while negotiating accords with Russia (in 1907 and 1910) that effectively divided Manchuria into northern and southern zones of influence. No international outcry greeted the Russo-Japanese accords. They represented no departure from actions taken by the other foreign powers in China. In fact, the British viewed the accords as a positive development. Possessors of exclusive rights in central China and newly allied with Japan, they were well pleased to see the United States rebuffed and some form of stability achieved in Manchuria through Russo-Japanese peaceful expansion.[65]

The fact that his An-Feng role is all Kawashima boasts of in the years 1906-1911—he was not one to hide his accomplishments—is again evidence that while the Chinese might have made him a high ranking officer in their bureaucracy, they intended to limit the extent of his influence. His champion, Prince Su, may have become wary of the Japanese. Su probably found the rapid expansion of SMR enterprises and new Russo-Japanese detente worrisome trends. He began to explore the prospects of German aid. He probably also saw Kawashima as a useful friend, informant, and police academy administrator but not someone he would consult on internal Qing politics in a time of crisis.

The Qing court had bowed to the inevitable in 1901 and launched a series of far-reaching reforms, hiring foreigners like Kawashima for their knowledge of modern institutions and systems. Now, in the years after the Russo-Japanese War, people outside government, the majority of them Han Chinese, were not only demanding a faster pace of change but questioning the competence and good faith of government leaders, most of them Manchus, particularly their willingness to share political power. It was becoming evident that the court was trying to use the reform agenda as a way to re-centralize political control in the hands of a Manchu-dominated central government. This meant altering the traditional Chinese/Manchu balance in top political posts by placing the newly created, "reform" ministries in the hands of the Manchu elite, including the highest ranking "princes of the blood" such as Prince Su. Su was appointed Minister of Civil Administration in 1907 in a cabinet made up of nine Manchus and four Han. The preponderance of Manchus remained the same in the cabinet formed after the deaths of the empress dowager and the emperor—mysteriously within 24 hours of each other—in November of 1908.

While the court's Manchu-first strategy made ethnicity more of an issue than it had been for centuries, at the top levels of government there were factional splits along other than ethnic lines. A Japanese political analyst writing at the time of the imperial deaths identified two major factions, one headed by the Manchu princes Chun (the twenty-five-year-old regent for the child emperor Puyi), Su, Gong, and Natong, and the Han Chinese elder statesman, Zhang Zhidong, the other by Prince Qing and Yuan Shikai. Kawashima personally knew princes Su, Natong, Qing, and Chun as well as Yuan Shikai, and one can be sure that his "take" on these figures and their relative power was relayed through diplomatic channels to Tokyo, a fact that may have induced Prince Su to keep him at arm's length. The key question for Tokyo policymakers was where these people stood on relations with Japan. Though Yuan Shikai had hired a whole cadre of Japanese advisers to help him with institutional development in Zhili, he was no friend of Japan when it came to Manchuria and, in fact, was inclined to invite U.S. involvement in the region. After observing Yuan's negotiating style on Manchuria railway issues, Kawashima, for one, came to thoroughly detest him.[66]

Zhang Zhidong reportedly opposed what the Japanese called Yuan's "pro-U.S." stance, preferring to bar U.S. investment in Manchuria and take his chances on a deal with Japan. Zhang's death and Yuan's forced retirement, both in 1909, reduced Han Chinese influence in top leadership councils and strengthened the authority of Prince Chun, the young regent. Again, however, there was no unified Manchu position regarding relations with Japan. Prince Chun clearly relied on the counsel of the consistently pro-Japanese Prince Su, twenty years his senior, but was no easy mark when it came to negotiating the An-Feng rail extension with the Japanese, as Kawashima found out to his annoyance.[67] It is possible that Kawashima's ultimate success in securing the concession resulted from behind-the-scenes lobbying by Prince Su.

The full story has yet to be told of the various Manchu princes and what foreign and domestic policy positions each represented in the political maneuvering that went on following the death of the empress dowager. Prince Su had a distinct Japan bias, but was well regarded in the foreign community as a whole, in part because he had unequivocally opposed the Boxers, in part because he had demonstrated in word and deed his commitment to Manchu reform. Even the acerbic London *Times* correspondent G.E. Morrison, a total skeptic when it came to Manchu royalty, referred to Su as "one of the best princes."[68]

Morrison, though well informed, was speaking generally based on secondhand sources. Kawashima, who knew Prince Su personally, was no doubt aware that Su, ever pragmatic and open-minded, was unusual among the princes in his evident interest in trying to understand and deal with the growing opposition to Manchu rule coming from various elements of the Han elite. He was not only receptive to power-sharing overtures from the exiled constitutional monarchists, Kang Youwei and Liang Qichao,[69] but kept channels open to Chinese revolutionaries in Japan. It seems that both Su and the revolutionaries put out feelers in 1908 and 1909 to explore possible collaboration, this at a time when the racist, anti-Manchu rhetoric coming out of the revolutionary camp was at its height and Manchu princes themselves were targets of terrorist attack.

Prince Su got a close look at revolutionary terrorism in 1909 when Wang Jingwei, editor of the Tokyo-based revolutionary journal, *Min Bao*, was captured and jailed for his part in an abortive attempt to assassinate the prince regent. As head of the Ministry of Civil Affairs, the supervisory agency for the Beijing police, Prince Su was responsible for conducting the investigation and trial. He decided to handle the matter personally, not because it was a complex case—Wang was clearly guilty as charged—but because it was a chance to find out firsthand what was on the mind of the revolutionaries. He had been following their views in print, he told Wang, through the pages of *Min Bao*. Su was impressed with Wang's keen intellect and the depth of his conviction that the Manchu-designed constitutional monarchy was mere window dressing, that only revolution led by the majority Han Chinese could save the nation from foreign domination. Whether he was trying to send a conciliatory message to the revolutionaries or simply thought that such a talented young man could be rehabilitated and recruited for a different cause, Su commuted Wang's expected death sentence into life imprisonment. In a conversation with one of Prince Su's sons in Japan in 1939, Wang acknowledged that he owed his life to Su. The following year Wang, the rescued revolutionary, became head of Japan's puppet government in Nanjing.[70]

Prince Su was astute enough to realize when he sat in the prison cell arguing politics with Wang Jingwei—the young, bright, articulate, Han intellectual—that Manchu reformism was in trouble. What looked like serious changes from his perspective—public security reforms, new educational opportunities, a "modern" constitution modeled after the Meiji constitution—were clearly not enough to satisfy the Wangs of the world now punctuating their verbal attacks on the Manchus with acts of terrorism. Also, he was well aware that while Wang's was an extreme form of opposition, negative feelings about the Manchu regime and the workability of its reform program were becoming increasingly pervasive, even among the regime's purported political allies, some of them Manchus. Clashes between the prince regent and the new, largely court-appointed national parliament highlighted the extent to which power sharing itself had become the issue.

For all his awareness of the depth of opposition sentiment—or perhaps because of it—Prince Su went ahead full tilt with the court's version of authoritarian reform. He had a great personal investment in Manchu recovery and revitalization. Exploring the mind of a terrorist was only a slight diversion from the main task that engaged him on a day-to-day basis in the spring of 1909: military reorganization. This was the capstone of the Qing effort—and a relatively successful one—to reassert control from the center with ethnic Manchus rather than Han regaining a preponderance of top positions. Su, after all, was part of the inner circle. He wanted to keep himself in power. Though he was more broadminded than many of his fellow imperials, he bet his future on the belief that they as a group had the political will to maintain stability while carrying out top-down and meaningful economic and social reforms.[71]

Kawashima thought otherwise. When he returned to Japan in the summer of 1911 for a much-needed rest, he made it his mission to warn Japanese policymakers of impending trouble in China. In a meeting at the Peers Club in late August, he and the prominent politician Inukai Ki offered sharply differing assessments of what was likely to happen in China in the near term. Kawashima described China as politically unstable and vulnerable to armed uprising. Inukai disagreed, pointing to the success of military restructuring as proof that the regime was in control and capable of moving ahead as scheduled to make China a constitutional monarchy. "It's a mistake to assume that because military preparations have been made riots will not occur," Kawashima shot back. On October 10, disturbances in the Wuhan tri-city touched off a revolution that brought the dynasty to an end.[72] Writing fifteen years later about the waning years of the Qing, Kawashima was harshly critical, probably more so than he was willing to be in a public forum at the time:

> When I was in China in the last days of the Qing dynasty, I saw that the political body was already rotten to the core, a mere skeleton functioning only out of inertia. It would collapse in no time with the least provocation. On the other hand, Japanese foreign ministry officials and others thought that enlightened new policies were being carried out by the Qing dynasty and were optimistic about the future. Then all at once, with little resistance, the structure toppled over completely.[73]

Kawashima was ready to board a steamer to China when the first reports came in about the uprising at Wuchang on October 10. While official Japan withheld comment, uncertain how events would unfold, Kawashima was immediately out in front pushing a dual China policy: non-interference in south China and support for a Manchu monarchy in the region north of the Yellow River. He changed his travel plans, going first to Seoul to get support for his north/south proposal from the resident general Terauchi, then on to Beijing to sell the plan to Japan's minister to China, Ijuin Hikokichi. Should the revolutionaries be successful in gaining control of South China, Kawashima reasoned—and he clearly thought this likely—the Manchus, already in a panic, would be eager candidates for Japanese military assistance. "Act quickly to get the Japanese government to go along with the plan," Kawashima told Ijuin. "I'll be ready at the first opportunity to take the lead in pushing the plan with the top Qing leadership. For that to work out it would be better if the disturbances become a bit more serious, don't you think."[74]

Ijuin was on board for the moment, but there was a fly in the ointment: Yuan Shikai. By the end of October, with the crisis deepening, the court turned for help to Yuan, top-ranking Han Chinese dismissed from high office three years before in the court's bid to firm up central power in Manchu hands. Now Yuan seemed the only person who could hold the nation together. A nationally known figure, he was a major force behind China's military modernization program and a successful reformer of civilian institutions, the latter an important factor in mollifying progressives skeptical of Manchu sincerity in promoting change. As Yuan's name came to the fore and the court made efforts to coax him out of "retirement," Ijuin lost interest in Kawashima's north/south policy. Backing Yuan Shikai, betting on his ability to work out a solution to keep the country intact and save the dynasty, seemed to Ijuin to be more in line with Japanese long-term interests than a policy that might lead to a north/south partition. His personal relations with Yuan were good, and the foreign community in general was cautiously receptive to a Yuan comeback.

Kawashima was outraged. He was convinced that bringing Yuan back into a position of power was a big mistake for the revolutionaries, for the Manchus, for Japan. Unwilling to compromise, he refused to meet further with Ijuin, who responded by having him watched and tapping into his telephone conversations. The Yuan issue split Japan's official community in Beijing into two camps, a pro-Yuan group of diplomats headed by Ijuin and the decidedly anti-Yuan Kawashima joined by his colleagues in the Japanese military. For Kawashima, the question of whether to back Yuan was not a mere difference of political opinion that could be papered over. It was a showdown over power, Japan's and his own, a test of the success or failure of ten years of cultivating Prince Su whom he regarded as the most promising of the younger generation of imperial princes. In Kawashima's view, only Manchu progressives like Su and some of lower rank, many of them Japan-trained, all receptive to offers of Japanese aid, had any hope of developing a sense of national commitment among the Chinese, a people motivated by nothing more than narrow special interests. Inviting Yuan back into government jeopardized this picture of Japan-led development. Kawashima responded to moves to reinstate Yuan with harsh words and extreme tactics, even masterminding plots to kill him, all of them bungled failures.[75]

Kawashima's extreme hostility toward Yuan stemmed from long observation and personal encounters. He found Yuan a dangerous character, not to be trusted by Japan. He had no such bias against the revolutionary party; in fact, many of his Japanese friends—Toyama Mitsuru, for example—were longtime supporters of Sun Yatsen. His objection to the revolutionaries was that they were out of touch with reality. Echoing the view of most Western observers at the time, Kawashima felt that China was not ready for a republic.

> Intellectuals who support the recent revolution call for such things as constitutional government, a republic, national sovereignty, and popular rights, an indicator, it would seem, of how politically advanced they are. But what looks like political sophistication is really nothing more than some overseas students importing half-understood terms remembered from two or three years spent in a daze in foreign classrooms, trying to be trendy in showing off their new knowledge, all for the sake of publicity and personal gain. And in the end, like aggressive businessmen, all they've done is to compete with each other to create a climate of confusion. It's no different in substance from the unreasonable arguments offered by disaffected scholars in the past . . . To ignore 5,000 years of

> a country's national character and conditions, to undermine all possible moral values, ethical codes, customs, and suddenly to try to construct a republican form of government borders on insanity—it's really beyond belief.[76]

Even if the revolutionaries succeeded in gaining nominal authority over China, Kawashima said, they would not be capable of maintaining unity. "Considering the signs that even Yuan Shikai, the consummate Chinese politician, has little prospect of holding China together, I'm ready to state unequivocally that no one—Sun Yatsen or Huang Xing replacing Yuan or anyone else—will in the end be able to make a success of a unification policy."[77]

Kawashima's steady drumbeat of advice fell on deaf ears. As events played out from October through January, he saw his entire vision of a Japan-backed Manchu monarchy crumbling to pieces. Yet he could only watch from the sidelines as the Japanese government, in concert with the British, refused to intervene, offering to mediate only if requested by Yuan, the court's newly appointed prime minister.[78] Kawashima's worst fears were realized. The entire country was out of control. Imperial troops clashed with the rebels' New Army in central and south China; racist attacks against Manchus by Han Chinese left thousands dead; and provinces one after another declared in favor of a republic.[79]

Yuan's job as the court saw it was to bring order out of chaos, to negotiate a compromise to maintain the Qing regime, which on its part would agree to an accelerated path to constitutional monarchy. However, as peace talks between the court and revolutionaries went forward under Yuan's direction, it became clear that most people with political clout, even some of the court's own representatives, favored a republican framework of government. Reflecting this, Yuan in the end brokered an agreement that restored some semblance of order but meant political disaster for the dynasty he was supposed to save. In a bizarre announcement on February 12, 1912, the court itself sanctioned establishment of a republic and announced the abdication of six-year-old emperor Puyi. The tradeoffs were personal and financial: freedom from reprisals for top echelon Manchus, recognition of racial equality, and generous allowances for members of the court. It was a quiet and inglorious end to 2,000 years of imperial rule. A few days later, with the blessing of Sun Yatsen and the national assembly, Yuan Shikai, the dynasty's last hope, became the first president of China's first republic.[80]

Kawashima, Prince Su, and the Politics of Manchu Separatism

Even as disaster was overtaking them in the months after October 10, Prince Su and his colleagues had been slow to react, apparently banking on Yuan's loyalty to the dynasty he had served so long. It was only in late December, as Yuan and the revolutionaries began to discuss not whether to abdicate but the terms of abdication that Su dug in his heels. He knew he could lose everything he had worked for since the launching of the post-Boxer reform program ten years before. At a series of contentious imperial council meetings, he, Prince Gong and some of the Mongol princes, notably the Prince of Karachin, suddenly took a hard line position, urging their colleagues to oppose abdication in any form at all costs. To buy time, they insisted that a national convention be convened to decide the question of a constitutional monarchy versus a republic. The council as a whole accepted this position and Yuan's plans for a quick settlement in mid-January were abruptly derailed.[81]

His options dwindling, Prince Su suddenly brought Kawashima back into the picture to discuss the crisis, raising the possibility that the council of princes might request Japan to take "appropriate measures" to intervene. Beginning on January 22, Kawashima sent a flurry—sometimes three a day—of cables to the military's General Staff Office in Tokyo, urging the military to respond quickly to Prince Su's apparent new interest in Japanese assistance. But the situation was deteriorating too rapidly for Su and his supporters to maintain credibility as an opposition force. On January 26, a key member of the group, the imperial clansman Liang Bi, was assassinated, reportedly a preemptive strike by Yuan Shikai's men to prevent a planned attack on Yuan. Liang, described by Morrison as "the most bellicose of all Manchus" but "an exceedingly able man," had studied at Japan's Military Academy and was a close friend of the Japanese military attaché, General (formerly Colonel) Aoki.[82]

Yuan's scare tactics worked. More of the top imperials threw their support behind abdication. A few days later, Prince Su with the help of Kawashima and Japanese officers with the legation guard fled Beijing for South Manchuria, traveling disguised as a Chinese businessman. Skilled in the politics of intimidation, Yuan responded by ordering his troops to surround Su's Beijing villa, terrorizing family members left behind. Kawashima in turn threatened to expose Yuan's "uncivilized behavior" to the international community, in this way managing to secure the family's safe passage to Japanese-occupied Port Arthur (Lushun) and Su's undying gratitude. By mid-February, as abdication was announced, Prince Su, his princess, four secondary wives and thirty-two children had moved into his new residence, formerly a Russian hotel, now the property of Japan's Kwantung Army. A villa overlooking the sea notwithstanding, Su's new existence was something of a comedown. The family had only ten servants by contrast to the 200 they were used to in

Beijing, which meant that the royal children had to pitch in with domestic work. Kawashima's wife of ten years, Fuku, helped the princess manage the household.[83]

Yuan played rough politics but he was right to worry about Su and some of the Mongol princes who, unlike most of their fellow clansmen, had no intention of quietly resigning themselves to the loss of imperial power. The strategy they hoped to work out with the help of Kawashima and the Japanese military was to establish an independent authority in Manchuria and Mongolia, a base from which to compete with China or even to retake China at some point in the name of a restored Qing dynasty.

Selling the merits of this strategy to the Tokyo General Staff was Kawashima's prime objective in the series of cables sent in late January early February. Prince Su and the Prince of Karachin, he told his superiors in Tokyo, had the leadership qualities, the commitment, and the local base of support to make it work. The benefits to Japan of an independent Manchuria-Mongolia regime were obvious: a de facto Japanese protectorate as a buffer against Russian aggression and a match for the claims on China made by other powers. The General Staff found Kawashima's arguments convincing enough to give him free rein, albeit with limited logistical and budgetary support, to see what he could accomplish. At the end of January, even before the fleeing Prince Su had reached Port Arthur, Kawashima and Kawahara Misako's old friend, the Prince of Karachin, had signed a written agreement outlining plans to recruit men and buy weapons for a new, locally based army. The prince was in charge of the enterprise with Kawashima named as chief adviser.

The General Staff may have regarded Kawashima as something of a loose cannon in this operation to wreck the Chinese republic, but he did have important backers within the Japanese establishment. It appears that the major source of financing for weapons purchases was Iwasaki Hisaya, president of Mitsubishi Ltd. The two men first met in 1908 at the home of Iwasaki, who had initiated the contact, presumably hoping to use to good business advantage Kawashima's close ties within the Manchu government. It took some coaxing on Iwasaki's part but Kawashima eventually managed to overcome his great antipathy to businessmen in the interest of securing the support of a powerful patron. As soon as Prince Su fled Beijing in early 1912, Kawashima sent Iwasaki a cable requesting financial help. Funds for the Manchuria-Mongolia (Man-Mō, in contemporary parlance) project were issued in the form of loans on the security of mines and pasturelands owned by the Prince of Karachin in Inner Mongolia.[84]

Neither the notion of Manchu/Mongol independence nor the building of a separate state based on non-Han ethnicity originated with Kawashima or his Japanese colleagues in the military. It was an outgrowth of the ideology and politics of the Chinese Revolution. Revolutionary thinking as it evolved in the decade before 1911 was predicated on two converging attitudes toward the Manchus: first, that they were political incompetents whose weak leadership had left China prey to foreign economic domination, and, second, that they were racially distinct from and inferior to the Han Chinese, ruling only because they had the advantage militarily at the time of the Ming decline. Simply removing a particular governing body—the princes' imperial council of which Prince Su was a member, for example—was not enough for radical nationalists shouting anti-Manchu slogans, whether they did so primarily for rhetorical reasons or not. For these people, there were no "good" Manchus in government. Prince Su may have hoped he could change this perception by dealing personally and leniently with Wang Jingwei, editor of *Min Bao*, the most influential of the revolutionary magazines spewing out anti-Manchu racial invective.

If so, he was too late. The revolutionary mindset was fixed on the Manchus as an obstacle to progress that must be swept aside. "Unless the Manchus are driven out," wrote Zhang Binglin, the revolution's theoretician on race relations and another *Min Bao* editor, "we will be unable to create an independent nation, free from foreign domination. We will, instead, sink by degrees to the status of slaves of Europe and America . . . If the inferior breed is not exterminated the superior breed will not prosper. Isn't it absurd to expect that China's revival will occur automatically, without our first seizing a big broom to sweep out the filth from our native home?" Where "the filth" would go in this version of ethnic cleansing is not spelled out, but the implication is that they should return to their "native home," Manchuria.[85]

Though most revolutionary party leaders, Sun Yatsen included, shied away from endorsing such an extreme solution, Zhang's negative stereotyping of the Manchu people provided the party a convenient rationale in its call to remove Manchus from all positions of power and influence in China. But this was a double-edged sword. As the leadership was well aware, assertions that the Han Chinese should have the exclusive right to govern, couched as they were in the language of racism, carried the huge political risk of encouraging secessionist movements among China's minorities, Tibetans and Uighurs as well as Manchus and Mongols. China's northern border areas had been slipping out of the Qing orbit of control since the Boxer Uprising. Manchuria was the site of conflict and competing claims between Russia and Japan. In Mongolia, Qing action in 1902 to encourage Chinese in-migration as a foil to Russian expansion contributed to a rise in ethnic tensions as Han Chinese laid claim to choice pastureland.[86] Separatist activities were in evidence as well in Tibet and in Xinjiang, homeland of the Uighurs, again with the involvement of foreign powers, in this case Britain and Russia. Neither Sun nor Yuan Shikai wanted to contemplate the new Republic as a truncated version of empire surrounded by breakaway, non-Chinese states vulnerable to foreign influence.

With the outbreak of revolution in 1911, the parties negotiating the exit of the Manchus began to speak in more conciliatory fashion of a republic composed of five races. As part of the abdication arrangements of February 1912, the new government under Yuan issued a formal statement, the Manchu-Mongol-Uighur-Tibetan Articles of Favorable Treatment, guaranteeing minority groups the same protections of property and persons as the majority Han Chinese. It was an admission of concern about what was happening on the ground. Already in December of 1911, local leaders in the western part of Mongolia had declared Outer Mongolia independent, an action that provoked immediate Russian intervention. When the Prince of Karachin, representative of the eastern Mongol princes, met with Kawashima in January 1912, he offered his own simple logic for separatism. Mongolia's allegiance had been to the Qing dynasty, not to China, he said. With the Qing gone, Mongolia had the right to claim independence—and to seek Japanese assistance in making it a reality.[87]

For Prince Su and the Prince of Karachin, part of the court's progressive faction opposed to abdication and now targeted as dangerous elements by the new Yuan Shikai government, separatism was a strategy for political survival, a means to regroup for an eventual push to restore the Qing dynasty. Given the shaky hold the new republic had over myriad competing forces in the Chinese body politic, its bid to transform the northern border areas into a Qing-led breakaway state was not mere grasping at straws. The princes had reason to see themselves as heirs to power in the region. For one thing, it was their ancestral homeland. For another, they had at the time what appeared to be solid claims to ownership of local resources. Prince Su, at the top tier of the Qing elite, held title to an estimated 5,000 acres of land in Manchuria, supposedly rendered inviolable by terms of the abdication agreement.[88] The combined weight of historical legitimacy and wealth might reasonably have been expected to persuade fractious local warlords, who were constantly switching sides, to join the cause of restoration.

Opportunity seemed at hand when Zhang Zuolin, the one-time bandit who was emerging as the region's paramount warlord, reacted to the political upheaval of 1911 by declaring himself a staunch monarchist strongly opposed to both the revolutionary party and Yuan Shikai. From his new home in Dalian Prince Su lost no time in contacting Zhang with an appeal to help restore a Qing state centered on the old Manchu capital of Shenyang. Whether Zhang was wary of power sharing with Su's Japanese friends is a question. What is certain is that Zhang's loyalty could be had for a price. When Yuan Shikai, whose politics Zhang supposedly abhorred, offered a higher sum than Su, Zhang quickly shed his royalist sympathies and agreed to back the Yuan-controlled republican regime.[89]

Like Prince Su and the Mongol princes, Kawashima based his strategy on the expectation that China was headed for political collapse, a scenario that would invite a stepped up level of foreign intervention. To ensure Japan's parity in this inevitable power grab, he favored a preemptive move to establish a controlling position in the northeast, a strategically critical area where just seven years before Japan had sacrificed 80,000 lives to block a Russian takeover. But Kawashima argued against large-scale Japanese military involvement. Bringing in an occupation force would come at too high a cost in his view. It took years to pacify Taiwan, and the northeast was far more vast and undeveloped. Not only that, a show of military force would be highly provocative, triggering immediate interventionist responses on the part of the other powers.

As Kawashima saw it, Japan could best establish its regional influence through action behind the scenes, supplying weapons and advisers to help Manchu and Mongol leaders develop an indigenous military capability that might lead to an independent monarchy under Prince Su or the former boy-emperor, Puyi. With a strengthened military, this new entity could conceivably mount a challenge to China proper, moving troops southward, breaching the Great Wall, much as the seventeenth century Manchu-Mongol warriors did in establishing the Qing. Japan would reap rewards from backing Manchu-Mongol separatist aspirations. The emerging Man-Mō state, Kawashima argued, would become increasingly dependent on Japan, a de facto Japanese protectorate serving Japanese economic and strategic interests. As a matter of fact, of course, exercising influence indirectly through a "friendly" indigenous regime represented nothing new in international power relations then or since. What is striking is how much of what Kawashima was proposing in 1912 became reality in the state of Manchukuo twenty years later.[90]

Kawashima, now in his late forties, worked tirelessly over the next four years to promote Man-Mō independence. It was a typical Kawashima performance, a tenacious, against-all-odds effort that included badgering his high-level contacts for support. Mitsubishi offered the most consistent backing, providing loans for arms purchases and operational expenses beginning in February 1912. The Japanese government was less forthcoming. Directly challenging the Yuan Shikai regime by openly supporting a breakaway state along China's northern borders would put Japan at odds with the rest of the international community, which was leaning toward recognizing Yuan as the legitimate head of the new Chinese Republic. In taking a cautious, wait-and-see stance, Japan's civilian leadership put the lid on a group of young China experts with the Army General Staff who agreed with Kawashima's anti-Yuan stance though not, as Kawashima would have it, to establish a Manchu-Mongol state but as an assist to China's revolutionary party. The best Kawashima was able to get out of the General Staff was a no-objection decision when three of its mid-echelon officers, already on assignment in China, extended their brief to advise Kawashima and his Mongol and Manchu friends.

Using his meager resources, Kawashima recruited a small Japanese team to direct the covert operation known later as the "first Man-Mō independence movement." Most in the thirty-man group, which included one of Kawashima's brothers, were either recent graduates of Japan's military schools or Japanese working in China as teachers and advisers at Chinese military schools. On the local side, the Prince of Karachin headed a mixed Mongol-Chinese-Manchu volunteer force of several hundred men, including two of Prince Su's sons, who had attended military school in Japan.[91] Kawashima's plan was to provide these local fighters with Japanese weapons and training, creating an elite corps whose evident military superiority would help to convince local commanders that the Japanese-backed independence movement was a cause worth joining. It was a daring but not implausible way to spark a local insurgency.

In the spring of 1912, an arms shipment from Japan sent to Kawashima at the port city of Dalian was loaded onto an SMR freight car bound for Changchun, about 400 km to the north. At a small station south of Changchun, rebel troops transferred weapons and ammunition to horse-drawn wagons, concealing them under farm implements and produce destined for sale at towns to the west in Inner Mongolia. Until now the operation had gone without a hitch, but the journey west posed new problems. No matter what goods were being transported, a caravan of thirty heavily loaded wagons moving slowly over the grasslands was an inviting target for roving bandits and Chinese government troops looking for contraband. After fending off several bandit attacks, rebel troops were stopped at a Chinese checkpoint, their weapons discovered and seized. A skirmish broke out with heavy loss of life. At the end of June, Kawashima was ordered back to Japan at the request of his old friend from Nagano, General Fukushima, now deputy head of the General Staff.

What Kawashima expected to hear from his Nagano colleague was that the army planned to extend additional aid to Man-Mō separatist activities. Instead he was informed that while Fukushima personally agreed with him, the Japanese cabinet had ordered a halt to all operations. Incredulous, infuriated, Kawashima stormed in to see the foreign minister, letting loose a tirade on the importance to

Japan of seizing the moment to cement alliances with ethnic groups in north and northeast China. The foreign minister explained, patiently at first, that the cabinet now deemed it in Japan's best interests to cooperate with the Western powers in extending loans to the Yuan Shikai government. More firmly, he pointed out that no matter what Kawashima had to say, the cabinet decision would not be reversed. "If you insist on defying the order to cease operations, I'll have no choice in my official capacity but to impose sanctions." Realizing he could lose all credibility, Kawashima at last backed off and agreed to cease and desist in exchange for two assurances from the minister: first, that Tokyo would continue to provide Prince Su safe haven in Dalian and, second, that in order to maintain the network of trust built up among Manchu and Mongol leaders, it would retain Kawashima's services as chief liaison at the local level.[92]

In late summer 1912, twenty-six years after he landed in Shanghai to begin his China career, Kawashima left Dalian to take up residence in Tokyo. With him was his wife, who had helped the Su household with the move to Dalian, along with one of Prince Su's sons bound for school in Japan. In the dozen years Kawashima had known Prince Su, there was a marked change in the relative status of the two men. Su, once a powerful prince of the blood, Kawashima's patron, was now a political hopeful on the sidelines, forced to rely on Kawashima's loyalty and skills in presenting his case to government and business in Japan. That Kawashima would remain steadfast in his support of Su, there was no doubt. Switching sides would have been out of character. Besides, he had no use for either of the credible alternatives. He was skeptical of Sun Yatsen and utterly distrustful of Yuan Shikai. In Kawashima's political calculus, the only way for Japan to further its interests in China was to undercut Yuan and install a Japan-backed Manchu-ruled state in the north and northeast.

Kawashima was no doubt heartened by the sharp criticism of the government's pro-Yuan policy that began gathering momentum in the press and the Diet within months of his return to Japan. Many felt that in joining the foreign loan program to assist the Yuan government, Japanese interests were ill served. Funds were tied up, yet, as a secondary power, Japan was unlikely to play a decisive role in international decision making on China. More immediately worrisome, the sudden loan windfall emboldened Yuan to launch a crackdown on dissent in China aimed to erode the power of Sun Yatsen, easily the most pro-Japanese of all the candidates contending for leadership of China's new republic.

Outmaneuvered by Yuan for the presidency, Sun had agreed to accept the lesser post of Railway Minister, then arranged to visit Japan in the spring of 1913 for technical talks. Sun spent some of his time in Japan meeting with rail experts, but his main goal in making the trip was to win the backing of Japanese politicians and businessmen in his power struggle with Yuan Shikai. Sun's declarations of faith in Asia for the Asians themes and promises of special economic concessions to Japan struck the right chord with influential Japanese. Sun, on his part, returned to China well satisfied that Japanese support would prove a key asset in his upcoming fight with Yuan Shikai.

But his attempt to spark a second revolution in the summer of 1913 fizzled. Foreign loan assistance, which included Japan's contribution, had worked only too well to make Yuan's position unassailable. Sun and his supporters fled to Japan to regroup for another political comeback. Over the next few years, the exiled Sun mounted an intensive lobbying effort to secure Japanese financing for a campaign to oust Yuan Shikai. His hatred of the Yuan regime led him to offer the Japanese huge concessions in a future China in return for their support, questionable behavior for a Chinese patriot in the eyes of his countrymen. In 1915 when Japan issued the 21 Demands, designed to make such concessions a reality, Sun was roundly condemned by Chinese of all political persuasions for refusing to line up with Yuan in at least a nominal display of Chinese solidarity.[93]

What type of regime would replace the old Qing dynasty was a political conundrum in the years immediately following Kawashima's return to Japan. Furthermore, uncertainty in China as Yuan battled with groups opposed to the trend toward dictatorship was matched by uncertainty in Japan as to how to respond not only to Yuan but to the ebb of Western power in China in the wake of World War I. Issuance of the 21 Demands, a display of clumsy diplomacy on the part of the world's newest imperialist power, was meant to settle the China problem in Japan's favor with one bold stroke. What it did was to raise the level of anti-Japanese sentiment among the Chinese.

Further complicating Chinese-Japanese diplomacy was Yuan's decision in late 1915 to abandon the Republic entirely and install himself as China's new emperor. Japan reacted cautiously at first, seeking to coordinate a response with the Western powers. It then switched to funneling aid to China's anti-Yuan elements, the revolutionaries aligned with Sun Yatsen. Against the backdrop of this unsettled state of affairs, Japan's political leaders looked with renewed interest at the pro-Japanese Prince Su and his plan for a revived Manchu monarchy in northeast China. To many, a two-China solution, Su in the north, Sun in the south, now seemed the best hope of ensuring China's stability and advancing Japan's regional interests.

On matters pertaining to Prince Su's restoration campaign, Kawashima was the person to contact. He was Su's chief spokesman, strategist, fundraiser, and lobbyist. He was on Su's payroll. He was a financial adviser of sorts, helping to determine the allocation of loan funds from Mitsubishi and Ōkura industries and the cash received from the sale of Su family heirlooms. On a personal level, he was a frequent visitor to the Su family home in Dalian. In Nagano he played host to several of Su's sons, supervising their Japanese schooling. There was no turning back for Kawashima and Su. Now approaching fifty, in the final phase of their careers, they needed each other for success in achieving lifelong political goals—for Kawashima, to make Japan the number one power in China, for Su, to guide China into the modern world with a strong Manchu hand on the reins. What made the Kawashima-Su relationship uncommon was that apart from a shared political agenda, the two were old friends. As Kawashima saw it at least, they had a unique personal bond made explicit that winter morning in 1906 when Su proposed fraternal friendship, leaving Kawashima dazzled by a gesture that seemed suddenly to erase differences in rank and nationality.[94]

Prince Su in exile, around 1915. (Aida Tsutomu, *Kawashima Nanwa Ō*; Tokyo: Bunsuikaku, 1936)

Prince Su once again made a dramatic commitment to Kawashima and Japan in 1914 when he gave up for adoption by the Kawashimas one of his fourteen daughters, a little girl about seven named Jin Bihui. Adoption of Chinese youngsters by Japanese families was not unheard of at the time. What was unusual about this arrangement was that it involved a member of the Qing royal family. According to Kawashima, the idea was entirely Prince Su's, a sensitive gesture to the childless Kawashimas, particularly to his wife Fuku who had been depressed and bored after returning to Japan. Since Fuku knew the Su family well, Kawashima was probably reporting what he assumed to be the case when he noted that the child, later known by her Japanese name, Yoshiko, was happy at the prospect of going to Japan.[95]

No doubt there were also political reasons for what amounted to a public endorsement of Kawashima by a member of China's imperial family. The intention may have been to improve Kawashima's standing as Su's official representative in Japan. Imperial connections meant something in Japan and, while Kawashima's access to people in high places had been remarkably good over the years, he was still a commoner whose star had dimmed after the independence movement debacle. The Su-Kawashima alliance looked good on the other side too, especially to some of the lesser Mongol princes who were interested in aid from Japan. It may well have been, as one writer has suggested, that Kawashima originally hoped to adopt one of Su's many sons, stronger testimony to friendship than the gift of a daughter, but that Qing house laws prevented changing the family name of any male heir. Or it may have been that Su and Kawashima saw the worth of a female in cementing future Man-Mō-Japan alliances. Reportedly, the adoption plan included the possibility that Yoshiko might eventually marry one of the sons of the Mongol prince, Babojab.[96]

For the small girl, torn suddenly from her family and thrust into a Japanese environment, the experiment in cross-cultural adoption proved a personal disaster. Politically it was also of questionable value. Timing, rather than symbolism, likely prompted the Ōkuma cabinet's sudden receptivity to Kawashima's ongoing appeal for Japanese aid to Man-Mō separatist activities. Yuan Shikai was no friend of Japan and his move toward imperial dictatorship in late 1915 worried the Japanese government and public alike. Concerns about Yuan and his pro-Western tilt made attractive allies of local power holders in Manchuria and Mongolia who had tenaciously resisted centralizing efforts from Beijing since the republic was founded. As London *Times* correspondent G. E. Morrison wrote in December 1913: "Things in Mongolia are in a bad way. China has 60,000 troops along the frontier and they are being held in check and persistently routed by some 3,000 Mongols. China has brought the trouble upon herself and has only herself to blame."[97]

As Kawashima tells it, when he met with Prime Minister Ōkuma in the spring of 1916, the latter was expansive in his offer to aid a second Man-Mō independence movement. You handle the military side and the government will take care of financing and diplomacy, Ōkuma reportedly said. Given the green light, Kawashima was soon back in the business of providing arms and military advice to anti-Yuan resistance fighters in the north, certain as ever that creation of a new Qing state encompassing Inner Mongolia, Outer Mongolia, and Manchuria was the key to regional stability. Japan's closest allies in this effort to restore the Qing and curtail Yuan's power were Prince Su and the Mongol Babojab, who each had at his disposal forces of several thousand men. Kawashima's account suggests that as many as 20,000 local troops were ultimately involved.[98]

Kawashima Naniwa (front row, center) with colleagues involved in the second Man-Mō independence movement, 1916. (Aida Tsutomu, *Kawashima Naniwa Ō*; Tokyo: Bunsuikaku, 1936)

With Japanese government backing, this second independence movement had more chance of success than the first, which had been an exercise in the go-it-alone Kawashima style. Yet it too ended in failure, for reasons that defied its planners' best efforts to consider all possible contingencies. Yuan Shikai died suddenly in June of 1916, taking with him the threat of a tightly controlled regime hostile to Japan. Japan in turn withdrew support from the Man-Mō venture, preferring to sound out the intentions of Yuan's successor in Beijing. Deprived of arms and logistical support, resistance forces retreated south, Babojab was killed, Prince Su returned, broken in spirit, to his life of exile in Dalian. This dismal outcome was a matter of fate not flawed strategy, Kawashima argued. Undercut by the government's change in policy, even the greatest general could not have made a success of the operation.[99]

The collapse of the Man-Mō venture in 1916 marked the end of Kawashima's direct involvement in politics on the China mainland. But, like the old household steward under the Qing—and, no doubt, similarly, for a fee—he continued to manage Prince Su's financial affairs, starting with another round of fundraising. Reportedly, Japan's army in South Manchuria contributed an initial amount, acceding to Kawashima's demand that Su be compensated for loss of personal assets used to finance the recent campaign. In what seemed a questionable move even at the time, Kawashima invested the entire fund in Japanese oil exploration and mining schemes, all of which failed miserably. As Kawashima tells it, Su spared him reproaches. These financial losses were but "small defeats," he said. "Though our Restoration Party has experienced reversals and setbacks of all kinds, we must not abandon hope as long as there's life still in us. If it comes to the point that you give up on our long-cherished goal, I'll have no hope that we'll achieve our mission in our present lifetime. The only thing for me to do is to drown myself in the sea at Lushun."[100]

Prince Su not only deferred to Kawashima on financial matters, he also entrusted him with the task of arranging a Japanese education for a dozen of his thirty-two children, nine boys and three girls, who used Kawashima as their contact point during their years in Japan. In addition, Kawashima organized schooling in Japan for several of Babojab's sons, taken into the Su household after the death of their father in the 1916 independence campaign. Babojab's second son and Kawashima Yoshiko were married briefly and unhappily in the late 1920s. Su's increasing dependence on Kawashima both to manage Su family affairs and to pursue the dream of Man-Mō separatism was in part a reflection of his political weakness. It was in part also because, along with Su's fortune, his health was declining. In February 1922 when Kawashima heard that the fifty-seven-year-old Prince Su was dying of kidney failure, he rushed to Dalian to be at the bedside of his old friend. As Kawashima described the death scene, Su took his hand and, with the little energy he could muster, urged him to keep the dream alive.

> I'm wracked with illness and about to die without the satisfaction of having restored the Qing tombs and the imperial state. How can I face my ancestors in the next world? You, my dear brother, are my only real friend. Of all my followers, again, only you have stuck with me. I beg you respectfully, from the bottom of my heart: do not take me to be disloyal and ungrateful as I, the younger of the two of us, depart this world before you.[101]

In his will, Prince Su named Kawashima head of family, giving formal recognition to a role Kawashima had been performing in fact for some years. In a family of five wives and thirty-two offspring there was considerable room for contention over matters of inheritance, and not everyone liked the idea of delegating to Kawashima even greater control over disposition of assets than before.[102] Whether some of Su's sons, resentful of Kawashima's autocratic ways, were responsible for spreading rumors of an improper relationship between Kawashima and his adopted daughter, Yoshiko, is impossible to tell, but not unimaginable.

Kawashima Naniwa with foster daughter Yoshiko and some of her brothers entrusted to his care after the death of Prince Su. (Kamisaka Fuyuko, *Dansō no reijin*; Tokyo: Bungei shunjū, 1984)

That Yoshiko was a victim in some sense is beyond doubt. Like the bride in an arranged marriage, she was given over to strangers for reasons of family alliance not personal happiness or welfare. Her adoption was meant to affirm not only Su's confidence in Kawashima, but also the importance he placed on ties with Japan. Yoshiko was to be the poster girl for the Japanese-backed Man-Mō separatist cause. The failure of the 1916 independence movement, the second attempt to restore Qing power, was a devastating blow to the longtime aspirations of Su and Kawashima. To nine-year-old Yoshiko it probably meant one simple, hurtful thing: she could not rejoin her family in Dalian. The break with the past was complete with the death of both her parents, her mother, aged thirty-seven, at the end of 1921 followed by her father, the prince, a few months later.

Yoshiko's reactions to these events, her inner turmoil, can only be imagined. What was observable was that she was a troubled teenager, willful, bright, rebellious, and sexually active at an early age. At seventeen she cut her hair short and began to wear men's clothing. There were reports of a botched suicide attempt; a bullet removed from her shoulder years later seemed proof enough. Ugly rumors circulated—supported by her ten-year-old brother also living in the Kawashima household—that she had tried to take her own life after being raped by the elderly Kawashima who had been lusting after her for years. It was suggested that Kawashima's wife, who moved out at the time, had left him over the Yoshiko affair.

Kawashima's friends countered by citing Yoshiko's failed romance with an army officer as the cause of her immediate despair and suggesting that she was manipulative and given to hysteria. Certainly Yoshiko demonstrated certifiably bizarre behavior during her subsequent career in Manchukuo, but there is no way of knowing whether this was triggered by Kawashima's sexual predations or simply evidence of a deep-seated psychosis that impelled her to claim such. Kawashima's official biographer attributes Yoshiko's cross-dressing tendencies to her intensely competitive nature, a trait that drew admiring comments when she was young, leading her to chafe against the restrictions on women in Japan of the 1910s. Beyond a simple denial of impropriety, Kawashima said little publicly about the Yoshiko affair—no countercharges against Yoshiko or claims to be a target of a smear campaign by Yoshiko's brothers.

Whatever the nature of their relationship, there was no breach between Kawashima and Yoshiko. Yoshiko married one of Babojab's sons in 1928 with Kawashima's blessing and divorced him in 1930 against Kawashima's wishes. By then she had secured a place in a man's world as head of a Mongol brigade, a flamboyant figure suited up in officer's garb. Kawashima, now in his sixties, permanently based in Nagano, was no longer directing field operations as a paid adviser to the Manchus in exile. But he was still in the business of trying to shape official and public opinion on Japan's China policy. He served as informal mentor to some of the army's young Asia experts. He gave speeches in Nagano and Dalian. He wrote articles, books, memos to the government, the insistent voice of an old China hand, certain he knew what was wrong with China and what Japan should do about it.[103]

Reflections of an Old China Hand

Kawashima had lived in China for twenty-five years, a dozen of them as a civil servant working within the Chinese bureaucracy. A dedicated student of Chinese history and language since 1882 when he entered the China Department of the

Tokyo Foreign Language School, he spoke Chinese with the fluency of a native, wrote Chinese like a member of the educated class. Yet his summary of his China experience was tinged with bitterness, as if he felt that for all the effort he had expended, China had somehow failed him in the end. "Based on my unique position in China," he told a Japanese audience in Dalian in 1926,

> I had the opportunity to experience with the utmost clarity what the Chinese people were really like, not only on stage but behind the scenes. After spending so many years as a China watcher, I came to grasp the truth of the Chinese national character. It was like someone who had never had wine, tasting wine for the first time. Such insights into national character led me—someone who had been deeply sympathetic towards China as the key to the revitalization of Asia—to come to the painful conclusion, sad to say, that the Chinese people are beyond hope.[104]

Beyond hope, in Kawashima's view, because they were like "loose sand," unable to coalesce for a larger political purpose, lacking any sense of reciprocal relationships, focused only on family and immediate selfish interests, prey to military cliques motivated by power and greed. In fact, said Kawashima, of all the Chinese—here he used the term broadly to include the Manchus—he knew well, only Prince Su had not let him down. Kawashima was probably aware that Sun Yatsen employed the loose sand image in much the same way in his critiques of Chinese political behavior, but Kawashima identified Sun and colleagues as part of the problem, not the solution. The 1911 Revolution was a sham, Kawashima said. Though the "American-bred Sun Yatsen" and the Chinese students in Japan "chanted the mantras of sovereign power, national power, legal rights and popular rights, this was not a product of earnest conviction. Leading public figures, as well, paraded such views as their stock in trade out of pure self-interest; there was nothing in it of sincere, passionate patriotic sentiment."[105]

Kawashima painted a dreary picture of post-1911 China. After fifteen years of warlord fending off warlord and men with guns constantly reinventing loyalties, China was now stuck in a cycle of disorder, leaving it vulnerable to disruptive elements from communist Russia ready to stir up a second wave of Boxer-like anti-foreignism in the name of rights recovery. Politics, in his view, were thoroughly corrupt. "However much the public coffers are depleted," he said, "the private purses of China's military cliques, which will do anything to rake in the money, are filling up to a disgusting degree."[106] And he was certain that Guomindang (GMD) leader Chiang Kaishek, engaged at the time of writing in a military campaign in the name of national unity, would turn out to be just another warlord:

> Lately the GMD-backed southern army has launched a campaign. There are those who take the view that if the GMD wins, the scourge of military cliques will be eradicated and China will achieve stability. But this is superficial thinking. To be sure, in the event of a GMD victory, some of the militarists active to this point will be wiped out. However, because by then the GMD army will have become a military clique par excellence, its allies on all sides will withdraw troop support and start the internecine struggle once again. Like an image in a mirror, China persists in being China. The GMD militarists are now emphasizing the Three People's Principles. But, because they have absolutely no sincere interest in anything like what's good for the Chinese people, this is not a set of beliefs that will be carried out. Always calculating what is in their self-interest, they have no compunction about double-dealing, taking it as a matter of course. What they say is no more reliable than the seductive words of a prostitute. It is really troubling that there are many honest Japanese who, regardless, place great stock in the professed beliefs and verbal arguments of the Chinese and seriously sympathize with them. Until now such Japanese have repeated again and again the mistake of holding China views which have proven false in every case.[107]

What Kawashima wanted his Japanese audiences to understand was that there was an alternative to Japan's frustrating and fruitless efforts to work with the various double-dealing Chinese warlords. This was the policy, which he had been pushing since 1912, of supporting the secessionist aspirations of China's ethnic minorities, particularly Mongols and Manchus, who welcomed Japanese aid. His experience with the Mongols had convinced him of their effectiveness as a fighting force. He was not entirely complimentary about the Manchus. They had so mindlessly allowed themselves to be swamped by Chinese culture that they were now "even more incompetent than the Han people," he said. But he saw potential there. "If they change their political circumstances and improve their leadership, there is hope of renewing the vitality of the Manchu past."[108]

With Japanese assistance, that is, the Manchus might be able to reinvent the effective political-military structure which three centuries before had helped them conquer their far more numerous neighbors to the south. A show of force from China's border states was the most likely way, in Kawashima's view, to jolt the Chinese out of the current cycle of warlord violence. "In general, in the absence of something like Manchu power threatening the adjacent central plain as happened in the past," he wrote, "it is not possible to get the fractionalized Chinese to coalesce for any length of time and avoid political disintegration. In other words, what's called for on our part is a policy of using force in their best interests. Taking this course of action will lead directly to the happiness of the 400 million inhabitants of China and is the way to achieve stability in Asia as a whole." This was vintage Kawashima, the moralizing authoritarian, convinced that Japan had a mission to rescue China from its own political mistakes. "While presenting the hard face of a temple guardian statue, we must act in the self-sacrificing spirit of a Bodhisattva," he said.[109]

Kawashima's call for Japan to act unilaterally in Asia applying military force if necessary went against the grain of mainstream Japanese foreign policy thinking in the mid-1920s, which stressed disarmament and international cooperation. Kawashima later recalled that people at the time laughed when he talked about "Japan's spiritual mission." But he had watched the game of thrust and parry among China, the Western powers and Japan since his arrival in Shanghai in the 1880s, and it seemed to him that now, at last, Japan had the edge morally as well as politically.[110]

The mass slaughter of World War I caused many Japanese—and Chinese—to view with cynicism Western claims to the superiority of its value system and the rightness of its civilizing mission to poorer parts of the world. Kawashima, anti-Western to the core—he had turned his back on Western culture as a teenager when it was not the popular thing to do—was more than most primed to go on the attack, no doubt feeling vindicated in his long-held views. The world was now at a crisis point, he claimed, engaged in nothing less than an East-West clash of civilizations. If Japan, inheritor of the best of eastern values, managed to curb harmful influences coming from the West such as socialism, anarchism, communism, hedonism, there was a chance that Eastern civilization could surpass and replace its Western rival. What the Europeans called civilization, he said, was really just an unusual burst of scientific achievement resting on a morally and spiritually weak foundation. Referring to the war, he wrote: "In their reverence for the individual, Europeans thought of human happiness in terms of ego gratification, and so they put all their energies into promoting material things. The result was a temporary florescence of culture, but because it was something achieved with the desire for material gain as the underlying motive, inevitably it gave rise to conflict, starvation, and, in the end, dragged humanity into hell."[111]

To Kawashima, the war proved that Western belligerence was too ingrained ever to cease despite all the talk in Europe and America, "a country hypocritical in the extreme," about the importance of international organizations to maintain peace. "I believe that without question unless a grand and powerful force based on universal moral principles makes its appearance in the world and acts as a stable, overarching mechanism to control nations and guide humanity, true peace will never be achieved. No other country except our Japan is endowed with the capacity to provide this kind of fundamental mechanism in the future."[112]

To Japanese in the interwar period, the devastation in Europe fresh in their minds, their own war machine soon to kill millions more as yet unleashed, the idea that Japan had the cultural capacity to lead the region, even the world, to peace and stability, did not sound as farfetched as it might to us now. Kawashima in his lifetime had witnessed Japan on the rise, a nation of ever more prosperous, law-abiding citizens, victorious in "just" wars even by European standards. Establishing a Japanese foothold in Manchuria and Mongolia, he argued, was not aggression, but part of a larger program of freeing Asians from Western domination and extending the Japan model of good governance to a world torn apart by war.

> We will liberate various Asian peoples from their enslaved state, placing them under the management of first-class national governments. Rallying them all into a unified bloc, we will free them from the unjust, aggressive chokehold of the white peoples, making our emperor Asia's great leader. Using the weight of his authority, we will curb the unjust, inhumane, thoroughly evil actions, which have been undertaken by the Europeans. In turn, we will assist the various European peoples to achieve their potential. Furthermore, once Japan's influence prevails worldwide, nations will be encouraged to practice justice, not mutual aggression, and people will be inspired to create a single, global peaceful society based on moral principles, not on conflict.[113]

Embedded in these post-World War I assertions of the superiority of the Japanese value system were the same old concerns about power and race—Japan's struggle to survive and thrive in a rapacious world—that had driven Kawashima to seek a China career path in the first place. Japan, he said, must establish a strong presence on the mainland as part of "a major effort to restrain the Powers and determine a top ranking position among them . . . One misstep and Japan will be the loser in the arena of global competition over the Pacific and forever on a downward cycle."[114] He lashed out at Europeans and Americans for pursuing their own goal of world dominance while citing international law to thwart the regional interests of Japan.

> I believe that we ought to put a stop to what's happening—namely, that a minority race is dead set on securing for itself a majority of the world's land. Japan's present posture in Manchuria and Mongolia is backed by natural law, which affirms the right to make claims on the world's unoccupied territory. Unoccupied territory perfectly suitable for Japanese settlement is available in such places as Northern Manchuria, Eastern Mongolia, and Siberia. Of course, we must give international law the highest possible respect as a means to guard

> against the outbreak of conflict. However, in my humble opinion, it makes no sense to adhere rigidly to this principle to the point of letting the Japanese people die of starvation. There are plenty of examples of the European and American powers ignoring international law. Even worse, the anti-Japanese conduct of the United States of America is a flagrant violation of the treaty between the two countries. The unfaithful, so-called "new men" among us who slavishly stick to the two-faced pacifism of the Europeans and Americans without regard to the plight of the Japanese ought to be driven from the ranks of the Japanese people.[115]

War with the United States was inevitable, he said, but Japan should first dispose of the "red menace" by expelling Russia from its controlling position in Outer Mongolia.[116]

Given his preaching in the mid-twenties, Kawashima might have been expected to wholeheartedly applaud the army's occupation of Manchuria and establishment of the "independent" state of Manchukuo in the spring of 1932. But what unfolded did not precisely fit the scenario he had in mind, and, true to form, he was quick to express his dissatisfaction publicly. As Kawashima had expected, former Qing emperor Puyi got the nod from official Japan to head the new state. He was already on the scene in Lushun, staying in Prince Su's old villa, surrounded by a collection of courtiers, Manchu, Chinese, and Japanese, including none other than Kawashima Yoshiko, back home at last. But there was a major issue that had to be resolved. What form of government would Puyi head in Manchukuo, a Qing-style monarchy or a more citizen-responsive republic? Puyi himself lobbied hard to don imperial robes as the first emperor of a revived Qing. For the moment, Japan's military leaders were unconvinced. Puyi had to make do with the title "chief executive" as Japanese on the right and left continued to debate the question of Manchukuo's governance.[117]

Mere mention of the term "republic" triggered a volley of objections from Kawashima. The Manchus and Mongols were ill prepared for and not even desirous of a republic, he said. There was no way for government to express the will of thirty million people whose concerns were entirely local. Sun Yatsen had tried to force a republic on China with disastrous results. The type of multiethnic representative government some were proposing for Manchukuo, far from achieving stability, was an invitation to political breakdown and ethnic conflict. The whole idea of the equality of peoples, he stormed, was one of the bad influences coming out of "Red' Russia," where it served as political cover for a small group intent on seizing power.

Only a monarchy could restore peace and stability, Kawashima insisted, a monarchy that derived its legitimacy from its Qing connections and its power from ties with Japan. Manchukuo in 1932 was clearly what Kawashima had hoped to achieve in 1912 and 1916. Only now the man of the hour was Puyi, a young man of twenty-five, instead of Prince Su, who would have been sixty-seven. Now, too, Kawashima sought to justify the enterprise not only politically but in broad moral terms that played well with a certain segment of the Japanese public. The new Man-Mō state would be built on the foundations of the Japanese values of consensus and community responsibility rather than self-indulgent notions of human rights coming out of the West. Puyi got the post he coveted, Emperor of Manchukuo, in 1934. He and his Japanese "advisers" paid a visit to Emperor Hirohito in Tokyo the following year. Seventy-year-old Kawashima, steadfast Qing supporter, received a letter and gift of money from Puyi, last representative of the Qing ruling house.[118]

Citation and award extended to Kawashima by emissaries of Puyi, last Qing emperor, new Kangde emperor of Manchukuo, on Puyi's state visit to Tokyo in 1935. (Aida Tsutomu, *Kawashima Naniwaō*; Tokyo: Bunsuikaku, 1936)

Even apart from the issue of monarchy versus republic, Kawashima had problems with the governance of Manchukuo. He had long been out in front in asserting the justice of Japan's claim to dominance in Manchuria. But he felt that Japan could most effectively exercise its influence, institutional and ideological, through cooperative working relationships with local leaders who genuinely viewed Japan as a good and useful ally. In other words, Kawashima saw the Manchukuo enterprise as a fulfillment of his efforts to forge mutually beneficial partnerships with people like Prince Su, the Prince of Karachin, and the Mongolian leader, Babojab. The heavy-handed behavior of the Japanese occupying force in Manchuria left him suddenly alarmed. "Our military authorities now stationed in Manchuria," he wrote in June of 1932 as the takeover was in progress, "must ease up on the excessively interventionist approach they have assumed in the affairs of Manchukuo and restore cooperation as the operating mode in Japanese-Manchurian relations."[119] Alienating the Manchus and Mongols would be counterproductive, he warned: "If in our zeal to capitalize on patriotic passions to effect an immediate territorial settlement we turn our backs on the enduring ideals of imperial Japan and do nothing more than reenact the evil deeds of the European and American powers, there will be repercussions. We will not see the day when we can make definitely clear to Asians and other peoples of the world Japan's true spirit and gain their heartfelt allegiance and trust."[120]

Kawashima continued to criticize Japanese officials in Manchukuo for their insensitive behavior and administrative ineptitude. Most were insufficiently prepared to institute Japanese-style justice and order, he said, using the current buzzword, *ōdō*, literally, "kingly way," to refer to the Japanese model of nation building.[121] But this was quibbling around the edges. After years of shouting from the sidelines about the need for a strong presence in Manchuria and a show of force to knock the Chinese to their senses, Kawashima now found himself part of the mainstream, a chorus of enthusiastic voices supporting the Manchukuo enterprise.

He was glad to be consulted as someone who knew the Chinese mind, to be respected for his early interventions on behalf of Manchu-Mongol independence. Never known for his modesty, he took every opportunity to point out how right he had been all along. "Over the past twenty years," he wrote in a memo to an unnamed general in 1937, "I have strongly emphasized the need to establish a foothold in Manchuria and Mongolia and to take preparatory steps that would enable us to reach final a settlement of the China situation." The Japanese military supported his plan in 1912, he was careful to note, but the pro-Yuan Shikai foreign ministry—Uchida, Ijuin, and others—ordered a stop to his activities. "Twenty years later the situation became more and more critical. Because my thinking had gradually over time gained currency among people in various quarters, a single night of action ignited a spark that has now produced the kind of Manchu state I had in mind, and we're in a position to deal with China. In every respect this is a realization of my previous predictions; it's something those people could not have imagined."[122]

Japan's war in China had begun when Kawashima wrote these words, apparently in response to a request from the military for advice on how to govern the Chinese after their expected defeat. This memo together with responses to questions put to him by the Cabinet Planning Board in 1938 was published in 1941 under the title, *Mr. Kawashima Naniwa's Views on China*. What Kawashima had to say here was in part a rehash of his previous arguments justifying Japanese intervention in China. Lawlessness and disorder in the region threatened Japan's security. The Boxer-like wave of anti-Japanese incidents in China had to be stopped. British-backed Chiang Kaishek would lead China into another round of uncontrolled warlordism. It was Japan's mission to replace China's special interest driven politics with the Japanese version of just, stable government. Japan, in other words, had no other option but to use force to solve the China problem.

As to governance of postwar China, Kawashima envisioned a variant of the Manchukuo model in which the Japanese military, while essential to maintaining security, would not dominate every aspect of administrative decision making. He recommended instead that a single civilian agency be given the power to supervise both military personnel and civilian experts, the latter responsible for developing resources and institutions in the twenty or thirty years it would take to reintroduce Chinese imperial rule. He cautioned that experts sent out from Japan must be carefully chosen so that they would not succumb to the corruption endemic to Chinese politics. As usual, Kawashima had nothing good to say about the Chinese; assuming they were like the Japanese was a big mistake, he said.[123]

This was the message to the Japanese public from one of Japan's long-time China experts, someone who had worked with the Chinese for decades and could legitimately claim to understand Chinese politics and society. He had not always been so bitter. He undertook his assignment with the post-Boxer government with enthusiasm, fully confident that by directing public security reform he could do great things for both China and Japan. But the truth was that with the possible exception of Prince Su, who had his own agenda, the government that hired Kawashima in 1902 regarded him simply as another paid contractor whose technical skills were useful for a particular time and purpose. The intensely competitive Kawashima—on his own behalf and Japan's—increasingly felt used, hemmed in, marginalized. Any hope he might have had of developing a working partnership with the Chinese evaporated in 1912 when Japan withdrew support for the Qing, squandering, as he saw it, the opportunity to replace Western prescriptions for China's political health with Japan's own. Never one to compromise, Kawashima soldiered on, taking up the cause of ethnic separatism and Qing restoration, aligning with Manchus and Mongols against the Chinese.

In 1943, in a volume dedicated to fallen soldiers at Guadalcanal, the Eastern World Press published a speech Kawashima had given at Tokyo's Imperial Hotel in 1924 entitled, "The Root Causes of China's Illness." This, readers were told, was the most cogent account available of the conditions of political breakdown in China that ultimately forced Japan to take military action. Kawashima himself, nearing eighty and in frail health, had no comment. He had been a vocal supporter of a tough policy toward China. He had predicted war with America. But after six years of slaughter, privation, and devastating destruction, a horrible reenactment of the conflict in Europe he had so roundly condemned, he could not have felt anything but profound pain. Worse still was the agony of the two years to follow, watching Japan's steep fall from world-class status—the Meiji dream and his own in ruins. "A darkening haze hangs ominously over East Asia," he had written in 1886 as he sailed for China for the first time. He was referring then to the threat of Western domination. Now darkness had closed in on Japan. The West had won.

As his world collapsed, personal crisis also intruded, reminding him of his past, piling failure upon failure. Yoshiko, his adopted daughter, had spent the war years in Manchukuo doing intelligence work for the Japanese military. In Japan she was considered a hero, another Mata Hari. At war's end she was arrested by the Chiang Kaishek government and put on trial for treason, a Chinese spy for the Japanese in wartime, a charge punishable by death. It was a yearlong trial, and a sensational one, drawing wide press coverage at home and abroad. She was, after all, the daughter of a Manchu prince, someone with good connections, even within the Nationalist regime. Besides, she was a theatrical figure, an attractive woman, usually in men's garb, pet monkey in tow, a woman known for the breadth and variety of her sexual liaisons and a volatile personality that combined bewitching charm with fits of rage. She was also a clever liar, a dangerous thing postwar for anyone caught in her web. In short, Yoshiko was too high-profile a figure to be denied a full review of her case.

The specific charge against Yoshiko was that she was, literally, a "traitor to the Han race" (*hanjian*), an ironic choice of words since, strictly speaking, she was a Manchu. Her defense was that since she had gone through a legal adoption process in Japan, she was neither Han nor Manchu but Japanese so that she should not be charged with treason but with war crimes, a charge that carried a lesser penalty. She also claimed, stretching credulity, that the prosecution had her age wrong. She was not forty but only thirty and therefore too young at the time of the Manchurian Incident to have been responsible for her actions. She wrote to Kawashima, her "dearest father," pleading for his help, asking him to verify her statements on both counts. He replied in kindly tones that, yes, she had been properly registered and was a legal citizen of Japan, and, no, as far as he knew, she was now forty years old. Yoshiko was angry, but continued the correspondence. She was sentenced to be shot to death. The last letter she wrote before her execution date, March 25, 1948, was to Kawashima.

Yoshiko continued to confound. Rumors began to circulate that she was not executed, that hers was not the body displayed in international press photos but that of another Chinese prisoner whose parents had agreed to substitute their daughter for the price of four gold bars. Two shots fired into the back of the head of the victim made full identification impossible, and the body had been carted away immediately by a Japanese priest for cremation. U.S. army intelligence in Japan had a small file on Kawashima Yoshiko dating from 1945. It was marked "case closed" in December 1947. However, a year later, with rumors mounting that she had escaped execution, the Americans reopened the case, tracking down people who knew her, including Kawashima Naniwa. It was the American view that if the person they referred to as "the Mata Hari of the Orient" were still alive, she posed a "dangerous threat." Kawashima was described in several interviews as cooperative, but in poor health and so hard of hearing that little was gained from the conversations. It was recorded, however, that he believed his foster daughter to be alive, this despite the fact that in September 1948 he had deposited the urn supposedly containing Yoshiko's ashes in the Kawashima family altar in Matsumoto City. For him, however ambivalent at a personal level, it was symbolic evidence of the end of the quest, the death of hope that a new Qing state, taking form in Japan-backed Manchukuo, would sweep down into China to start an Asian revival under Chinese-Japanese power. Kawashima died June 14, 1949, aged eighty-four.[124]

Before Yoshiko's sentencing, Kawashima had written to her defense lawyer, a former Chinese student in Japan. It was a dignified letter, a letter designed to elicit sympathy but also providing a glimpse into Kawashima's mood after Japan's defeat, his feelings for Yoshiko, his attitude toward Japan's military leadership, his prescription for the future.

> I've reached the advanced age of eighty-three and am increasingly worn out in mind and body, a childless, lonely old man who continues to hope beyond hope that Yoshiko might be released and return home. I appeal to

you, with your sense of fairness and compassion, to please make every effort on her behalf. Some day, at the conclusion of a peace treaty, I look forward to offering you my heartfelt thanks in person on another visit to Beijing, a city of fond memories where I spent a dozen years as a high-ranking official of the Qing court.

What led to the recent hostilities between Japan and China was that those involved in the Manchurian Incident, in pursuing their own personal ambitions, distorted the real intention of Japan's great mission in Asia. The fact that they obscured Japan's true purpose by a show of aggression was very likely the root cause of their great blunders. The Japanese people must reflect on what happened and get back on the right track. It is imperative that the Chinese people also come to realize that in the final analysis the path to Asian security lies in Japan and China joining hands and acting with complete solidarity.[125]

Chapter V

Ariga Nagao and Japan's Internationalism

When Japan installed Henry Puyi, the last Manchu emperor, as head of its client state in Manchuria in 1932, Kawashima Naniwa was once more in the news, cited for his pioneering efforts on behalf of Manchu-Mongol separatism twenty years earlier. The message was clear. Manchukuo as a multiethnic state had a history as a shared idea, Japanese-Manchu-Mongol, and therefore a legitimacy to it that defied the skepticism of the international community. It is true that in the Kawashima-Prince Su arrangement, leader and follower roles were blurred. Japan was in equal measure encouraging and responding to the separatist aspirations of China's minorities unleashed in the political turmoil after 1911. But somewhat lost in the image making of the 1930s was the low level of actual support given the Kawashima-Prince Su schemes by the Tokyo government in 1912 and 1916—and with good reason. For all the appeal of his anti-Yuan Shikai stance, Prince Su was the representative of a failed dynasty whose support even in his home base of Manchuria was uncertain. Had Tokyo been determined to oust Yuan, an option with much greater promise would have been to back Sun Yatsen. By contrast to Prince Su, Sun represented the new China—1911 was his revolution. He had a substantial political following in China's national assembly, a core of opposition to President Yuan. He was also a known quantity in Japan with a web of contacts among Japan's political and business elite developed over years of residence there. In 1913, in a campaign to reverse his political fortunes at Yuan's expense, Sun was in Japan, politicking for Japanese aid, offering major concessions, control of Manchuria among them, in return for that aid.

Ultimately, Sun was as disappointed in Japan as Prince Su. The drawback for both was that the Europeans and Americans had put their considerable weight behind Yuan Shikai as the man most likely to bring stability to post-Qing China.

Japan at this point had neither the will nor the resources to stake out an independent course with respect to China, contravening its alliance with Britain, the leading power in Asia. Rational minds in Tokyo prevailed. Japan would follow the least risky course: to press its interests in China to the hilt within the framework of the international treaty system. Other options where Japan had a comparative advantage—backing Sun or even Prince Su—were never completely written off, but joining the international community in support of the Yuan presidency would be the main event.

President Yuan on his part was as eager to accept foreign aid as the foreign powers were to give it. Foreign backing gave him political advantage over competitors such as Sun Yatsen. The £25 million loan provided by major European governments and Japan to finance his Beiyang Army was a case in point. The new President's decision to use foreign advisory help in state building efforts was also good politics, a reassuring sign of continuity with Qing policy and Yuan's own programs as provincial governor. What was different in 1912 was the scope of work offered a select few of the foreign experts: not simply to provide professional advice to one or another ministry, but to get to the heart of the matter and help draft a new constitution for a new China. In keeping with the Qing tactic of diversifying foreign advisory sources, Yuan informed several foreign governments, including the Japanese, of his interest in hiring experts to work with him and his inner circle in this enormously important task.

Thus it was that in the summer of 1912, as Kawashima was packing his bags to leave Beijing, his twenty-five-year China career behind him, Ariga Nagao (1860-1921), Waseda University law professor, was in the throes of deciding whether to go to Beijing as an adviser to the Yuan government. At fifty-two, Ariga was at the peak of his professional career. He had an international reputation; he had participated in world conferences and published in French and English. The enormously influential G.E. Morrison, twenty year China correspondent for the London *Times* and a key member of Yuan's staff, knew Ariga personally and put his name forward as the best candidate for the Japanese advisory slot. No doubt Ariga's vast knowledge of European political systems did much to recommend him for the constitution drafting role. But equally important, his was a respected name among the Chinese. Many on the president's staff knew Ariga from their student days at Waseda. Others were familiar with his work from a series of lectures on constitutional law he and his colleagues had given to visiting Chinese officials in 1906 and 1908.

When the Foreign Ministry in Tokyo contacted Ariga about the China job, he was at his cottage in the mountains of Shiobara where he routinely escaped for summers of uninterrupted research and writing. In the summer of 1912 he was working at a slower pace, still recovering from a serious stroke he had suffered the year before. Ariga was a first-rate candidate, but not the only candidate with the achievements and experience demanded by Tokyo and Beijing. Fellow professor at Waseda, Takada Sanae, was approached first by the Foreign Ministry, but turned down the position, recommending Ariga instead. Ariga hesitated for several weeks then declined the offer in late July for reasons of health and a commitment to a lecture series he was preparing on Japan's imperial institution. The Foreign Ministry then turned to Minobe Tatsukichi, much respected Tokyo University professor of constitutional law, and got another refusal.

In December 1912, Ariga was again approached and pressed hard by Takada Sanae, leading political figure Ōkuma Shigenobu, and China's minister to Japan acting on behalf of Yuan Shikai. As China's parliament was about to convene, they argued, it was critical to have a Japanese in place on the team of foreign experts to advise on the constitution for the new republic. This was the appeal to national duty. Also persuasive was a matter of symbolic and practical importance that had been worked out in the intervening months: the question of salary and benefits. The Japanese government for reasons of prestige, and certainly Ariga who was not well paid as a professor at a private university, wanted a salary commensurate with that of the other foreign advisers. Morrison had set a high standard, though it was acknowledged that his salary reflected his role as political mediator along with constitutional advising. As a compromise, Tokyo and Beijing agreed that Ariga would be paid slightly less than Morrison, but be provided with a Manchu villa, renovated Japanese-style, plus utilities which in Morrison's case came out of his own pocket.

Ariga finally accepted the China job in January 1913. Once the decision was made, he felt a surge of optimism that China was the right choice. The assignment had the potential to add a new dimension to his career, until now focused on Europe. Personally it would allow him to pursue his keen interest in Chinese art history and possibly give him time to complete a translation project long on his agenda. As friends and students waved him off on the Tokyo-Kobe train on February 28, 1913, to start his initial five-month contract, Ariga sensed that things would go well. Quite fortuitously, Sun Yatsen was on the same train and had time to brief him on China's constitutional issues and actors. He was pleasantly surprised, too, by the calm seas encountered on the voyage from Kobe to China's port at Tianjin, normally a rough crossing. At Tianjin, it seemed propitious again that a fierce north China dust storm that could have delayed the ship from docking struck only after he and his party were safely on the train to Beijing.

Things continued to look good after arrival. Ariga knew something of north

China from his field experience in the Sino-Japanese and Russo-Japanese wars. But Beijing was new to him. He was awed standing in Tiananmen Square thinking of 270 years of Qing history. He was surprised by the good order in the city so soon after the revolution and found things to commend Beijing over Tokyo, helpful street signs and comfortable rickshaws among them. He immediately called on G.E. Morrison, who received him kindly, noting that he had Ariga's publications in his collection. He had a one-on-one meeting with Yuan Shikai followed by dinner with Yuan's newly appointed cabinet, many of them with Japan connections. Two ministers knew Ariga from the constitutional study mission of 1908. Two delegates to China's newly elected upper house, both Waseda graduates, cornered Ariga to pick his brain on how to proceed with revisions to the hastily crafted provisional constitution. He was delighted that Yuan's young staff seemed to want to talk about work and nothing else. By mid-March, Ariga and his family, brought along to monitor his health, were installed in a spacious villa, equipped with electricity and running water, on a quiet street near the president's office. On the road to recovery after a serious illness, selected to work on a major constitution writing task at a higher rank than all foreign advisers except Morrison, well-paid and well-regarded, Ariga could be forgiven his optimism that China would be the capstone of an already successful career.

The Making of an Internationalist

Ariga Nagao both represented and helped create a new profession for a new Japan, that of teacher and practitioner of international law. What this required in a country recently emerged from relative isolation was someone with the uncommon ability to put the world under his scope. Ariga was a kind of Meiji polymath. Even those colleagues who found him difficult to deal with, a real curmudgeon by many accounts, had great respect for his towering intellect, the range and depth of his scholarship, and his internationalist activism.

As longtime friend Takada Sanae remarked, Ariga's scholarly bent was almost a genetic trait. He was born in 1860 into an Osaka family that had produced generations of teachers and scholars. His father was a well-known *waka* poet and specialist in Japanese cultural studies.[1] Of modest income but highly respected, the Arigas managed to make a smooth transition to new elite status after 1868 when so many of their fellow samurai, Kawashima Naniwa's family included, slipped into debt and obscurity. And not all of the senior Ariga's sons followed the academic route. Ariga Nagao's younger brother Nagabumi was destined to become director of Mitsui Gomei and president of Mitsui Bank.[2]

Two essential ingredients of career success for the early Meiji generation were learning a foreign language, English, German, or French preferred, and study abroad. However traditional Ariga's father was in his own profession, there was no doubt in his mind that in 1870s Japan he would do well to enroll his eldest son in the Osaka English language school. Pledged to "seek wisdom throughout the world," the new Meiji government had clearly signaled the kinds of tools required of the next generation of leadership. And very quickly, for the most gifted students, the various English-language middle schools became feeder schools for Tokyo Preparatory School and Tokyo University, founded in 1877. Ariga entered preparatory school in 1876 and university in 1879, aged nineteen. According to Ariga's classmate Takada Sanae, Ariga was always impressively studious, consistently at the top of his class. He was especially loved by the American professor from Boston, Ernest Fenollosa, very likely, Takada added, because he was the only student capable of understanding Fenollosa's lectures on philosophy. His unusual facility in English, a requirement for university entrance, gave him a natural advantage.[3]

"Be cosmopolitan" was the underlying message of the government's fledgling university, a small collection of science and humanities departments that started out with just 100 students. The plan was to provide a select group of Japanese youth with advanced training under the tutelage of specialists from Europe and America followed by a period of overseas study, the ultimate product being a cadre of new leaders for the new Japan. During Ariga's university days, 1879-1882, foreign-hires were the predominant element on the university faculty, accounting for about two-thirds of the forty-man teaching staff. The small student body meant that everyone was in close contact with the foreign faculty members and the new ideas they brought with them. And the impact was felt well beyond the university classroom. When Edward Morse, American zoology professor, gave a lecture at Japan's Biological Society in 1882 using Ariga as his interpreter, 1,500 people were in the audience.[4]

As everyone knew at the time, the small but influential group of foreigners on the university faculty was but a fraction of the total number of foreign advisers then in Japan. In any given year in the seventies and early eighties, the high point of Japanese openness to outside assistance, some 500 foreign contract personnel were plugged in throughout the government bureaucracy, helping to propel Japan's great leap forward to modernity even as the advisers themselves were influenced in lasting ways by the culture and practices of Japan. Educator William Clark (of "Boys, be ambitious" fame); Horace Capron with the Hokkaidō Development Commission; Josiah Condor, British architect; Henry Dyer pioneer in engineering education—all were part of this mutually enriching process. Some advisers worked for years in Japan. Herman Roesler, legal expert attached to the Foreign Ministry, then the Cabinet, spent fifteen years there. Perhaps the prize for longevity goes to Henry W. Denison, hired in 1883 to advise the Foreign Ministry, who stayed on as a fixture until 1914. Most of the foreign advisers were remarkably well qualified considering they got their jobs not through a vetting process but a combination of happenstance and personal contacts. In the case of Ariga's mentor, Ernest Fenollosa, timing was everything. Uninspired by his job at the Boston Art School, Fenollosa jumped at an invitation from Harvard classmate Edward Morse to join him on the Tokyo University faculty.

Both Fenollosa and Morse represented a peculiarly American phenomenon in the 1870s and 1880s. As Christopher Benfy so elegantly puts it, they were part of a "wave" of New Englanders post-Civil War seeking spiritual renewal in the culture of old Japan at the very time Meiji Japan was rejecting that culture in favor of Western modernity. Zoologist Morse was as passionate about discoveries of ancient pots and fossils in the caves of Kyushu as Henry Adams was excited by the shrines at Nikkō, William Bigelow and painter John LaFarge by Japanese woodblock prints, and Ernest Fenollosa by the entire canvas of Japanese art, literature, and philosophy.[5] From their prominent place among East Coast intellectuals, they introduced Japan to America as a place of culture and sophistication, Japonaiserie as objects of admiration sought after by elite collectors, Japanese artistic style as worthy of emulation. And their influence worked the other way, particularly in Fenollosa's case. Teacher of Western philosophy and American resourcefulness, Fenollosa was also a student of Japanese culture, converting to Buddhism, spending all his free time, as Ariga recalled, scouring Kyoto and Nara temples for sculpture and paintings and searching through old manuscripts to piece together the art history of Japan and China. Through his passion for the arts of old Japan he re-engaged his students in their own culture to lasting effect.

Fenollosa who, like most of his New England colleagues, knew little Japanese, hired two of his students as translators: Ariga Nagao and Okakura Tenshin. Both had excellent English-language skills. Both had first-class minds. Beyond that, they were quite unalike, Ariga a sober-minded philosophy student from a solid scholarly family, Okakura an art enthusiast with a flair for getting on in the world learned from his father, a smalltime entrepreneur of fluctuating fortunes. Okakura became Fenollosa's principal assistant, then colleague in a joint endeavor to create a new art for a new Japan, a synthesis of traditional and Western techniques, definitely modern but identifiably Japanese. For a Japan uncertain of its place in the world, the Fenollosa-Okakura proposal to establish a national art school on the grounds that "a great nation must have a great art" struck a responsive chord with the Ministry of Education. In 1887 funds were provided to send Fenollosa and Okakura on a year-long study tour to Europe and the United States to evaluate the variety of organizational models and pedagogical approaches then in vogue. The immediate product was the Tokyo Fine Arts School, which opened in 1889.

Beyond this single achievement the two men played a major role in making Japanese culture part of world culture: Fenollosa celebrated for his writing on art, philosophy, and Nō plays and for his art acquisition on behalf of the Boston Musuem of Fine Arts, where he became curator, Okakura for promoting among his American friends a peaceful pan-Asianism of spiritual values distinct from the material West, for his writings on the tea ceremony and Asian ideals generally, and for his role in museum management in Tokyo and Boston. Okakura was above all a "phenom" with his impeccable English and flashy kimonos, a hint of romance and sadness about him, the darling of Boston female society, especially of patron of the arts Isabella Stuart Gardner. He did as much by his very person to promote a positive image of Japan among America's northeast elite than all of the writings on his résumé.[6]

Ariga graduated from Tokyo University in 1882, two years after Okakura. There were twelve in his graduating class, including Takada, "the best and the brightest" as the press described them, young men chosen on merit for higher-level training and expected to play a sizable role in Japan's future. Working with Fenollosa had been an eye-opening experience for Ariga as it had for Okakura, stimulating his interest in Western intellectual traditions as well as the arts of China and Japan. Along with his small researcher's salary, he had acquired new skills as a translator and interpreter, new habits of thought, and a confidence in dealing with non-Japanese. When Ariga joined the Tokyo faculty as an assistant professor immediately upon graduation, it appeared he was headed for a promising career in academia. But the independent mindedness that defined his character got the better of his caution and two years later he found himself without a job and the essential income it provided.

Where Ariga ran aground was over the issue of academic freedom. Tokyo University was a public institution, the nation's first and only university. By the early eighties it absorbed 40 percent of the Ministry of Education's budget, and plans were for rapid expansion. From the government's standpoint, efficiency demanded uniformity. University professors should be classified as civil servants, subject to the same rules and regulations of other members of the bureaucracy. On the other side was the small university faculty arguing the case for academic autonomy. When the Ministry issued a ruling in 1884 designed to discourage liberal-leaning academics from criticizing government policies, Ariga and a few others responded defiantly, publicly. Ariga spoke out at a student forum vigorously defending the notion that advances in scholarship could only occur in an unfettered environment where adherence to universal principles took precedence over government controls. Whether these utterances alone would have sealed Ariga's fate is unlikely. But when students gathered to celebrate the emperor's birthday went on the rampage destroying school property, Ariga's defiance was linked to their anti-establishment actions, and he was advised by school authorities to resign his post.

Still, the twenty-four-year-old ex-professor was highly regarded. The head of the emperor's chief law-making body who knew Ariga as Fenollosa's interpreter took pains to assure him that once the incident blew over he could expect to be back on a positive career track. Meanwhile, there was the question of income. Fenollosa was all too happy to increase the work hours of his brilliant student who came daily to his official residence to translate colophons while he took notes. Ariga in temporary disgrace was relieved to have the means to support his parents, a central concern of his until their deaths some thirty years later.[7] His debt of gratitude to Fenollosa remained deep in his consciousness until the end of his life.

Ariga was not out of favor for long. In 1886 he won a government scholarship to study law in Germany and Austria, joining Konoe, who was still at university in Bonn; Mori Ōgai, a medical student in Berlin; and another of Fenollosa's products, Inoue Tetsujirō, who was in Berlin continuing his studies in philosophy. Ariga's shift from philosophy to law, he recalled later, was a direct result of his clash with university authorities. Evidently he found the study of law the best refuge for the independent thinker he was and the public critic he wanted to become. Ariga's two years abroad were central to his career. He became conversant with European politics and current legal thinking and developed an unusual degree of fluency in both German and French. Yet curiously Ariga makes no reference to these years in later reminiscences, by contrast to his long accounts of his early friendship with Fenollosa. Perhaps the hint of scandal connected with his stay in Germany kept him silent. A short story by university classmate Tsubouchi Shōyō about a Japanese student in Germany whose German girlfriend followed him home causing turmoil in the family was rumored to be based on Ariga's own story. Whether embellished on or not, it was not the kind of public notice Ariga wanted.[8]

On his return to Japan, Ariga was tapped by Itō Hirobumi for the job of secretary to the Privy Council, the emperor's top advisory body. He also joined Takada Sanae on the Waseda (then known as Tokyo Senmon Gakkō) faculty where he remained until his China assignment in 1913. Waseda, a private university with lower salaries but fewer constraints than Tōdai, was a hospitable place for Ariga. The bureaucracy was not. Once he had paid back the obligation he had assumed as a scholarship recipient, he resigned to devote full time to teaching and writing. Ariga's record of publications starting even before he went abroad is nothing short of astounding, a veritable outpouring of monographs, compilations of lectures and translations, several per year. Topics from the 1880s ranged from Spencer's sociology, to Roman law, analysis of the Meiji constitution, Japanese domestic law, economic history, and educational psychology. His translations were from English to Japanese—several works by Johannes Johonnot, popular American educator—or German to Japanese, some jointly done with his friend from college days Inoue Tetsujirō. In the nineties, Ariga began to publish works on diplomatic history and international law, some written by him in French then translated back into Japanese. Inevitably, he came in for criticism by some in academia for deviating from the usual track of pursuing a single specialty. Takada's response was that only Ariga was brilliant enough to shift from philosophy to international law and diplomacy over his lifetime without becoming superficial.[9]

Lessons from the Battlefield

Ariga was a prototype of the new-style academic. He was a real world problem-solver rather than a pure researcher, a practitioner eager to maximize his public impact by assuming roles beyond teaching and research at a single academic institution. The most critical issues facing Japan in the 1880s and 1890s were in the area of foreign relations—treaty revision with the Europeans and Americans and the standoff with China over Korea chief among them. Yet public understanding of law and diplomacy was almost entirely lacking. Given Ariga's personal preference for applied research, his remarkable fluency in foreign languages, and Japan's need for expertise in foreign relations, it is not surprising that he would shift from philosophy to international law and try to broaden his professional role beyond teaching at Waseda.

In 1890, in addition to his Waseda duties, Ariga accepted a position as instructor at the Japanese Military Academy, Japan's elite training school for career military.[10] Founded in 1874, the academy was highly regarded both within and outside Japan. No less a military expert than General Ulysses Grant, visiting Japan in 1879, had good things to say about Japan's service academies, indeed about the country's education system in general: "The progress they have made in the last twelve years is almost incredible. They have now Military and Naval Academies, Colleges, Engineering schools, schools of science and free schools, for male and female, as thoroughly organized, and on as high a basis of instruction, as any country in the world."[11] There was another "almost incredible" feature of the military training program that made it unique in the world. Beginning in the late eighties, along with weaponry, tactics, and strategy, students were required to take a law course featuring the first of the international conventions dealing with wartime behavior, the 1864 Geneva Convention for the Amelioration of the Condition of the Wounded of the Armies in the Field.[12]

The person responsible for introducing humanitarian law into the army curriculum was a professional soldier, General Ōyama Iwao. Ōyama was one of the wonder boys of the new Meiji government, the talented few destined for long service as part of the emperor's advisory circle. At the start of the Franco-Prussian War in 1870 Ōyama, age twenty-eight, was sent to Europe to observe firsthand how modern wars were fought. What he saw were massive armies of mobilized citizens, the technological prowess of a rising Germany, and a test case for the recently formed Red Cross societies operating under Geneva Convention guidelines. The Red Cross performance was only a mixed success. Coordinating volunteer relief efforts with military operations proved more difficult than imagined by the humanitarian activists promoting the Red Cross movement. Still, to Ōyama and other Meiji leaders engaged in building a conscript army from the ground up, the concept of minimizing battlefield deaths through reciprocal delivery of aid by both parties to a conflict seemed rational, an efficient use of resources, and, not least, up-to-date and humane.

The start of a brief but bloody civil war in Japan in 1877 prompted the Meiji government to organize a relief society that, much to the surprise of Europeans, carried out the evenhanded treatment of war wounded envisioned in the Red Cross ideal. Ōyama, his experience as war observer topped off with two years of study in France and Germany, was by then back in Japan fighting insurgents as brigade commander in Kyushu. By1884 he had risen to the position of army chief of staff and again traveled to Europe, this time specifically to study the organization of army medical services by the Red Cross in various countries. According to Ariga, it was at Ōyama's urging that the Meiji government signed the Geneva Convention in 1886, only four years after the United States. On this basis, the International Committee of the Red Cross (ICRC) accepted Japan as a member in 1887, and the 1877 relief society became the Japanese Red Cross Society (JRCS), a privately funded organization managed by the army ministry headed by none other than General Ōyama. On his order, copies of the simple, ten-article Geneva Convention were immediately distributed to Japan's active and reserve troops. Following up on Japan's formal accession to the ICRC, Ōyama dispatched a delegation to the fourth ICRC conference held in Karlsruhe in September 1887.[13]

This quiet action was in fact a momentous event. This was the first time Japan had participated in an international forum. Moreover, it was doing so in post-Franco-Prussian War Europe, a time of uncertainty about the feasibility of trying to regulate wartime conduct through the Geneva Convention and the Red Cross, uncertainty even more fundamentally about how to define the boundaries between national sovereignty and universal human rights. In other words, humanitarian law was then a new and evolving science in its European setting, and the Japanese model was partly adaptive but also possibly a contributor to the world stream of experience.

Ariga was just the right person to brief Japan's officer corps on the latest Western thinking on conduct of war issues. When he was hired at the Military Academy in 1890, he was fresh back from several years of study in Europe, fluent in French, German, and English and a brilliant and rare commodity in the developing field of international law. In 1894 he wrote a law handbook, including a translation of a French standard text on international law, as teaching material for the officers training course. General Ōyama contributed the preface.[14] Ariga's teaching was not confined to the classroom. Prime Minister Itō called him in for consultations in the months prior to the Japan's declaration of war on China in August 1894. Another job possibility opened up when the second army corps, now on war alert, began hiring legal experts to advise on conduct of war questions.[15] Japan's acceptance of the idea that in place of variable chivalric traditions, modern wars should be fought in accordance with universally agreed upon rules was a first for any military organization in Asia, a sad irony in light of the conduct of Japan's military fifty years later.

The outbreak of war between Japan and China in 1894 after ten years of tension over control of Korea was the first chance for Japan's small cadre of international law experts to engage in real work on the ground. Given his connection with the Military Academy and General Ōyama, who assumed command of the second army, Ariga was a natural choice for one of the field positions. How much, or even if, he had to be persuaded to accept the assignment, which he did within a month of the opening of hostilities, is not clear. Given the national mood at the time, patriotism likely played a part in his decision. Of equal importance no doubt, given his love of empirical research, was the fact that the assignment presented a unique opportunity to test firsthand whether Japanese battlefield behavior would conform to the requirements of the Geneva Convention. However the decision was made, within a couple of months the life of classroom teaching had faded, and Ariga in army uniform was at the front lines in Manchuria surrounded by the sounds of artillery and scenes of carnage.[16]

In the most decisive land battle of Japan's victorious campaign in China, the second army under General Ōyama captured Port Arthur at the southernmost point on the Liaodong Peninsula in November of 1894. As Japanese news dealers reaped a profit selling woodblock prints of battle glories, reports began to filter out from foreign journalists on the scene of Japanese atrocities against Chinese defenders of the city, including noncombatants. Ariga, acting as army spokesman, was singled out for criticism in the foreign press for suggesting in response to questioning that such reports were exaggerated.[17] In the climate of negative publicity, various European foreign ministers lodged formal complaints with Japan's Foreign Ministry, thus raising the issue to the level of an international incident. Ariga's own response to Western condemnation of the Port Arthur atrocity came quickly after the war ended in the spring of 1895. Based on his extensive field notes, he produced in six months a 300-page account of the conflict written in French entitled, *La Guerre Sino-Japonaise au Point de Vue du Droit International* (The Sino-Japanese War from the Point of View of International Law). Along with detailed discussion of Japan's reasons for going to war and treatment of non-combatants, prisoners of war and the like, the book devoted a chapter to Japan's actions at Port Arthur. The book was published in Paris by A. Pedone Press in 1896.

Ariga gave the Japanese army high marks overall for prosecuting the war in accordance with international law. Europeans and Americans agreed. Japan was not only universally praised postwar for its advanced military technology and training but generally described as "civilized" in its battlefield behavior. It was only the Port Arthur massacre that prompted outrage, and here Ariga presented a carefully crafted argument to explain but not entirely excuse Japanese actions. Ariga was in the employ of the army, yet his judgment disagreed in certain important ways with the report of General Ōyama's own fact-finding commission on the incident.

Ariga was at a field hospital on November 19, three days before the capture of Port Arthur, when he heard reports of a Chinese atrocity against Japanese troops. According to eyewitness accounts, after a gun battle the previous day Chinese soldiers had hacked off the heads and disemboweled the bodies of fallen Japanese, leaving the gruesome remains in the path of advancing Japanese troops. Among the observers were Western journalists who had their own horror stories to tell. James Creelman of the New York *World,* described Japanese soldiers coming upon "the heads of their slain comrades hanging by cords with the noses and ears gone." Creelman's point and Ariga's, too, was simply that the Japanese army was in a vengeful mood as it advanced on the city of Port Arthur.

Ariga entered the captured city mid-morning November 22 "before the generals" where he witnessed firsthand the immediate aftermath of the Japanese side of the atrocity equation: bodies of Chinese lying on doorsteps, obstructing the alleyways, floating in the sea channel—by Japanese count a total of 2,000 dead, about 1,500 of them non-combatants. Most of the dead were young men. Ariga reported seeing only two women. There was no continued mayhem. He saw a column of Chinese being led away to execution but also a group of Chinese wearing tags exempting them from death sentences.[18]

General Ōyama's investigative commission came to two major conclusions: first, that in conditions of what we now call urban warfare it was difficult to distinguish between soldiers and civilians, thus making a certain number of non-combatant deaths inevitable; second, that for the protection of Japanese troops it was essential to shoot to kill in the case of prisoners trying to escape. On the first point, Ariga was in partial agreement. As a new city, he argued, Port Arthur had few real natives. There were no physical features or dress or dialect to distinguish young locals from enemy troops who were themselves guilty of looting and destruction. And many local residents were in fact assisting the Chinese army by concealing soldiers and weapons in their homes. Particularly in the dim light at sunset when the fighting began, it was difficult to tell innocent residents from armed troops. In short, he agreed with the official finding that while the Japanese attack was directed solely at the Chinese army, in the confusion and crossfire, non-combatants were often the unfortunate victims.

But Ariga raised a more fundamental question. Was it necessary at all to use massive force to take Port Arthur? There was not much resistance coming from the city, and enemy numbers were small. Nor did it make sense to launch the attack in the early evening when the risk of involving non-combatants was high. On these primarily tactical grounds, Ariga concluded that "it is impossible not to acutely regret the Port Arthur incident from the point of view of the laws of war." He differed also with the Ōyama commission on the treatment of prisoners of war and on the underlying question, the big elephant in the room, of whether revenge killings were part of the death count of non-combatants. Situations occur in wartime everywhere in which soldiers outraged at the abuses of the enemy respond in kind, he pointed out. These are "the instincts of human nature." But while this may explain the actions, "they are not a sufficient reason to violate the laws of war." He acknowledged the logic of the claim some Japanese made that the laws of war should not apply at all in this case since the Chinese were not signatories to any of the conventions outlining *jus in bello* practices. Yet at the end of the day, he concluded, Japan's own commitment to act in accord with "civilized nations" carried with it the obligation to respect the laws of war, one-sided or not. On the question of treatment of enemy detainees, he noted that Japan's current military codes were based on Western precedents that included a prohibition on use of force against unarmed prisoners. In Ariga's opinion, a shoot to kill order applied to prisoners trying to escape was not, as the Ōyama commission report suggested, allowable under international law.[19]

As one of Ariga's colleagues later recalled, *The Sino-Japanese War from the Point of View of International Law* with its informed discussion of conduct of war issues—and written in French, the language of diplomacy—was the perfect vehicle to convince the foreign reading public that Japan was serious in its commitment to international law.[20] The book had prestigious backing. Both Sir Thomas Barclay of the Institut de droit international, Europe's leading think-tank in the field, and Paul Fauchille, chief editor of the professional journal *Revue generale de droit international public*, helped with manuscript preparation, including editing Ariga's French, assistance Ariga gratefully acknowledged in his introduction. Ariga worked directly with the two men bringing the book to press during the several months he spent in Paris from late 1895 to early 1896.

Fauchille wrote an enthusiastic preface. Like many Europeans in the aftermath of the Sino-Japanese War, he was excited by the notion of an exceptional Japan, a Japan that by virtue of adopting European institutions and norms was becoming ever more civilized, "the equal of the most civilized nations"—more like us, in other words. For this distinction, Fauchille told readers, Japan had been justly rewarded by the powers even before the war when they agreed in principle to end extraterritoriality, the jurisdictional privileges enjoyed by foreigners in Japan. Japan's battlefield conduct provided added proof that Europe's confidence in Japan was not misplaced, that unique among non-European nations, it was committed to "the principles of civilization." Japanese troops showed themselves to be "inspired by the most humanitarian ideals," Fauchille claimed, in conformity with the terms of the 1864 Geneva Convention. Fauchille clearly admired Japan for its remarkable progress. Still, there was a bit of unwitting condescension, typical of Europeans of the 1890s, in his assumption that *his* side set the standards as to what was civilized. And the question of standards posed a dilemma on the receiving end as well. As Martti Koskenniemi has summed it up, "In order to attain equality, the non-European community must accept Europe as its master—but to accept a master was proof that one was not equal."[21]

In Fauchille's view, Ariga was unique as Japan was unique. He could think of no one better qualified to assess Chinese and Japanese wartime behavior from a legal standpoint than Dr. Ariga, professor of international law at the Japanese Military Academy, embedded legal expert with the army in the field. Ariga was someone well versed in both the theory and practice of international law or, in Fauchille's words, "the rules as called for by science and those imposed by practical necessity."[22] He recommended Ariga's account of the conflict as the first study of international law written by a Japanese, scrupulously documented, backed by evidence from the battlefield, and evenhanded in citing Japan's violations of humanitarian law as well as China's.

Fauchille's warm endorsement of Ariga, Ariga's note of gratitude to Fauchille, the speed of publication, all suggest an easy collaboration that was to repeat itself in years to come. Rising stars in their mid-thirties, both men appreciated the differing experiences they brought to the project. Fauchille, the scholar-publicist at his desk compiling legal precedents into European case law was intrigued by Ariga, fresh from the battlefields of Asia where he had engaged in the real business of monitoring compliance with the Geneva Convention. Ariga, soon to return to civilian life and academia, saw in Fauchille the impact that a private individual could have on public policy through publication of a professional journal like the *Revue du droit international public.*

They were like-minded in their approach to international law. Theoretical issues were not at the top of their list. What concerned them was how the law functioned and could be imagined as a set of tools to assist in diplomacy and global governance. They thought of it as a practical science, universal and transferable, not culture bound and static. Just as Japan had become a legal-minded nation in thirty years, presumably any nation or people—Chinese, Arabs—could choose to join the international legal regime, sign the Geneva Convention, and, should war be necessary, fight the good fight according to common rules of engagement. Just peace or lawful war, Fauchille and Ariga shared the belief common among Europeans at the time that a world of internationally accepted standards would be a better, more orderly place.

Fauchille praised Japan for what he saw as its largely successful effort to comply with existing wartime conventions, convincing proof to him of the broad applicability of Western legal thinking beyond the borders of Christian Europe. Ariga, too, had compliance in mind when he spoke of Japan's ascension to "civilized nation" status, but he was less Euro-centered in assessing what this achievement meant. Though he agreed that following rules devised in the councils of Europe was worthy of notice, for him, Japan's real contribution to current *jus in bello* discussions was its decision to go-it-alone on compliance, to stick to the rules unequivocally, unilaterally, even in the face of an enemy that had not signed on to the Geneva Convention or joined the ICRC. Nothing in current just war prescriptions required this kind of asymmetrical morality, Ariga argued in Chapter I of *The Sino-Japanese War from the Point of View of International Law*. Leading European jurists were on record as saying that the rules must be mutually agreed to have binding force. Therefore, as Ariga saw it, Japan's decision to fight justly regardless of the Chinese response indicated a degree of commitment to humanitarian and rational action unusual even among the ranks of civilized nations.[23]

Ariga could take some personal credit for the disciplined action of Japan's officer corps. Many were recent Military Academy graduates who had taken his required ethics course. But the point he wanted to make in the book was not simply that Japan had fought a lawful war, but that it had managed to do so without ceding the advantage to an enemy who was fighting—to use a current term—an irregular war. It was this experiment that Ariga pronounced as being "of great scientific interest" to Europeans and Americans who likewise, he cautioned, might find themselves one day bogged down in irregular warfare in Asia. Ariga's self-assured analysis that extended even to questioning his own country's actions at Port Arthur, struck a new tone in Japan's internationalism: that the world ought to look for more in Japan's modernizing experience than lessons learned from Europe.[24]

What is so perplexing to historians struggling to explain atrocities committed by Japan's military in the 1930s is that key initiatives to bring Japan into the European mainstream of international and humanitarian law—the army legal unit of which Ariga was a part and the Japanese Red Cross Society (JRCS) on whose board he actively served—came from *within* the military itself. Ariga was in Paris in late 1895 not in his academic persona but as an adviser to the army. Producing the definitive book on Japan's wartime conduct was one part of his assignment. The other was to develop recommendations to improve the field efficiency of the JRCS. No one was better equipped than Ariga to evaluate JRCS field operations or more willing than he to consider input from European colleagues on possible organizational changes. The phrase he used to characterize the institutional flexibility of the JRCS, "restless inventive energy," was in fact an apt summation of his own pragmatic approach to change.

At the same time, Ariga strongly believed that the transfer of institutional experience also worked the other way, that the JRCS had a message for its European counterparts when it came to the issue plaguing all the Red Cross societies at the time, namely, should they engage in non-partisan humanitarian work or serve the particular interests of national military structures? Japan's Red Cross was unique, in Ariga's view, in having achieved an effective balance on this score, patriotism and humanitarianism observed in equal measure. It put country first but with scrupulous adherence to the Geneva Convention in part in the hope of reciprocity, in part simply because it was the right thing to do. Indeed, on the humanitarian side, foreign journalists in north China had praised the ICRC's only Asian member for providing good quality hospital and nursing care to Japanese and Chinese soldiers alike under unusually difficult field conditions. Ariga also highlighted another JRCS success which was the envy of its European sister organizations: its membership drive on the home front. From a prewar figure of 37,000, the number of JRCS paying members had soared to an astounding 160,000 immediately after.[25]

Nothing could have been more surprising to the European philanthropists promoting growth of national war relief societies than this sudden flourishing of the JRCS less than ten years after its acceptance to ICRC membership. Their expectation was that Red Cross societies would thrive only in countries like the United States and Britain where principles of Christian giving and volunteerism were strongly ingrained. Yet it was there that the organizations failed to take hold, while in Japan where there was no tradition of religiously based charitable relief associations success was achieved early. As was the case more generally with institutional transfers from the West to Japan post-1868, evolution of the JRCS structure owed as much to innovation as imitation, to use Eleanor Westney's terms. In the absence of grass-roots charities the state took the lead, supplying imperial patronage and an organizational home within the military structure. The JRCS was among the first of the national Red Cross societies to treat the organization as part of the war effort in a larger sense, not only to supply aid and comfort to wounded soldiers but to mobilize public support in wartime. Concerned about medical skill levels and skeptical of volunteerism, the Japanese moved quickly to professionalize JRCS service by using paid personnel in permanent positions with "ladies" volunteer groups filling in as needed and only on the home front. Ironically, it was only after the United States and Britain adopted some of the features of the centralized, professionalized Japanese model that their Red Cross societies took off, and this not until after 1905.[26]

Ariga's reputation got a huge boost from publicity about his wartime experience and the book that emerged from it. Viewed as a legal first abroad, *The Sino-Japanese War from the Point of View of International Law* also caught the public eye at home, attracting interest beyond the small community of academics conversant in French. General Ōyama himself authorized its translation into Japanese for use as a textbook at the Military Academy,[27] presumably as new supplementary material for Ariga's ethics course. Ariga was also asked to prepare a summary of JRCS wartime activities (*Le service de secours de la Societe de la Croix-Rouge du Japan, pendant la guerre de la 27e-28e anne de Meiji)* to present to the sixth International Red Cross Conference held in Vienna in 1897. This was just the third time Japan had participated in the world meeting since the founding of the JRCS ten years before.[28] It was Ariga's first chance to take part in an international forum. Sitting with European jurists, conversing in German, French and English about international humanitarian law, Ariga, the sole Asian delegate and still a relatively young thirty-seven could be expected to count the experience a success for himself and Japan.

But Ariga was thinking beyond kudos that might accrue at Vienna. Like many Japanese, his pride in the performance of Japan's armed forces was tempered by concern about the path ahead, particularly on the diplomatic front. Yes, Japan by 1897 had secured a timetable from the Europeans and Americans for ending the unequal treaties, a thorn in the side of the public and politicians for thirty years. And, as he found on his trips to Europe, now that Japan was victorious on the battlefield it was regarded as one of the civilized nations, an up-and-coming power. But Ariga questioned whether Japan had the capacity over the long haul to manage its new status as the first Asian nation to join the Western treaty regime, this "historic first experiment in human society," as he called it.[29] He believed that successful integration into the world community required a strong foreign policy establishment and public support base well-informed about Western politics and diplomacy, not only what the rules were but how they had evolved historically. In his characteristically blunt way, Ariga made it known that on this point he felt Japan was seriously deficient.

Gaikō Jihō: Creating a Public Voice in Foreign Relations

Ariga's mission to overcome what he perceived to be a public knowledge gap in international affairs was the genesis of a project that would be his all-consuming passion for the next fifteen years. In February 1898 he founded the magazine *Gaikō jihō* (Revue diplomatique), published by Tōkyō Senmon Gakkō, predecessor of Waseda University. Modeled after Paul Fauchille's *Revue generale de droit international public*, the new publication made a dramatic debut. It was Japan's first foreign affairs magazine. It had no government or political party affiliation. The freedom to criticize or editorialize was a position that Ariga as editor-in-chief insisted on throughout his long tenure in the job. With its staff of international law professionals, *Gaikō jihō* functioned as a kind of think-tank whose self-appointed job was to enlighten the public about the conduct of diplomacy around the world. Touting the magazine prior to publication, Ariga made known his intention to provide not only informed commentary on diplomacy, law and politics, past and present, but translated documents and topical articles from the foreign press.

Gaikō jihō was new and so was its premise—that issues in foreign relations should be the public's business. When Ariga spoke in favor of "people's diplomacy" (*kokumin gaikō*), however, he did not mean, as the term might imply, popular participation in foreign affairs decision making. He acknowledged and accepted the fact that under the Meiji constitution the power to make war or peace was the sole prerogative of the emperor and his delegated advisers, thus outside the reach of Japan's elected body, the Diet. At the same time, Ariga was well aware that the nebulous entity "public opinion" was at the center of European discourse on the workability of international law, and this at a time when the publics of Europe were no better educated and scarcely more enfranchised than the Japanese. As he explained to his readers, for the modern nation-state, furthering the interests of the public or the national community was what external relations were all about. The people counted. The state was only as strong as the people on whose behalf it was acting.[30] Ariga saw public opinion as a potent force that must be shaped, at times even consulted—at least the elite part of it—because in the end the success of what was wrought through diplomacy depended on the support of the people at large.

The peculiar feature of the Meiji constitution which made foreign relations—as military affairs—an exclusive imperial prerogative not subject to Diet oversight left unclear as a practical matter which agencies would handle the day-to-day conduct of diplomacy. There were a number of competing actors, some of them purely advisory and extra-legal like the all-powerful body of elder statesmen (genrō), others with a degree of constitutional validity like the Privy Council, the Prime Minister's office, and the Ministry of Foreign Affairs.[31] Ariga reserved judgment on the workings of the apparatus as a whole but had a lot to say about the Ministry of Foreign Affairs. The ministry was Japan's face to the world. It was meant to function as a modern bureaucracy on the European model. Ariga himself was training university students for diplomatic service. He believed the ministry could constitutionally and should practically assume a more prominent role in managing the complex problems emerging in the post-Sino-Japanese War years.

Ariga was never one to hide his opinions. The professor in the classroom easily cast himself in the part of *Gaikō jihō*'s ombudsman and Foreign Ministry critic. Right from the start, in the second issue of the magazine, he challenged the ministry in an article deploring the excessive secrecy of its foreign affairs reporting. Release as many documents as possible as they do in European countries was his advice. An informed public was likely to be a supportive public. Three issues later Ariga expanded his brief in an article that bore the sweeping title, "Refashioning Diplomacy." Here he argued the pressing need to upgrade staff. He conceded that Japan's diplomats could hardly be expected to match their European counterparts in skill and sophistication overnight, a "physical impossibility," he said, using the *katakana* syllabary to sound out the English. After all, the Ministry had only been engaged in full-scale foreign relations for seven or eight years and was notably deficient in speakers of Chinese and Korean much less European languages. But he pointed out that the military had on its own initiative instituted an internal regulatory system to ensure high-quality personnel. He saw no reason why the Foreign Ministry could not similarly introduce organizational changes to deal with its personnel problem, in this case a deficit in language and area expertise. Ariga's solution was to create a Foreign Ministry advisory council. This was not to be a council of elder statesmen. What Ariga had in mind was a group with well-defined monitoring and reporting responsibilities made up of young professionals, international law experts with overseas experience and foreign-language capabilities.[32] The profile was remarkably his own.

When Ariga spoke of advisers he meant Japanese advisers exclusively. In an angry tirade in the September 1898 issue of *Gaikō jihō* he blasted the ministry for continuing to employ its longtime American legal adviser, New Hampshire native, Henry W. Denison. Ariga acknowledged that when Denison took up his post in 1883 foreign advisers served a legitimate purpose, particularly in a field like international law where Japanese expertise was lacking. What bothered him was that fifteen years later when this was no longer the case, Denison, whose skills were limited to reading English-language sources, was still ensconced in his high paying post in the Ministry, growing increasingly out of touch with the latest developments in the field. It would make more sense to employ a recent graduate of one of our universities, Ariga complained. Besides, now that Japan was regarded as a real contender on the world stage, the Ministry should unquestionably shape its own foreign policy without the perception of conflict of interest that Denison represented. Ariga advised Japanese officialdom to honor Denison's service however limited its value and send him on his way.[33] Ariga was free to give advice but nothing came of it. Denison lingered on in his post for another eighteen years, a prominent figure in diplomatic negotiations at the highest levels.

The Japanese press gave *Gaikō jihō* a warm reception. Ariga was praised for his expertise, the magazine for filling a critical need. *Kokumin shimbun* declared it a must-read for the Japanese public ill-informed as they were in foreign affairs. The only note of skepticism among reviewers was whether the magazine was taking on too much, whether it could meet its goal of global coverage and still maintain accuracy in reporting.[34] Reminiscing about *Gaikō jihō* in the 1930s by which time the magazine had dozens of competitors, Ariga's former colleagues emphasized its huge public impact at the outset when it was a one-of-a-kind operation and virtually a one-man show with Ariga at the center.[35] Ariga worked tirelessly on the magazine. He viewed it very much as his own. The magazine had a regular stable of writers drawn from colleagues and students, but Ariga put his stamp of approval on all articles, and until his China assignment in 1913 every issue included several of his own contributions. While Ariga dominated the scene and pulled no punches with his tough editorial comments, he also hired people who disagreed with his positions, and these differing views were aired in the magazine. At the monthly editorial meetings, usually held at a Western restaurant in Tokyo, again, Ariga was chair and ultimate decider, but the conversations were free ranging with everyone participating. Often Ariga invited an outside expert to keep things lively, Takada Sanae or, as China lurched toward political crisis in 1911, Kawashima Naniwa.

In the history of the Japanese press, *Gaikō jihō* represented a new product, a hybrid of professional journal and news magazine. On the one hand, it was published by Waseda University, its writers were mostly professors, and its target audience was the educated elite. It contained no commercial ads, only notices for new books. At the same time, *Gaikō jihō*'s writers were no ivory tower academics. Most were active in the public sphere beyond the university campus, several of them, like Ariga, practitioners of international law. With Ariga leading the way, their goal for the magazine was essentially a practical one: to provide access to information and analysis not only to shape public opinion on foreign affairs issues but to help Japan's leadership make foreign policy decisions that were effectively in the national interest.

Gaikō jihō's global coverage was unprecedented; there was nothing like it in the Japanese daily newspapers. The range of Ariga's own contributions reflected the vast amount of reading he did in French, English and German and the network of contacts he had abroad. Occasionally the topics he chose to write on seemed slightly off-message as if something fascinating had come across his desk that he felt he must pass on to readers whether it related to foreign affairs or not. Did it fit his purpose to give his audience an account of the U.S. Civil War, one wonders, or a brief history of the Zionist movement? Usually, however, the connection was clear. Subjects as diverse as British colonial rule in Egypt, the completion of the Vienna-Baghdad rail line, the British-French rivalry in East Africa, and the crisis in the Balkans were chosen to provide lessons for Japanese policymakers not only in what was happening in the world in general, but how the Western powers who, after all, *were* the international order, managed their competing global interests.

The world at the turn of the twentieth century, as Ariga himself liked to point out, was run by about forty nation-states, now including Japan. All of them, with the notable exception of Russia, had constitutional governments. Just as the rule of law held sway over these national polities in the form of written documents, it governed relations among them through a loose collection of generally accepted norms and procedures known as international law.[36] The task that Ariga set out for himself and his *Gaikō jihō* colleagues was to explain how this Western-based system, itself evolving and changing, worked to the advantage of participating states or, in other words, how nations used international law to augment their power and influence. He was a realist and a pragmatist. He was not proposing any grand ideology in foreign policy. Nor did he attach any moral opprobrium to the expansionary aims of the powers. Indeed, that a nation would expand if it could expand was axiomatic in his time, easily justified, if need be, using the civilization word. As Theodore Roosevelt said about turn-of-the-century France, England, Russia and the United States, "every expansion of a great civilized power means a victory for law, order, and righteousness." Applied to the U.S. takeover of the Philippines in 1898, Roosevelt assured the public that America would carry through with its duty to govern the islands, "so that one more fair spot of the world's surface shall have been snatched from the forces of darkness."[37]

Snatching fair spots like Hawaii and the Philippines alarmed the Japanese. In an editorial written in August 1898 Ariga suggested that there was less of moral duty than greed in U.S. expansion into the Pacific, though he conceded that U.S. governance would be an improvement over Spain's. But his reason for opposing permanent annexation was pragmatic, not moral. With the United States controlling the Philippines Japan would have to "abandon entirely the idea of spreading its wings to the south." [38]

A more immediately pressing foreign affairs question for Japan when *Gaikō jihō* was launched in February 1898 was how to deal with the West in China. The year began with the Chinese government granting Russia a twenty-five-year lease to the Liaodong Peninsula, the selfsame territory denied Japan at war's end by the joint intervention of Russia, Germany, and France. An obvious slap in the face to Japan, this action was but one of a rash of Western concession-grabbing moves in China and consequent weakening of the Qing regime that heightened anxieties in Tokyo. Everyone was talking about the possible breakup of China into permanent Western dominated blocs.

Ariga went over this ground in several editorials written for *Gaikō jihō*. Though he named no names, his argument on China was a clear answer to Konoe Atsumaro's call for a new Asia for the Asians strategy. Japan was lucky to have an alternative to Euro-Asian alliances when it came to responding to the dangerous game being played in its neighborhood, Ariga conceded. And certainly thinking long-term it made sense for geographic and economic reasons to strengthen ties with China. But the reality of the moment, he argued, was that there was no reliable political group in China to partner with. Absent that, the only rational course for Japan was to work with the Europeans and Americans in tried and tested arrangements—whether these should be by collective guarantee or guarantee by alliance, he examined in excruciating detail—to prevent China's partition and maintain equal access to the China market.[39]

In February 1898, on the eve of publishing *Gaikō jihō*, Ariga had written to Konoe to get his endorsement for the new venture.[40] They had interests in common. They were both German-educated and cosmopolitan in outlook. Ariga was an occasional visitor to the Konoe mansion for meetings on treaty revision, international law, and the Japanese Red Cross. But they differed on China policy. Konoe was thinking regionally, bilaterally, even idealistically in arguing for a "soft power" approach, making cultural ties the foundation of commercial and political partnership. He envisioned the possibility of a future regional bloc, Japan-led and supported by modernizing forces in China, to counterbalance Western interests in Asia. He was open to contacts with an array of potential future leaders in China, from young Manchu imperials to senior Chinese governors to the reformist coup leader Kang Youwei.

Ariga, committed Europeanist, cautioned against anything that looked like unilateral intervention in China. When Kang fled to Japan in November 1898 with a price on his head, Ariga agreed that granting him political asylum was warranted under international law. But taking sides in China's factional disputes, in his reading of the law, was not. Nor was it politically wise. Kang had terribly misjudged the strength of the forces arrayed against him; he hardly looked deserving of Japan's backing. Ariga warned those dealing with Kang's asylum status—and that included Konoe—that going overboard in support of the failed coup leader ran the risk of alienating some of China's progressive governors, the very people then engaged in enacting local-level reforms on the Japanese model.[41]

The article on Kang was typical Ariga, practical and lawyer-like in its presentation of the facts of the case, the limits of the law, and the implications for Japan's national interests. Ariga's *Gaikō jihō* was Fauchille's *Revue* in a Japanese setting, "professional-technical and avowedly nationalist," to use Martti Koskenniemi's words.[42] With its December 1898 issue, 898 pages after launching, *Gaikō jihō* had secured a place in the Meiji publishing world and Ariga was hitting his stride as a public figure. Teaching at three institutions—Waseda, the Military Academy, and the Naval College—writing books, scrambling to meet monthly deadlines at the magazine, attending conferences at home and abroad, his life was nonstop work. He allowed himself a summer retreat to Shiobara where with a monetary award for service in the Sino-Japanese War he built a cottage, but this was simply intensive work in a different setting. Above all, *Gaikō jihō* was his baby, focus of his professional attention and on occasion a place to record the color of his life, his emotions on the battlefield, reactions to colleagues, feelings about family. It functioned as his diary.

Often in small print as the preface to articles, Ariga discussed the health of his aging parents to whom he was singularly devoted. They always accompanied him and his family to Shiobara. Enjoying their company was the one thing that drew him out of his study. Ariga was known among his colleagues for his genuinely caring attitude toward his parents. Filial piety was a virtue he urged Chinese youth not to abandon and a trait that softened Ariga's image as a brilliant but brusque academic.

Giving Peace a Try

On April 8, 1899, Ariga Nagao got government clearance to travel to Europe to attend The Hague Peace Conference. This was a plum assignment. Two years before, Ariga had represented Japan at the Red Cross meeting in Vienna, itself a prestigious gathering of European nations plus Japan to discuss improved treatment of the war-wounded and other aspects of humanitarian law. But the upcoming conference at The Hague in the Netherlands was a notch above, a conceptual breakthrough in international diplomacy that in fact set the stage for the League of Nations and the United Nations decades later.

It was truly international. Twenty-six nations, less than half the world's total but controlling three-fourths of the world's resources and population, were sending delegations of which five represented non-Western nations: China, Japan, Persia, Siam, and Turkey. The Hague spirit reflected a new determination to make international rules enforceable, to create permanent international instruments to resolve disputes or at least mitigate the effects of wars that were becoming demonstrably more global in reach, costly, and devastating in effect. There was even hope of progress on arms reduction, an issue never before tackled in an international forum. Finally, though the European powers in fact dominated the proceedings, what heartened the second-tier nations invited to attend was that each delegation was entitled to but a single vote on conference resolutions, a recognition of sorts of national equality for countries like Japan and China. No wonder that this first Hague Peace Conference, its efforts long forgotten now, roused public excitement at the time, both cynics ready to see it as a tool of the big powers and idealists, who heralded its coming as "the Parliament of Man, the Federation of the World."[43]

Ariga had little time to prepare for his trip but it was an assignment that he was unlikely to turn down. On April 14, six days after receiving his travel orders, Ariga and two fellow delegates boarded the *Empress of China* bound for Vancouver where they got a train the next day to New York City via Montreal, arriving on May 2. There was no lingering in New York either, only a night's rest at the Waldorf Astoria where Ariga unexpectedly ran into Prince Konoe whom he had seen off at Yokohama just a month before. Quite coincidentally both men had booked passage the next day on the White Star Line's *Majestic* sailing from New York to Liverpool. Konoe, after a taxing two weeks in the United States, looked forward to a full month in England. Ariga immediately pressed on to Paris where he spent a day or two in consultations with Japan's minister to Brussels, the second ranking member of the Japanese delegation. He reached The Hague at last on May 15, just three days before the conference opened.[44]

Ariga arrived exhausted but grateful that his health had held up. He was exhilarated by the atmosphere, the flags of attending nations fluttering from lampposts, the comings and goings of the one hundred delegates who had commandeered some of The Hague's finest hotels, the reunions with old friends from Paris. The conference site was the Huis ten Bosch, the House in the Woods, former summer residence of the royal family. It was located about a mile from the city in a spacious park at its best now in springtime with its tall trees in new green and the air filled with the aroma of lilacs. Sessions were held in the ballroom, the Oranje Zaal, a majestic hall with fifty-foot ceilings and walls hung with paintings of the finest Dutch masters, including one depicting the Peace of Westphalia, a portent, it was hoped, of conference success.

Here at The Hague, in surroundings evocative of European culture and power, Japanese delegates shared the conference table with notables from Europe and America. In their place among the "Hundred Chosen" as the delegates were labeled, the Japanese played an active role. Not so, the Chinese. In the words of one contemporary observer, the Chinese delegates "regarded [China's] presence as more or less complimentary." Japan's representatives were in fact cosmopolitan by background. And unlike the Chinese delegates in their mandarin attire, they looked the part as they sat for an official photograph in one of the gardens, all impeccably dressed in Western suits, cravats and ties, the two wives present stylishly got up in Victorian gowns and fancy hats. Behind Baron Hayashi, Japan's handsome, distinguished First Delegate seated with top hat in hand, stands Ariga Nagao, a man of medium height, pudgy face with glasses, thick curly hair now growing gray.[45]

By the time the conference was over in late July, two months after it started, daylight stretched until nine at night, and Ariga was feeling enervated by the humidity and especially grateful for the occasional Japanese meal at the Japanese consulate. He immediately left for Paris where he spent a few weeks compiling a report on the Japanese Red Cross to be submitted to the organizers of the next year's world exposition to be held in Paris. Then he was faced once again with the long voyage home from Le Harve to New York, across Canada by train, over the Pacific to Japan, where he arrived on September 26. Back in his office at *Gaikō jihō*, Ariga pondered what kind of report he should write for the magazine. He could not publish a detailed insider's account without the permission of Japanese authorities, which was not forthcoming. On the other hand, as a conference delegate and editor of Japan's only foreign policy journal, he was now besieged with questions about a meeting the Japanese press in its meager coverage portrayed as a general disappointment. Ariga's answer was an article carefully drawn from information already made public in Europe entitled, "The Hague Peace Conference: One Success and One Failure."[46]

Ariga Nagao (back row, far right) with fellow delegates at the Hague Peace Conference, 1899. (Courtesy of the United Nations Office at Geneva [UNOG] Archives)

Ariga acknowledged up front the failure of the conference on the critical issue of armaments. However, he argued quite correctly that before the meeting convened its Russian sponsors had tried to ratchet down expectations from disarmament to the more modest goal of an agreed moratorium on arms expansion. But even proposals along the latter lines—to maintain troop force and military budgets at current levels—failed to get a consensus, not surprisingly, Ariga added, given the extreme complexity of arriving at a fair-minded formula reflecting various national interests and strengths. Besides, he sensed an underlying distrust of Russia's role as honest broker on the issue arising from its own blatantly expansionary aims in Asia. Ariga translated for readers the disappointing outcome of the much-anticipated Hague arms talks, a simple agreement-in-principle that cutbacks in military expenditures were "extremely desirable" for the welfare of mankind.

But failure on arms control, Ariga contended, by no means rendered the entire conference a useless exercise as some observers were suggesting. Quite to the contrary, Ariga cited the two-month-long meeting as an unprecedented success in getting international agreement on other measures to make warfare less likely and less lethal. The three weapons bans passed by the conference—on launching explosives from hot air balloons, the use of projectiles carrying asphyxiating gases, and the use of exploding or "dumdum" bullets—were hardly on the scale of arms reduction, but a step forward nonetheless in a world in which nations rarely addressed such issues at all. (Ariga duly noted that the United States had reservations on all three, opposing outright the prohibitions on poison gas and dumdum bullets.)

But what excited Ariga as a landmark event, signaling "tremendous progress in the history of international law," were the three conventions passed by the Hague conference. Two of these extended and codified previous laws and customs of land and sea warfare, the other established a Permanent Court of Arbitration, an institution that still, in 2012, operates out of The Hague to adjudicate dispute cases voluntarily submitted by member states. In 1899, for the first time ever, Ariga informed readers, procedures for mediation, adjudication, and arbitration, hitherto ill-defined and variably applied, had been clarified and codified into universally recognized law. Under these new agreed rules, two nations on the brink of war had an obligation to attempt a peaceful resolution. Should talks break down, third countries had an obligation to intervene to try to reconcile the dispute.

This was exciting stuff for Ariga who was seeing real-life enactment of beliefs he shared with Paul Fauchille that international law, based on universal not exclusively Western experience and applied impartially, had the potential to maximize peaceful resolution of disputes between states. Ariga agreed that when all else failed a nation like Japan, constitutionally bound to act on behalf of the people at large, might legitimately resort to war to protect its vital interests. But as the twentieth century unfolded, he wrote in "Wars from Now On," an article adapted from one of his Military Academy lectures, "might makes right" was no longer an accepted operating principle among advanced nations. The notion of the just war had taken hold. There were limits to the use of force. On the principle that wars were between states not peoples, internationally agreed upon laws required humane treatment of civilian populations along with wounded and captured enemy combatants.[47]

The fine sentiments and high hopes of the Hague Peace Conference were immediately put to the test in conflicts brewing in the North China-Manchuria region. As Ariga back in Tokyo resumed teaching his courses on military ethics and diplomacy in the spring of 1900, Japanese residents in Beijing, Hattori Unokichi among them (Chapter II), began writing home about the Boxers whose terrorist tactics were worlds apart from notions of rules-based wars discussed at The Hague. Ariga was willing to acknowledge that this anti-Christian, anti-foreign insurgency, backed by some factions within the Chinese government, was not an entirely irrational reaction to foreign concession grabbing since the Opium War. But there was no question in his mind about how the international community must respond. Boxer violence and terrorism violated all international norms and must be stopped through the use of force. Japan was right in his view to join the international military effort now being organized to march on Beijing, even at the proportionally higher troop levels the Europeans were proposing. Logistically this made sense, though like Hattori, Ariga did not miss the irony that non-Christian Japan was being asked to contribute in a big way to put down a movement whose primary target was Christian missionaries.

This was a critical moment for Japan, Ariga told his *Gaikō jihō* readers. "At this juncture, given our geographical position and historical ties to China, we have no choice but to leap beyond the comfortable brand of diplomacy we've been practicing and plunge into the stormy seas of world diplomacy." Yet, he conveyed deep reservations about the ability of Japan's policymakers to manage the transition to big-league diplomacy. They must make it clear to the Western powers, he warned, that Japan's participation would come at a price, at the very least an assurance that there would be no separate deal-making with the Chinese government once the Boxers were brought under control.[48]

Ariga's metaphor was on the mark: navigating the currents of international diplomacy in the aftermath of the "summer's madness" of 1900 was no easy task. Most historians since then have focused their attention on the event as a local phenomenon, trying to explain the origins of Boxer terrorism, the perplexing behavior of the Qing government, and the enduring use of the Boxers as symbol and myth in subsequent periods of heightened Chinese nationalism. But in fact the Boxer uprising had critical repercussions internationally as well. It revealed some ugly truths about the Qing government, that it was bitterly divided politically, that it harbored deeply anti-foreign elements, that it was capable of reckless behavior, all signs of a fatal instability that worried nations with economic interests in China. Even more fundamentally, at the level of popular perception, the Boxer frenzy of violence and atrocity fueled negative images of the Chinese people as a whole, not only in Tokyo but in Western capitals as well. Hattori's account of the siege of the legations was matched by those of Lancelot Giles, Ernest Morrison, and W.A.P. Martin. Distrust of the Chinese, distrust of each other marked the mood of the international community as the new century opened.

Once the Boxers were defeated, the big problem for most of the allies was how to restrain Russia. Russia had sent troops to Manchuria at the start of the uprising to protect Russian-held rail lines from Boxer attack. Now at the end of the conflict in the fall of 1900 about 100,000 men remained stationed in Manchuria, a virtual occupying force with no timetable for departure. It was to counter this evident challenge to their own interests in the north China/Korea region that Britain and Japan soon opened talks leading to the signing of a mutual security pact in 1902. In Japan, the issue was not only diplomatic but emotional. Humiliation over the "loss" of Liaodong in 1895 was deeply felt. Russia's claims to control not only this territory but the rest of Manchuria provoked strong public anger.

Before the year was out, an intensely worried Konoe Atsumaro had organized a group of prominent public figures to urge the cabinet to press Russia hard on the issue of troop withdrawal.[49] Joining the effort were a number of Ariga's fellow law professors, at least three of them writers for *Gaikō jihō*, who gained quick notoriety by confronting top leaders personally with arguments for taking military action, a dramatic gesture that appealed to Japan's generally pro-war public. Ariga was as ready as his colleagues to level criticism at Japan's foreign policymakers for diplomatic missteps, lack of transparency and generally making a mess of things, but he parted company with them when it came to timing on the use of force.[50] Fresh back from the Hague Peace Conference, Ariga was thinking arbitration, negotiation, conflict resolution, not an immediate resort to war. Even in the late stages of the Russo-Japanese negotiations at the end of 1903, Ariga continued to see hope for a diplomatic solution. He called for the appointment of a high-ranking special envoy to lead a new initiative to internationalize the Manchuria issue, to press Western nations with interests in Manchuria—Britain, France, Germany, the US—to take collective action to end the Russian incursion and preserve equal access to Manchurian resources. In a final push for compromise, some in the Tokyo government floated a reciprocal-interests-track proposal—recognizing Russia's paramount position in Manchuria in exchange for Japan's in Korea. Ariga was skeptical but not, like Konoe and what were known as the "seven pro-war doctors," unalterably opposed.[51]

A strong believer in academic freedom, Ariga defended fully his colleagues' right to mount a public campaign against the government's post-Boxer Russia policy. At the same time, he made clear his own professional commitment to the ideal of problem-solving through international mechanisms like the Hague Conference which, in fact, was the product of a Russian initiative. So it was that as Ariga's colleagues heated up their "war now" rhetoric after 1901, he began making preparations to attend the Seventh ICRC Conference in St. Petersburg where he was scheduled to present a report on the performance of Japanese Red Cross personnel during the Boxer conflict. In May 1902, just two years after his trip to The Hague, he was on a ship bound for the Suez Canal and Marseilles, this time feeling a sad weariness at being so far from home. Two weeks in Paris revived him. He liked the Japanese minister to France, his kind of diplomat, thoroughly knowledgeable about European affairs and with a wife and children who spoke both French and Italian. He was welcomed by his old friends Barclay and Fauchille who were ready to assist him with the French publication of his Red Cross report. Barclay arranged for Ariga to stay in a small family hotel near his law office.

The Russia trip was a personal setback. Ariga had always prided himself on fitting in, on being respected and accepted by his European colleagues. At the Red Cross gathering in St. Petersburg he hoped to build on his contact with Russian delegate Fedor Fedorovich Martens, conference host and someone he had gotten to know at the recent Hague meetings. Ariga expected the camaraderie from The Hague to continue and to be greeted as a fellow scholar and delegate. On his own home turf, however, Martens made it clear that he was not just any international lawyer but a top government official far outranking a lowly representative from Japanese academia. Ariga was deeply offended. He made no attempt to paper over his anger, publicly denouncing Martens in the pages of *Gaikō jihō* as an arrogant fraud, repeating the rumor circulating among Red Cross delegates that Martens' reputation in international law was based on the mere fluke that he happened to share the same surname of the great French legal scholar, Georg Friedrich Martens. No doubt Ariga's account played well with an increasingly anti-Russian Japanese public.

The Martens snub did not dampen Ariga's interest in Russia. On the long journey back to Japan over the Trans-Siberian railway, he got to know a Russian traveler and his wife also bound for Tokyo. Once home, Ariga took the Russian visitor under his wing, finding him a teaching job and hosting him for the summer at Shiobara though he could scarcely afford the expense of the extra lodgings. Ariga and two of his children then spent the summer studying Russian.[52]

A Necessary War?

Konoe was only a month in the grave when Japan broke off diplomatic relations with Russia on February 6, 1904, and two days later delivered a surprise attack on the Russian navy at Port Arthur. Within days war was formally declared by both sides, and Japan led off with a series of early victories on land and sea in Manchuria and Korea. By summer, Ariga was contacted by the army's legal service to play the same monitoring role he had during the Sino-Japanese War. He was reluctant to go. His father at eighty-seven and mother aged seventy-seven objected to having their eldest son once again in the line of fire in a war that was producing high casualties. He on his part was in his mid-forties, well occupied with teaching, publishing, and research. But an order was an order and, with his younger brother interceding with the parents, he was off to Hiroshima in August to join the army transport vessel bound for the South Manchurian coast. As he rode the troop train south, he began to take heart from the crowds of patriotic well-wishers lining the tracks along the way:

> How stirring—the chorus of hurrahs from the villagers
> Cheering on the Imperial Army with all their hearts!
> Even I, not a military man, think to myself,
> I won't return home without accomplishing something.[53]

Ariga was deeply moved by the display of wholehearted popular support for the war with Russia. But he was also well aware that he had a tougher assignment ahead of him than ten years before when he deployed with the army to fight the Chinese on the same Manchurian terrain. The 1894 war, equally popular with the public, was short and mostly glorious, a string of victories by Japanese land and sea forces against a poorly trained, outgunned Chinese military. Russia, in stark contrast, was a major Western power with a modern military machine. War against the Russians was a horror on a much larger scale with new, gigantic artillery, deadly mines, and precision torpedoes wreaking enormous casualties on both sides, a rehearsal, as it turned out, for the massive bloodletting of World War I. Japanese casualties in the eight-month long Sino-Japanese War were around 13,000 in total. When Ariga got to the front in August 1904, six months into the war with Russia, the Japanese casualty figure was nearly that number already. The siege of Port Arthur, begun that month, was to add 60,000 more.

It was a point of pride with Ariga that the Japanese military employed legal experts, one per field army, in the first place. The Russians did not. His immediate task as he defined it—and he apparently had the discretion to do so—was to assess from battlefield observations whether the two sides were adhering to current international rules on warfare. Both Russia and Japan were signatories to the recent Hague conventions which set limits on killing methods, prohibited the targeting of civilians, and required humane treatment of POWs. Ariga felt certain that the Japanese, at least, would wage a "civilized war," so thoroughly had officers and men been briefed on the Hague requirements. Beyond specific monitoring functions, Ariga hoped that the unique circumstances of this particular war might point the way to new, universal applications of international law, new thinking on rules of engagement.[54]

Ariga was with the army as an embedded legal expert, so to speak, for seventeen months, from August 1904 to December 1905. A photograph taken at the front in the last month of his assignment shows him in the company of three other, apparently junior officers. Only Ariga truly looks the military part as he sits with one hand resting on a small table, the other lightly touching the unbuckled sword at his side, medals prominently on display, calf-length leather boots well worn. His face, now bearded, has taken on a rugged look as if the rigors of camp life have taken a toll. His gaze away from the camera makes him appear particularly somber, detached. This was a long way from the Hague Peace Conference.[55]

Ariga Nagao with army officers at the front, Russo-Japanese War, 1904. (*Gaikō jihō* 7:85 (November 1904))

Ariga had served in the Sino-Japanese War, but the present conflict, he told *Gaikō jihō* readers, was of a different order of magnitude. A major offensive to take the southern tip of Manchuria began within a week of Ariga's arrival at the front in mid-August, masses of Japanese and Russians, an estimated 200,000 in total, moving against each other like two giant killing machines. He described huge artillery guns that shook the ground with earthquake force and shattered the night sky with the brightness of daylight. The Japanese death toll on a single day of fighting was more than 10,000, Ariga was told by an army doctor. Many wounded soldiers were left to die in trenches, impossible to retrieve. When people urged him to move back from the front lines, however, he declined. "For a scholar of international law, advancing with the front line is an extraordinary privilege. It's unprecedented among nations to have a war on this scale. From the beginning of my career I've wanted to sacrifice myself for the sake of learning and teaching. If I were to fall back to the rear wouldn't it invite criticism that in the conflict between Japan and Russia the study of international law was the first to retreat?"[56] Most people writing about wars did so from the comfort of their desks, he added, but would probably wish for the same opportunity to experience the realities of the battlefield.

Japanese soldiers awaiting attack from Russian cavalry, Manchuria, Russo-Japanese War. (Courtesy of the Library of Congress)

Appalled as Ariga was by the brutality around him, he nevertheless portrayed the conflict as a necessary war in his first dispatch from the front. He had heard all the arguments for abolishing war when he attended the Hague Peace Conference, he explained to readers. But even after witnessing the horrifying spectacle of the late August offensive, he felt that in the case of a country like Russia whose continued aggression showed a total disregard for international norms, resorting to war was the only way to safeguard peace. Just as England and France had stepped in during the Crimean War to check the Russian threat to Europe, so Japan now must do its part to stop Russia's advance into North Asia. Japan was not acting solely in its own interests, Ariga argued, but in the interests of the international community as a whole.[57] In fact, the international community agreed. Japan had the tide of world opinion in its favor on the *jus ad bello* issue. Far from condemning Japan for its surprise attack on Port Arthur, most foreign press reports pointed out that had Russia not been delayed in deploying troops it would have attacked Japan first.[58]

When he revisited the Liaoyang battle site in July 1905, Ariga was in a darker mood. He had requested permission to go rabbit hunting, a diversion meant to relieve his gloom, but it only increased as he wandered the hills, passing abandoned forts, finding skeletal remains of bodies unclaimed in the fierce firefights, stopping to read the grave markers of those properly buried, a generic "died in battle defending Lushun on behalf of his country and emperor." Gone for the moment were legal justifications for going to war, distinctions between Japanese and Russian policy. Weighing heavily on Ariga instead were images of the huge human cost, not just to *our* young men but to *their* young men as well. "What a pity. The Russians also know about loyalty to sovereign and love of country; our soldiers don't have a complete monopoly on devotion and a sense of public duty." How to extract meaning from the deaths of honorable individuals sent to do battle over the competing moral claims of nations was the gripping question for Ariga as he gazed out at the bleak landscape of tombstones. "Is it perhaps that war is the way to convince people to strive for permanent peace?"[59]

There was no repeat of the 1894 Port Arthur atrocity in this "well-watched war," as it has been aptly called. Foreign journalists covering the fighting praised Japan for its civilized behavior, agreeing with Japanese artists who showed their soldiers treating Russian wounded with unusual compassion. Beyond individual instances of humanity, the press reported favorably on the Japanese Red Cross for its well-organized, evenhanded care: "The Japanese was carried along on a stretcher close to the Siberian infantryman, the one shot through the leg, the other in the side." Japan's more than 2,000 Red Cross nurses drew special Western notice even as they were celebrated in woodblock prints in Japan. Ariga described Japan's medical services as "among the best in the world," citing a British Royal Army source for confirmation. Building on its experience first during the 1894-1895 War, then in the Boxer Uprising, Ariga wrote, the Red Cross by 1904 was noted for its well-trained personnel and efficiently-managed ambulance and hospital resources. He calculated that by war's end Japan had treated a total of 662,523 sick and wounded combatants, about 20 percent of them Russians.[60]

The human cost of the war Ariga witnessed firsthand weighed heavily on his mind: remains of Russian troops killed near Port Arthur, 1905. (Courtesy of the Library of Congress)

Ariga's battlefield experiences had a searing impact on his memory, but his day-to-day routine over his seventeenth-month assignment as army legal adviser was usually less harrowing. Based at army headquarters in Lushun he monitored POW treatment, prisoner exchanges, and the organization of military tribunals while providing guidance on the larger question of how Chinese Manchuria was to be administered by the Japanese occupying force. On the purely *jus in bello* issues Ariga used the Geneva Conventions as a constant reference point. By contrast, he explained, how to administer occupied Manchuria represented something new in international law. Since China had declared itself neutral in the Russo-Japanese conflict, Manchuria was not enemy territory but neutral territory. There was no legal playbook to guide Japanese military authorities in structuring relationships with local Chinese inhabitants and officials so critical to security, troop maintenance, and military operations. Especially troublesome was how to deal with locals who chose to aid and abet the enemy. Regulations were crafted to meet every new contingency, some reflecting Ariga's opinions, others the competing judgments of fellow legal advisers.[61]

Ariga (front row, first on left) and Baron Ōzawa, vice-president of the Japanese Red Cross Society (third from left) with their Russian counterparts, Port Arthur, 1905. (Ariga Nagao, *La Guerre Russo-Japonaise*; Paris: A. Pedone, 1908)

As a natural corollary to these activities, Ariga drafted a book on postwar planning for Manchuria with the provocative title, *Discussion of a Mandate for Manchuria* (Manshū inin tōchi ron). The book was published by Waseda University Press on March 18, 1905. At the time of writing, presumably late February-early March, Japan was enjoying a series of battle successes. Very likely at this juncture, with victory seemingly in the offing, someone in the high command requested Ariga to provide his legal assessment of Japan's postwar options.[62] Ariga is not clear about this though certainly he was independent minded enough to have taken up the topic on his own initiative. In either case the discussion was premature. There were still major land battles to be fought. The Russian fleet was not destroyed until the end of May. Only in June was President Roosevelt's offer of mediation accepted by Japan and Russia, beginning a summer of negotiations over peace terms.

Mandate for Manchuria is predicated on the "if not now when" argument, namely, that Japan must strike a bargaining position immediately while the facts on the ground were in its favor. Among the reading audience in Japan, the book drew praise for being on the mark, criticism for being too academic to influence policymakers (to which Ariga, characteristically, replied that he *was* an academic and he would say what he liked). But his prescription for postwar Manchuria could not fail to carry weight at home in the official deliberations and public debate over how to frame the peace terms. Not only was Ariga one of Japan's leading international law experts and editor of a major publication but his was the rare, authentic voice of someone serving with the army in the field.

Ariga was also unique among political commentators in offering a total scenario for postwar Manchuria that took into account international law, the interests of the powers, Chinese politics, and Japan's capacity to govern. Most other contributors to the debate then raging in Tokyo focused more narrowly on what demands to make of Russia in the event of victory. This was a tactical question for the government, which knew the limitations of Japan's military staying power, and an emotional matter for the general public, less informed, driven by the desire to extract a high price for its sacrifice and suffering. Ariga had doubts about war as an instrument of dispute resolution. He had favored a diplomatic solution until the eleventh hour and despaired over the battlefield slaughter he witnessed firsthand. Yet he shared the view of the overwhelming majority of his countrymen that this war was a necessary war. He believed that justice was on Japan's side in the fight to end Russian occupation of Chinese sovereign territory, a threat to China, Japan, and the other powers as well. And he was quick to point out that only Japan bore the cost in this conflict that benefited others, a financial and human toll of enormous proportions.[63]

In making his case for postwar Manchuria, Ariga introduced a theme raised also by Chinese political opposition groups at the time and heard repeatedly in the decades after: that China's failures of governance were as much to blame for the mess in Manchuria as Russian aggression. Ariga's characterization of Manchuria prefigures the "contested borderland" image described in the recent scholarship of Prasenjit Duara and others. It was a region in transition, no longer an exclusive Manchu preserve, not yet part of a Chinese nation, whose uncertain frontier status was a magnet for the competing interests of outside powers. As Ariga put it, apart from a few Manchu imperial princes with little clout, no one in the Chinese leadership was working on Manchuria's behalf. China's Han Chinese leaders, their roots in the south, were indifferent to development of this northern frontier region. Not only that, they had shown a willingness to bargain away rights in Manchuria to the Russians both before and after the Boxer Uprising. Indeed, Ariga's point is reminiscent of a line from the League of Nations report on Manchuria in 1931, "China, at first, showed little activity in the field of development in Manchuria. She almost allowed Manchuria to pass from her control to that of Russia . . ."[64] But what could be stated blandly in 1931 was a hot issue for Ariga writing in wartime 1905. As he saw it, China's failure to develop and defend Manchuria had propelled

Japan on a course toward war and military occupation. The question now, with occupation a reality, was what sort of settlement should Japan aim for once peace talks began?

Troop withdrawal from the whole of Manchuria was not an option for Ariga or any other Japanese citizen. The blood and treasure spent on the war required some form of compensation, as a bottom line transfer to Japan of the Russian-held lease and railway concessions that would require a residual force to protect. Ariga's proposal for "at least a partial mandate" over Manchuria implied this and more. He reflected the concern of most Japanese about maintaining security in a region still under Russian threat and poorly governed by China. Preventing renewed instability, in his view, required a continued Japanese presence, growing out of what had obtained of necessity during wartime, sanctioned by international law.

In an era of European protectorates, trusts, and mandates, all neatly conditioned to justify extension of state sovereignty to overseas territories, appropriate models were not hard to find. Ariga based his mandate argument on two existing cases of territories long held in trust by outside powers, British-controlled Cyprus and Bosnia-Herzegovina administered by Austria-Hungary. The analogy was a compelling one. Pre-trusteeship Cyprus and Bosnia were, like Manchuria, strategically important areas weakly governed by a weakening empire, in this case Ottoman Turkey. Assumption of administrative control by Britain and Austria-Hungary in the late 1870s with the goal of Russian containment was sanctioned by Turkey, which retained nominal sovereignty, and by the rest of the European powers, who saw it as justifying rather than impeding their own colonial ambitions.

To Ariga, Cyprus-Bosnia seemed the perfect model for Manchuria. While still formally part of China, Manchuria would be given over to Japan to run in exchange for protection against Russia. Treaty arrangements would be spelled out with full transparency, which Ariga saw as a marked improvement over the recent secret deal-making between the Russians and the Chinese. All the powers would benefit from consistent application of the open door policy, again a plus. However, the Cyprus-Bosnia model failed Ariga on the key issue of rights transfer. He conceded that he could find no precedent at all in international law that would require a defeated Russia to turn over to Japan rights previously acquired by agreement with China, a declared neutral party to the conflict. He could only say that facts on the ground—Japan as occupying force in Manchuria—entitled Japan to push for rights transfer in the expectation that Russia would sooner or later agree.

Viewed in retrospect, citing Cyprus-Bosnia precedents might seem nothing more than clever argument on Ariga's part, dressing up a Japanese power grab in the fashionable cloak of legality. Indeed, there were enough examples of asymmetrical power at work in Ariga's world—mostly European acquisitions in Africa and Asia—to make references to international law seem altogether a bit of cynical manipulation. As Martti Koskenniemi has said about the Cyprus-Bosnia deals, "It was striking how the European States continued to pay lip service to the inviolability of the Ottoman Empire while constantly occupying and bargaining among themselves over large chunks of it."[65] The same might be said about the Chinese empire.

However, focusing on this truth alone would overlook the real debate going on among legal experts such as Ariga and his French colleagues about the application of the rule of law and humanitarian ideals to international relations. How to develop a rules-based system to govern relations among nation-states, how to minimize conflict, how to fight the just war should arbitration fail, how to incorporate less developed parts of the world into an international system, were all part of an ongoing discussion about sovereignty, power, human diversity, and humanitarianism. International law and internationalism were not static but dynamic and evolving. To be sure, consensus on issues was elusive and governments tended to talk justice and use force. It was difficult enough at the Hague Peace Conference to get agreement on banned weapons much less on the big issue of disarmament. Yet the very fact that such a conference was held—along with the series of Red Cross conferences—attests to a broad public concern about mitigating the lethality of war and somehow rationalizing inter-state relations. The fact that conference organizers invited five non-Western nations, including Japan and China, reflects a growing awareness that world order to some extent depended on the world beyond Europe, Russia, and America.

Ariga was originally drawn to international law as science, a universally applicable set of tools intended to allow pursuit of national goals while curbing the excesses of nation-state power in an increasingly complex and competitive world. No one knew better than he, participant at the Hague Conference, the limitations of the system when it came to conceding sovereignty in the interests of the collective good. Clearly it was easier to get agreement on how to fight wars than how to prevent them. Clearly the dominant powers continued to dominate. Yet, imperfect as it was, this evolving set of rules was the best, indeed the only, system the human imagination had to offer at the time to try to promote stability on a global scale. Like other Western organizational patterns it appealed to Japanese such as Ariga because it was rational, workable and not culturally exclusive. Japan could learn and join and benefit in the same way as, for example, nations today ready to sign on to current trade rules have gained entry to the WTO and the advantages of collective bargaining globally.

In his proposal for Manchuria Ariga took an independent stance. He rejected the views of Japan's civilizing mission proponents and colonial expansionists alike, arguing that imposing cultural norms in the one case and expropriating land in the other would do nothing more than trigger local opposition on a scale that would invite a second Russian intervention. Ariga was as strong a supporter of expanding Japan's influence in Manchuria as anyone. He simply believed that this could be achieved more effectively if Japan's leaders thought long term and provided the local population with what China had failed to provide: efficient administration and improved services in such areas as agriculture, health, and education. He noted by way of example that almost every young person he encountered in Manchuria bore the marks of smallpox, sad testimony to the low level of health care. Bringing tangible benefits to the population in the form of clinics and vaccination programs would, with time and patience, he argued, translate naturally into increased popular support for a Japanese presence in the region.[66]

The China Factor

The treaty ending the Russo-Japanese War, signed in Portsmouth, New Hampshire on September 5, 1905, got Japan only a scaled down version of Ariga's "partial mandate," namely, the transfer to Japan of Russia's lease over southern Manchuria and rights to a swath of territory along the Chinese Eastern Railway (quickly renamed the South Manchurian Railway) running from Changchun to Port Arthur. On this score the Japanese public was satisfied. What drew protest demonstrations of unprecedented size—30,000 turned out at Hibiya Park—was the government's failure to press for war reparations. As Ariga saw it from the field, however, seeking an indemnity was unrealistic from the start. The Russian military was down but not out. Massive reinforcements were on their way to the front. And it was questionable whether Japan could match this force and avoid a pushback. Ariga faulted the government in Tokyo for keeping the public in the dark about Japan's problematic negotiating position, not preparing people for likely disappointment on the issue of recovering war costs.[67]

Ariga remained in Manchuria throughout the fall of 1905, his services needed to translate official peace into arrangements between the two armies in the field. On September 13 a small contingent of Japanese and Russian officers, Ariga among them, set up camp tables along a rutted dirt road outside Chahotse Village to work out terms of a cease fire. A month later he was photographed in a more formal setting at a conference table somewhere in the city of Sipingjie (eastern Jilin Province) where his team of five and their Russian counterparts signed an agreement on evacuation of troops.[68] It was not until late December that Ariga arrived back in Japan after nearly seventeen months in military uniform. He was glad to be released from his commission, glad to find his aging parents—his father now eight-eight—in good health, to greet a new grandchild, and to see his second daughter happily married.

Ariga Nagao (center with arm behind his back) engaged in armistice talks with the Russians in the field, September 13, 1905. (Ariga Nagao, *La Guerre Russo-Japonaise*; Paris: A. Pedone, 1908)

It had been Ariga's intention from the start of his wartime assignment to write an account of the Russo-Japanese War from a legal perspective. No doubt he realized at war's end that this would be a bigger task than writing up the Sino-Japanese War. The conflict with Russia was of longer duration and the legal issues more complex. Not only would any account need to consider the new conduct of war conventions coming out of the 1899 Hague Peace Conference, it also must address a legal gray area: treatment of locals in neutral Manchuria. Ariga was well aware, too, that the world was sitting in judgment on Japan. "To put it succinctly, the extent to which Japan observed the rules of civilized warfare in this great world war at the start of the twentieth century is not exclusively an internal Japanese question but a world question, and relevant evidence ought to be shared with the world rather than being made available only in Japan."[69]

In May 1906 Ariga was given a contract by the General Staff to tackle this "world question." His scope of work was broad, requiring months of effort to research the full record of the war in the military archives and to corroborate his professional judgments with those of fellow legal advisers, some of whom had already published wartime accounts. It was not until March of the following year that Ariga completed his book on the Russo-Japanese War *La guerre Russo-Japonaise au point de vue continental et le droit international d'après les documents officiels du Grand Ètat-major Japonais*, a nearly 600-page assessment documenting Japan's compliance with the Geneva Conventions and other international norms in its conduct of the war. This was the proof, if proof were needed, that the Japanese had, as the world already believed, fought fair in this horrific conflict. In June Ariga traveled to Europe, first to present a paper, "The Japanese Red Cross and the Russo-Japanese War," at the eighth International Red Cross conference in London, then on to Paris where he spent the next six months laboriously translating his book into French with the help of Paul Fauchille. As he had in the case of Ariga's volume on the Sino-Japanese War, Fauchille supplied a preface and the book was issued by A. Pedone Press in 1908.[70]

A well-respected figure in international circles with yet another major publication to his credit—one that would win him a special award from the emperor a few years later—forty-six- year-old Ariga's career would seem to have been flying high. Yet there was increasing competition in the changed post-Russo-Japanese War world. Ariga *was* a delegate to the ICRC meeting in London, but there were other higher-ranking Japanese present, including General Ōyama Iwao, who stole the show, something Ariga acknowledged as only natural given the importance of the Anglo-Japanese Alliance, renewed in August 1905. Far more disappointing was the fact that Tokyo had not selected him to attend the second Hague Peace Conference, in session from June to October 1907 at the very time he was living in Paris, a six-hour train ride away. As he pointedly remarked, the conference agenda was dedicated to the very issue at the heart of his long career in foreign relations, building international mechanisms to reduce the likelihood or, at a minimum, the brutality of war.[71]

Another professional uncertainty that Ariga faced on his return to Japan after the war was whether to continue publication of *Gaikō jihō* scheduled to put out its 100th issue in March 1906. The magazine no longer owned the foreign affairs space. The demand for war news had driven the Japanese print media generally to step up foreign coverage, particularly of events in China, Manchuria, and Korea. Ariga wondered if there was a continued niche for a magazine which had been founded specifically to inform Japanese readers about the Euro-American side of the story. His staff came back with a resounding yes, that far from disbanding, the magazine ought to expand its original mission to include analysis of Japan's growing regional interests within the global context.[72]

Korea was the immediate issue. The American-brokered Portsmouth Treaty acknowledged Japan's paramount position in Korea but only in general terms. When Japan immediately strong-armed the recalcitrant Korean ruler into signing a more detailed "treaty of protection" with Japan there were cries of protest in the Korean press and criticism from Western capitals as well. Just back from a war to save north Asia from Russian aggression, Ariga reacted indignantly to what he saw as Western hypocrisy. For decades Western nations had been colonizing parts of Africa and Asia, intervening militarily as deemed necessary, all under the umbrella of international law. Why, he wondered, should Japan's mere threat of the use of force, a negotiating tactic to secure what had been granted in an internationally recognized treaty, be treated as a violation of the law? Korea's new status as a Japanese protectorate, still sovereign but relinquishing foreign policy decision making to Japan, got the tacit acceptance of the Powers in 1907 when the Hague Peace Conference refused to seat a separate Korean delegation.

Ariga could see a bright future for Korea as a protectorate, its institutions remaining intact, guided along to modernity by Japanese working within the existing structure. He was alarmed by intimations from Tokyo in 1910 that, like Taiwan, Korea would be made a Japanese colony. In a series of *Gaikō jihō* articles he urged Japan's leaders to consider the costs and benefits of alternative, less politically complex arrangements already put to the test in the European colonial experience. At the end of the day, however, he well recognized that the sovereignty of weak nations could be breached with impunity when it was in the interests of the international community to do so. The actions of the British in South Africa and the Americans in Cuba and Panama proved the point, he told readers. As long as Japan continued to allow equal trade access to Korea and showed some military restraint, the Western powers would raise no objection even to outright annexation.[73] He was correct.

To boost *Gaikō jihō*'s China coverage, Ariga brought in Chinese-language and area specialists like Aoyagi Atsutsune, his former student, now a political science professor at Waseda. For all Ariga's deep knowledge of Chinese art and classical Chinese, he in no way considered himself a China expert. He was the first to say that in late Meiji Japan that designation belonged to people like Aoyagi—and Kawashima Naniwa, he might have added—who were fluent in spoken Chinese.[74] Yet, at the same time, contemporary China and its problems increasingly intruded on Ariga's time and consciousness. When Chinese officials came to Japan to study

Meiji institutional models as they did in increasing numbers after 1905, Ariga Nagao was on the list of people to consult along with top educators Kanō Jigorō and Shimoda Utako.[75] Ariga's role was to supply lectures on the comparative workings of constitutional government in Japan and Europe, a critically important topic in the years between 1906 and 1908 when the Qing court was laying the foundations for a shift from imperial absolutism to some form of constitutional rule.

Ariga also encountered more Chinese in the classroom after the war. With Japan's victory—the first Asian nation to defeat a Western power—the number of Chinese students coming to Japan surged dramatically from around 3,000 in 1904 to an estimated 10,000 in 1906. Several hundred a year enrolled in Ariga's classes at Waseda and read his works in Chinese translation, eager to understand the secret behind Japan's demonstrated capacity to adapt, to innovate, and to move forward rapidly with resource development. Ariga's views on the subject probably disappointed some of them. New technology was all very well, he agreed, but he disapproved of "Fukuzawa-ism," his way of referring to Fukuzawa Yukichi's much-touted notion that joining the technologically advanced European world required a priori abandoning patterns of thought and human interaction identified with a uniquely Asian past. In Ariga's opinion, Japan had paid a price in rejecting the past to rush to the new, namely a degradation in family values and morality. Chinese students should think twice about what they hoped to learn from Japan. "Dear students, please learn only the latest in scholarship and technology from the Japanese. By no means emulate our public morals. On that score, what you have long-established in your own country is of excellent quality."[76]

What was excellent about China's past, in Ariga's view, was Confucianism. He spoke admiringly of Confucius as "a great artist" (*daibijutsuka*) who had directed his creative urge to constructing an ideal, peaceful society based on explicit norms to govern relations among men. A rational thought system with respect for authority at its core and collective welfare and stability as its goals, Confucianism had proven its worth as a cultural binding force for 2,000 years of China's history. Reason enough, Ariga insisted, that the present generation of Chinese should make Confucianism the starting point for the institutional transformation that China must make, as Japan had before it, to survive in a world dominated by Western powers. Rather than replacing tradition as they might be inclined to do, he told the young Chinese, they should transform it into a worthy modern *Chinese* alternative to Western beliefs, which focused exclusively on the primacy of individual interests and scientific analysis.

In stressing national particularity, Ariga cautioned visiting Chinese against wholesale adoption of either European models or their new Japanese versions.

What they should learn from Japan was method, namely, how Japanese leaders had managed the transition from old to new without tearing the country apart. He advised the Chinese to take note of two things: first, that Japan's imperial house, the very repository of tradition, had eased the way by giving full support to the Meiji reform effort, and, second, that the reforms themselves were a product of Japan's past and a global present, not a rejection of one in favor of the other. Chinese students, he argued, should continue to study the Chinese classics and value their message of family-based ethics.[77]

Ariga's words fell on receptive ears. Chinese students in Japan were anti-authority but not, as they were to become after 1915, anti-Confucius. Visiting Chinese officials, proud of the Chinese past, liked the message that the new should be built on a core of native ideals. Chinese imperial leaders agreed. When they announced their nine-year constitutional preparation program in 1908, it was the Japanese model constitution and slow phase-in process they selected, a tribute no doubt to the convincing arguments of Ariga and his fellow legal scholars.[78] On Ariga's part, briefing Chinese visitors added a new dimension to his résumé, which was otherwise geared to Europe and international concerns. He had long talked up the virtues of traditional Chinese family values—he was a living example of filial piety—but he now gave a nod to Japan's China hands in speaking of the importance of a Japanese-Chinese special relationship.

Yet Ariga's pro-Chinese sentiments had their limits. China's tough stance on railway negotiations clearly annoyed him.

> In the Russo-Japanese War, Japan put all its national resources into deploying a huge military force. In service on behalf of our countrymen 220,000 people were wounded, 236,000 suffered illness, and 80,000 died either on the battlefield or in hospital. The country was filled with parents who lost sons, wives who lost husbands. As if this were not enough, because of the expansion of foreign loans, taxes were increased putting a heavy burden on people. Today people throughout the entire country are still in a state of constant grief. And the reason they're in this situation was to drive Russia out of Manchuria. Because of this sacrifice by the people of Japan, China did not lose a single soldier and has been able to maintain sovereignty over Manchuria. All Japanese are deeply conscious of this. And so everyone expects that China ought to express its special gratitude to us in terms that go beyond the language in a treaty.[79]

When it came to trying to make sense of China's internal politics, Ariga left matters to Aoyagi and his contacts with old China hands like Kawashima Naniwa. Kawashima's intimate friendships with Manchus, Mongols, and Tibet's Dalai

Lama as well as his insider's view of the Chinese bureaucracy made him a popular person to consult at a time when China's central government appeared to be fracturing along ethnic lines. Kawashima was the featured guest at *Gaikō jihō's* monthly dinner meeting in May 1910. What sort of person was the Dalai Lama, Ariga and his staff wanted to know? "A great guy who was raised in the mountains," Kawashima replied, adding that this most revered religious figure had only recently been persuaded that he could do more for his country if he studied in Japan rather than staying in his landlocked country reading sutras. Relations between the Dalai Lama and Beijing were not good, Kawashima told his audience. "Tibet has always been a hotbed of opposition." Now that the Dalai Lama had fled to Mongolia, home of fellow Lamaists, one could expect further trouble for China's central government, itself an increasingly fragile coalition between Han and Manchu. When asked how the vastly outnumbered Manchus were still able to control the Han Chinese, Kawashima replied simply, "It's inertia (*jōryoku*)."[80]

The year 1911 was one of revolution in China and personal crisis for Ariga Nagao. Always inclined to overwork, suffering from chronic insomnia, Ariga was under particular pressure as the year began to meet deadlines on two major book projects in addition to carrying on with his usual teaching and editing jobs. In late March, with the April issue of *Gaikō jihō* off to the printer, Ariga and his wife decided to go to Kyoto for a short spring break. He was in a Kyoto bookstore browsing through rare books when he suddenly collapsed and was rushed unconscious to the city hospital. He had suffered a stroke, doctors concluded, although there were no impairments except for his fragile emotional state. Once stabilized, Ariga was sent to Hakone for rest and recovery. *Gaikō jihō* apologized to readers for his absence. Ariga, still a relatively young fifty, took his near-death experience more personally. Health worries began to loom large in his decisions about lifestyle and career.[81]

In October Han Chinese insurgents in south China finally struck a mortal blow to Manchu central authority, drawing Ariga back to his desk to editorialize on what Japan's response should be to the likely death of dynastic rule. International law, he declared, clearly favored non-intervention on this issue of regime change engineered through revolution. This is what national autonomy was all about, ". . . the right of the people of any nation to establish the form of government they believe will most adequately fulfill their own national development goals. This includes the right to overturn a longstanding government that is not acting in the national interest or to seek independence from it."[82]

Over the next months there occurred a dizzying succession of power plays in China, all, significantly, finding expression in various constitutional documents.

Even the Manchu leadership, the most absolute of imperial regimes, tried to write itself out of crisis by shifting from the Japanese to the more liberal British form of constitutional monarchy. But to no avail. By the time Ariga was in serious negotiations about his China assignment in the summer and fall of 1912, the Manchus had formally abdicated in favor of the new republic, the provincial assemblies formed after 1908 had elected a national legislature that endorsed a presidential system, and Yuan Shikai, lead negotiator with the defeated Manchus, had taken on the role of president of China both North and South. What was needed to hold this fragile political body together was a permanent constitution to replace the provisional one the national legislature issued in March.

Ariga was interested in being involved in the drafting process, but had other commitments. He was engaged in preparing a lecture series for Tokyo University on Japan's imperial system. Even on a reduced writing schedule for *Gaikō jihō*, he was responsible for much of the magazine's European coverage and was writing several articles on the deteriorating situation in the Balkans. Besides, for someone in precarious health the China job posed risks, not least undue stress in a time of political turmoil. Within weeks after Ariga's arrival in China March 1, 1913, a leading politician opposing Yuan's top-down modernization policies was assassinated. According to rumors, the assassins took their orders from Yuan himself.[83]

China Bound

Whatever misgivings he might have had initially, Ariga's reports from China during the first months of his appointment as legal adviser to President Yuan Shikai reflect a sense of renewal and excitement. Writing a constitution for a newly emerging republic as part of a panel of paid foreign advisers was an unprecedented event anywhere in the world. For Ariga, this involvement in what we would now call nation-building offered a chance to take his career in a new direction, to move from academic, analyst, publicist to the hands-on experience of designing a real-world political system to lasting effect. For someone so recently reminded of his own mortality the possibility of contributing at this level was a boost to the spirits. It was also personally gratifying to Ariga to be working on a fully collegial basis with a group of highly regarded Western experts, people like G. E. Morrison, celebrated correspondent for the London *Times*, Frank Goodnow of Columbia University, soon to become president of Johns Hopkins, and Georges Padoux, formerly adviser to the governments of Tunisia and Siam. Ariga particularly valued his association with Morrison whom he described as having, "a more thorough knowledge of Chinese realities than the Chinese." It was a point of pride with

Ariga that within the group of six or seven legal advisers only Morrison outranked him. Ironically, Morrison had recommended Ariga to Yuan with the argument that Ariga was as well-regarded in international legal circles as recently deceased Russian jurist, Fedor Martens, the same fellow who had so offended Ariga at the Red Cross Conference in St. Petersburg in 1902.[84]

Ariga had an advantage over his Western colleagues. He had a ready-made network of professional contacts among the Chinese. As Morrison remarked to a *Times* colleague about Ariga upon his arrival in March: "His appointment is interesting because a considerable proportion of the Chinese who will have seats in the Senate and in the House of Representatives, both of which meet in April, will be former students of Ariga's." President Yuan himself, in his first meeting with Ariga observed that among the ten most promising figures in the new Chinese Republic, seven or eight were Waseda graduates who had pressed for Ariga's appointment by citing the importance of Chinese-Japanese friendship. When some of these Japan-trained leaders invited Ariga to a dinner in his honor a few days after his arrival he felt compelled to attend despite doctor's orders to avoid evening engagements for health reasons. It was a warm welcome for this first-time visitor to Beijing whose previous overseas stays were in Paris, Berlin, The Hague, and St. Petersburg. Ariga's Chinese hosts conversed in Japanese with one exception, the European-trained head of the Legislative Bureau. Ariga spoke with him in German.[85]

Ariga had no trouble communicating in written and spoken English, French and German, which facilitated his occasional meetings with Morrison and other members of the foreign advisory group. Chinese was another matter. Like Hattori Unokichi, Ariga read classical Chinese texts with ease but neither spoke Chinese nor was familiar with the contemporary written language. For these tasks he was provided with an official interpreter, *Gaikō jihō* China expert and Waseda University colleague Aoyagi Atsutsune. Aoyagi was present at Ariga's initial meeting with President Yuan Shikai but to his surprise and dismay as an observer only. The job of interpreting had been commandeered by the young Japan-trained politicians surrounding Yuan "either to benefit their own positions or their factions." In fact, nothing more sensitive than Ariga's health and their common insomnia problems came up at this first courtesy call. But Aoyagi was alarmed about future exchanges on constitutional matters in which the choice of words would be all-important. He put Ariga on notice after the meeting that henceforth he intended to take on the interpreter's task himself, "for the sake of protecting the reputation of a Japanese scholar and maintaining transparency in the friendship between Japan and China."[86]

Yuan Shikai's management style was to deal with his foreign-hires separately and to use their advisory services sparingly, the better to keep decision making entirely in his own hands. Goodnow reportedly worked only four hours a week. Morrison complained loudly about not being consulted often enough, which he attributed to Chinese suspicions of foreign interference: "The Chinese appoint a foreigner and never trust him," he fumed. The feeling of being underutilized was pervasive. Ariga's colleague on the infrastructure-building side, Rensselaer Polytechnic-trained Dr. Hirai Seijirō, seconded to China from his post as head of Japan's Imperial Railway, also grumbled publicly about the slow pace of his advisory work. Ariga reacted differently. His health still shaky and fearing a second stroke, he welcomed this sudden break from his past frenetic life. He now had time to go cherry blossom viewing with his family, to pursue his hobby of collecting stone rubbings, and to mull over his draft translation of Fenollosa's book. His salary was substantial and the work low pressure, so how was this not a good deal, he asked Aoyagi.[87]

Slow and steady, Ariga nevertheless expected to accomplish great things. He had the backing of the president's office. He had been asked to work with a small task force made up of young Chinese, most Japan-trained, to review and revise the provisional constitution. President Yuan made a positive impression. Not a first tier leader but a highly competent politician, Ariga concluded, surely China's best hope at a time when north-south divisions and ethnic tensions on the border threatened to tear the country apart.[88] In his optimism about Yuan, Ariga echoed Morrison, dean of foreign advisers in China, who likewise pinned his hopes on Yuan's proven record as a reformer and administrator. For those many Japanese who had a negative image of Yuan, it was not his reformist credentials that were in question but his trustworthiness. Suspicion of Yuan's motives and intentions toward Japan was what fueled the anti-Yuan vehemence of people like Kawashima Naniwa.

When "friends in the President's office" asked Ariga to extend his initial five-month contract beyond July he gladly accepted. A September re-start date allowed him to take his elderly mother on their usual summer retreat to Shiobara. Waseda agreed to grant him a second leave of absence. Life seemed good. The last three months working over constitutional drafts with Chinese colleagues had been "my happiest time in Beijing," he reported to *Gaikō jihō* readers in the July 20, 1913, issue. "I did nothing else over the three month period from April through June but devote my complete energy to designing a republican form of government worthy of recognition as the very best for the future of the Republic of China." He professed surprise at the violence of the anti-Yuan insurgency in the south—the failure of which sent Sun Yatsen and associates fleeing to Japan—but saw his role as assisting Yuan, not taking sides in internal political battles. "I was hired as a scholar," Ariga told readers, "and I've made every effort to maintain a scholarly attitude."[89]

Ariga had spent his entire career as an independent voice. No matter what his role— professor, columnist, ex-officio diplomat, adviser to the military—he had reserved the right to appraise or criticize based on his own reading of the evidence before him. A thorough conservative in his bedrock loyalty to the Meiji state structure, he also had the passion for inquiry, knowledge of the world, analysis, and questioning that marks the liberal mind. Ariga favored the role of public intellectual, influencing national policy while staying clear of politics and political activism. Even in the run-up to the Russo-Japanese War as many of his colleagues publicly and passionately argued the case for war, he had kept his own anti-Russia sentiments in check to provide *Gaikō jihō* readers with carefully reasoned assessments of the pros and cons of making that fateful decision. Ariga was not always loved, particularly within the Foreign Ministry, a frequent target of his attack, but he was always respected for his scholarly erudition and integrity.

In the messy politics of China in 1913, however, Ariga's style of engaging in real-world problems while avoiding political entanglements was a trickier thing to manage. He had some inkling of this from the outset when he learned through Morrison that Yuan had initially hesitated to hire him out of concern for political appearances. As Morrison explained to a British colleague, ". . . Ariga came from a country essentially monarchical and [Yuan] feared that his appointment, especially in connection with the drafting of the constitution, might strengthen the fears of the Chinese who were suggesting that Yuan Shikai himself was aspiring to monarchical powers." Indeed, Ariga not only came from an "essentially monarchical" country, he had provided input to the 1908 constitution adopted by China's failed imperial regime.[90]

Ariga, who clearly wanted the China job, credited Morrison with overcoming Yuan's misgivings by presenting him as a world-class jurist as knowledgeable about republican political structures as constitutional monarchies.[91] Once in Beijing Ariga sought to allay any residual concerns by publicly citing the American and French constitutions as the models he planned to work from. He also signaled his complete loyalty to Yuan and his intention to work collegially with both Yuan's staff and the other foreign advisers, especially Morrison and Goodnow. What Ariga failed to factor in adequately was the difficulty of balancing loyalty to Yuan Shikai with loyalty to leaders of his own government in Tokyo.

Yuan Shikai himself was difficult to read. He was the ultimate imponderable element in the fractious political scene after 1911. How far would he be prepared to go with political reforms and reforms in general? To what extent would he take Japan as the dominant model for change? On the one hand, there was some evidence in Yuan's record in the ten years previous that both reform and the Japan connection were important in his thinking. In the North China provinces under his control, Yuan had worked to modernize the school system, the military, and the public security apparatus using Japanese models and Japanese experts as the chief, if not exclusive, agents of change. He was a key figure in central government decisions pre-1911 to institute a Japanese-style constitutional monarchy and to hire Japanese legal experts to help their Chinese counterparts, many of them Japan-trained, in the enormous task of writing civil, criminal, and commercial law codes for a modern China. In fact, work on the law codes, critical to China's internal governance and acceptance internationally, was ongoing, uninterrupted by the Revolution. Okada Asatarō, who had arrived in China in 1906 to draft a new criminal law code, was on hand to greet Ariga Nagao on his arrival in Beijing in the spring of 1913.[92]

On the other hand, nothing in Yuan's pre-1911 record suggested a statesmanlike figure with a vision for China's future as a nation-state, much less a republic. Nor was there evidence to indicate that he had chosen Japanese advisory help over the years for other than pragmatic reasons. Japan was a relatively low-cost, accessible source of new technology and institutions. "Same culture" arguments were not heard from Yuan's lips. In fact, trust was a rare commodity on both sides. What Yuan's career had shown in spades was the success of a highly shrewd politician, a consummate careerist who had managed his rise from ordinary soldier to the top ranks of the civil service through intelligence and guile and a willingness to play for broke using strong arm tactics to eliminate rivals. Yuan's most urgent goal was to maintain his power at all costs. His reforms were to good effect—improved public security to prevent another Boxer-like outbreak, for example—but his motives in launching them were to enlarge his area of influence, not to advance a national agenda. By 1912, only Yuan had the clout to ease the Manchus out of office, thus avoiding the spread of civil conflict. Managing the transition was Yuan's best act, but it was not a high-minded one. Leveraging to his advantage the plight of his former imperial patrons was an exercise in political expediency.

When it came to constitutions, Yuan knew very little, only that China had to have one to establish its bona fides as a republic in the eyes of the international community. Ariga on his part felt confident that he could quickly educate Yuan and his supporters in the fundamentals of constitutional law and government. Reminiscing about Ariga's China service years later, Japan's military adviser in Beijing at the time called this crash course in comparative law Ariga's biggest contribution.[93]

Yuan Shikai assuming the presidency of the Republic of China, February 1912. (Wikimedia Commons)

Ariga's job, as he and his employer Yuan Shikai agreed, was to produce a permanent constitution that would best accord with Chinese political culture as it existed in 1913: absent a monarchy, with a compromise president and fledgling elected councils, yet still steeped in beliefs about governance and societal relationships that reached back two millennia. This would have been challenging enough in a situation of political stability. But in fact the country was on the brink of chaos, strapped for cash and increasingly polarized into Yuan's northern faction seeking to centralize power in the presidency and Sun Yatsen's southern coalition demanding a stronger voice for parliament. Foreign opinion at the time was entirely divided on Yuan and Sun, their various schemes, programs, and personal idiosyncrasies. Sun, unlike Yuan, generally got good press in Japan, though one Western journalist who interviewed him concluded, "He is mad!"[94]

History has been far kinder to Sun than Yuan on the question of patriotism. Clearly Sun was more ideologically driven, but neither one had a problem with money in politics, even if it meant bargaining away China's assets in return for foreign loans. Sun was notably cavalier in offering rights in Manchuria as an enticement to his Japanese backers. For those actually living the messy politics of 1913 there seemed no convincing path to order and progress. Most in the foreign community found it hard to envision a republic functioning well in China, at least in the short term. "As I read the attitude of the Powers toward China at the moment," Ariga wrote in June of that year, "there is no one who believes that the Chinese

Republic ought to create a republican form of government from the beginning."[95] Whatever the merits of this view with its implied need for strong central controls, scholars in recent years have cited it as evidence of the patronizing attitude of foreigners.[96] Ariga's American colleague, Frank Goodnow, has come off especially badly, criticized as being not only naïve but almost un-American for advancing the not-ready-for-democracy argument. Yet even Sun Yatsen himself, leader of the revolution, champion of a socialist-style economy, declared China ill-prepared for democracy, hence his prescription for an unspecified period of "political tutelage" under the guidance of his own Nationalist Party.

A typical researcher, Ariga came to Beijing with a briefcase full of constitutional models to draw on for guidance in writing a charter for China's new republic. There were no ready templates. In the pre-1914 world where constitutional monarchies governed most of Europe and empires held sway over much of the rest, examples of viable republics were hard to find. Aside from tiny Switzerland, only France and the United States could claim enduring commitment to constitutional rule free of any vestiges of inherited monarchy. Ariga was fully versed in the history and legal traditions of both countries, particularly France, where he had lived and knew people in the legal community. But this knowledge only reinforced his conviction that China was a different case entirely.

True, he acknowledged, there appeared to be a parallel in the birth of all three republics, the exit of old monarchy in the face of popular revolution. But more fundamental, he argued, was a profound difference. The Chinese republic could not claim to represent the will of the entire people. Minority groups in China's border areas opposed formation of a republic, a self-styled Han Chinese republic, declaring their continued loyalty to the Manchu imperial house. What tipped the balance, he explained, was the emperor's abdication document, which formally transferred sovereignty to the republic. In other words, the Chinese republic had come into being as a result of an act from above, a brokered deal between top Manchu imperials and Chinese revolutionaries, not as an expression of the will of all peoples within the borders of the vast Chinese empire.[97]

Based on this distinction, it was possible to argue that the new republic lacked the legitimacy to govern China's ethnic minorities, including most Manchus. This is precisely the argument Kawashima Naniwa used to justify support for Manchu separatism. Ariga was not a separatist. He stressed the uniqueness of the republic's birth as a concession from the monarch rather than a popular rejection of monarchy for quite another reason, that is, to suggest caution in relying too exclusively on American and French models in writing China's draft constitution.

> I'm not saying that because the Chinese Republic owes its very existence to the consent of the Qing emperor it needs to take on organizational features of a monarchy. I'm trying to make another point entirely; namely, as I said before, that the history of the founding of the Chinese Republic is completely different from that of other republics. Therefore, not only on the matter of the election law but other important matters as well, there is no logical necessity for the Chinese constitution to follow American and French models. For example, on the formation of the upper house and laws relating to presidential authority and the election of the president, China must devise a scheme unique to the conditions in China itself.[98]

Ariga did not contest China's choice of an American-style system with a president, a cabinet, and a bicameral representative body. This was fine in outline form. His focus was on giving the system operative substance, on defining and limiting the powers of the various branches of government. When it got to specifics, he believed the Chinese needed to think beyond outside models to craft something of their own.

For years Ariga had been telling his Chinese students at Waseda that they must construct a modern society out of their own traditions and standards. Not everything about Japan was worth emulating, he had warned them, particularly when it came to public morals. Now in his role as China adviser there was a chance to give these ideas reality in the new constitution and to point out where he believed the Japan model *was* in fact relevant, namely, as an example of how to manage the transition to modernity by adapting indigenous beliefs to new institutional patterns from abroad. This was not an easy sell to the young Chinese serving with Ariga on the constitutional task force. Though he cautioned them that after 270 years of Qing monarchy, China was unlikely to switch to a liberal republic (*jiyū kyōwa*) overnight, they were impatient to get a structure in place even in the absence of a consensus on how democratic it should be. Nor did he find them as committed to producing a distinctively Chinese constitution as he thought they should be. "The gentlemen now prominent in Chinese political circles and involved in discussing the constitution are all young people forty and under," he complained. "Those middle-aged and above are not generally admitted to the group. Not a single person engaged in deliberations on the constitution is a true, bona fide China scholar or thinker."[99]

It was frustrating to Ariga that these young politicians, the educated elite, most of them Japan-trained, appeared to have forgotten the essential lesson of Meiji Japan, that fusing Asian values with Western organizational patterns had proved an unbeatable way to achieve stability and spectacular economic growth. He reminded them that the Meiji constitution writers not only had firsthand knowledge of European models but also solid grounding in native Japanese studies and Chinese learning. He urged them likewise to give weight to the Chinese past in writing their own national charter. What better binding material to hold together the fragile new republic than the Confucian ideals of moral governance and respect for authority and order that had been part of the Chinese psyche for centuries? He reminded his young colleagues, too, that identifying core values was especially critical in the case of China where, unlike Japan, there was no imperial institution to serve as a legitimizing force.

To those who might suggest that writing traditional ideals into the constitution would somehow compromise its modern character, Ariga cited the recent constitutions of Norway and Sweden where recognition of state support for Christianity coexisted with clauses guaranteeing freedom of religion. Further afield he noted that the 1908 Turkish constitution did the same for Islam. He was careful to acknowledge that these countries were constitutional monarchies and thus not bound by the separation of church and state concept characteristic of the modern republic. But even in republican America, he argued, no matter what was written in the Constitution, Christian teachings were being promoted in every public school in the country. (Ariga would have found interesting the argument still made by some American Christians today that Jefferson was wrong in insisting on a "wall of separation.")[100]

Apart from its function of providing moral authority, Ariga found immediate pragmatic reasons for encouraging Confucian conservatism. Though he said he understood why the southern revolutionaries, long at the forefront of fighting Qing oppression, wanted to cap their success by jettisoning anything connected with the past,[101] there was no doubt in his mind that to do so would deepen internal political divisions with disastrous consequences for China's future. As he explained in an article in *Gaikō jihō*:

> What concerns me is this: if the weaknesses of the revolutionary politicians are exposed in all their true colors just as China's old ideology resurfaces and sparks renewed interest, it would be virtually impossible to handle the anti-revolutionary backlash. The danger of this combustible mix is really the last thing we want to have happen. Therefore, rather than waiting until such a reaction takes shape and China is on the brink of disaster, isn't it in every way better to start now before violence breaks out to utilize those longstanding, underlying conservative influences, put some curbs on the excessive zeal of reform through revolution, and achieve stability centered on a republic of law and order.[102]

Ariga's words were not only spoken behind closed doors in the office of the constitutional committee. His advice and the details of his draft proposals were well publicized in both the Japanese and the Chinese press. His *Gaikō jihō* readers had come to expect this kind of editorializing from Ariga Nagao whether he was writing as a representative to the Hague Peace Conference or as an embedded legal adviser to the army in Manchuria. He was an old pro at using the magazine to shape public opinion, in this case to try to convince a largely skeptical Japanese public that Yuan and his brand of neo-conservatism were best not only for China but for Japan as well.

What was different this time was that Ariga was an employee of the Chinese government. As a member of Yuan's staff, he felt duty-bound to present Yuan in the best light to the government in Tokyo. He also sought to score a win for conservatism and Yuan with the audience in Beijing, both Chinese and foreign. Ariga had the ear of the older generation of Chinese, which included Yuan himself. It was the under-forty generation he was targeting with his arguments about retaining Confucian core values. He hoped to rouse them from indifference by pointing out that there was no better alternative at a time when consensus building was critical. Ironically, the biggest supporters of his conservative message were his colleagues in the foreign advisory group. No one, even his American counterparts, he liked to point out, offered a defense of liberal democracy.[103]

Certainly Goodnow, who knew little about China on his arrival, ended up sounding like an Ariga convert. Writing for his American audience, he said that China's problems of governance, "must be worked out carefully and slowly in the light of Chinese traditions and history and in such a manner as to conform to the peculiarities of Chinese life" and that Chinese youth studying abroad faced ". . . the danger of becoming denationalized, of losing their reverence and respect for all that is good in China because of their admiration, often not discriminating, for the new civilization to which they are introduced . . ."[104] Japan, by contrast, had done things right. Speaking of Europe's "subjugation of Asia" over the past 200 years, Goodnow explained, "The one Asiatic country which has come out of the contest unscathed is Japan. And Japan is also the one Asiatic country which has made a successful attempt to combine the Asiatic and European political principles in her state organization."[105]

Goodnow, citizen of democratic America, concluded that constitutional monarchy was the most suitable form of government for China. Ariga, subject of a monarchical country, accepted the Chinese republic as a fact of life, its existence legitimated by the imperial institution it replaced. But he argued that for a republic to succeed in China's fractionalized political culture post-1911, it had to retain a key feature of the traditional Chinese state structure—strong central authority. In the draft constitution that emerged from Ariga's pen, the president once selected reigned supreme, his powers unchecked by decisions of party cabinets or no-confidence votes of parliament. Parliament's function was not to challenge the executive branch but to enable its smooth operation. Whether it was Ariga's advice that led Yuan to his controversial decision to dissolve an intractable national assembly as he did in the fall of 1913 is unclear, but Ariga's position on executive authority no doubt made it easier to do so. Ariga was skeptical of China's readiness for representative institutions in any case, a sentiment surprisingly common among reformers and even revolutionaries in the early years of the republic. The 1911 Revolution, after all, was an elitist revolution. On the question of voter eligibility, Ariga made his views plain in the title he chose for the relevant constitutional draft chapter: "Warding off the Abuses of Socialism in Establishing China's Constitution."[106]

To twenty-first-century ears Ariga's passionate defense of elitism has a jarring, off-key quality. Not entirely so in 1913, pre-World War I, when voting rolls around the world were restricted, even in America. Ariga's argument was straightforward. No matter what the standard attributes of a republic might be, in actual fact giving China's huge, poor, illiterate population the vote would be a dangerous thing, both for China and for Japan as China's near neighbor. China's ill-informed laboring class would become the easy prey of politicians advancing their own partisan interests rather than a national agenda. Empowered workers, clamoring for a redistribution of resources, would engage in strike activity, disrupting the flow of capital to industry so essential to sustained economic growth. As Ariga described it, this was precisely what had happened in France and America, whose constitutions and general election laws were being touted as models for China to follow.

France since the revolution had been beset by parliamentary instability and worker protests, the unfortunate result of what Ariga termed the "domination of politics by the dissatisfied underclass," given electoral clout through the socialist party. America, with its limitless resources and high labor demand, had escaped the pernicious effects of socialism, but even there labor strikes were recently on the rise. And in California, worker empowerment through the ballot box had other deleterious effects, namely voter pressure on legislators to pass anti-Asian discrimination laws damaging to U.S.-Japan relations. Closer to home, Ariga worried about the possible negative impact on Japan's working class if a socialist movement took hold in China.[107]

The only way to avoid what Ariga saw as the inefficiencies and risks of parliamentary politics was to limit voter eligibility to the lower house by age, education, and tax-paying status and to make the upper house an appointive body drawn from the top echelons of those with wealth and overseas training. It was the elite who would run China—as they were running Japan and most of the rest of the world in 1913. At the same time, Ariga insisted that the Chinese Republic was inherently democratic, first, because it did not discriminate on the basis of race, class, or religion and, second, because the opportunity to join the voting rolls was open to all qualified Chinese males over the age of twenty: ". . . Even members of the lower class, when they take it upon themselves to act independently and fully assume the tax paying burden vis-à-vis the state, deserve at that point to have the right to participate in government."[108] This was not to be a random event left to chance. A firm believer in the Confucian notion of self-improvement, Ariga supported giving legal heft to the principle of equal opportunity:

> Once you specify voter qualifications by law, you necessarily open the way for anyone who works hard and meets these requirements to have the right to vote. Otherwise, the system is less than democratic. It is precisely in the interest of fairness that we add to the constitution the following clause based on the principle of access to free education found in the Belgian constitution: "The people have the right to a general education."[109]

Ariga Nagao, international-minded academic, and Yuan Shikai, local political strongman, were poles apart by background and experience. But they saw eye-to-eye, one analytically, the other viscerally, on what was best for China: Confucian authoritarianism moderated by limited but potentially expanding citizen participation in governance. Parliamentary checks on executive authority allowed under the provisional constitution were completely reversed in Ariga's new version while voter eligibility was defined with such precision to ensure a restricted franchise. But whatever the judgments of later critics, Ariga's defense of this kind of guided democracy under one-man rule—he would have objected to the term "dictatorship" later applied to Yuan's tenure in office—was an entirely reasonable response from a member of the Meiji elite witnessing the unstable state of China in 1913. More surprising was the degree to which Goodnow and Morrison shared Ariga's views. But all three were writing as nationalists, essentially concerned with the potential threat to their nations' interests if China dissolved into civil war. Concentrated power, a constitution guaranteeing citizen rights, however limited, seemed a start on the way to stability. Timing was important. Ariga urged speed in getting a constitutionally sanctioned parliament up and running to tackle China's urgent budgetary crisis. With its taxing and spending mechanisms ill-defined, he feared China remained vulnerable to dependence on foreign loans or worse, foreign intervention.[110]

Ariga had traveled the world and visited Versailles and The Winter Palace at St. Petersburg. But to his eyes neither was as awe-inspiring as the Hall of Great Harmony (Taihedian) in Beijing's Forbidden City where Yuan Shikai was inaugurated as president of the Chinese Republic on October 10, 1913. For Ariga the sense of history was palpable. In this very spot under the massive winged roofs, tiles gleaming red-orange on a gray rainy day, centuries of Qing emperors had received foreign missions submissive and respectful before the all-powerful empire. He could feel what he had been putting down on paper, the continuity between past and present, the seamless transition from monarchy to republic. Morrison and other Westerners who were present caught something of the political symbolism of the event but none shared Ariga's excitement about China's future:

> Here for the first time I felt China's great power. It occurred to me that compared to the grandeur of China Japan seemed just a world in miniature. China was like a giant— unflappable, methodical—Japan a clever little fellow who, because he got a head start, easily defeated the giant. But I think that the giant will in fact come to his senses confronting us with the full force of his unflappable, methodical brainpower and we will be no match for him. [111]

Reversal of Fortunes

In a letter to a British diplomat in August 1916, Morrison described a conversation he had with one of Japan's top leaders on the subject of Ariga Nagao:

> I was struck by Viscount Kato's hostility to Professor Ariga, the Constitutional Adviser in Peking. I said that I had recommended the appointment, having been advised that he was the most distinguished of Japanese Jurists. He said he *never was that*. Yet Ariga was attached as adviser to Oyama during the China Japan war and to Nogi during the Russo-Japanese war and capitulation of Port Arthur, and when appointed by Yuan Shih-kai the Japanese minister insisted that he should be given a salary of £4,000 a year and a five years contract. Viscount Kato even attacked his moral character and suggested that his integrity was doubtful. [112]

Morrison's apparent surprise at Katō's angry outburst was itself surprising. Morrison was in regular contact with Ariga. Not only that, he had always made it his business to follow the political rumor mill, particularly important for a China-Japan expert who knew neither language. In this case, however, Ariga and Morrison's other English-speaking sources evidently failed to clue him in to what he would have sensed on his own had he been able to read *Gaikō jihō*. Ariga had helped derail Katō's career.

Baron Katō Takaaki (Morrison had mistakenly raised his rank to viscount) was on an unwavering trajectory of professional success when he accepted his fourth stint as foreign minister in 1914. Two time ambassador to London, Japan's most prestigious overseas posting, chief steward of Japan's alliance with Britain, the world's leading power, Katō was also the new "bureaucratic politician," heading up one of Japan's major political parties. As Katō took up his post in the Ōkuma cabinet in April, he believed he had both the clout and the duty to challenge Japan's elder statesmen (*genrō*) for the lead role in foreign policymaking. A dramatic test of this new Foreign Ministry activism came on August 4, 1914, with Britain's decision to intervene on the side of France and Russia in the escalating war against Germany. Without consulting the genrō, Katō began pushing the Japanese cabinet to respond with its own declaration of war on Germany under the terms of the Anglo-Japanese Alliance. In Katō's vision of global politics, a swift show of support for Britain, long the dominant foreign power in Asia, now tied down in a major war in Europe, offered Japan an unprecedented opportunity to advance its vital interests in China and Manchuria. At a cabinet meeting on August 7, with the reluctant concurrence of the elder statesmen, Katō got approval to inform the British government of Japan's intention to declare war on Germany.

Britain's reaction was mixed. On the one hand, should Germany attack Hong Kong or another British asset in East Asia, Japanese military assistance would be essential. On the other, Katō made it plain that there was a *quid pro quo,* a free hand to take possession by force if necessary of German-leased territory in China's Shandong Province. Wary of Japan's great-power pretensions in China as a threat to their own, the British mulled over the costs and benefits of Japanese participation, concluding ultimately that Japanese assistance to counter the German navy in the Pacific was worth the risk of advantaging a rival on the continent. The big payoff in naval assistance in fact came not in 1914 but in 1917 and not in the Pacific but in the Mediterranean, where Japanese destroyers provided protection to British merchant shipping, a little-known sideshow to the main European theater of operations. On August 15, 1915, Japan issued an ultimatum to Germany to cede to Japanese control its lease to Jiaozhou in Shandong. Germany recalled its ambassador from Tokyo. Japan followed with a formal declaration of war on August 23, 1914. A joint Japanese-British attack on German-occupied Jiaozhou began four days later.

Ramming through his policy of leveraging the Anglo-Japanese Alliance to maximize gains in China cost Katō some political capital. While it represented a win for Foreign Ministry autonomy, it meant a breach with Japan's elder statesmen, offended at being outmaneuvered but, more to the point, convinced that Katō's Anglo-centrism was a constraint to developing a successful China policy. In the diplomatic arena, Foreign Minister Katō outclassed his British counterpart in negotiating skills but at the price of adding another layer of distrust to an already fraying alliance. Katō's less than two years as foreign minister, 1914-1915, were to prove the most fateful turning point for Japan since the Meiji Restoration.[113]

Writing from Beijing in the fall of 1914, Ariga could have been mistaken for a Katō supporter. Like Katō, he believed absolutely that Japan should stand with Britain in the war against Germany. He had spent much of his professional energy promoting the notion that global stability depended on a world run by agreed rules and structures, and that threats to international order must be met first by diplomacy, then as a last resort by force, preferably collective action. Germany's offensive against France and Belgium appeared to constitute such a threat to order, or, perhaps more cynically, in hindsight, a threat to the monopoly of British interests on two continents, European and Asian. For Ariga, declaring for Britain was simply what was demanded of Japan as an international player with clear treaty obligations and a commitment to the Hague Conventions. Reports of German atrocities on the Belgian front—"violations of law and custom which have left an unimaginable blot on the character of the German people"—seemed to confirm that Japan, a nation "that has always observed the laws of war," had made the only decision possible. [114]

Ariga also supported Katō's position on Jiaozhou, the ultimatum, then the invasion, as a means to strike at German power in the Pacific. He was a realist in this, no different from Katō and most of Katō's colleagues and British counterparts. It is fair to say and important to remember from the present vantage point, that pragmatism, not ideology dominated foreign policymaking before World War I. Strategic calculations came first, moral commitments a distant second. Indeed, it would have been hard to find firm moral ground in a matter that involved taking from the Germans what the Germans had already taken from the Chinese. More to the point for decision makers was what was allowed under international law. Besides, the Chinese raised no serious objections, mollified for the moment by vague assurances from Tokyo that Jiaozhou would eventually be returned to China.

What most concerned Ariga was not the morality or even the legality of Japan's seizure of German rights—after all it was reminiscent of the forced transfer of Japan's claims in Liaodong to Russia after the Sino-Japanese War—but that the parties engaged in the Jiaozhou campaign respect China's status as a neutral nation as defined by international law. China had declared its neutrality as soon as the conflict in Europe began in early August, almost certainly on the recommendation of

Ariga, the most experienced of Yuan Shikai's legal advisers. Ariga later compiled a highly detailed account of China's complex negotiations with the three belligerents covering this period as well as China's eleventh-hour declaration of war on Germany in 1917. Written in French with a foreword by Paul Fauchille, the 340-page *La Chine et la Grande Guerre Europèenne au Point de Vue du Droit International* was published in Paris in 1920 by Ariga's old publisher, A. Pedone. The book concluded, first, that Germany was the first to violate China's neutrality thus justifying subsequent Japanese-British incursions, and second, that Chinese diplomats had acquitted themselves very well in their dealings with the three foreign powers. The Great War, Ariga said, showed the new Republic "capable and determined to act in conformity with the rules contained in the law of nations."[115]

Supportive of the broad outlines of Katō's foreign policy in the fall of 1914, Ariga also showed signs of becoming an irritant. In an article submitted to *Gaikō jihō* in October, he discussed using the good offices of Sweden and the United States to settle the European conflict, an interesting proposition at a time when the conflict was heating up. But it gave him an opportunity to raise an issue much on his mind, namely, that Japan must start planning immediately for a postwar peace conference whose task it would be to recalibrate the balance of power worldwide. While being allied with Britain was a "stroke of good fortune *(gyōkō)*," as Ariga called it, Japan had no experience negotiating critically important issues at a multinational level. Most difficult of all, Ariga emphasized, would be finding the right people to attend. They must have the rank and career experience that would entitle them to sit at the table with top world statesmen. But over and above this, they ought to be open-minded, willing to think multilaterally, "eminently capable of broadly assessing from various perspectives the interests of all nations, exploiting them to our advantage where possible as the means to achieve our national goals." It was a job description for an internationalist—like Ariga Nagao. But he was not simply touting his own credentials. By suggesting that qualified people were rare, Ariga was also taking a not-too-subtle swipe at the Foreign Ministry, a consistent target of his criticism since *Gaikō jihō* first appeared in 1898.[116]

More irritating than this poke in the eye at the diplomatic corps from someone who was, technically speaking, the Foreign Ministry's own man in China and a highly visible figure at that, were articles Ariga published in the magazine in November and December 1914. Japan had just secured Jiaozhou with British help and taken over German islands in the Pacific in a joint operation with Australia and New Zealand. Foreign Minister Katō was ready to launch his next move, a diplomatic offensive to get Chinese government agreement not only on the future status of Jiaozhou but on the entire range of Japanese interests in China, including

Manchuria and Mongolia. Historian Frederick Dickinson argues that the political battle at this juncture between Katō and the genrō over defense spending and the approach to the China negotiations was not really about differing foreign policy visions but about who should control the process. And Katō won on both counts, blocking the increased military budget sought by the genrō and slapping a list of demands on the Chinese government, an opening negotiating tactic so cleanly executed that it even brought favorable initial reviews from the genrō who had cautioned moderation.[117]

This would not be the first or last time that aggressive action abroad would be used to force consensus on the domestic front. But what Ariga had to say on the subject of Japan's wartime involvement suggests that essential differences in foreign policy outlook were at least as important as domestic political considerations in the buildup to the 1915 negotiations with China. China was the case at hand, but the real question was whether Japan should think in global alliance terms in its foreign policy formulations or proceed unilaterally and regionally. Ariga invited controversy along these lines in his November editorial entitled, "Questions about Japanese Troop Deployment to Europe." Taking his cue from a British publication questioning the level of support Britain could expect from its Japanese ally, Ariga proposed that Japan send a 250,000-man volunteer force to Europe to join the fight against Germany.

To say this was provocative is an understatement. Proposing that a force this size, Japan's first-ever volunteer army, serve outside Asia was an idea bound to, and most certainly intended to, create a stir. Critical reviews appeared in major newspapers. Closer to home, Ariga took a round of criticism from one of his fellow *Gaikō jihō* writers who raised issues of logistics, provisioning, and the problematic of recruiting a volunteer army. Foreign Minister Katō expressed his displeasure in a press interview where he insisted that while Japan was bound by the alliance to help degrade German power in the Pacific, it could not sustain the costs of a major troop deployment elsewhere in the world.

Always ready for verbal combat, Ariga countered by arguing that as much as Katō might like to limit Japan's involvement to the Pacific, Japan's decision for war on the side of the allies was a commitment to fight Germany on all fronts. Certainly Germany on its part regarded Japan's attacks on Jiaozhou and the Pacific islands not as minor infringements of leased property but as an invasion of its sovereign territory and rights. Germany, Ariga warned, would retaliate against Japan at this major level of grievance at the first opportunity should its military remain intact at war's end. Apart from what the state of hostilities meant for Japanese-German relations, Ariga emphasized Katō's shortsightedness in assuming that it was even possible for Japan to insulate itself selectively from the war as it spread from the main show in Europe to fronts in Africa and the Middle East. The interests of all the belligerents, including Japan, would suffer grave consequences if shipping through the Suez Canal were disrupted or if British troops had to be redeployed from India to Europe and other hot spots, leaving South Asia unsecured.

Ariga supplied the international framework for the argument against Katō's policy of limited engagement. But he made it plain that when it came to laying out the rationale for committing Japanese troops to the allied effort, he had relied on conversations with several "military experts" whose names he was not free to disclose. Indeed, Ariga had close relations with people in the military, having served in two major wars and taught at both service academies. He was well acquainted with Yuan Shikai's Japanese military adviser, Colonel Banzai Rihachirō, posted in Beijing since 1911. He was particularly close to General Ōyama Iwao, for twenty-five years his mentor, his field commander in the wars against China and Russia—and one of the genrō currently doing battle with Foreign Minister Katō over the direction of foreign policy.

As Ariga framed it, this "first world war" which was Japan's war, too, presented an unprecedented opportunity for Japan to broaden its alliances and become a real global player. A sudden infusion of Japanese troops, even a division or two, on the front lines in Europe could break the current impasse in the fighting, enabling a swift and complete allied victory that would eliminate the German threat entirely. There were challenges, he acknowledged, providing the troops with a Japanese diet, coordinating field operations in two languages among them, but these were manageable. The sticking point was Tokyo's opposition to the required budgetary outlay, an estimated 300 million yen or 30 million British pounds. While a large absolute figure, this was only 5 yen per capita, Ariga reminded his readers, a reasonable amount when measured against the enormous benefits that would accrue to the nation long-term. If the Ōkuma cabinet failed to approve this expenditure and Germany managed to rearm in the near term, "we have to say that it will really bear considerable responsibility." Ariga's plea for army expansion appeared in the December 15, 1914, issue of *Gaikō jihō*. At the end of the month after a convoluted political drama, Katō prevailed and the genrō-sponsored army bill went down to defeat.[118]

As Katō dispatched Minister Hioki to Beijing in January to open secret talks with the Yuan Shikai government, he could not have been happy to think that Ariga Nagao was there serving on Yuan's advisory staff. Ariga had questioned Katō's competence and challenged his foreign policy vision publicly in the pages of *Gaikō jihō*. He was aligned in his thinking with at least some of Katō's genrō rivals in favoring multilateralism over Katō's more Anglo-centric view. While it was not clear if the straight-talking Ariga could be a problem in the ensuing negotiations, indications were that he would if he could. Had Katō been able to foresee the disaster to come over the next few months, he might have tried to bring Ariga and his considerable expertise into the process rather than leaving him in the role of sideline critic.

Katō's attempt to effect a comprehensive resolution of all outstanding issues between Japan and China—the so-called 21 Demands—has come to symbolize a uniquely Japanese form of aggressive diplomacy. Frederick Dickenson quite rightly points out, however, that in pursuing its China interests Japan was acting within the accepted operating framework of the other Powers in China, trying to legitimize through treaty provisions specific spheres of influence, in this case, Japan's generally recognized special position in Shandong, Manchuria, and Fujian and in iron mining activities in central China. Even Group V, the notorious "desiderata," on hiring Japanese as government advisers in all key areas of administration, fit the long-term practice of providing foreign advisory help that Yuan Shikai himself had welcomed and sought out.

The problem for Yuan was more a matter of timing and perception than the specifics of the demands themselves, which did not surprise him. His worry was that having given in to Japan on neutrality and the Jiaozhou transfer, he might weaken support for his presidency were he to follow up immediately with further concessions. For Yuan, as Katō, the outcome of internal political rivalries was critically linked to the diplomacy over the 21 Demands. Unsure of how to respond to the package presented in a confidential note on January 18, Yuan's office promptly leaked news of its existence to the press. The initial reaction of the Powers was mild. Their overriding concern was how to maintain equal access to the China market. The war in Europe was the main event. Britain's ambassador to Japan cautioned against introducing "a jarring note in our hitherto harmonious relations [with Japan] since war has drawn us so close together."[119]

As the talks continued into February and March without resolution, foreign diplomats began to take a closer look at the demands relative to their own China interests. Japan's credibility took a hit when the Foreign Ministry denied that Group V existed and then was forced to retract. The British foreign office voiced new concerns, but concluded that Yuan should be encouraged to settle with Japan, Britain's ally, in the interests of stability on the Asian front. Only the United States, which had yet to declare war on Germany, raised an alarm about Japanese aggression, fearing encroachment on its commercial interests in Fujian and Manchuria. Japan's Foreign Ministry faced its most serious scrutiny at home. The pages of

Gaikō jihō came alive with critical comment about Foreign Minister Katō and the conduct of Japanese diplomacy. Historians are not in accord on whether Katō was pressured by the Japanese military to take an increasingly hard line with China or he tripped up in an excess of zeal to seize the foreign policy-making function from the genrō. But there is agreement that his was a piece of bungled diplomacy that did irreparable damage to Chinese-Japanese relations.

Gaikō jihō's spring editorials on the China negotiations did not appear under Ariga's by-line. Very likely, as someone working in the president's office, he felt he knew too much about the talks from the China side to attach his name so brazenly to criticisms of his own foreign ministry. But the opinions contained therein were vintage Ariga, longtime critic of Japanese diplomacy now acutely concerned that his current project of consensus building over a new constitutional order in China might be wrecked in the growing crisis. Freedom of the press seemed alive and healthy. The government was attacked for its excessive secrecy, for heavy handedness in pushing Group V, for inflaming anti-Japanese sentiments among the Chinese, for failing to anticipate the negative fallout now occurring internationally as Japan was perceived as taking advantage of the war in Europe to press its claims in China. Moving Japanese troops into China was deemed an unnecessary provocation. Foreign Minister Katō was held directly responsible for the mess, charged with dealing with the Chinese in bad faith and committing a major diplomatic blunder. Minister Hioki was derided as incompetent. From Ariga's vantage point in China's capital, years of frustration with what he viewed as the narrow-mindedness of the foreign ministry, its unwillingness to think globally, seemed magnified many-fold. "Asia is not Asia's Asia," *Gaikō jihō* declared. "It's the world's Asia. The notion of an Asian Monroe Doctrine is in the end just fanciful thinking." This was Ariga's answer to Konoe Atsumaro. A unilateral China policy would simply not work.[120]

In March 1915 Yuan Shikai sent Ariga to Tokyo to argue China's case before the genrō, bypassing Katō and the Foreign Ministry. China was willing to make concessions in Shandong, Manchuria, and Mongolia, Ariga explained, but would hold the line on Group V, which represented an infringement on China's right to run its own government. Drop Group V and back off from the threat of force, he argued, or risk not only damaging Japan's China relationship but diminishing allied support for Japan's positions at a future peace conference. The genrō found Ariga's argument convincing, not least because British and American opinion was turning markedly anti-Japanese. In late April, the genrō authorized Ariga to inform Yuan that Japan would not only drop Group V but restore Jiaozhou to China.

Ariga had knowingly jumped into the middle of the turf battle between the genrō and Foreign Minister Katō, taking advantage of the bureaucratic rift to press his case for the wisdom of moderating the 21 Demands. No matter what the personal risk, he was opposed on principle to Japan taking unilateral steps against China and to Katō making policy on his own without resort to the usual consensus building system centered on input from the genrō. Furious with Ariga for altering the course of the talks, Katō charged him with being a spy for Yuan Shikai. Ariga was no doubt prepared for the Foreign Minister's angry reaction having sparred with him repeatedly. He may not have anticipated, however, the level of vitriol his efforts on behalf of China would stir up among right-wing fanatics who not only denounced him in public meetings but tried to kill him. It was a weary sounding Ariga who penned a commentary on war and diplomacy for *Gaikō jihō* on May 6, 1915:

> To escape the current mess in Tokyo I've left home without any plan and put myself on a train north. If I'm tired I just get off and stop at an inn. In my wandering mode I don't have with me any of the materials I ought to consult. But, on second thought, considering how ominous the skies over Tokyo look off in the distance, I decided to depart from my usual practice and be so bold as to give only general opinions rather than providing precise discussion based on history or the evidence before us.[121]

Beyond personal danger, the "mess" that Ariga chose to escape included the final round of confrontational meetings between the genrō and Katō on what to do about China. The genrō held firm on their objection to Group V and castigated Katō for a failure of diplomacy, but from Ariga's vantage point the damage had already been done. Japan had lost credibility with both the Chinese and the international community. What came out of the meetings did nothing to salvage Japan's image. On May 7, as Ariga traveled north, the Cabinet instructed its representative in China to deliver an ultimatum to the Yuan government that it had until May 9 to agree to provisions in Groups I-IV of the Demands or face uncertain consequences.

As yet unencumbered by war, the Americans sought allied support for "a friendly but earnest appeal to Japan and China to continue their negotiations in the spirit of patience and friendship . . ."[122] The proposal got nowhere. The allies saw no reason to offend Japan, already a partner in the European conflict. Pointing out that none of the European powers was in a position to come to China's aid, Britain's representative to China urged Yuan to recognize the "necessity of giving an absolutely unconditional acceptance" to Japan's ultimatum. This was done on May 9 in a series of Sino-Japanese agreements. The allies were relieved that conflict had been avoided. Yuan felt he had made the best of a bad situation. The Chinese public was outraged. The rise in anti-Japanese sentiment that Ariga and others had warned about for months edged upward. China still commemorates May 7, the day the ultimatum was presented, as a day of "national humiliation."[123]

The genrō forced Katō Takaaki's ouster as foreign minister in August 1915. Their dissatisfaction with Katō was present from the outset of negotiations, but Ariga's March-April mission on Yuan's behalf tipped the balance against him at the critical hour. Katō's name was now associated with diplomatic failure, his career under a cloud. No doubt Morrison touched a raw nerve when he mentioned the word "Ariga" in a conversation with Katō a year later. Ariga did not escape unscathed either. For the first time in his professional life, he had gotten himself entangled in politics and diplomacy at the working level. It was a minefield for the uninitiated, and not surprisingly Ariga soon paid the price.

Why Yuan Shikai chose, in the wake of the 21 Demands debacle, to revive the idea of a constitutional monarchy with himself as China's new emperor has never been entirely clear. Though Morrison spoke of his "mad ambition," more likely Yuan's decision to scrap the Republic was rational and calculated, a bit of bold political theater designed to impress the world that he had the prestige and power to withstand further acts of aggression from Japan or the Powers jointly. He was given encouragement in his imperial pursuit from an unlikely source, his American adviser Frank Goodnow. In a much-publicized essay, "Republic or Monarchy?" Goodnow had flatly stated that "a monarchy is better suited than a republic to China."[124] Once his words were seized upon by Yuan backers, he tried to explain that he was speaking in a theoretical rather than programmatic sense, but it was too late. Whatever the intent of the analysis, it had the effect of lending credibility to Yuan's cause.

The immediate foreign reaction to Yuan's plan as it unfolded beginning in August 1915 gave Yuan reason for optimism as well. Senior officials from Tokyo to London declared the shift from republic to constitutional monarchy a matter for the Chinese to decide. As long as foreign economic interests were protected, Emperor Yuan was as acceptable as President Yuan. Over the next two months, however, amid growing opposition within China to Yuan's imperial bid, Japan backed off from the non-interventionist approach favored by its European allies and the United States. Business and army leaders convinced the Ōkuma cabinet that there was an opportunity to be had in supporting the various anti-Yuan forces. Yuan had never shown any pro-Japan proclivities. In fact, he was backpedaling from some of the provisions agreed to in the May settlement. The opposition, on the other hand, consisted of longtime friends of Japan, revolutionaries such as Sun Yatsen who had promised better than the 21 Demands, or the Manchu Prince Su who could deliver a secure Manchuria.

With few resources, diplomatic or otherwise, to devote to China for the moment, Britain, France, Russia, and the United States joined Japan in the fall of 1915 in advising Yuan to postpone his plan to become emperor until after the conclusion of the war in Europe. When a defiant Yuan publicly accepted the throne in December, Japan began a concerted campaign to depose him, fueling China's opposition forces while fending off European and American proposals to recognize the new monarchy. Arms sales to Sun increased. Kawashima Naniwa (see Chapter IV) was given the go-ahead for his Manchuria-Mongolia independence movement. Yuan renounced the throne in March, but the opposition within and the Japanese without pressed him to retire from politics entirely. He was spared the humiliation of resignation by his death in June 1916. "So Yuan is no more," Morrison exclaimed. "What a tragedy that monarchical movement was!"[125]

Ariga was uncharacteristically silent during the Yuan Shikai drama. For reasons that are not entirely clear, he stopped writing for *Gaikō jihō*. Possibly the people now in charge of the magazine found Ariga too controversial. More likely Ariga himself decided to withhold comment. He had backed Yuan to the hilt over the 21 Demands at the cost of making some powerful enemies. But he genuinely believed that the Group V desiderata were excessive and counterproductive. Yuan's imperial bid, on the other hand, presented a real dilemma. Like Morrison, Ariga had been a big Yuan supporter, seeing him as someone with statesmanlike potential. Suddenly and publicly opposing this leader he had so recently championed risked bringing into question his judgment in supporting him in the first place.

Yet endorsing Yuan's plan was not a good option either. However much Ariga might like to have seen pre-1911 China develop into a constitutional monarchy, his advisory work for Yuan on a post-revolution constitution was based solidly on the premise that China was an internationally recognized republic. Ariga had spent two years trying to help shape a republic that fit China's traditions and current needs as he saw them; namely, a republic with a strong executive and weak legislature. Yuan as strongman was fine. Yuan as emperor meant undoing Ariga's work and raised all sorts of legal and institutional issues quite apart from inviting civil war. Ariga warned Yuan at the start of his imperial venture that the move was of questionable legality, echoing Morrison, who reproached Yuan for inviting political disaster with his "ill-advised and inopportune movement for the restoration of the monarchy." Whether, as one scholar has suggested, Ariga, out of loyalty to Yuan, wavered in the end on the Emperor issue seems highly unlikely given his principled personality and unshakable belief in the primacy of the law.[126] Even

Yuan worried about preserving his image as a legitimate ruler, as witness his effort to promote the fiction that he had been "elected" emperor.

In trying to dissuade Yuan Shikai from moving ahead with monarchy, Ariga and Morrison were acting from personal conviction. They could do so comfortably, knowing that Yuan had no real champions in Tokyo or London either at this juncture. At the same time, Yuan was not passive in the face of outside pressures to deter him from his chosen path. He continued to try to change minds among the foreigners in his midst—Goodnow had already proved a sympathizer, after all, and Ariga a useful tool—with better-the-devil-you-know arguments and appeals to friendship. He sought to cozy up to the British and Americans by contributing to the war relief fund. He sent the British Minister to China a porcelain etching of King George set off in a bejeweled frame, and presented Ariga with a rare Song dynasty stone rubbing to add to his prized collection. It was over this modest gift that Ariga committed a political gaffe, a seemingly small misstep that damaged his career.

The circumstances were innocent enough. In response to Yuan's gift, Ariga wrote a formal letter of thanks in Japanese, which he signed "*shin Nagao.*" As Banzai recounts the incident, this was just after Yuan had accepted his "election" to the throne and since Ariga had heard people in Yuan's office referring to him as "your majesty," he accordingly chose what he thought was an appropriate closing, "your humble servant Nagao." Unfortunately, the same character, *shin* in Japanese, *chen* in Chinese, can also mean "minister." The Chinese translator took the opportunity to render the term as "Foreign Minister Nagao," implying that Ariga not only endorsed but envisioned a role for himself in Yuan's new imperial government. How the possibility of misinterpretation escaped Ariga's notice and that of his own translator, Aoyagi, is not clear. Ariga never referred to the incident. But in what has a decidedly contemporary ring to it, Yuan's office leaked Ariga's personal letter to the press which gave it wide distribution as evidence of Japan's behind the scenes support for the new regime. Tokyo was not happy.[127]

If Yuan's idea was to use Ariga to exploit divisions within Japan, as had happened during the 21 Demands, the plan backfired. But Ariga once again, this time unwittingly, became the target of Japanese outrage for contravening official policy. Stunned and embarrassed, he hunkered down in his house near Yuan's office to ride out the storm. Banzai who was himself carrying mixed messages from Tokyo to Yuan on the monarchy issue, painted Ariga as a victim of political inexperience. Nothing in Ariga's background, Banzai asserted, however cosmopolitan it was, had prepared him to navigate the political intrigues surrounding Yuan Shikai. Ariga's boyhood friend Takada Sanae, chimed in sympathetically that it was almost inevitable that the highly principled Ariga would come to grief working for a corrupt politician like Yuan.[128]

Within six months of the "Foreign Minister Nagao" incident Yuan was dead. But the damage to Ariga's reputation and career was lasting. After years of carping at the Foreign Ministry for its ineptitude, Ariga could find no sympathy there for his public humiliation, as witness Katō's cutting remarks. Nor could he find it among his academic colleagues, with a few notable exceptions like Takada and Aoyagi. Early on Ariga had chosen conscience over comradeship and his brilliant but suffer-no-fools-gladly temperament brought more schadenfreude than support in his time of trouble. No longer could he hope to join the Japanese mission to the upcoming peace conference, a dream that once seemed within reach. Nor did he find returning to Japan and rejoining his colleagues at Waseda immediately appealing. But if Ariga had lingering regrets about taking the China assignment in the first place he said nothing about it publicly. Still, one wonders if he felt like his good friend Morrison whose frustration mounted as he watched Yuan's monarchical movement careen toward disaster: "Yuan Shih-kai has made an awful mess of things, and I realize more than ever what a blunder I committed in joining his service with so much enthusiasm."[129]

Final Accounting

When Yuan's successor, Li Yuanhong, took over in June 1916, Morrison, Goodnow's replacement Westel Woodbury Willoughby, and "Dr. Ariga," as Morrison deferentially called him, were all on hand to tender advice on constitutional questions. We are simply a resource, Ariga told Li. You tell us what you want built and we will supply the design. A few years and a couple of Chinese presidents later, Ariga struck a defensive pose looking back at the work of the foreign advisers. A republican constitution based on an American-style presidential system had shown every sign of working in China, he asserted. Reforms of the military, local administration, financial institutions were already under way during Yuan's first years as president. What went wrong was not the fault of the system shaped by Yuan's advisers, but of the monarchical movement. When that failed, the entire reform enterprise broke down as well.[130]

But China's problem was more than the botched experiment of the Yuan Shikai presidency, Ariga told *Gaikō jihō* readers as he reflected on his seven years' service. More fundamental was the failure of China's leadership to accept the rule of law. This was no doubt something of a personal disappointment. Though a supporter of the Confucian model of authoritarian rule, he had with equal passion sought to convince the Chinese that modern laws, uniformly applied, were essential to good governance and international respect. China, he had said repeatedly over the years, was as fit and entitled to join the international legal regime as any nation. Progress was discernible but slow. Writing in 1920 at the height of the warlord lawlessness following Yuan's death, Ariga was forced to conclude that finding authoritarian leaders also committed to making China a nation of laws would require time and persistence. "China is a country that for thousands of years has relied on the rule of men not the rule of law. So in this way it's very different from the nations of Europe and America that directly and indirectly have been influenced by Roman law. Nor is it like Japan where during the 300-year Tokugawa period laws began to take precedence over men."[131]

China had made good use of Ariga. He had coached a generation of Chinese students in modern law and Yuan Shikai in constitution building. His attempts to internationalize China, to bring it into the mainstream of Western law, and to moderate Japanese pressure at the time of the 21 Demands worked to China's advantage. Yuan and his political supporters repaid the favor by playing Ariga for a fool, a neophyte in politics, which he was. Yet there was nothing in Ariga's subsequent public utterances to indicate bitterness on his part, the kind of disillusionment with the Chinese as people so obvious in the case of Hattori Unokichi or Kawashima Naniwa. He stayed on in China (as did Morrison and Willoughby) to advise a series of weak Chinese presidents following Yuan and Li, ever tinkering with the constitution that oddly remained the hope of a unified republic even as the country shattered into civil war among competing military factions. He felt that he still had a useful role to play. It was not true as some insinuated, he told Morrison, that he was staying on simply because it was financially attractive.[132] More to the point, Ariga had few options at this stage. He had come to China with high hopes of fleshing out the China dimension of his career in international law while enjoying his sideline passion for Chinese art. Several years later, with Chinese politics in turmoil, his judgment and integrity questioned at home, his writing for *Gaikō jihō* much reduced, he could not reasonably contemplate a new high-profile job. And age was a factor. Like Morrison, Ariga was already in his mid-fifties.

And so, responding creatively to his shrinking options, Ariga turned to China scholarship as both refuge and outlet for his formidable intellectual energies. His book on the legal basis for China's entry into World War I, *La Chine et la Grand Guerre,* published in Paris in 1920, was a highly technical case study in international law, a wrap-up of issues he had worked on with Morrison and the Chinese over the past six years. Available only in French, the book had limited appeal in

Japan except among Ariga's law colleagues. But for those who took the trouble to read it, the book provided a positive view of China's progress in joining the international legal order. In his writings for a Japanese audience, Ariga also chose to present China as a glass half full, warlord violence a mere blip on the screen of the enduring China, the China of fine art and Confucian culture. His belief that the past offered a reservoir of values on which to build a bright future represented both a reprise of his work with Ernest Fenollosa in the 1880s and affirmation of Okakura Tenshin's views on the equal worth of Eastern and Western civilizations. It was also a message Ariga had tried to get across to his Chinese colleagues without complete success in 1913.

Ariga's *A Correct View of China* (Shina seikan) published by *Gaikō jihō* in 1918 provided readers with a synthesis of his views on *bun* and *logos*, Confucian humanism and Western scientific rationalism. This translated into no immediate prescription as to how the Chinese Republic should proceed, but clearly he had come full circle in his own thinking about the need to fuse the humanist and scientific traditions. And his was an authoritative voice. As an advertisement for the 1920 edition pointed out, Ariga could draw upon his practical experience as constitutional adviser in China as well as his scholarly work in philosophy dating back thirty years.[133]

Mary Fenollosa had contacted Ariga in 1910 about revising and translating her late husband's *Outline History of East Asian Art*, then in manuscript form. He was too busy at the time, particularly to take on a major project with no certain prospect of remuneration. His stroke intervened the following year when the book was published in London in a handsome edition, beautifully illustrated. The best Ariga could do was to take the manuscript with him to Beijing in 1913 where he worked on it in his spare time over the next few, crowded years. By the time he left Beijing for good in August 1919, he had prepared an annotated version ready for translation.

In a meeting with people at the Tokyo Arts School, Ariga agreed to complete revisions and translation in time for a Fenollosa memorial scheduled for November 1920. He was now in regular contact with Mary Fenollosa over a host of matters including publication rights and transferring her husband's remains from London for interment in Tokyo. He saw the Fenollosa assignment as an honor that would have been Okakura Tenshin's were he still alive. But clearly Ariga wanted the challenge and knew he was uniquely qualified. It was a job that required knowledge of Chinese and Japanese art, history, philosophy, and religion along with first-class skills in translating from English to Japanese. It involved nothing less than the mediation of cultures. And it was not politically risky.

At the personal level, Ariga also had a strong sense of obligation to his early teacher. His own history was tied to Fenollosa's. As a man of sixty reflecting back on his career, he was ever more aware of his debt to Fenollosa for kindnesses during his student days and for opening up to him not only the world of Europe and America but the Chinese and Japanese past. The project was indeed a labor of love on Ariga's part. He was not and did not expect to be recompensed for his efforts. Yet the psychological satisfaction he derived from the chance to tie up the loose ends in his life, to affirm the filiality he so much believed in, and to cement his bona fides as a China scholar, was also enormous.

And the project with its short time frame for completion saved him from thinking too much about the Paris Peace Conference, in session from January 1919 to December 1920. He was too busy to comment, he said, and he may well have meant it. But one is left to wonder if Japan might have been better served at the conference had the Japanese delegation included a man of Ariga's caliber, fluent in English, French, and German, thoroughly versed in international law, and, while a firm Japanese nationalist, not unsympathetic to China's current struggles for unity. Would he have come down differently on the issue of returning Shandong to China? Perhaps not; he was a stickler for treaty obligations, and China had acknowledged Japan's claims to Shandong in a secret agreement in 1918. Would he have been able to convince Western delegates of the justice of Japan's proposed racial equality clause, which went down to defeat at the hands of the British, Australians, and Americans? His arguments might have helped. Pursuit of common humanity in scholarship and law regardless of race and culture had been at the core of his life's work.

Ariga's biggest problem would have been dealing with Tokyo, not his strong suit. As it turned out, among all gathered at Paris, the Japanese delegation was the most hamstrung by micro-management from the home government. Had Ariga not already clashed with key parts of the bureaucracy over the 21 Demands and the emperor incident, he surely would have done so over the discretion allowed delegates at Paris. In the end, Ariga's presence on the team may not have affected political outcomes. But almost certainly it would have countered the general Western perception that Japan's delegates were provincial, secretive, and sly with clear evidence of at least one delegate who was smart, outspoken, and cosmopolitan—in short, "one of us."[134]

By this point, however, not only was Japan regarded with increasing suspicion by the rest of the world, but the Japanese on their part were becoming more cynical, questioning whether the robust internationalism promoted by Ariga and other first generation Meiji thinkers was working to Japan's advantage. Ariga was the very personification of the notion that adherence to law was a global ideal and that Japan's best interests were served through steady, peaceful integration within the Western international system. But as China spun out of control and war in Europe showed the essential frailty of international law and the alliance structure, many of his countrymen began to wonder if unilateral self-protection was the better course for Japan. Even Ariga, seeing the world through the China lens, appeared more willing to consider common culture themes that would have warmed the heart of Asia for the Asians partisan Konoe Atsumaro. His work on the Fenollosa translation reflected a reaffirmation of the East Asian heritage.

Ariga worked like a driven man once he returned from Beijing to Tokyo in August 1919, finally retreating to Shiobara to get away from the demands of his newly activated social life. It was December when he started his "winter hibernation," as he called it, huddled at his desk in the drafty, unheated house dressed in padded clothes and a fur jacket purchased in Beijing. He worried that the strain of intensive work would bring on insomnia and result in a stroke as had happened in 1911 when he was trying to finish up two books. To his surprise, Spartan living and a country diet helped him sleep better. For this, he said, he had Fenollosa to thank.

It was the kind of obsessive work schedule that Ariga enjoyed. He completed the translation on schedule, much to the gratitude of Mary Fenollosa. Ariga had been right that he still could pour on the effort to meet a deadline. He was wrong about the impact on his health. The stress of his heroic burst of work landed him in the hospital with a second stroke. He died on June 17, 1921, aged sixty-one.[135]

Conclusion

Making Sense of It All

When Ariga Nagao died in 1921, Konoe Atsumaro was already seventeen years in his grave, his life cut short in January 1904, just a month before Japan's surprise attack on the Russian fleet at Port Arthur. Konoe knew in the final agonizing weeks before his death that war was likely. Any hope of a Russo-Japanese accord over the status of Manchuria and Korea had dissipated after a year of frustrating negotiations, pushing both sides closer to military confrontation. But it was not the prospect of war that worried Konoe. It was the possibility, however slight, of a last-minute compromise. His greatest fear was that Tokyo would strike a deal with Russia allowing Russia's 100,000-man force to remain in place in Chinese territory south of the Amur River. As he saw it, anything short of total withdrawal would be a dangerous concession to Western power in a region where Asian interests should predominate. It was a view that resonated with an anxious public. By December 1903 most Japanese agreed that a war to protect Japan's security, China's sovereignty, and regional integrity was not a war of choice but a war of necessity.

But the war itself, the staggering casualties from use of new, high-tech weapons, would have appalled and saddened Konoe, as it did Ariga Nagao witnessing the carnage from the battlefield. Civilian pursuits had always been the focus of Konoe's energies: building a first-class education system at home, the projection of "soft" rather than "hard" power in China. He was making headway on both fronts from the mid-1890s on with the help of a growing network of like-minded colleagues. In China, the Tō-A Dōbunkai presence with its message of Asian partnership was contributing to Japan's improved standing among Chinese progressives inside and outside the government. When the government got serious about reform after 1900, Japanese were the first to be hired to assist with institutional change. Hattori

Unokichi, Kawahara Misako, Kawashima Naniwa, and dozens more Japanese were working in advisory positions in China by 1902. When tensions with Russia worsened the following year, an important segment of China's future elite, the twenty-something students, favored Japan and were not afraid to say so loudly, publicly. Official China was more cautious, choosing neutrality as the better part of valor in this impending war over disposition of its own territory. Still, there were subtle signs of a tilt toward Japan. The Manchu court was making more than a personal gesture when it graced Konoe's memory with a special service at Beijing's Yonghegong Temple in January 1904.

Japan's early victories over the Russians on land and at sea generated an excitement among China's youth that would have warmed Konoe's heart. They wrote admiringly of Meiji achievements, citing Japan's success in battle not only as proof of Asian military/industrial potential but of the superiority of constitutional government over autocracy. It was a long slog to war's end, and some students began to worry about Japan's continental ambitions. But there is no doubt that Japan's demonstrated strength in this first colossal conflict between East and West fired up Chinese imaginations about the kind of nation China could become. In fact, Japan's defeat of a major Western power had an electrifying impact on nationalist sentiment in the East more broadly defined. Marius Jansen recounts to dramatic effect the experience of revolutionary leader Sun Yatsen as he passed through the Suez Canal on his way from Europe to Asia in July 1905. Sun met "an Arab" who told him of Russian troop transports filled with soldiers returning home, sure evidence, the fellow thought, that the Russians had lost the war. "The joy of this Arab as a member of the great Asiatic race," Sun recalled, "seemed to know no bounds."[1]

Sun's final destination on his 1905 trip was not Hong Kong or Singapore but Tokyo. News of Japan's victory had triggered an amazing jump in the number of Chinese students in Japan. The 1,000 students Konoe and Kanō Jigorō could point to with pride in 1903 had risen to nearly 10,000, a politically restive group eager to take advantage not only of a Japanese schooling but also of a freer atmosphere in which to vent about reform and revolution in China. Sun's hope was to breathe life into his faltering revolutionary movement by capturing the support of student dissidents. It was not an easy sell, but six years and many recruits later the core group Sun cobbled together in Tokyo helped put an end to imperial rule and make China a republic.

That revolution happened in China in 1911 would hardly have surprised Konoe. He knew of the deep anger among China's political elite at government corruption, incompetence, and mismanagement of foreign policy. He had discussed the failure of the 1898 reform movement with the coup leader himself, Kang

Youwei, who had barely escaped with his life to Japan. He was well aware of the restless energy and anti-government writings of the Chinese students in Tokyo. Tō-A Dōbunkai representatives stationed in China kept him briefed on local business and politics, including the activities of the renegade Sun Yatsen, and he spoke directly with China's provincial leaders about their efforts to remedy institutional weaknesses. In other words, Konoe had his finger on the pulse of Chinese politics at a time of domestic unrest.

But beyond this, Konoe himself was doing what he could to promote political change in China. He had lived through the uncertain days of early Meiji and been part of the bold restructuring that had transformed Japan from a third-rate country into a competitive nation-state in his lifetime. Call it reform, restoration or revolution, he believed that what had happened in Meiji Japan should happen in Qing China and could do so rapidly with Japanese help. He was convinced that a strong partnership between the two rising Asian nations was in their mutual interest at many levels, particularly as a counterweight to Western dominance in Asia. This was the message of Asia for the Asians. He liked to call the new policy an Asian Monroe Doctrine, and indeed the non-interference principle was at the heart of it. But Asia for the Asians was intended to be less hegemonic than the U.S. version. It had a development assistance emphasis that struck a positive chord with some of China's politicians, notably Sun Yatsen, who spent years seeking Japanese aid for his vision of revolution in China. There was more pragmatism than sentiment involved in Sun's much-publicized visit to Konoe's grave in 1913.

China's slippage from instability into fully-blown warlordism after 1911 and the Yuan Shikai debacle flummoxed Tokyo's politicians who knew so much—much more than their Western counterparts—about conditions on the ground, as we like to call them, in China. Pursuit of multiple options simultaneously, often through clandestine means and imposition of ultimatums, eroded much of the goodwill Japan had managed to build up in some quarters in China during the decade previous. Whether Konoe might have provided a steadier beacon on China policy had he lived beyond his fortieth year is difficult to say. His high rank made him politically unassailable; his reputation as man of complete integrity and public-mindedness lent special credibility to his positions, including his support for a special relationship with China. He might well have agreed to become Japan's prime minister in a time of crisis. And the value he placed on the *mutual* gains to be had from the Chinese-Japanese alliance might well have affected the course of events in a positive way.

But it is equally true that Japan's world grew increasingly complex in the years after Konoe's death. What none of Japan's leaders could possibly have imagined from the vantage point of 1903 or 1905 were the global reverberations of Russia's defeat, secondary effects that further complicated the already treacherous landscape of decision making. Not only did Japan's defeat of Europe's last pure autocracy give a symbolic boost to Chinese radicals calling for constitutional government. It also inflamed anti-tsarist sentiment in Russia, paving the way for revolutions in 1905 and 1917, the latter giving rise in Japan to fears of a new threat from Russia in the form of Soviet Bolshevism. There were secondary effects on Japan, too, from the changing balance of power in Europe after the Russo-Japanese War. As Russia's stock plummeted, Germany's rose, encouraging new alignments, with Britain, France, and Russia in one camp and Austro-Hungary and Germany in the other, thus setting the stage for World War I.[2] For four years the war in Europe was the main event, the position of the powers in Asia a sidelight, and it was at this point that Japan launched its 21 Demands, the opportunistic China policy that deepened the distrust on the part of Japan's allies and fueled the hostility of the Chinese. There was much in the world to be cynical about. For Japanese, the war itself, destruction on a scale never before witnessed in human history, seemed to prove the hollowness of Western systems and values that for so many in the Meiji generation were the source of lessons on how to modernize.

Reorienting Japan

Reliving the careers of our five Meiji Japanese as if a journey unfolding, destination unknown, gives us a revealing perspective on the larger story of Japan's transformation in the last decades of the nineteenth century. All five were born in the years between 1860 (Ariga Nagao) and 1875 (Kawahara Misako) when the violence attending the opening of Japan to foreign trade was fast giving way to a new unity of purpose under the imperial banner. They were the first children of the Meiji Restoration, that epic event that was in fact a revolution—and a young man's revolution, at that. After 1868 leaders still in their thirties and forties moved quickly to reshape Japan, launching national-level reforms that were breathtaking in their scope and impact. Efforts to construct a Western-style military were matched by a range of firsts in the civilian sphere: Asia's first national public school system, Asia's first constitution, Asia's first elected parliament, Asia's first commercial press, and on and on. It was a time of unprecedented opportunity, innovation, and societal energy. There was a spirit of optimism in the air. Had a Pew Global Survey been conducted in the 1870s or 1880s when Konoe and the others were growing up, the majority of Japanese would no doubt have responded that Japan was heading in the right direction.

Family background and status still counted in getting ahead in life after 1868, but much less so than before. Japan's commitment to wholesale change raised the prospect of new types of jobs, and increasingly routes to success were open to the bright and ambitious whatever their origins. The Hattoris, Kawaharas, Kawashimas, and Arigas were typical of the families whose children became prominent in Japanese public life in the 1890s through the 1910s: people of substantial education but little means, searching for ways to survive the passage from old certainties to open-ended challenges. For the youth of early Meiji, the feeling of hope in a time of reform was tempered by a keen awareness of how precarious life could be and how much their future security and that of the nation depended on their own determination to excel in their working lives. Even Konoe Atsumaro, who might have coasted along on his imperial connections, took nothing for granted when it came to career. He got his top slot in the new parliament while still in his twenties in part through personal drive and insistence in the face of opposition at court to pursue the study abroad opportunities available to his generation.

Expansion of educational opportunity was the single most important factor shaping this generation of Meiji youth. The 1872 education act, which suddenly mandated an entire system of public schools from primary level to university, for men and for women, set the markers for a nation rushing to modernize. Not surprisingly, the system was imperfect in financing, operation, and coverage at the start and buffeted by the shifting views of educators for decades after. Still, the spirit of the reform was clear from the outset: faith in the capabilities of ordinary people, irrespective of status, in building the nation, a search for talent based on merit, and, at higher levels, education for public service. It was a policy that invited, indeed required, all citizens, from the privileged Prince Konoe to Hattori Unokichi, Kawahara Misako, Kawashima Naniwa, and Ariga Nagao, to join a national effort to catch up with the advanced powers of the world. William Clark captured the mood in sound bite terms when he exhorted his students in Hokkaido in the 1870s, "Boys, be ambitious."

We know the outcome. By the turn of the century our five Meiji Japanese had become visible figures in the new establishment. Japan's bold plan for education had yielded literacy and school attendance rates comparable to those in Europe and America. However, it was not as easy along the way as these summary results might suggest. In the early days of Meiji, both educational planners and families of school-age children had to try to project what mix of skills would be needed in a modern workforce. What should people be trained *in* was the question. The new public school curriculum gave equal weight to Japanese-language and humanities courses and so-called Western studies—English, math, and science.

English-language study had been a draw from the time of the Perry mission in the 1850s. Like today's Internet it was regarded as the gateway to new knowledge, institutional and technical. Taking the Western part of the curriculum beyond the primary school level, however, was problematic at a time when there was limited space in public schools. In urban areas, families such as the Hattoris typically enrolled their youngsters in various private academies, often on a short-term basis, to get the sought-after English and other Western subjects. The result was individual programs, Western, Chinese, public, private, cobbled together in ad hoc fashion to try to gain an edge over the competition. It was hard to buck the popular trend in favor of Western studies. Kawashima Naniwa's teenage rebellion against learning English caused a crisis in his family, convinced as they were that some degree of modern training was essential for future success.

Kawashima was unusual in his uncompromising rejection of Western studies in favor of total immersion in Chinese. But even for those inclined to "seek knowledge throughout the world"—the *Western* world as the Meiji founding charter implied—and to go along with the government's curriculum, China remained an important source of foundational, humanistic values. For Japanese in the post-1868 world, the study of the Chinese classics continued to be the hallmark of an educated person just as the study of the Greek classics was for contemporary British. Konoe was tutored in Chinese by his eminent grandfather, Kawahara by her father, the others in private academies; the level and quality of training varied, but all had this basic experience of China. By their middle teens all were able to read Chinese and relate to China of the past. The best had developed a degree of fluency in both Chinese and English. Ariga Nagao helped with family finances during his university years by doing translations from Chinese into English for his major professor, Ernest Fenollosa.

When Ariga passed the entrance exam to enter Tokyo University in 1879 there were no more than 100 students enrolled, and two thirds of the forty-man teaching staff were foreign-hires. In 1887, when Hattori entered, enrollment was around 450. While Japanese had begun to replace foreign faculty, the university model still centered on the study of European languages and an open, liberal arts approach to learning. Ariga tangled with education authorities over the issue of academic freedom. Hattori grumbled about measures to regulate student conduct and standardize the curriculum. But neither disagreed with the underlying goal of the university which was to produce leaders to guide and govern the emerging nation. If this sounds overly pragmatic and out of tune with our own present context, it fit the vision of education in the advanced world generally in the late nineteenth century. Theodore Roosevelt's message to graduates of Harvard and Yale in 1890 that "they should stand foremost in the honorable effort to serve the whole public by doing their duty as Americans in the body politic"[3] would have translated well into Japanese.

Ariga was a gifted linguist. His contact with Fenollosa sharpened his proficiency in spoken English to the point that Fenollosa used him as one of his regular interpreters, along with Okakura Tenshin. His reputation as a brilliant student earned him a scholarship to study in Europe where he perfected his German and French, and more, his understanding of the dominant political systems and ideological debates engaging the attention of European intellectuals. Study abroad was regarded by both the Education Ministry and individuals with ambition as the capstone of a solid education. Konoe who skipped the Tokyo University track, spent five years studying in Germany to prepare for a future role in politics. Both Kanō Jigorō and Shimoda Utako, supporting characters in our story, went to Europe for mid-career training. Kanō had already made a name for himself as head of Tokyo Teachers College when he was awarded a yearlong grant to observe teaching methods in France and Germany. Shimoda was similarly an educator of established reputation when she managed to get the government to finance her extended study tour to England; she argued that firsthand observation of the lives of Victorian women would be of direct benefit when it came to shaping new programs to educate Japanese women.

Hattori's case is a revealing variant on the Euro-American bias in study abroad. His post-graduate scholarship specified a year of study in China to study the spoken language and make contacts with Chinese China scholars followed by three years in Germany to study German and German historical writing on China. Of course, it did not work out so neatly, as we know. The first year was indeed a learning experience, though being trapped in the foreign legations while the Boxers rampaged about was hardly the kind of study Hattori and his sponsors in the Education Ministry had in mind. But the important point is that while Hattori, like Ariga, had studied European languages and intellectual traditions at Tokyo University, his major professor was not Fenollosa from Boston but Shimada Jūrei, celebrated *Kangakusha,* China scholar. Because Western studies were "in" did not mean that China studies were "out."

What I call Japan's "reorientation" was a much more subtle, dynamic process. It involved on the one hand experimenting with various Western models—shifting from French to American systems in school reform, for example—and innovating on these models by giving them a special Japanese stamp. Shimoda's modern Asian education for women with its emphasis on morals courses and traditional domestic arts and Kanō Jigorō's judo, which might be termed a Japanese-like sport, are but two examples. On the other hand, with regard to China, reorientation involved reinterpreting and revaluing Chinese traditions, already changed in their Japanese setting, to give them new force in dealing with the problems of contemporary life. One of the prime movers in this effort to keep China studies relevant in Japan's more cosmopolitan intellectual environment was Shimada Jūrei, Hattori's mentor and father-in-law. Hattori's scholarship plan with its two-country focus mirrored the older man's interests, and very likely Hattori ultimately became what Shimada intended: a hybrid, a European trained China scholar who had real world experience of China and Europe. Though his career path was entirely different, Hattori with his intellectual cap on showed the permanent imprint of Shimada Jūrei. He followed in Shimada's footsteps as a professor at Tokyo University similarly engaged in demonstrating the continued vitality of Chinese classical traditions to modern life.

Kawashima Naniwa had no interest in the overseas study route favored by so many ambitious young men of his generation. He was a difficult teenager. He insisted on majoring in Chinese at a time when studying European languages was the popular thing to do, and then when the university track was closed to China majors he refused to consider alternatives such as business school or the military academy. He expressed his anti-Western bias so dramatically as to make it seem an affectation, though his underlying bitterness was real. He resented Japan's—and China's—humiliation at the hands of the Western powers just as he resented his family's precarious financial situation and the pressures on him as the eldest son. Internal tensions as much as anything drove his grand idea of fashioning a career as a China expert, not as an old-style scholar but a new-style specialist in contemporary China. He managed to get a good foundation in the spoken language at the Tokyo Language School before abruptly deciding to strike out on his own for Shanghai in 1886. Over the next fifteen years Kawashima acquired such extensive knowledge of China—its country and its people—that his skills were at a premium. He was a self-made old China hand when he was hired by the Chinese government in Beijing in 1901.

Kawashima Naniwa and Professor Hattori's wife, Shigeko, were among the well-wishers watching Kawahara Misako and her small caravan disappear over the horizon beyond Beijing's city walls on a December day in 1903 at the start of their uncertain journey to Karachin. Kawahara, a single woman in her late twenties, was, like the others whose lives we have traced, emblematic of Japan's quest to chart out a unique place for itself as Asia's first modern nation, a mediator of cultures East and West. Though not of the prominence of Hattori's father-in-law Shimada Jūrei, Kawahara's father was also a China studies teacher, a respected figure in Nagano intellectual circles. She got her early impressions of China from him: an appreciation of China's past culture, a concern for China's political future. He fit the mold of the modernizing *Kangakusha* who lacked firsthand experience of China but was convinced of the continued relevance of Chinese ideals to constructing modern life. Kawahara senior was also a modern parent, encouraging Misako, his daughter and only child, to get the best education available to women in 1890s Japan. At sixteen she studied to be a teacher, a sure path to an independent life for young women. At twenty, she was admitted to the highly selective Tokyo Women's Teachers College, which she attended briefly before withdrawing because of illness. When it came to pursuing the career she wanted, teaching Chinese students, Kawahara found her father totally supportive. He facilitated her contact with the highly placed Shimoda Utako, who was only too delighted to find an enthusiastic young ally in her own efforts to help shape China's modern education.

All of these young people growing up in early Meiji Japan—Konoe, Hattori, Kawahara, Kawashima, Ariga—felt the presence of China in their lives. Yet China spoke to them in different ways across time and place, always in the context of competing voices, European and American, and the need to arrive at a satisfying sense of what it meant to be Japanese. It was not a question of a clash of values, East and West, but of a constant weighing and considering of old and new, outside and homegrown. Their early experiences convey an aspect of the Meiji period often overlooked in the search for an oppressive hand: the great diversity of thought. Japan was at its most open-minded then. The climate of the times encouraged choice, risk taking, public service, and a search for meaning in the wider world.

Why Did China Beckon? Why Did They Go?

The face of Meiji Japan was outward looking after two hundred years of relative isolation. Japanese were eager to take advantage of new opportunities to study in Europe or America where they could observe the workings of advanced societies firsthand. The appeal of China was entirely different; it was the excitement of being able to visit a country that had existed only in books and perhaps to play a pioneering role in its development. Americans who studied China in the 1960s on National Defense Foreign Language fellowships—this author included—and only years later, after China's opening, had the chance to travel and work there—with the World Bank in my case—can relate to the feelings of awe and wonder experienced by Ariga Nagao standing in Tiananmen Square for the first time or Kawahara Misako approaching the port of Shanghai.

China was the place to fulfill personal dreams and professional aspirations.

How this played out with our five Meiji figures had to do as much with personal circumstances and personality as with society's emphasis on contributing to the national good. To the young and restless Kawashima, China represented escape from a troubled adolescence and the chance to expand Japan's influence and his own. To Ariga, a standout student eager to expand his mental horizons, China was fixed in place as a respected cultural artifact, Fenollosa's passion not his own. It was Europe with its embrace of multiple subjects, methods, and truths that charged Ariga's imagination. Only later did China take center stage in his life. Hattori's experience was just the reverse. For him China was the object of scholarly fascination during his university years, Germany a topping off for a well-educated young professor slated to get ahead in academia. Young Konoe, getting his first glimpse of China on a ship bound for Europe in the 1880s, worried about China's political survival in the face of Western pressures. The pragmatic concerns about regional policy that consumed him in the late 1890s greatly outweighed any fleeting sentiments he felt about the old China. Kawahara, very much her father's daughter, quite simply saw China as a backward place in need of the helping hand of a Japanese feminist.

What is striking is the extent to which China was a choice for our Meiji Japanese, rather than a decision directed by some central agency. To be sure, the Japanese military was glad to use Kawashima's language skills once he made it plain he had them; the foreign ministry was instrumental in arranging the terms of Hattori's and Ariga's China advisory work, and Kawahara's teaching job originated with the respected establishment figure Shimoda Utako. But as our chronicle of their lives reveals, they could have chosen options other than China along the way. Kawashima could have studied Western languages or business as his teachers recommended, Hattori might have built on his German experience, Ariga had the choice of turning down his China assignment on the grounds of poor health, Kawahara could have continued to teach school in Nagano rather than seeking out Shimoda. In time, after working in China, their attitudes toward China took on layers of complexity, but its appeal at the start was as a place where the ambitious might dream big dreams.

Within our group of China-oriented people, Konoe and his Tō-A Dōbunkai were the closest thing to the government getting directly involved in expanding Japan's influence in China. At the same time, the originating idea for the organization came from outside government and was meant to stir government to a more proactive Asia policy; Konoe prided himself on his independent, non-partisan status. And, although the Tō-A Dōbunkai received a government subsidy, it was largely privately funded, mostly by Konoe himself. As mentioned in Chapter I, the Tō-A Dōbunkai, as originally conceived, was remarkably like today's Asia

Foundation, no more, no less. Its expansionary vision took the benign form best expressed by Konoe in his Asia for the Asians formulation: that Japan should pursue its commercial and political interests in China vigorously but using what we would now call "soft power" means—overseas study, official study tours, advisory assistance—areas where Japan appeared to have advantages culturally and linguistically over the other foreign powers competing in China. The broadscale cultural borrowing he was encouraging was precisely the approach Japan's own leaders had adopted after 1868 in their earnest effort to modernize every aspect of government and economic organization. By the 1890s Japan had, in effect, graduated from its learn-from-abroad program. Fewer students were going abroad for study and fewer foreigners were working in the Japanese bureaucracy. As Ariga Nagao complained at the time, it made no sense for the government to retain the services of so-called experts like Henry Denison when capable Japanese were available to fill their posts.

A great deal has been written over the past sixty-five years about Japan's push to expand its influence in China from the late decades of the nineteenth century on. Certainly the efforts of our five Meiji Japanese can be made to fit this format though with the exception of Kawashima, whose record was mixed, the soft power qualifier must be applied. On the other hand, rather little attention has been paid to the pull factors, that is, China's interest in Japan. This is one of the casualties of China's postwar sensitivities. Though published in 1954, Marius Jansen's scholarly exposé of the decades-long friendship between the father of republican China and his Japanese political backers, *The Japanese and Sun Yatsen,* is still a blockbuster of a book, revealing how assiduously Sun courted Japan in the years before and after the 1911 Revolution. It is still stunning to read of Sun's willingness to bargain away Manchuria in return for Japanese aid.

Jansen's book featured Sun's associations with Japanese "professional adventurers and full-time plotters"[4] who served as indirect channels to the funding he hoped to secure for the cause of revolution in China. Pragmatic to be sure, but Sun's pursuit of Japan was not solely directed to a search for aid. He quite sincerely shared with his Japanese friends a belief in the logic of pan-Asianism. This is an intriguing mix of motives. Were it not for the tragedy of China and Japan's subsequent history, the story of exiled Chinese dissidents and their Japanese supporters might well have drawn more than the passing interest from research scholars than it has gotten in recent years. And this is only the radical political side of the encounter. Equally understudied is the larger phenomenon of which the Chinese-dissidents-and-their-Japanese-friends segment is just a part: the willing collaboration with Japan from the 1890s on of mainstream Chinese elites from businessmen to intellectuals to progressive-minded government officials.

What caught the attention of this broad group was not the promise of Japanese alliance but the attractive power of Japan's modernity. While most Chinese in the 1870s and 1880s were convinced that they knew all they needed to know about Japan, that attitude changed after China's double defeat—by Japan in the war over Korea and by the Powers jointly in the war against the Boxers. The sense of crisis produced by these events carried much the same punch as the crisis over economic stagnation of the late 1970s. It propelled the Chinese government, the Zhang Zhidong-style progressives in the first case, Deng Xiaoping in the second, to undertake reform programs that were national in scope and willing to upset old verities. While Deng turned to the West for aid, Zhang and his fellow progressives took a new look at Japan. Japan on the rise, a near neighbor with a similar written language and with experience mediating Western institutional models, suddenly presented itself as the best source of a low-cost, modern education. From Japan's standpoint, taking on the role of teacher seemed an ideal way to compete with the West for influence in China. It was a pragmatic decision on both sides that had mixed results. Some of the Chinese who came to Tokyo to study, including those tutored by Ariga at Waseda, retained warm feelings for Japan, others raged against Japanese imperialism. And while the ranks of China's modern-trained increased so did the incidence of dissidence against the Chinese government. When it comes to study abroad, this is not an unfamiliar storyline, anytime, anywhere.

When Konoe met with Zhang Zhidong and Liu Kunyi on his first trip to China in late 1899 he did not need to argue the case for increased teacher-student exchange programs. Both readily agreed that this was in China's best interests. Zhang's grandson was already enrolled in school in Japan. When it came to politics, however, the attitude of the two senior leaders was not quite so clear-cut. Liu made a point of emphasizing his pro-Japanese views, citing the fact that twenty years before he had willingly yielded to Japan on the issue of sovereignty over the Ryūkyūs. Zhang, on the other hand, made it plain that while he was open to more contact with Japan he did not welcome Konoe's frank commentary on China's domestic politics. He bristled when Konoe told him that international law protected exiled dissidents like Kang Youwei and waved him off when he inquired about Sun Yatsen. As a piece of political theater, the Zhang meeting was designed to impress, to insist on deference not simply to Zhang as the much senior in age but to Zhang as the symbol of Chinese grandeur and power. Konoe was aware of Zhang's sensibilities and annoyed with himself for letting things get out of hand with his sharp retorts on Japan's right to harbor Chinese dissidents. That he, an imperial prince with a degree from a German university, head of Japan's upper house, having just completed a year-long tour of Europe from London to St. Petersburg, might have expected some probing questions from Zhang on how politics and society worked in Europe or Japan seemed not to have entered his head. Instead, he went along with his host and politely reviewed Zhang's industrial projects and his German-trained officer corps. Zhang was in charge.

When Konoe visited China in July 1901, not quite two years later, China was struggling to recover from the Boxer trauma, Zhang and Liu had established "opening to the outside world" as reform doctrine, and Japan was in favor as a source of lessons in how to achieve rapid growth. This is the essential point: while the Japanese were keen to educate Chinese in these years, the Chinese were equally drawn to the idea, similarly for reasons of national interest. Getting the Japanese involved in institutional upgrading had the advantages of cost efficiency and reduced dependence on Western know-how. The initiatives to send some thousand Chinese officials to Japan for short-term training and to invite several hundred Japanese with special expertise to work in China long-term grew out of a convergence of views.

When it came to hiring Japanese advisers, the relationship was essentially contractual. Chinese central or local entities and the Foreign Ministry and Education Ministry acting for Japan vetted candidates and negotiated arrangements at the working level. Agreed terms were included in written contracts that spelled out what the Chinese were willing to pay in salaries and travel costs and the length of the contract period. While a measure of idealism and certainly excitement played into decisions to work in China, it was, in plain terms, a *job* the candidate was applying for, a source of income, and so salary was a key consideration. The Chinese paid well, though Japanese were on a lower salary scale than their European and American counterparts. Sometimes professional pride was at issue. Ariga argued for a high salary, not only because, as a low-paid Waseda professor he needed the money, but because he felt he was worth as much professionally as China's top-ranked foreign adviser, London *Times* correspondent G.E. Morrison. Contracts were usually short-term—Ariga's first contract was for only five months—with renewal subject to performance review, a device that enabled Chinese employers to maintain control over the people they hired. In a word, the Chinese were pragmatic, chose their Japanese candidates carefully, and managed them closely. There is no evidence that they were disadvantaged in the matter of hiring or firing or ever felt themselves to be so. For example, when Hattori tried to expand his advisory brief after six years in China, the Chinese turned him down, eliminated funding for his position, and he returned home.

In hiring Hattori, Kawahara, Kawashima, and Ariga the Chinese were getting top-quality people. When appointed education adviser in 1902, thirty-five-year-old

Hattori Unokichi had just been made a full professor at Tokyo University (the Chinese insisted on the professorial rank) where he had trained in European philosophy and China studies. He had worked in Japan's Education Ministry and taught at a public school in Kyoto as well as Kanō Jigorō's Tokyo Teachers College. He had studied in Germany and lived in China—during an unfortunate period, to be sure, but he knew China and had contacts within the bureaucracy. Other educators in Japan at the time, particularly those who had studied pedagogy in the United States, might have seemed better qualified to design the new teacher training program at Beijing University. Hattori had the edge, however, precisely because of his greater knowledge of China, his expected cultural sensitivity in the matter of training future teachers for a system still steeped in traditional values. He was probably viewed as a safe pick by the Chinese doing the hiring. This was also true of Kawahara Misako, who arrived in China just a week before Hattori to teach at a private girls' school in Shanghai. No doubt she was an unusual young woman, the epitome of the Meiji "new woman," ambitious, outgoing, and determined—at least for a time—to pursue an independent career path as a single woman. When she accepted the Shanghai teaching post in 1902 at age twenty-seven, she had several years of teaching to her credit, first at a high school in Nagano, then at a Chinese girls' school in Yokohama. She was self-taught in Chinese and French. But her biggest asset from the standpoint of the Chinese hiring her was that she came highly recommended by Shimoda Utako, whose approach to women's education—progressive in its commitment to expand opportunity, traditional in hewing to the idea of service to family and state goals—held great appeal for Chinese educators at the time.

Kawashima Naniwa had two major skills to recommend him for the job as director of the new Beijing Police Academy, which he assumed in the fall of 1901: first, he knew how to run an effective public security operation, and second, he had native-level fluency in spoken and written Chinese. His unique language proficiency and knowledge of the country had gained him much respect in the years since his stay in China in the mid-1880s but not a clear career path. Instead, he had bounced around from job to job—as an army interpreter during the 1895 war, as supervisor of a drug suppression unit in occupied Taiwan, as a language and literature teacher at the Military Academy and Kanō Jigorō's Tokyo Teachers College.

His big break came in the aftermath of the Boxer siege when he was hired as a contractor by the Japanese peacekeeping forces to train the old Beijing gendarmerie in modern police methods. As the streets became safer, Kawashima's reputation for getting things done caught the attention of China's senior leaders concerned about keeping the city clear of terrorist elements after the withdrawal of international troops. Kawashima's fluency in Chinese was an asset in his job as police trainer; it also helped him gain entré to key politicians in the Manchu-led government. Convinced that the Japanese model for the police made sense, Prince Qing appointed Kawashima to head a new Police Affairs Bureau, a post he held for only a few months before strong protests from Western members of the foreign coalition forced him to resign. While placing a Japanese national in a high-profile leadership position was clearly unacceptable to the other powers competing for influence in China, no objections were raised when the Prince subsequently offered Kawashima the less visible post as public security adviser and director of the Beijing Police Academy. As a mark of special favor he was made a civil official of the second rank within the Chinese bureaucracy.

Kawashima was thirty-six when he took on the task of developing a modern police system for China. A decade later he was still at it though the scope of his responsibility had been curtailed over that period in response to an upswing in Chinese nationalist sentiment and a souring political mood toward Japan. He thought the program of authoritarian reform he had signed on to assist was in trouble and he warned Tokyo to that effect. When revolution came in 1911 it proved a career-changing event for him just as the Boxer Uprising had been. The difference was that this time he risked being sidelined as he gambled away his China connections not on the New China but on the faltering cause of Manchu separatism. The year 1911 had a different message for Ariga Nagao. For him, the New China opened up a new career opportunity that looked both personally and professionally promising.

Were he to accept the position of constitutional adviser to the developing republic, however, Ariga felt he deserved the same salary and benefits as G.E. Morrison. Based on a comparison of résumés, Ariga had a valid point. Personally, Ariga was a great Morrison admirer. As he remarked publicly, Morrison knew more about China than the Chinese. Indeed, as the London *Times* man in Beijing Morrison was enormously influential in shaping British public opinion and policy on China. He had a huge rolodex, to use the current term, as well as a sensitive ear for political gossip and an insiders' command of facts and details. He wrote about China with sympathy yet certainty that the British presence there was a force for good. President Yuan Shikai was a big fan of his and this was reciprocated—at least at the outset. Yet Morrison could not read Chinese at all or even speak it fluently. Nor did he have the depth of understanding of comparative political systems or the administrative experience that would equip him to guide the new nation on the perilous path of institutional change.

When Ariga decided to take the China position, he was already in his early fifties and at the peak of a distinguished career in academia, publishing, and the practice of international law. His spoken Chinese may have been no better than Morrison's but he read classical Chinese with the fluency of a scholar and he was thoroughly versed in Chinese art and philosophy. He was a Europeanist by background and training, one of Tokyo University's earliest graduates, who went on to do post-graduate work in Germany. He was fluent in German, French, and English and a capable translator of works in diverse fields from pedagogy to political science. He wrote original works in French on his major subject, international law. He taught military ethics at Japan's military colleges and law and comparative politics at Waseda University where his students included Chinese youth and visiting officials.

But there was life beyond academia. Ariga was founder, editor, and managing director of Japan's first journal of foreign affairs. He was on the board of the Japanese Red Cross Society and had served as a delegate to the Hague Peace Conference in 1899. He was a legal adviser to the Japanese army during two wars, the Sino-Japanese and the Russo-Japanese. Ariga brought an impressive résumé to the table in 1912 when the Chinese raised the idea of hiring a Japanese national to help structure the new state. Morrison recommended him to President Yuan Shikai as "the most distinguished of Japanese Jurists." Whether Tokyo University's Minobe Tatsukichi, whose primary specialty was constitutional rather than international law, might have been a better match for the job is a moot point. When approached after Ariga's initial refusal, Minobe said he was not interested. The breadth of Ariga's experience seemed an advantage in any case, a chance for the Chinese to learn not only about Western political systems but the current rules of global politics.

Ariga was a committed internationalist. He had long argued that the only way that Japan as a latecomer to power could advance its interests in a European dominated world was to play by the rules of the international system already in place. The problem was that to play by the rules Japan needed to know the rules, and here he felt that both the Japanese public and Foreign Ministry diplomats were seriously deficient. Overcoming this perceived knowledge gap was his reason for establishing the foreign policy journal *Gaikō jihō* (Revue diplomatique), in 1898. Foreign relations under Ariga's baton became a professional field of study. He intended *Gaikō jihō* to have a teaching function, providing a kind of self-study curriculum in diplomatic history, comparative political systems, and international case law for senior policymakers and diplomats. He targeted youth with a similar array of courses at Waseda and the military academies. Japan, he believed, needed to be prepared to deal with the world as it was. If in this "knowledge is power" respect, Ariga was thinking pragmatically, there was a strong strain of idealism in his internationalist outlook as well. He shared the hope and belief of his French colleagues that the end result of building a rules-based international system would be a just and fairer world in which the only wars would be necessary wars.

Humanitarian law was the starting point for Ariga's career as an internationalist. In 1890 General Ōyama Iwao recruited the brilliant young student just returned from Germany to teach ethics at the Japanese Military Academy. A few years later, as the China conflict heated up, Ōyama assigned him to the newly created post of legal adviser to the army in the field, a commission he was given again a decade later in the war with Russia. In light of Japan's appalling record of atrocities in World War II, there is great irony in the fact that the impulse to adopt international standards in fighting modern wars came from within the military. The idea of soliciting legal opinion on actions in the field sounds remarkably contemporary. Yet this and the early stage of Japan's internationalism in general have not been well researched. Realities sometimes have a way of inconveniently blurring conventional pictures, in this case the negative take on the process of Meiji state building.

General Ōyama's strong views on conduct of war issues stemmed from his experience in Europe before and after the Franco-Prussian War of 1870. His was the guiding hand directing Japan to follow the European lead in establishing a Red Cross affiliate. Japan signed the Geneva Convention in 1886, only four years after the United States, and the Japanese Red Cross Society was founded a year later. Ariga was Japan's delegate to the 1897 international Red Cross conference in Vienna and the one in 1902 in St. Petersburg. During the Russo-Japanese War, the Society drew international praise for providing high quality medical services to both Japanese and Russian wounded. In fact, international observers were well satisfied not only with Japan's treatment of war wounded but how the war was conducted as a whole. There were no reports of violations of the Geneva Conventions and many reports that highlighted Japanese restraint and magnanimity. Not so in the earlier case of the Sino-Japanese War, where the reviews were mixed: admiration that Japan had managed to put together an effective fighting force so quickly and condemnation of the Port Arthur atrocity in which Japanese troops massacred some 2,000 Chinese soldiers and civilians. General Ōyama organized a commission to investigate and Ariga was asked to provide his own independent assessment of the incident.

Ariga's book, *The Sino-Japanese War from the Point of View of International Law,* published in 1896, provided a full-scale review of how Japan conducted the war, including a section on the events at Port Arthur. It created something of a sensation. Drafted in French by Ariga himself, it told the international community that Japan was serious in its efforts to comply with universally accepted standards—and that

Japan spoke the language of diplomacy. Translated back into Japanese at Ōyama's request for use as a textbook at the military academies, it boosted Ariga's reputation at home as someone with cutting edge knowledge of the laws of war. Port Arthur was a sticking point, a blot on the military's otherwise clean record. It raised an issue that still confounds us today: how to fight an enemy who does not observe the Geneva Conventions and has no compunction about committing atrocities of its own. The Ōyama commission was inclined to give the Japanese military a pass precisely on those grounds. Ariga had a different view. He concluded that while China's practice of irregular warfare might appear to justify Japan's brutal reaction at Port Arthur, it was not a sufficient reason. Japan had agreed to international standards governing battlefield conduct absolutely, not selectively.

Ariga did not bring in the "civilization" word to condemn China for atrocities against Japanese troops though he was careful to note the fact that those had occurred. For him, international law was not culture-bound or exclusively Western. It was simply a set of political tools for global governance, and agreeing to use them was a matter of choice for any nation—Japan, China, Persia, Turkey. Japan had chosen to enter into the Western-sponsored world order because it judged that doing so was in its national interest; other nations would follow suit as circumstances demanded. Ariga also saw international structures and norms as dynamic and evolving. He expected Japan not only to adapt to the existing system but to help shape the international relations agenda in the future. It was this kind of thinking that took him with enthusiasm to the Hague Peace Conference in 1899. It inspired him to judge the outcome of the conference, much criticized by some, as a glass half full. No, the Hague negotiators had not achieved their broad disarmament aims. But he argued that the fact that an international gathering was held at all for this purpose, the first-ever truly international conference in history, was cause for optimism about the future. And the meeting had managed to agree on new rules for new weapons—a ban on launching projectiles from hot air balloons, for example—and on establishing mechanisms for arbitration of international disputes.

Konoe Atsumaro mentions in his diary a chance meeting with Ariga in New York as they embarked on the *Majestic* bound for Liverpool, Ariga headed to The Hague, Konoe on the first leg of his round the world tour. They were both cosmopolitan in outlook: German-trained, well traveled, and attuned to world opinion. But they differed in their foreign policy vision and China's place in it. And they used the press, Ariga the pages of *Gaikō jihō* launched in 1898, Konoe an announcement in *Taiyō* that same year, to try to convince the public and policymakers of the soundness of their views. Ariga believed that building strong alliances with Western nations should be Japan's core objective, with China relations shaped in accordance with Western patterns and precedents. Konoe argued that for reasons of culture and geography partnership with China should be Japan's foreign policy linchpin, the better to balance off the long entrenched China interests of the Western powers.

Thinking in Asia for the Asians terms, Konoe was tolerant of Chinese dissidents, possible future leaders after all, citing international law as justification for providing them safe haven in Japan. Ariga agreed with the legal part but worried that giving comfort to dissidents might damage Japan's position with the Manchu-led government which had the backing of the Western powers. When Boxer violence spread in North China in 1900, Konoe urged restraint even after the murder of a Japanese diplomat in Beijing and rumors that Manchu officials were secretly funding the Boxers. He feared the destabilizing effects of foreign military intervention on China's fragile central government and the possible setback to Tō-A Dōbunkai-sponsored partnerships with progressive elites in South China. Ariga questioned whether Japan was up to the big league diplomacy required in the aftermath of a joint operation and acknowledged that Boxer rage against Christians and foreigners was not entirely unjustified. But he was firm in his belief that Japan had no choice but to throw its forces behind an international coalition to put an immediate stop to the Boxer threat. Terrorism could not be tolerated under international law.

Once the Boxers were defeated and the victorious allies began to depart Beijing, Ariga and Konoe began to worry about a countertrend they might have predicted: the buildup of Russian troops in Manchuria in violation of the phased withdrawal agreed with China. But there were important shades of difference in their response. Konoe campaigned strenuously against compromise and tradeoffs with Russia, believing that protection of China's sovereignty and Japan's interests was a sound regional strategy. Ariga was equally distrustful of the Russians, but he declined to join the anti-Russian hardliners aligned with Konoe. Instead, with the spirit of the Hague Peace Conference and internationalism fresh in his mind, he called for collective action, a meeting of the Powers with interests in Manchuria, to mediate the dispute.

In proposing a mechanism for conflict resolution, Ariga was being true to his internationalist ideals. But once negotiations with the Russians broke down and the Japanese attacked Port Arthur in February 1904, he was as good a Japanese nationalist as anyone. As he had done a decade before, he accepted an assignment as army legal adviser, assessed Japan's compliance with the Geneva Conventions from a frontline vantage point, and produced a volume on Japan's conduct of the war in light of international law. In his first message to *Gaikō jihō* readers from the front, he echoed the sentiments of virtually the entire Japanese public that this was a necessary war, not a war of choice. Just as Britain and France had gone to war in the Crimea to check Russia's advance into Europe, Japan was now acting in the interest of world peace by trying to halt Russian aggression in East Asia. World opinion was on Japan's side.

Ariga had no trouble justifying to the world Japan's reason for going to war or its battlefield conduct. Yet witnessing the reality of thousands of young men slaughtered in a day in the name of patriotism drained Ariga emotionally, making such distinctions as legal and illegal seem for a time quite meaningless. His writing, rational analysis packed with details, reflected the sense that the world had grown more complicated for Japan over the decade, as it was as well for Ariga with his vast, intricate knowledge of legal precedents and tangled alliances. He was the man who knew too much. Nowhere is this more palpable than in his prescient tract on what to do about postwar Manchuria, entitled, *Discussion of a Mandate for Manchuria.* Western-devised rules of the international game of monopoly allowed for, even encouraged, occupation of overseas territories deemed by the Powers to be badly administered and strategically important. British-held Cyprus and Austria-Hungary-controlled Bosnia provided Ariga with neat parallels. The partial mandate for Manchuria that Ariga proposed was meant to allay Japanese concerns about continued instability in a region of Japanese—and world—interest. Ariga also cast himself in the role of development advocate, advancing an argument repeated in later decades: that only Japan had the special capacity to develop this frontier region long neglected by an unimaginative Chinese leadership. As we know now from the American experience in Iraq, occupations are more easily justified than effectively implemented.

G.E. Morrison and President Yuan Shikai were almost certainly well aware of what they were getting when they brought Ariga onto the China advisory team in the spring of 1913. His writings were well publicized. He was always clear and forceful in his opinions. Many of his former Chinese students at Waseda were in key positions in the new Republican government. The big question was how Ariga the Europeanist would manage in the Chinese political environment.

Taking Stock: The Prospects and Limits of Partnership

Today there is a self-consciousness and anxiety in outsiders' attempts to understand China in its Asian context and to predict its future impact on us. Politicians and economists puzzle over China's stake in the global economic system and wonder about the viability of regional blocs such as ASEAN plus three or eight.

Businessmen worry about patent protection and the Chinese proclivity towards "re-innovating." Human rights advocates debate the relevance of Chinese values, particularly the legacy of Confucianism, to principles defined under the Western-inspired international human rights regime. Political scientists argue for or against the likely survival of China's resilient authoritarianism. Historians survey the broad sweep of history, seeing the present as a watershed moment marking a global shift of power from West to East. Or they engage in theoretical discussions—for example, is Asia One as Ariga's classmate Okakura Tenshin argued, or not?—in which concepts and isms seem to float about unanchored to the human beings who thought them.[5]

My own approach as a historian has been to take individual human lives as the starting point and to hold back overarching judgments, waiting and watching instead to see what is revealed. Thus, for example, I have not focused on imperialism, a topic of considerable interest currently, simply because Konoe and the others were not thinking "imperialism" when they set off on their life's endeavors, nor did they make it a topic of discussion. There were people who did talk about it—for example, Ariga's colleague at Waseda liberal scholar Ukita Kazutami—but more often than not as a system to promote world order and progress, a stage in national development to aspire to, not to condemn.[6] Judging from the actions and rhetoric of the five people whose lives I have traced, they did support Japan's overseas expansion or expansionism in a general sense, seeing this as a natural extension of nation building and a force for good. There was and is nothing new about putting a positive spin on one's own country's efforts to spread its influence abroad. As our reality-check Theodore Roosevelt pronounced in 1899 as justification for America's invasion of the Philippines, ". . . every expansion of a great civilized power means a victory for law, order, and righteousness."[7] And how many times were we told that the American occupiers of Iraq would be greeted as liberators?

It is not that our Japanese figures were not debating such fundamental issues as the meaning of Asia and Japan's regional role. Ariga, for example, questioned Tokyo's decision in 1910 to make Korea a colony. And both he and Hattori Unokichi devoted a great deal of thought over the years to defining the place of Chinese-inspired values in the modern life of China and Japan. But theirs was a practical approach to the world. Ariga's reservation on the colony option was that it was likely to come at too high a political cost. He and Hattori urged Chinese and Japanese to revisit Confucianism because they believed that Confucian beliefs in order, loyalty, the extended family, and the importance of education could be applied usefully to present problems of governance. They did not over-intellectualize these issues as our current theoretically inclined historians are wont to do, making neat distinctions among "regionalisms," "regionalizations," "regional imperialism," and the like, disengaging quickly from hard evidence and reality.

Our five Meiji Japanese were above all doers. They went to China to accomplish something—or many things. The stories of their China encounters are dynamic and moving, hard to pigeonhole in value terms. They lie in the realm of people-to-people interactions in which attitudes inevitably shift, not necessarily along a good-bad spectrum, but in terms of what is workable and what is not in a different cultural context. They went to China in what most would consider the best frame of mind for an overseas experience: knowing the language, admiring the civilization, and eager to make a positive difference. They were not the condescending sort that Konoe worried about in the late 1890s. Assessing the results of their efforts in purely pragmatic terms, one can say that all five contributed in concrete, lasting ways to China's institutional development, suggesting the potential for constructive collaboration. Konoe was personally involved in all aspects of educational exchange. He was the inspiration behind the whole notion of regional partnership that long outlived him. As advisers in the field, Hattori launched China's first teacher training program, Kawahara provided a prototype of women's primary education that was quickly replicated, Kawashima established core training for an entirely new public security system, and Ariga helped the Chinese write their first modern constitution. These were no small accomplishments.

Yet for all their real contributions, none of the five left China feeling satisfied with a job well done. Konoe, who traveled there twice on official missions, probably came closest. He was pleased to get China's top leaders to endorse Japan's educational initiatives, though his diary entries reflect frustration at his inability to break through the arms length mode of his Chinese counterparts. The other four, who went to China as foreign-hires, were disappointed that their sought-after advice was not fully utilized, that their achievements were limited in scope. They grew frustrated with their Chinese counterparts, all the more so because they had expected that knowledge of language and culture would facilitate a unique working relationship denied Western advisers in China.

Ironically, at the personal, everyday level Konoe and the others felt or came to feel no less foreign among the Chinese as the Europeans and Americans. Konoe with his cropped hair, Western business suits, and cosmopolitan interests moved confidently and comfortably in English and German elite circles. Yet traveling to China for the first time he was ill at ease, put off balance by a society that seemed as difficult to penetrate as the minds of the old-style Mandarins presiding over affairs from inside their walled compounds. Hattori's first tour of China proved an even more dramatic demonstration of cultural difference. He found to his dismay that being a fellow Asian was no advantage when it came to Boxer violence. The Boxers saw him as much a foreigner as the Westerners who were the essential targets of their anger. This initial impression stayed with him for a lifetime as it did with the Westerners caught in the legation quarter, but it was layered over with other experiences, both positive and negative, during his second, much longer tour of China. Hattori, Kawahara, Kawashima, and Ariga were not just travelers to China. They lived and worked in China and this real interaction on the ground, so to speak, made them at once more understanding of China's problems yet less optimistic about how to solve them.

Westerners and Japanese today are shocked and alarmed by China's relentless pursuit of outside technology. "Digesting and re-innovating" is what the Chinese call the process of partnering with foreign high tech firms, studying the technology—whether it be high speed trains, power-generating equipment, or advanced military aircraft—then retooling it into a made-in-China product. What outsiders see as disregard for intellectual property rights the Chinese see as ingenious reverse engineering. Addressing China's modernizers a hundred years ago Hattori Unokichi decried precisely the opposite tendency: a Chinese reluctance to look for best practices outside China or even to consider that such might exist. He warned that in a competitive world this was a recipe for decline. He was talking here in terms of both science and institutions, and he laid the blame for the tendency on a deeply ingrained intellectual arrogance in which the very idea of an outside product being superior represented a threat to China's cultural self-image. Japan, Hattori believed, offered models of modern systems that were especially worth considering, not because they were imitations of Western counterparts but because they were realistic adaptations in the Asian context.

Ariga Nagao also pinpointed what Hattori referred to as Chinese close-mindedness as an issue, though he was careful not to call it that. Instead, he urged the Chinese leadership not to worry about the specifics of Japanese models but to take as the lesson of development Japan's willing embrace of an innovative mindset. No need to be like us, he cautioned, except in taking an open-minded, flexible view of best practices available both elsewhere in the world and from within Chinese tradition. For Ariga, the constitution writer, this meant considering European constitutions on the one hand, and, on the other, going back to first principles, *Chinese Confucian* principles, in devising a cohesive state ideology. This was the message he had for his Chinese students at Waseda who were, in his view, too quickly inclined to toss out the best in their own culture. Hattori was in accord, emphasizing that training in Japan for students from Beijing Normal was intended to help the Chinese devise their own, culturally compatible system of teacher training.

Hattori, Ariga, and eventually Kawashima, too, after twelve years on the government payroll, found it frustratingly difficult to deal with the Chinese bureaucracy. Policymaking was opaque. Determining who was in charge in the tumultuous years between the war with Japan in 1895 and Yuan Shikai's death in 1916 is a challenge even now with the advantage of hindsight, much less at the time. When Hattori proposed establishing a school for women, he was given the diplomatic runaround, advised by one of the princes, no less, to take the matter to a higher level. He complained to no avail that the government was not giving its Japan-trained students responsible positions. His bid to extend and expand the scope of his contract met with a negative response on funding grounds, possibly true though he sensed that more likely it reflected the waxing and waning of pro-Japanese elements within the government. Where Japan stood at any given moment relative to the Western powers was hard to discern amid the factions contending for power—Han, Manchu, liberal, conservative, and various combinations thereof. Yet, for development to work, Hattori believed, China needed to make a consistent commitment to what he hoped would be the Japanese model. After Hattori left China in 1909, the Chinese government awarded him an honorary degree in recognition of his services; he came away from his long years there with some lasting professional friendships. On a personal level, however, he had to concede that he had changed his mind over time: it was not really possible to get to know the Chinese in any close, meaningful way.

Ariga's position was even more difficult. He had been hired to work at the very center of power in President Yuan Shikai's office without having anything in his background to prepare him to navigate the hidden shoals of Chinese politics. No doubt he suffered the consequences of political inexperience, though even the politically savvy Morrison eventually threw up his hands in disgust that he, Yuan's political adviser, was kept out of the loop when it came to internal decision making. Still, the cost to Ariga was higher. He stuck his neck out on the issue of the 21 Demands in 1915, opposing his own government in an effort to soften the terms imposed on the Chinese. Obviously Ariga felt this was the right thing to do, though he was acting more on rational than moral grounds. As Yuan's employee, he believed he should be working in Yuan's interests. More important, he agreed with Japan's elder statesmen that delivering an ultimatum to the Chinese as Foreign Minister Katō decided to do would prove counterproductive, angering the Chinese and alarming the international community. He was right. Yuan's reaction to Ariga's principled behavior was to spread the false rumor that Ariga favored Yuan's bid to become emperor, a bit of political chicanery that caused Ariga enormous public embarrassment. Both he and Morrison stayed on in China until 1919, advising Yuan's successors, watching China disintegrate into warlord rule. Neither was invited to attend the Paris Peace Conference.

Kawashima was in the unique position of not just working *for* the Chinese government but working as a two-star ranked bureaucrat *within* the Chinese government. As he described his dozen years of service, he had the authority to hire, fire, and promote thousands of Chinese subordinates while interacting collegially with Chinese of the same or higher rank. He savored his position as an insider. This was a role Ariga and Hattori never sought to achieve, however much they believed that their China knowledge and cultural sensitivity equipped them well for the jobs they had been hired to do. Instead they saw themselves as serving within the ranks of the other foreign professionals, bringing a special Japanese perspective to the process of opening China to the outside world, to use the Deng-era formulation. Only Kawashima thought he could push China to Japan's version of modernity from the inside, by essentially becoming Chinese. As he said, "I tried to adapt to Chinese practices and customs, to assume an attitude of ready acceptance of the other culture."[8] This approach is perhaps not as unusual now with our Peace Corps awareness and concern about stakeholders' input, but it set Kawashima apart then. He was gratified when the Chinese "view of me as a foreigner nearly faded away."[9]

All the more bitter, then, was Kawashima's disappointment when he was edged out of his insider role and the influence he so highly prized nearly faded away. Addressing a Japanese audience in 1926, he described himself as "someone who had been deeply sympathetic toward China as the key to the revitalization of Asia" now being forced to conclude that the Chinese were "beyond hope."[10] What he meant by this, he explained, was that the Chinese were like "loose sand," incapable of joining together in a common national purpose, motivated instead by short-term self-interest and materialistic goals.

The charge was not unusual at the time. To Meiji era Japanese brought up to prioritize public service, patriotism, and the common good, China's fractious politics and particularistic interests were baffling at best and at worst not a hopeful sign for the future. Evenhanded as he tried to be, Konoe grumbled about the lack of Chinese concern for public goods and public space and the apparent inability of China's top leaders to come together to solve China's underlying problems. Hattori laid some of the blame for the Boxers' hatred of foreigners on the Chinese failure to understand that certain people—the Western missionaries, in this case—were motivated by something other than personal material gain. Ariga complained about the Han Chinese majority's selfish inattention to the lagging status of minority groups in Manchuria. After a year teaching at a girls' school in Shanghai, the notably nonjudgmental Kawahara came away frustrated by her students' focus on material things and their evident willingness to remain nothing more than household ornaments, as Naruse Jinzō liked to say. Some prominent Chinese were equally critical. Sun Yatsen himself famously agreed with the loose sand image circulating among foreign observers, Japanese and Western. To him it signified the lack of national solidarity that was the proximate cause of China's inadequate response to foreign oppression.

Kawashima was in more than his usual angry mood in the mid-1920s. He railed on about the loss of China, calling the 1911 Revolution a sham, led by people like Sun who mouthed slogans about popular rights and national sovereignty as a mere cover for their own brand of special interest politics. He lashed out against China's warlords, including Guomindang leader Chiang Kaishek, as totally money-and power-driven without a sincere thought in their minds about what was good for the Chinese people. He was frustrated that so many well-intentioned Japanese were, in his view, willing to accommodate to a succession of warlords, blind to the fact that continued disorder in China would make it vulnerable to influences coming from communist Russia. He argued that only Japan could save China from itself. After engaging in the butchery of World War I, Western nations had no moral basis for claiming a leadership role in Asia. Besides, what Westerners called international law had been exposed as nothing more than fine-sounding rhetoric to justify establishment of their overseas colonies while trying to deny Japan the same.

By his own admission, Kawashima was on the fringes of Japanese public policy thinking in the 1920s. People laughed at his talk of Japan's spiritual mission to liberate Asia from white racist oppressors. They dismissed his complaints about double standards in international law and his persistent belief that Japan's best hedge against China's chronic instability was support for ethnic separatism, state-building under Japan's direction among the minorities in China's northeast. His call for a revival of the Chinese monarchy struck most Japanese as retrograde and self-serving coming as it did from the author of two previous failed attempts to bring "independence" to Manchuria and Mongolia. Yet just a few years later with the effects of world depression and instability pressing on Japan, Japanese had come to agree that Manchuria was Japan's economic lifeline and must be protected from Chinese lawlessness along the border. Expansion into Manchuria in 1931 and establishment of the Manchukuo puppet state the following year were greeted not simply with public approval but with public enthusiasm. Kawashima warned military officers stationed in the new state to tone down their arrogant behavior and demonstrate the cooperative spirit behind Japan's unique version of nation building. But apart from this scolding, he was clearly delighted that the public was now on his side in believing that taking strong action in China's northeast was an essential first step in negotiating from strength with China's new strongman, Chiang Kaishek.

This kind of shift in public sentiment is hardly uncommon. As we know so well, conditions of global economic downturn and political instability heighten public anxieties, excite protectionism, and make the possibility of a military response seem the reasonable, perhaps the only, solution. When Konoe in 1898 invoked the threat of Western expansionism and the likelihood of a future white/yellow racial struggle, he did so largely for dramatic effect to indicate the urgency of re-directing Japan's foreign policy toward East Asian concerns. The danger he posed was not immediate. The solution he proposed was benign: building an East Asian community, a modern political construct based on mutually beneficial regional partnerships with the China-Japan relationship at the center. Forty years later Ko-noe's articulation of Asia for the Asians principles had gained credence at top policy levels as the justifying rhetoric behind the Greater East Asia Co-Prosperity Sphere. But now the threat factor appeared real; it seemed quantifiable in the steady cutoff of raw materials, visible in the steady encirclement of Japan by the Western powers. In this new context not only Japan's leadership but an increasingly fearful public accepted Konoe's rationale but abandoned his faith in soft power, convinced that only direct intervention could stabilize China, foster Manchuria's development, and free Asia from the bonds of Western colonialism.

In the same pattern of undercurrents converging into a new mainstream, Ariga Nagao's carefully crafted proposal on what to do about Manchuria, written in 1905, seemed to bolster Japan's case for occupying Manchuria twenty-five years later. It was hardly Ariga's intention to lay the groundwork to support the state of Manchukuo. His point was simply that in the case of a war fairly fought and won, the victor had a legitimate right to preempt future threats from the contested region through some system of controls, particularly since international precedents existed to support such a scenario, in this case Western-occupied Cyprus and Bos-nia. Ariga showed occasional flashes of annoyance in 1910 over what he saw as the hypocrisy of Western colonialists criticizing Japan's position on Korea. But he was no Kawashima. He had devoted his career to understanding the workings of international law and believed deeply in the potential of international rules and in-stitutions to preserve global order. Still, an intriguing question remains: had Ariga been alive in 1933 would he have supported Japan's walk-out from the League of Nations over the issue of Japan's claims to Manchuria? Would he who helped write China's republican constitution have agreed with Japan's argument before the League that "China was not a state?" Certainly Ariga acknowledged and deplored

China's descent into lawlessness. Writing in 1920 at the height of warlord violence, he singled out China's failure to substitute the rule of law for the rule of men as its biggest problem.

However, to go the step of withdrawing from the League would have given him pause. The report of the League's fact-finding commission was moderate in tone. It recognized Japan's special interests in the region and recommended a negotiated solution, an undoubted point of appeal to the logical Ariga. As a confirmed pragmatist, he would likely have concluded that it was more sensible for Japan to stay in the League and thrash out a compromise than to cut off ties completely. Besides, with his old nemesis the Foreign Ministry behind the precipitate withdrawal, Ariga would have relished citing this decision as yet another example of bungled diplomacy.

Hattori, by this point suffering from Parkinson's, had retreated into academic research on China, having made his futile argument about the need to separate culture from politics. He continued to teach university students the importance of Confucian ethics in modern life. But it was hard to get the Boxer images out of his system or the public's. What he had written in his published diary more than thirty years ago seemed relevant now: a picture of China in disorder, prone to violence, unpredictable. Hattori, though enfeebled, had maintained his place in the public eye. Kawahara, on the other hand, had been out of Japan and the public limelight for years before the press brought her back to life beginning in the mid-thirties to feed the public frenzy of interest in books on Manchuria and Mongolia.[11] She was a reluctant media figure who protested that *Remembrances of Mongolia,* re-issued in 1943, was meant to chronicle her experiences in education not politics and certainly not her own brief role scouting out information for the military. But what could be read as the adventurous tale of a Peace Corps Volunteer in the 1910s became a new drama in wartime with Kawahara cast as female patriot and Japan as liberator of Manchuria first from Russian invasion and now from the corrupt and brutal rule of Chinese warlords.

Weighed in the balance, what our five Meiji Japanese said about China was as important as what they did in China. They were different in their outlook and experiences, though remarkably interconnected, in fact, to a degree I had not anticipated when I embarked on my reading of their lives. Konoe knew Ariga and Kawashima who knew Hattori and Kawahara who knew our two secondary figures Shimoda and Kanō and so on. They were all prominent figures. They taught and wrote books and articles and were quoted in the press. While they did not make policy, they intended to influence it. They helped shape a Japanese public perception of China, not unlike the dualistic view of opportunities/challenges we are given today by China experts concerned about the future of China and America. In the Japanese case, as external circumstances worsened from the late 1920s on and the Meiji generation moved off the stage, the challenges side of the discussion came to dominate: that China's shortcomings in development were primarily due to resistance to innovative thinking, that China's chronic political instability posed a particular threat to neighboring Japan, and that China could only be transformed with outside assistance.

If Konoe and the others left China in some frustration it was in part because they had more advice to offer than they were asked to give. With a concerted push from the China side, the Tō-A Dōbunkai might well have been able to organize a more vibrant teacher-student exchange program; as it was, it managed to keep its Shanghai business school for Japanese going until 1946. If Hattori had been invited to work within China's Education Ministry as some of his Chinese colleagues wanted him to do, he could have built quickly on his already substantial progress in establishing teacher training facilities. Kawahara probably would have been enticed to stay in China, her father's reservations overcome, had she been offered greater responsibility. Ariga had at his fingertips a world of experience in international law that could have been useful to China in its foreign dealings, but as in the case of Morrison and the other foreign advisers his expertise was sadly underutilized. Kawashima's case was more problematic. His evident personal ambitions signaled "handle with caution," though his ability to get things done was legendary. The Manchu reformers who chose to hire him erred on the cautious side. As to Kawashima's own decision to throw in his lot with them, it made sense around 1907 when the reform faction appeared to be gaining ascendancy, less so after 1911 when Tokyo chose to follow the lead of the Western powers in supporting Yuan Shikai.

As underscored by WikiLeaks 2010, diplomacy is a messy, complex business. All of the factors present now—personal innuendo, hidden agendas, cultural gaps—were present in the nineteenth century world as China and Japan tried to adjust to a new Western-imposed negotiating style. Clearly, China did not match Japan in quick mastery of international practices and efficient use of foreign advisers. Accounting for the difference has not been the subject of this book except through the eyes of our Meiji Japanese who attributed it largely to Chinese intellectual arrogance or failure of leadership. Still, the fact remains that China was under enormous pressure economically and militarily throughout the period we have considered, not only at the hands of the Western powers but a rising Japan as well. Playing off one foreigner against another was not just traditional policy. It may have been the only reasonable policy. At least no Chinese leader, beset with internal problems, was willing to risk all on a Konoe-style special relationship with Japan.

January 1948 marked the eightieth anniversary of the Meiji Restoration. Japan was under American occupation. The Tokyo trial had yet to hand down its judgment. Of our group of five, only Kawashima Naniwa was alive to survey the wreckage of the Meiji dream that had infused Japanese of his generation with such high hopes for the future. There is a sense of sadness remembering Konoe and the others from this vantage point. They valued their connection with China, emotional and professional. They were among Meiji Japan's best products—well educated, principled, hard-working—and they contributed in real ways to China's betterment. Had Chinese politics been less fractured, it is possible to imagine the fragile unfolding of a genuine East Asian community. Yet their words and opinions, however honestly delivered, also contributed to a negative Japanese perception of China, which in time of crisis fed into public support for war against the very country they had expended so much energy to study and to understand. Should we think of Konoe and the others as helpless, complicit, responsible? Reading their lives forward makes it vastly more difficult to render judgment. It clouds the picture of good and bad motives, moral and immoral behavior; it exposes the full complexity of Chinese-Japanese interactions, defies the rush to assign blame or to pin a guilty label on a government or faction or set of people. We are forced to question conventional narratives and to take a fresh look at the capacity of Meiji Japan to act as a cultural mediator. Human stories, after all, are the real stuff of history, and starting with them is a logical way to bridge gaps in "historical perceptions," as historians with the Japan-China History Committee like to say. True reconciliation will come, I believe, when historians plumb the depths of a range of such stories, when writing on war and the build-up to war centers on evidence, not predetermined moral judgments, and when wartime atrocities are viewed not as a single national tragedy but a shared human tragedy.

Notes

Notes to Introduction

1. See especially Gries, *China's New Nationalism*, 13-22, 43-53.
2. Coble, "China's 'New Remembering' of the Anti-Japanese War," 394-410.
3. Chang, *Rape of Nanking*; Fogel, "The Nanking Atrocity and Chinese Historical Memory," 267-284; Gries, *China's New Nationalism*, 83-84. Other excellent volumes in addition to the Wakabayashi and Gries books are: Fei Fei Li et al., *Nanking 1937: Memory and Healing*. Fogel, editor, *The Nanjing Massacre in History and Historiography*; and Yoshida, *The Making of the 'Rape of Nanking.'*
4. Note that from the China side the group is known as the China-Japan History Joint Research Project.
5. Jason Leow, "Nanking Efforts Examine Massacre, Seek Healing," *The Wall Street Journal* (August 13, 2007), A6. For a sample of articles in the press on the joint research project see: Murie Dickie/David Pilling, "Sino-Japanese Historians Battle to Find Common Ground," *Financial Times* (February 16, 2007), 2; Bu Ping, "Reexamining History," *Beijing Review* (February 15, 2007), 10; Bu Ping, "Bridging a Divide: Mission Impossible," *Beijing Review* (April 12, 2007), 16; Kitaoka Shin'ichi, "Nit-Chū rekishi kyōdō kenkyū no shuppatsu," 14-20; Bu Ping, "Nit-Chū rekishi kyōdō kenkyū igi to kadai," 207-210. For an interesting account of some of the challenges faced by participants in the project—this by a Japanese member—see Shoji Jun'ichiro, "Briefing Memo," 1-5. The discussion here is also based on the author's meeting with Ishitobi Takashi, Deputy Director, China and Mongolia Division, and Wakayama Kyōichi, Japanese Joint Study Secretariat, Japan Foreign Ministry, August 10, 2007.
6. Kitaoka Shin'ichi, "Insights into the World: Future tasks in the study of Japan-China history," April 18, 2010, www.yomiuri.co.jp/dy/columns/commentary/20100419dy01.htm.

7. "Japan Admits War 'Act of Aggression,'" *China Daily* (July 24, 2010), 1-3; Kitaoka, "Insights into the World," http://www.yomiuri.co.jp/dy/columns/commentary/20100419dy01.htm; Kitaoka Shin'ichi, "A Look Back on the Work," 6-20.
8. Tony Judt, "The Past Is Another Country," 157-183.
9. Barrett and Shyu, editors, *Chinese Collaboration with Japan*, 17.
10. Wakabayashi, *The Nanking Atrocity*, 19.
11. Cohen, *History in Three Keys*, 6.
12. Ministry of Foreign Affairs of the People's Republic of China, "Premier Wen Jiabao Holds Talks with Japanese Prime Minister Shinzo Abe," 2006/10/08 http://www.fmprc.gov.cn/eng/zxxx/t277536.htm
13. Ministry of Foreign Affairs of Japan, "Final Report." The report is available in Japanese at http://www.mofa.go.jp/mofaj/area/china/pdfs/rekishi_kk_j-2.pdf and https://memoryreconciliation.wordpress.com/
14. Nish, "Japanese Expansionism," 83.
15. See Harrell, *Sowing the Seeds of Change.*
16. Ferguson, Empire: *The Rise and Demise of the British World Order.*
17. Yamamuro, *Manchuria under Japanese Dominion*, Fogel, translator, vii-viii.
18. Prasenjit Duara, *Sovereignty and Authenticity*; Louise Young, *Japan's Total Empire.*
19. Townsend, *Yanaihara Tadao and Japanese Colonial Policy*, 8.
20. Fogel, *Articulating the Sinosphere*, 1.

Notes to Chapter I

1. *Nikki*, vol. 2, 195.
2. Konoe Fumimaro, "Chichi no koto," 2.
3. Oka, *Konoe Fumimaro*, 1. As head of one of the five regent families, Konoe was made a kōshaku or prince, the highest-ranking title in the new peerage created in 1884.
4. Seidensticker, *Low City, High City*, 28-29; Kudō, *Konoe Atsumaro Kō*, 313; *Konoe Kazan Kō*, 1-3. See entries on Konoe Tadahiro (1808-1898) in Beasley, *Meiji Restoration*, especially 134, 137, 180, 192, 288, 317, and in Keene, *Emperor of Japan*, 41-44, 63. A senior court noble, Konoe served as regent in 1862-1863. He was also related to the Satsuma daimyo through marriage.
5. Bird, *Unbeaten Tracks in Japan*, 13 (quote); Seidensticker, *Low City, High City*, 26-28, 42-44, 105-107.
6. Keene, *Emperor of Japan*, Chapter 28, 273-284. Quotation is on page 273. Keene goes on to say: "The war represented a great threat not merely to the evolution toward democracy desired by principal members of the government but to the very survival of the regime. At the start it was by no means certain that the Satsuma Rebellion would fail, and if it succeeded, the entire political configuration of Japan would undoubtedly have changed." Keene follows this opening paragraph with the best account available of the

rebellion led by Saigō Takamori, hero of the Restoration and loyal supporter of the monarchy itself (see page 281).

7. *Konoe Kazan Kō,* 1-5; Keene, *Emperor of Japan,* 3-4.
8. Kudō, *Konoe Atsumaro-kō*, 6-13.
9. Kudō, *Konoe Atsumaro-kō*, 13-18; Konoe Fumimaro, "Chichi no koto," 31-32; Oka, *Konoe Fumimaro,* 9. In his younger days, Saionji had studied calligraphy with Konoe's grandfather. On Itō's support for Konoe's study abroad plan, see also *Nikki*, Suppl. vol., 447.
10. Kudō, *Konoe Atsumaro-kō*, 18. Note that by the terms of the Treaty of Shimonoseki in 1895, Japan acquired the Pescadores.
11. Konoe Fumimaro, "Chichi no koto," 36. For a sampling of Japanese newspaper reports on the Sino-French conflict, see MHNS, vol. 5, entries for July-September 1884.
12. Kudō, *Konoe Atsumaro-kō*, 19-29; *Nikki*, vol. 2, 345; Oka, *Konoe Fumimaro*, 16-18. On letters home to grandfather, see *Konoe Kazan Kō*, 304 and *Nikki,* Suppl. vol., 556-605. For a copy of the thesis, see *Nikki*, Suppl. vol., 3-36. Paris mentioned in *Nikki*, Suppl. vol., 448.
13. Jansen, *Making of Modern Japan,* 389-395. Itō was made prime minister, Japan's first, under the cabinet system announced in 1885. For an excellent analysis of the working of the House of Peers, including Konoe's role, see Andrew Fraser, "The House of Peers," in the altogether first-rate study, *Japan's Early Parliaments, 1890-1905.* Both the Introduction and Conclusions are notably insightful. The authors make the convincing case that the House of Peers was an activist body for at least the first fifteen years of its existence, a useful corrective to the more conventional view of Japan's early democracy. *Nikki*, Suppl. vol., 449.
14. *Nikki*, Suppl. vol., 37-43, 449-450; Oka, *Konoe Fumimaro*, 3; Kudō, *Konoe Atsumaro-kō*, 28; *Nikki*, vol. 2, 187-192.
15. *Konoe Kazan Kō,* 313.
16. Oka, *Konoe Fumimaro*, 4. He is said to have remarked later that this deception made him feel "the world is full of lies."
17. *Nikki,* Suppl. vol., 701-702; Konoe Atsumaro, *Hokkaidō shiken*, 5; Fraser, "The House of Peers," 24-25; *MHNS,* vol. 9, 57-58.
18. Keene, *Emperor of Japan*, 467.
19. Mason, "Foreign Affairs Debates," 177-194; Keene, *Emperor of Japan*, 466-469.
20. *Nikki*, Suppl. vol., 449, 701-702; Kudō, *Konoe Atsumaro-kō*, 74-76, 267-269, Oka, *Konoe Fumimaro*, 2-3; Keene, *Emperor of Japan*, 424-428, 466-469.
21. Kudō, *Konoe Atsumaro-kō*, 267.
22. *MHNS*, vol. 9, 448-449; Keene, *Emperor of Japan*, 525.
23. Kudō, *Konoe Atsumaro-kō*, 269.
24. McClain, *Japan: A Modern History*, 227-230.
25 Kudō, *Konoe Atsumaro-kō*, 267; *Nikki*, Suppl. vol., 100-101; Keene, *Emperor of Japan*, 505-506.

26. Harrell, "The Meiji 'New Woman' and China," 110.
27. Calculated from figures given in *Education in Japan* (1904), 13-14, 32. See also discussion in Harrell, "Meiji 'New Woman'," 115-116.
28. Kudō, *Konoe Atsumaro-kō*, 287-290. See *Nikki* entries for Naruse, vol. 2-5; Kuni Nakajima, "Naruse Jinzo" in *Ten Great Educators of Modern Japan*, 67-87, and discussion of Naruse in Harrell, "Meiji 'New Woman'," 122.
29. "Japan's Women Growing Like Their American Sisters," *New York Times*, November 10, 1912, available at www.nytimes.com/ref/membercenter/nytarchive.html
30. Kudō, *Konoe Atsumaro-kō*, 288.
31. *The Works of Theodore Roosevelt*, Vol. XIII, 469.
32. Harrell, "The Meiji 'New Woman'," 111-112. Shimoda was originally Hirao Sekiko. She acquired Utako at court and Shimoda through marriage.
33. *Shimoda Utako Sensei den*, 339. Harrell, "Meiji 'New Woman'," 113-115.
34. Harrell, "Meiji 'New Woman'," 115-118.
35. Konoe, *Nikki*, Vol 1, entries under Shimoda; Keene, *Emperor of Japan*, 435.
36. Hearn, *Editorials from the Kobe Chronicle*, 168; Japanese National Commission for Unesco, *The Role of Education*, 350.
37. Japanese National Commission for Unesco, *The Role of Education*, 347-353; MHNS, vol. 9, 346-347; Harrell, "Meiji 'New Woman'," 120.
38. Konoe, *Nikki*, Vol. 1, 103-104, 112; *MHNS*, vol. 8, 473, vol. 9, 268; Duke, *History of Modern Japanese Education*, 184-186, 301-303, 251-252; Lincicome, *Principles, Praxis*, 64, 69, 195-196, 230-247.
39. Konoe, *Nikki*, vol. 1, 57, 113-114, 116-117, 122, 127-128, 137-139, 202; *Nikki*, Suppl. vol., 702.
40. For a sample of meetings with Kanō see Konoe, *Nikki*, vol. 1, 118-119, 120-122, 124, 138-140, 203; for Isawa meetings, vol. 1, 219, 243, 315, 319, 320, 329 and *MHNS*, vol. 9, 479; Kudō, *Konoe Atsumaro Kō*, 285-286: Konoe was a member of a number of educational organizations; in 1898 he resigned as president of the Imperial Education Association fearing he was spreading himself too thin.
41. Inoue, "The Invention of the Martial Arts," 164-167. On the press, see Harrell, "Meiji 'New Woman'," 110.
42. *MHNS*, vol. 8 (April 1891), 70.
43. Ibid.
44. Katō, *Kanō Jigorō*, 34 (quote), 21, 114-115
45. Literally, Tokyo Higher Normal School (Tōkyō Kōtō Shihan Gakkō). I believe that Tokyo Teachers College better conveys the meaning of the original in today's English.
46. Katō, *Kanō Jigorō*, 97, 99, 109, 118-119, 111, 122, 264-267; Inoue, "The Invention of the Martial Arts," 167.
47. Harrell, *Sowing the Seeds*, 1-2, 34.
48. *Nikki*, Suppl. vol., 62-63.
49. Ibid.

50. Ibid, 62.
51. Putnam Weale, *Re-shaping of the Far East*, vol. 1, 49; Konoe Fumimaro, "Chichi no koto", 36.
52. Oka, *Konoe Fumimaro,* 4; *Nikki*, Suppl. vol. 438, 448, 467; "Kichō shitaru Konoe Kō," (Prince Konoe on his return home), 47-51.
53. Harrell, *Sowing the Seeds,* 21-22, 30, 43; Reynolds, "Training Young China Hands," 212-227.
54. *Tō-A Dōbun Shoin Daigaku shi*, 16; Tō-A Dōbunkai, ed. *TSKKR*, vol. 2, 888.
55. Kudō, *Konoe Atsumaro-kō,* 225 passim; *Nikki*, vol. 2, 105, 117, 123, 125.
56. Kudō, *Konoe Atsumaro-kō,* 314; *Nikki*, vol. 2, 27.
57. *Nikki*, vol. 2, 123, 125.
58. *Konoe Kazan Kō,* 352; Arima, *Seikai dōchūki,* 92-93. Konoe contributed personal funds in large amounts to finance the Tō-A Dōbunkai and similar projects. Realizing that this was becoming a financial drain, some of Konoe's colleagues proposed establishing a fund to support all of his public activities. Konoe refused at first, reluctant to become involved in special interest politics as so many in the Diet were at the time. He finally relented, but was very strict in keeping his personal and professional accounts completely separate. Oka, *Konoe Fumimaro,* 2. Fumimaro notes that as a result of his father's large expenditures for public causes, the Konoe family was in financial straits after his death.
59. *Nikki*, vol. 2, 168, 175, 177-179, 184; Kokuryūkai, *TSSK*, vol. 1, 610-11; *MHNS,* vol. 10, 308-309. At the inaugural meeting, only China was mentioned as the focus of Tō-A Dōbunkai activities. Soon after, Korea was added to the agenda. Initially about 60 percent of Tō-A Dōbunkai funds went to China projects, the rest to Korea. See Reynolds, "Training China Hands," 226-229.
60. See *MHNS* articles on Kang, vol. 10.
61. *Nikki,* vol. 2, 195.
62. *Nikki,* vol. 2, 195-197 (quote).
63. *Nikki*, vol. 2, 239, 247-252, 272, 293-294, 299; *Nikki,* Suppl. vol., 703ff; *Konoe Kazan Kō,* 140.
64. *Nikki*, vol. 2, 306-307. For a fine account of the departure scene, see Jansen, "Konoe Atsumaro," 107.
65. Kudō, *Konoe Atsumaro-kō,* 236.
66. Morris, *Rise of Theodore Roosevelt,* 456, 579 (for quotes). For Japanese press coverage of events in Hawaii, see *MHNS*, Vol 15 (index), 458-459.
67. Kudō, *Konoe Atsumaro*-kō, 236.
68. *Nikki,* vol. 2, 311-321.
69. *Nikki,* vol. 2, 324.
70. *Nikki*, vol. 2, 322-337; remarks to Japan Society meeting, 323-324. See also Jansen, "Konoe Atsumaro," 109. For the British primer verse, see Adam Goodheart, "How to Expand the British Empire," *Civilization* (Library of

Congress), August-September, 1997.
71. *Nikki,* vol. 2, 339, 362-372, 350.
72. *Nikki,* vol. 2, 478.
73. *Nikki,* vol. 2, 357-375, 477-478; *Nikki,* Suppl. vol., 424; "Bei-Ō junkai no zakkan," 96-97.
74. *Nikki,* vol. 2, 477; *Nikki,* Suppl. vol., 424.
75. *Nikki,* vol. 2, 426.
76. Ōmori, "Tō-A Dōbunkai," 79; Tō-A Dōbunkai, *TSKKR,* vol. 3, 360-403.
77. Kokuryūkai, *TSSK,* vol 3, 377-379.
78. *Nikki,* vol. 2, 450-451, Beasley, *Japanese Imperialism,* 55-68.
79. *Nikki,* vol. 2, 431-432 (quotes), 453, 464, 473-474(quote); Harrell, *Sowing the Seeds,* 41ff; Peattie, "Japanese Treaty Port Settlements,"166-209.
80. Putnam Weale, *Re-shaping of the Far East,* 61-66; Chu, "Li Hung-chang," 269; *Nikki,* vol. 2, 442-443.
81. *Nikki,* vol. 2, 442-444. Quotes on 444.
82. *Nikki,* vol. 2, 445-446.
83. *Nikki,* vol. 2, 447-448.
84. *Nikki,* vol. 2, 455.
85. Ibid.
86. Ibid.
87. *Nikki,* vol. 2, 454-456
88. *Nikki,* vol. 2, 456-480.
89. *Nikki,* Suppl. vol., 424-425.
90. *Nikki,* vol. 2, 480, 488-495, 495, 497, 503-510, 512-513; *Nikki,* vol. 3, 16-18, 29, 65-70.
91. *Nikki,* vol. 3, 119-120.
92. *Nikki,* vol. 3, 184-185, 199-201, 211-213, 248.
93. *Nikki,* vol. 3, 204.
94. *Nikki,* vol. 3, 203-205 (quote).
95. *Nikki,* vol. 3, 119-121, 208-209, 211.
96. *Nikki,* vol. 3, 291-292; *Konoe Kazan Kō,* 156-157.
97. *Nikki,* vol. 3, 338-340 (quote).
98. *MHNS,* Vol. 11, 128, 168-169, 185, 200, 224, 294; Okamoto, *Japanese Oligarchy,* 58-59; *Nikki,* vol. 4, 81-83; Jansen, *Japanese and Sun Yat-sen,* 109
99. *Konoe Kazan Kō,* 361-362; *MHNS,* vol. 11, 169; *TSSK,* 901-902.
100. Harrell, "Meiji New Woman," 124-125; Harrell, *Sowing the Seeds,* 34-35; Katō, *Kanō Jigorō* , 124-128.
101. Harrell, "Meiji New Woman," 128-130.
102. Ibid., 130.
103. *Konoe Kazan Kō,* 361-362; *MHNS,* vol. 11, 169; *TSSK,* 901-902.
104. *Nikki,* vol. 4, 228-229; Suppl. vol., 68.
105. *Nikki,* vol. 4, 229-233; Reynolds, *China 1898-1912,* 69-78, 164-167.
106. *Nikki,* Suppl. vol., 71-72.
107. *Nikki,* Suppl. vol., 68.

108. *Nikki*, Suppl. vol., 70.
109. *Nikki*, Suppl. vol., 68-72.
110. *Nikki*, vol. 4, 237-274.
111. *TSKKR*, vol. 2, 903-905 (quote on 905); Hatano, "Historical Materials on Konoe," 279-295; Jansen, *Japanese and Sun Yat-sen*, 109-110 Okamoto, *Japanese Oligarchy*, 69-71
112. Konoe, *Hokkaidō shiken*, 1-82, (1902).
113. *Konoe Kazan Kō*, 363-364; *Nikki*, Suppl. vol., 489-490; Okamoto, *Japanese Oligarchy*, 62-67; Harrell, *Sowing the Seeds*, 133.
114. *Konoe Kazan Kō*, 366-372; *Nikki*, Suppl. vol., 469-471; *MHNS*, vol. 12, 96-98, 106, 114, 159 [obituary]; Okamoto, *Japanese Oligarchy*, 81; *TSKR*, 909.
115. Konoe Fumimaro, "Chichi no koto," 30; *Konoe Kazan Kō*, 372. As the latter source explains, since the mourning period for Konoe was announced on January 2, 1904, the date of his death is sometimes given as the 2nd rather than New Year's Day as in *MHNS* 12: 159; *Nikki*, Suppl. vol., 487.
116. *TSKKR*, vol. 2, 910-911.
117. As quoted in Okamoto, *Japanese Oligarchy*, 119. Casualty figures for the Russo-Japanese War are hard to determine. Official Japanese figures as reported by General Kuropatkin in his 1909 publication, *The Russian Army and the Japanese War* (Vol. I, 207), are 47,387 killed and 172,425 wounded. The total number of "killed, wounded and sick" is given as 554,885. According to the general, these numbers come from a report published by the "principal medical officer of the Japanese army." Okamoto (Chapter 5, 368n13) cites figures of 60,083 "killed in battle" and 21,879 "died from disease." No figure is given for wounded. Ariga Nagao who served as the army's legal expert and wrote a book on the war cites figures of 220,000 wounded, 80,000 dead at the front, and 236,000 suffering from disease. (See Chapter V, n72.) Arriving at an accurate count is difficult given the number of deaths from illness and war injuries that occurred after the war was officially over.
118. Reynolds, *China, 1898-1912*, 186-192; *Tō-A Dōbun Shoin Daigaku shi*, 27; Harrell, *Sowing the Seeds*, 195; Jansen, *Japanese and Sun Yat-sen*, 160.

Notes to Chapter 2

1. *TSKKR*, vol. 2, 910; Lillian Li, *Beijing*, 50-51, 78, 87, 148. Description also based on author's personal observation of Yonghegong.
2. Harrell, *Sowing the Seeds*, 1-2, 34-35.
3. Ibid., 35. Between 1902 and 1906, 1,959 Chinese graduated from Kōbun. *Kanō Jigorō* (Kanō Sensei denki hensankai, editor), 180 (quote).
4. *Kanō Jigorō choshakushu*, vol. 3, 1983, 293 (quote); Abe Hiroshi, *Nit-Chū kyōiku kōryū to masatsu*, 8-10.
5. Wang, *Zhongguo de jindai hua yu Riben*, 126-129.

6. Jansen, *Making of Modern Japan,* 329-332, 364-370; *HSK,* 2-3; Yoshikawa, ed., *Tōyōgaku no sōshishatachi,* 121-125.
7. *HSK,* 1-3; Yoshikawa, ed., *Tōyōgaku sōshishatachi,* 121-125.
8. Jansen, *Making of Modern Japan,* 329-330; Yoshikawa, ed., *Tōyōgaku sōshishatachi,* 4.
9. John Russell Young, in Tokyo for the Grant visit in 1879, as quoted in Seidensticker, *Low City, High City,* 34; see also, Ibid., 12-14.
10. Mehl, "Private Academies for Chinese Learning," 87-104.
11. *ZTSKKR,* 743; Seidensticker, *Low City, High City,* 62-63, 214; *HSK,* 4-6; Yoshikawa, ed., *Tōyōgaku no sōshishatachi,* 126-127.
12. Japanese National Commission for Unesco, *Role of Education,* 57-58; Mehl, "Private Academies for Chinese Learning," 90; Tanaka, *Japan's Orient,* 48; *HSK,* 5-6.
13. See, for example, *MHNS,* vol. 4, 411 and vol. 5, 179.
14. *HSK,* 6-8; *ZTSKKR,* 743-744. For a discussion of the military drill course, see Hall, *Mori Arinori,* 424-437. On Shimada, see Fogel, "Kano Naoki's Relationship to *Kangaku,*" 358-372, and Yoshikawa, ed., *Tōyōgaku no sōshishatachi,* 131-132. Figures for foreign and Japanese faculty at Tōdai from 1877 to 1890 when Hattori graduated are given in Marshall, *Academic Freedom,* 32.
15. Tanaka, *Japan's Orient,* 41.
16. *HSK,* 9-12; *MHNS,* vol. 9, p. 144, vol. 10, 146; *ZTSKKR,* 744; Takeuchi, *Kindai Nihon to Chūgoku,* 215.
17. *HSK,* 11-13; *MHNS,* vol. 10, p. 392. This was in May 1899 and concurrent with his position at the Normal School. See *ZTSKKR,* 744-745; for a summary of Hattori's career to this point, see also Shiba Gorō, *Pekin rōjō* and Hattori, *Pekin rōjō nikki,* 20. On Japanese sinologists and the new emphasis on spoken language competency, see Tao, "Shigeno Yasutsugu," 373-382 and Tao, "The Influence of the Tongcheng School," 151-163.
18. On the use of the designation "overseas student," note that some of the Chinese students already in Japan at this time were likewise well educated and/or high-ranking—e.g., Governor-general Zhang Zhidong's son and grandson.
19. *ZTSKKR,* 745.
20. Ibid.
21. Takeuchi, *Kindai Nihon to Chūgoku,* 213.
22. Hattori, *Pekin rōjō nikki,* 114, 199-200. Hattori published his diary in the fall of 1900 just after his return to Tokyo from Beijing. It was re-published in 1926 on the occasion of his sixtieth birthday in a volume that included Hattori Shigeko's (his wife's) account of managing the family in Japan while waiting anxiously of news of her husband trapped in Beijing under Boxer assault. Translations in the present chapter are from the 1965 version published by Heibonsha. This version replaces Shigeko's journal with that of Shiba Gorō, the Japanese colonel in charge of the Japanese legation defenders. Both the Shiba and Hattori diaries have been annotated, punctuated, updated in terms of place names, and supplied with maps and a chronology of the siege.
23. Quoted in Spence, *To Change China,* 125.
24. Hattori, *Pekin rōjō nikki,* 201.

25. Ibid., 204.
26. Ibid., 115.
27. Mathews' Chinese English Dictionary: "expel pernicious heresies in order to honor the truth."
28. Hattori, *Pekin rōjō nikki,* 114-116. Quote on 115.
29. Ibid., 120.
30. Ibid., 123-124.
31. Ibid., 125-131. Hattori quotes (131) the Qing prohibition order issued in response to protests from foreign diplomats, noting that it avoided clearly stating whether the Boxers were "good" or "bad" elements. In his view, by stating that officials would clamp down on bandits acting in the Boxer name, the order implied that the Boxers themselves were not a threat to national security.
32. Ibid., 132-133; Spence, *To Change China,* 233; Pearl, *Morrison of Peking,* 113.
33. Hattori, *Pekin rōjō nikki,* 133.
34. Ibid., 133-134.
35. Ibid., 133-136. The photo appears in preface to the book. Note that the volunteer list included Ishii Kikujirō, later of League of Nations fame.
36. Ibid., 136-139.
37. Ibid., 140.
38. Ibid., 143-144.
39. Ibid., 146-148.
40. Ibid., 150-152; Pearl, 115-116.
41. Hattori, *Pekin rōjō nikki,* 211-212; Pearl, *Morrison of Peking,* 118-119, 125; Fairbank, *East Asia,* 400-401; Putman Weale, *Re-shaping of the Far East,* vol. 1, 193-203.
42. Hattori, *Pekin rōjō nikki,*111, 212, 221-222.
43. Ibid., 157-158, 220-221; Pearl, *Morrison of Peking,* 118-119. Note that in his account Hattori was nowhere near as judgmental as Morrison who wrote of the Hanlin burning: "Other great libraries, the Alexandrian and in Rome, had been destroyed by the victorious invader, but what can we think of a nation that sacrifices its most sacred edifice, the pride and glory of its country and learned men for hundreds of years, in order to be revenged upon foreigners?" (Quoted in Pearl, *Morrison of Peking,* 118-119). For an additional account, see Smith, *China in Convulsion,* 281-285.
44. Hattori, *Pekin rōjō nikki,* 159 (quote), 207-208.
45. Ibid., 162.
46. Ibid., 167-170.
47. Ibid., 206, 174-184 (quote 178)
48. Ibid., 177, 181, 185.
49. Ibid., 186-195.
50. Ibid., 196-198.
51. Ibid., 184 (Japanese casualties as of July 26 were 10 dead, 20 wounded), 198, 222-223. On casualty figures, see Smith, *China in Convulsion,* 488-489. Such sentiments were echoed by many Western writers. See, for example, Putnam Weale, *Re-Shaping of the Far East,* vol. 1, 203, who said about the post-1900 occupation of part of the Su-wang-fu by the Japanese: ". . . if ever men deserved to hold a piece of ground by

right of conquest it is the gallant Japanese after the exploits of Colonel Shiba and his men. For it was they on this ground who fought for nearly two months until there was nothing much left of them or their positions. Another week or two and Chinese desperadoes, having pierced through this important outwork, would have been able to attack directly the British Legation—the base where were stored the women, children, and useless people during the siege—which would have been the beginning of the end."

52. Takeuchi, *Kindai Chūgoku to Nihon,* 214 (from an article in *Taiyō,* 12-13). On the size of the Allied relief force, the most reliable figure is 20,000, with 40-50 percent Japanese. Additional troops were brought in once the siege was lifted to handle mop-up operations in the Beijing-Tianjin region. Separately, the Russians poured additional troops into Manchuria which put it under virtual occupation. See Cohen, *History in Three Keys,* 54-55, and Preston, *Boxer Rebellion,* 207, 217. On the Russian troop buildup in the area, an article in the December 8, 1901 *New York Times* cited sources saying that, "No less than 200,000 Russian infantry and cavalry have been quietly mobilized in Manchuria, in other Chinese provinces, and in Southern Siberia . . ." www.nytimes.com/membercenter/nytarchive.html
53. *HSK,* 15-16; Ōtsuka, "Chūgoku kindai kōtō," 52-53; Abe, *Chūgoku no kindai kyōiku,*" 156. As mentioned in *Shimoda Utako Sensei den,* 415, Hattori left his children in Japan with his parents.
54. Putnam Weale, vol. I, 201-202 (quote) and chapter VIII, "Peking under the Foreign Heel," 194-211
55. Reynolds, *China, 1898-1912,* Appendix A for translation of January edict, 201-204; Harrell, *Sowing the Seeds,* 28-29; Hattori, *Pekin rōjō nikki,* 223.
56. Ōtsuka, "Chūgoku kindai kōtō," 53-54, and Xiao, *Beijing Daxuexiao shi,* 13-14, and chart, 323. From 1902-1909, the university was organized into preparatory (science and technology and government subdivisions) and short-course or accelerated tracks (teacher education and public administration) plus associated schools such as classics and medical schools and an attached higher primary school. What was referred to by Westerners and Japanese as Beijing University was literally, "jingshi daxuetang" or "capital university." Note Reynolds, *China, 1898-1912,* translates "shixue guan" as General Education Division. See Japan, Ministry of Foreign Affairs Archives (Gaikō shiryōkan) for contract (in Chinese) for Iwaya Magozō dated October 9, 1902, with note that same terms applied to Hattori. For a listing this and other official communications between the Chinese and Japanese governments regarding the hiring of Japanese teachers for Beijing University, see Eto, *Jindai zai-Hua Riren guwen ziliao mulu,* 2-10.
57. Xiao, *Beijing Daxuexiao shi,* 10.
58. Ōtsuka, "Chūgoku kindai kōtō," 53-54; *HSK,* 17-18.
59. Ōtsuka, "Chūgoku kindai kōtō," 45-47. See Liu, "Politics, Intellectual Outlook, and Reform," 88-110, for an earlier controversy over a proposal to have Hanlin scholars study Western science and technology. On the Board of Punishments official (vice-president), Li Duanfen, see Bailey, *Reform the People,* 20-24. Regarded

as a pioneer in public education in China, Li was the first to propose a national school system capped by a modern university.

60. Ōtsuka, "Chūgoku kindai kōtō," 49. *MHNS*, vol. 10, 348: The 2/1/1899 *Jiji Shimpō* report given here is slightly at variance with other accounts which speak of 100 students, e.g., Xiao, *Beijing daxuexiao shi*, 10. Note that Martin, in a bit of self-promotion, translated his title, zong jiaoxi, as "president." See Ibid., 7, on China's official endorsement of the Japanese school model.
61. Xiao, *Beijing Daxuexiao shi*, 10-11; Hattori, *Pekin rōjō nikki*, 135; Giles, *Siege of the Peking Legations*, 121-122; Smith, *China in Convulsion*, 267; Spence, *To Change China*, 158-159. For the comment on James, see Giles, *Siege of the Peking Legations*, 121.
62. Ōtsuka, "Chūgoku kindai kōtō," 49-52. Zhang Baixi dismissed everyone but Robert Coltman, medical missionary who was retained temporarily. See entry in Morrison, *Correspondence*, vol 1: Coltman wrote a book on siege of the legations in 1901 entitled *Beleaguered in Peking or Yellow Crime*. Xiao, *Beijing Daxuexiao shi*, 10-15; *Beijing Shifan Daxuexiao shi*, 2-3.
63. On Backhouse, see Trevor-Roper, *Hermit of Peking*, 37. From this fascinating account, it is clear that any qualifications Backhouse lacked he was more than capable of fabricating.
64. Ōtsuka, "Chūgoku kindai kōtō," 49-52; Bailey, *Reform the People*, 4-5; *Beijing shifandaxuexiao shi*, 9.
65. It is difficult to make a precise comparison. According to the Iwaya/Hattori contract, they were to be paid 600 Chinese taels per month to cover salary and household expenses but with additional allowances provided for lodging and travel. At the exchange rate of about 1.5 taels to the yen obtaining at the time of the Boxer indemnity calculations in 1901, this would be 400 yen/month. Assuming about 50 yen/month for living expenses, the salary would amount to 350 yen/month or 4200 yen per year compared to a salary range of 1000-3000 yen for full professors at Tōdai and Kyōdai (figures for 1890). However inexact this calculation might be, there is no doubt that the China jobs were financially very attractive. See Abe, *Chūgokujin no Nihon ryūgaku*, 158, for salaries of the Japan-hires at Beijing University, and Marshall, *Academic Freedom*, 42, for Tokyo University salaries as of 1890.
66. Foreign Ministry Archives (Gaikō shiryōkan), Iwaya Magozō contract.
67. *HSK*, 18; *Beijing Shifandaxuexiao shi*, 3. Note that this is the official founding date of the institution now known as Beijing Normal (Peking National Normal University). Ōtsuka, "Chūoku kindai kōtō," 53-54. The author asserts (1) that the Chinese were more administratively savvy than Hattori acknowledged, and (2) that Hattori, who had just signed his contract on October 9, claimed too much credit for a program that was launched only eight days later. On (1) while the Chinese working for Zhang Baixi may have been familiar with university programs, particularly as a result of study tours to Japan, they certainly lacked experience when it came to the nitty-gritty of organizing curricula, selecting book titles, purchasing equipment, outfitting classrooms and the like, activities that Hattori knew well

from his previous teaching/administrative experience at Tokyo Teachers College. On (2) while Hattori's formal contract signing was held on October 9, he very likely began his advisory tasks as soon as he arrived in Beijing early September, especially given the time constraint imposed by Zhang Baixi. Note that Abe, *Chūgoku no kindai kyōiku,* 157, says there were 160 students in the entering class.

68. "Benxiao huan'an Riben Hattori," 1.
69. *ZTSKKR,* 747.
70. *HSK,* 19; *ZTSKKR,* 747-748; Ōtsuka, "Chūgoku kindai kōtō," 54.
71. Hattori, "Shinkoku jigen," 90.
72. Ibid., 90-91.
73. See Fang, *Qingmo Minchu yangxue,* 61, listing of university faculty for 1906. Hattori is first on the list that included twelve Japanese teachers. Eight of the Chinese faculty members were returned students from Japan. Like a number of prominent educators in the late Qing and Republican periods, Fan Yuanlian (1875-1937) studied in Japan and the experience shaped his approach to educational development. On Fan, see Sanetō, *Chūgokujin Nihon ryūgaku shi,* 472; Cao Rulin, *Yisheng zhi huiyi,* 25; and entries in Bailey, *Reform the People,* and Reynolds, *China, 1898-1912.* Fan, in "Benxiao huan'an Riben Hattori," 1, mentions that he worked closely with Hattori for six months.
74. Ōtsuka, "Chūgoku kindai kōtō," 55-58; Hattori, *Shina kenkyū,* 298-299; *ZTSKKR,* 748; *Beijing shifandaxuexiao shi,* 10.
75. See *ZTSKKR,* 749, for an account of the bad behavior of some Japanese teachers in China at the time, something Hattori and others, notably Kanō Jigorō, found most deplorable. See *Beijing shifan daxuexiao shi,* 11-16, for anti-Russia activities involving Normal School students. On student teacher relationships see Ōtsuka, "Chūgoku kindai kōtō shihan kyōiku," 57. Cao, *Yisheng zhihuiyi,* 36, also mentions the students' exalted status. Students were well-treated, not only provided good quality board and room but issued winter and summer clothing and shoes. In addition, depending on their exam results, they were given cash awards. Still, some students continued to compete in the old exam system to hedge their bets. See Chiang, *Tides from the West,* for an account of new schooling combined with the old civil service exam system. Also, on the deference to students see *Beijing shifan daxuexiao shi,* 6-7. Takeuchi, *Kindai Nihon to Chūgoku,* 214, mentions carriage color as a status symbol among Chinese officials.
76. Harrell, "The Meiji 'New Woman,'" 136-137.
77. Ōtsuka, "Chūgoku kindai kōtō," 57; *Beijing shifandaxuexiao shi,* 16.
78. Ōtsuka, "Chūgoku kindai kōtō," 60-61, and Japan, Ministry of Foreign Affairs Archives (Gaikō shiryōkan), Cable from Minister to China Hayashi Gonsuke to Foreign Minister Hayashi Tadasu, confidential document no. 9, February 16, 1907. Fang Chao-ying, 61. On the promotion offices, see Abe, *Chūgoku kindai,* 1993, 141-146 (it is not entirely clear that the table on page 146 dates from 1905). Note that Yan founded Nankai University, Zhou Enlai's alma mater.
79. Ōtsuka, "Chūgoku kindai kōtō," 59.
80. Ibid.; *HSK,*19; *Beijing shifan daxuexiao shi,* 16-20.

81. Ōtsuka, Chūgoku kindai kōtō," 59; Japan Foreign Ministry Archives (Gaikō shiryōkan), memorandum from Minister Ijūin Hikokichi to Foreign Minister Komura Jutarō, December 1, 1908; Hattori, "Shinajin kyōiku ni taisuru shoken," 36-42.
82. *HSK*, 21.
83. Ibid., 40.
84. Hattori, "Shinajin kyōiku ni taisuru shoken," 36-42.
85. Hattori, *Shina no kokuminsei to shisō*, 81-106, 124-125; Hattori, *Shina Kenkyū*, 285. Dikotter in *Discourse of Race*, like Hattori in *Shina kenkyū* and other works, cites evidence of Chinese racism in a range of Chinese historical writings, drawing the same conclusions.
86. Hattori, *Shina kenkyū*, 300.
87. Ibid., 302.
88. Ibid., 302, 306-307, 315; Hattori,"Shinajin kyōiku ni taisuru shoken," 39-40.
89. Hattori, *Shina kenkyū*, 308-309.
90. *HSK*, 21; Yoshikawa, ed., *Tōyōgaku no sōshishatachi*, 150; Harvard University Gazette, Vol. X, February 27, 1915, no 23, p. 4; Harvard University Catalogue, 1915-16, HV 20.413: Hattori taught "Confucian Ethics and Japanese Life," "Confucius, His Life and Teachings," and "Schools of Confucian Thought in Japan." For exchange of letters on Hattori's contract, see President A. Lawrence Lowell's papers, UAI 5.160, folder 71.
91. Tanaka, *Japan's Orient*, 148-150; Hattori, *Shina kokuminsei to shisō*, 132.
92. Yoshikawa, ed., *Tōyōgaku sōshishatachi*, 138-145; *HSK*, 50-57.
93. Iriye, *China and Japan in the Global Setting*, 41-88. See Lee, "The Foreign Ministry's Cultural Agenda," 281, for a list of committee members.
94. *HSK*, 25-26.
95. "Benxiao huan'an Riben Hattori," 2.
96. Yamane, *Kindai Chūgoku no naka no Nihonjin*, 26-28. The committee was known as the Tōhō Bunka Jigyō Sōiinkai in Japanese and the Dongfang Wenhua Shiye Zongweiyuanhui in Chinese.
97. Yoshikawa, ed., *Tōyōgaku no sōshishatachi*, 144, 156, 161; Hattori, *Tōyōronri kōyō*, 1-2.
98. Yamane, *Kindai Chūgoku no naka no Nihonjin*, 27-32.
99. Hattori, *Tōyōronri kōyō*, 1-2; *HSK*, 28. According to Hattori, noted archaeologist/historian Luo Zhenyu, member of the Emperor Puyi's government in Manchuria, was one of eight from the Chinese side who proposed establishing such a center. Luo had longstanding Japan associations (Reynolds, *China, 1898-1912*, 11-5-116, 135-139) .

Notes to Chapter 3

1. Putnam Weale, Re-Shaping of the Far East, vol. 2, 282.
2. The 150 and 550 figures are the standard estimates given in Abe, *Nit-Chū kyōiku kōryū to masatsu*, 8-10, and Wang, Shinkoku oyatoi Nihonjin, 126. Li, "Shinhai kakumei jiki ni okeru Nihonjin komon," 4, gives a figure of 744 for 1907. See also Eto, Jindai zai-Hua Riren guwen ziliao mulu, 225-249.
3. Bailey, *Reform the People*, 20 n24, 34-35; Ogawa, "Shinmatsu no kindaigakudō," 105.
4. Bailey, *Reform the People*, 102, 115-116; Harrell, *Sowing the Seeds*, 73; and Lewis, *Education of Girls in China*, 34.
5. Ogawa, *Shinmatsu no kindaigakudō*, 108-109.
6. Kawahara, *Karachin ōhi to watakushi*, 109.
7. Ibid., 112-113.
8. *Shimoda Utako Sensei den*, 434-435; Harrell, *Sowing the Seeds*, 33f, 231n44; Kawahara, *Karachin ōhi to watakushi*, 22-24.
9. Kawahara, *Karachin ōhi to watakushi*, 22-24; 296-97.
10. Harrell, "Meiji 'New Woman'," 110.
11. Hani, "Stories of My Life," 330-353
12. Kawahara, *Karachin ōhi to watakushi*, 297-298. For information on normal school education, including the standard course of study at women's ordinary normal schools, see *Outlines of the Modern Education in Japan*, 61-67, 72-73 and Japanese National Commission for Unesco, 66, 96, 99-100.
13. Kawahara, *Karachin ōhi to watakushi*, 105-106, 298 .
14. Seidensticker, *Low City, High City*, 60-69; Rose, Tsuda Umeko, 60.
15. Harrell, "Meiji 'New Woman'," 111-112; Rose, Tsuda Umeko, 77; *MHNS*, vol. 8, 449 ; *MHNS*, vol. 6, 461; *MHNS*, vol. 10, 46-47.
16. Harrell, "Meiji 'New Woman'," 115-118; *MHNS*, vol. 10, 377, 471; vol. 13, 149; Ono, *Kindai Nihon to Chūgoku*, 406; *Shimoda Utako Sensei den*, 754-755, 760; Bacon, *Japanese Girls and Women*, 386. The Industrial Arts School became part of the Women's Practical Arts School in 1908.
17. Harrell, "Meiji 'New Woman'," 118-120.
18. On Shimoda's tutor, Ji Yihui, see Harrell, *Sowing the Seeds*, 34; Sanetō, *Chūgokujin Nihon ryūgaku shi*, 296-297, 306-307; *Shimoda Utako Sensei den*, 427-429; Ono, *Kindai Nihon to Chūgoku*, 206.
19. Ono, *Kindai Nihon to Chūgoku*, 206; *Shimoda Utako Sensei den*, 420. The rumor about the Shimoda-Sun meeting was oft-repeated: see *TSSK*, vol. 1, 673 + photo, vol. 2, 318, and vol. 3, 655; Young, "Chinese Leaders and Japanese Aid," 124.
20. Kawahara, *Karachin ōhi to watakushi*, 105-106, 298-299. On the Yokohama Datong School, see Harrell, *Sowing the Seeds*, 34; *Shimoda Utako Sensei den*, 435.
21. Kawahara, *Karachin ōhi to watakushi*, 107-108.
22. Ibid.
23. Kawahara, *Mōko miyage*, 4.

24. Kawahara, *Karachin ōhi to watakushi*, 124, 108-109; Kawahara, *Mōko miyage*, 6-7; 26. Lewis, *Education of Girls in China*, 26.
25. Bird, *Yangtze Valley and Beyond*, 24. Note that Bird insisted on visiting the native city and said that it was not any worse than other big Chinese cities. See Peattie, "Japanese Treaty Port Settlements ," 181-186, for a map and description of Shanghai. Westerners called the Wuben school the Strive for Duty School. See Burton, *Education of Women in China*, 112.
26. Kawahara, *Karachin ōhi to watakushi*, 128; Kawahara, *Mōko miyage*, 11.
27. Kawahara, *Karachin ōhi to watakushi*, 128.
28. Ibid., 125.
29. Kawahara, *Karachin ōhi to watakushi*, 116-117; Kawahara, *Mōko miyage*, 12-15.
30. Kawahara, *Karachin ōhi to watakushi*, 130-131.
31. Ibid., 137
32. Katō, *Kanō Jigorō*, 89.
33. Kawahara, *Karachin ōhi to watakushi*, 137-138.
34. Ibid., 138
35. Ibid., 139-140.
36. Ibid., 118.
37. Kawahara, *Mōko miyage*, 20-22. See *Shimoda Utako Sensei den*, 438: Kawahara wrote kana alongside the characters to assist in the Chinese pronunciation. See Bailey, *Reform the People*, 99, for a translation of a slightly different version of the song.
38. Kawahara, *Karachin ōhi to watakushi*, 117; Kawahara, *Mōko miyage*, 15-35.
39. Kawahara, *Karachin ōhi to watakushi*, 120-123; Kawahara, *Mōko miyage*, 23-25. On school regulations relating to bound feet, I am grateful to Joan Judge for the following citation: Wu Ruoan, "Huiyi Shanghai Wuben nushu" (Reminiscences of Shanghai Wuben Women's School), *Wu Ruoan koushu* (Wu Ruoan's Oral Narration), 1986 (reprinted in XZSL2:2, 602-609).
40. Kawahara, *Mōko miyage*, 59-60.
41. Ibid., 58, 108. Note that Kawahara is in error in attributing the practice of footbinding to the middle and upper classes only. See Fairbank, *Great Chinese Revolution: 1800-1985*, 68-73, for a discussion of the history of the practice, and, for a contemporary account, Bird, *Yangtze Valley and Beyond*, 237-238.
42. Kawahara, *Karachin ōhi to watakushi*, 129, 139; Kawahara, Mōko miyage, 33.
43. Kawahara, *Karachin ōhi to watakushi*, 123
44. *Mōko miyage*, 27, 67 (quote); *Karachin ōhi to watakushi*, 125.
45. "Prince" seems the most appropriate translation of ō (Japanese) or wang (Chinese) in the case of the Karachin ruler. He derived his status through marriage. His wife was a sister of Prince Su who held the top imperial princely rank of qinwang or prince of the blood of the first degree. Whether the idea for the Japan trip originated with the Karachin prince or the Japanese is not entirely clear, but given the county's strategic location close to Russia's expanding sphere in Manchuria, there were certainly political reasons on both sides for holding talks. But very likely an equally strong motivation for the visit on the prince's part was the chance for a firsthand look at a modern economy and educational system, a sought-after experience generally for

Chinese officials at the time. The period after the Sino-Japanese War marked the high point of Chinese study tours to Japan for professional development reasons. See Harrell, *Sowing the Seeds*, 40-44.

46. Kawahara, *Mōko miyage*, 131; Harrell, *Sowing the Seeds*, 43; *Education in Japan: Prepared for the Louisiana Purchase Exposition*, Part I, 31.
47. *MHNS*, vol. 12, 49. Note that the Osaka Exhibition opened April 21, so the prince must have visited some time after that, *MHNS*, vol. 12, 54. For the build-up to the war, see Okamoto's excellent account in *Japanese Oligarchy*, 57-102.
48. Kawahara, *Mōko miyage*, 67, 185-186; Kawahara, Karachin ōhi to watakushi, 29, 302. Japanese China watchers thought that of the more than 100 banners, Karachin was the most likely to be pro-Japanese.
49. Kawahara, *Karachin ōhi to watakushi*, 22-23, 162, 261-262. Note that the contract for Kawahara's services was drawn up between the legation and the prince of Karachin. A draft was sent to the prince for his approval; he replied with a note of gratitude for the legation's efforts and declared himself pleased after his first meeting with Kawahara.
50. Ibid., 145-146.
51. Ibid., 151
52. Ibid., 23-31; 163-164; 1909, 98-100.
53. Ibid., 21-28, 168-181, 262-263; Kawahara, *Mōko miyage*, 103-118.
54. Kawahara, *Mōko miyage*, 117; Kawahara, *Karachin ōhi to watakushi*, 180. Translation is from the former work with reference to the latter.
55. Kawahara, *Mōko miyage*, 144, 141-148; Kawahara, *Karachin ōhi to watakushi*, 198-200. Note that the 1909 version of the speech (reproduced in its original Chinese) makes the distinction between Chinese and Mongol, which the Japanese translation in the later published work does not. Another speaker, one of the Japanese military advisers, mentioned *ryōsai kenbo* directly.
56. The translation is from Kawahara, *Mōko miyage*, 118. See also, Kawahara, *Karachin ōhi to watakushi*, 181.
57. Kawahara, *Mōko miyage*, 125, 120-130. Note that from 1901-to-1907, the governor of the province (Zhili) of which Karachin was a part was the well-known Chinese military figure Yuan Shikai.
58. Ibid., 157-159; Kawahara, *Karachin ōhi to watakushi*, 209-211.
59 Kawahara, *Mōko miyage*, 159; Kawahara, *Karachin ōhi to watakushi*, 212-214. The characters read as Tōyō and meaning "Asia" or "Orient" in Japanese were used in Chinese (*Dongyang*) to refer to Japan only.
60. *MHNS*, vol. 12, 227 (April 9, 1904); Kawahara, *Karachin ōhi to watakushi*, 211; Kawahara, *Mōko miyage*, 158.
61. Kawahara, *Mōko miyage*, 187.
62. Kawahara, *Karachin ōhi to watakushi*, 52-52, 96, 245-246; Kawahara, *Mōko miyage*, 199.
63. Kawahara, *Karachin ōhi to watakushi*, 35-37, 41-53.
64. *TSSK*, vol. 1, 765-766; *MHNS*, vol. 13, 88; *TSKKR*, vol. 3, 1098-1099.

65. Kawahara, *Mōko miyage*, 194. Note that the version given in *Karachin ōhi to watakushi* softens the slur by saying simply that the soap will wash off their disguise, rather than their Chinese disguise.
66. Kawahara, *Mōko miyage*, 193-195; Kawahara, *Karachin ōhi to watakushi*, 35-37, 57-60, 241-242.
67. *TSKKR*, vol. 3, 1097-1098; *MHNS*, vol. 12, 240 (article of May 4, 1904 reporting Yokogawa's death).
68. Kawahara, *Karachin ōhi to watakushi*, 35-40, 59-90; *TSSK*, vol. 1, 739-786. Note that the latter account includes translations from Russian official accounts of the capture and trial. General Kuropatkin who had spent some time in Japan before the war as part of the Russian negotiating team had a high opinion of the Japanese, not only for their effective military organization but also for their fine moral character. See his fascinating account, *Russian Army and the Japanese War*, vol. 1.
69. The executions of Oki and Yokogawa appeared in newspapers in Japan at the end of April based on Reuters reports. See MHNS, vol. 12, 235, for the *Asahi Shinbun* report of April 24, 1904, on Oki's death; Ibid., 240, for the Asahi article of May 4, 1904, on Yokogawa's death; Kawahara, *Karachin ōhi to watakushi*, 39, 94-99. Note that a monument was later erected in their honor near Harbin. The celebrated poet Yosano Akiko visited the site in 1928, noting in her diary, "We then left the city proper to visit the site of the martyrdom of Yokogawa and Oki, where a monument had been placed." Fogel, *Travels in Manchuria and Mongolia*, 92.
70. Kawahara, *Mōko miyage*, 170-185; *MHNS*, vol. 12, 227.
71. Kawahara, *Mōko miyage*, 162-164; Kawahara, *Karachin ōhi to watakushi*, 215-217.
72. Kawahara, *Mōko miyage*, 132-133. Burton in *Education of Women in China*, 118-119, refers—with some inaccuracy in detail—to the princess and Kawahara when she writes: "The sister of Prince Su, who had married a Mongol prince, was eager to start a school for girls in her Mongolian home . . . When she left for her home she took with her a Japanese woman teacher, and soon had a school for girls in full operation."
73. Kawahara, *Karachin ōhi to watakushi*, 190.
74. Kawahara, *Mōko miyage*, 199-200.
75. Kawahara, *Karachin ōhi to watakushi*, 263.
76. Ibid., 262-264; Okamoto, *Japanese Oligarchy*, 105-107.
77. Kawahara, *Mōko miyage*, 208; Kawahara, *Karachin ōhi to watakushi*, 247-248.
78. Kawahara, *Mōko miyage*, 207-211; Kawahara, *Karachin ōhi to watakushi*, 246-249.
79. Kawahara, *Mōko miyage*, 232; Kawahara, *Karachin ōhi to watakushi*, 251. The photograph in *Mōko miyage* shows Kawahara and Hattori Shigeko flanking the princess and her sister-in-law with some of the princess's daughters standing behind them.
80. Ono, *Kindai Nihon to Chūgoku*, 215-218.
81. Kawahara, *Karachin ōhi to watakushi*, 250; Kawahara, *Mōko miyage*, 233-234.
82. Kawahara, *Mōko miyage*, 233-234; Kawahara, *Karachin ōhi to watakushi*, 250-251; MHNS, vol.13, 52. Kawahara's father apparently enlisted the help of General Fukushima who recommended that Kawahara cut short her stay.
83. Kawahara, *Karachin ōhi to watakushi*, 281-282.

84. Kawahara, *Mōko miyage*, 237.
85. Kawahara, *Mōko miyage*, 236-242.
86. Ibid., 2; *MHNS*, vol.13, 391; Kawahara, *Karachin ōhi to watakushi*, 281-285, 305.
87. *MHNS*, vol. 13, 52, 83, 211; Torii, *Torii Ryūzō zenshu*, vol. 12, 235-241.
88. Wang, *Shinkoku oyatoi Nihonjin*, 210-211; Abe, *Chūgoku kindai gakkōshi kenkyū*, 343-344.
89. Bailey, *Reform the People*, 35; Abe, *Chūgoku kindai gakkōshi kenkyū*, 245; Ono, *Kindai Nihon to Chūgoku*, 107.
90. Ogawa,"Shinmatsu no kindai gakudō," 109.
91. Ibid., 108-109; *HSK*, 15-16; Wang, *Shinkoku oyatoi Nihonjin*, 134. On numbers, Wang, 195, gives a figure of 414 teachers and educators out of a total Japanese advisory group of 549.
92. *MHNS*, Vol. 13, 150; Ono, *Kindai Nihon to Chūgoku*, 108-109.
93. Wang, *Shinkoku oyatoi Nihonjin*, 143-147. For a salary comparison, see Burton, *Education of Women in China*, 132-135. Foreigners teaching at the Fuchow Normal School in 1908 got between 10 and 40 dollars a month, native teachers 4-6, and native teachers with some English, 10-20.
94. Wang, *Shinkoku oyatoi Nihonjin*, 83-125. Note that Hattori's wife is listed as "Shinako" rather than Shigeko.
95. For an account of what is almost certainly this school, see Burton, *Education of Women in China*, 116-119; *Shimoda Utako Sensei den*, 422-423. One of Kimura Yoshiko's students was the infamous Kawashima Yoshiko, the daughter of Prince Su, who was adopted by Kawashima Naniwa (see Chapter IV of present work).
96. Wang, *Shinkoku oyatoi Nihonjin*, 120, 126; Ogawa, *Shinmatsu no kindai gakudō*, 107-110.
97. For excellent shorter discussions, see Tam, "Meiji Japan and the Educational and Language Reforms," 61-77, and Reynolds, *China, 1898-1912*, 131-150.
98. Abe, *Chūgoku kindai gakkōshi kenkyū*, 141-145; Bailey, *Reform the People*, 138, 141. Yan Xiu was a key education official in Yuan Shikai's Zhili Province, in 1911 part of Yuan's first cabinet (*MHNS*, Vol. 14, 490), later President of Nankai University. Note that Wu Rulun died shortly after returning to China following his Japan trip.
99. Lewis, *Education of Girls in China*, 34.
100. Kawahara, *Karachin ōhi to watakushi,* 285-286.
101. Kawahara, *Karachin ōhi to watakushi*, 291, 287-291.
102. Ogawa, "Shinmatsu no kindai gakudō," 107.
103. Shimoda *Utako Sensei den*, 583, 764-768.
104. Young, *Japan's Total Empire*, 55-114.
105. Kawahara, *Karachin ōhi to watakushi*, 294-296.
106. Ibid., 276-278. Note that Kalaqin (Karachin) was on China's list of poor counties in 1989. *Outlines of Economic Development in China's Poor Areas* (Agricultural Publishing House), 1989, 32.
107. Kawahara, *Karachin ōhi to watakushi*, 31-32.
108. Ibid., 28, 32.
109. Ibid., 260.

Notes to Chapter 4

1. Garrett, *Chinese Dragon Robes,* 11-17, 31, 51-55; Garrett, *Mandarin Squares*, 25-29, 35-37, 47-52.
2. Aida, *Kawashima Ō*, 11.
3. Aida, *Kawashima Ō,* 12-13; *TSSK*, 213; *MHNS*, vol. 2, 245, vol. 5, 467, vol. 6, 419; Seidensticker, *Low City, High City*, 70, 214.
4. Aida Tsutomu was Kawashima's authorized biographer, producing a work which, while not a diary, presented Kawashima's life in his own words. See his account, *Kawashima Naniwa Ō* cited throughout this chapter. *TSSK*, vol. 2, 214-216; Oketani, *Futabatei Shimei*, 212.
5. *MHNS,* vol. 4, 167, 181; Sato, "Kō-A kai ni kansuru ikkōsatsu," 399-410; *TSSK*, vol. 2, 216.
6. Tao, "Shigeno Yasutsugu," 374.
7. *TSSK*, vol. 3, 2-6, 61, 360, 688-689; *TSKKR*, vol. 2, 1230-1232, Tao, "Shigeno Yasutsugu," 382.
8. Tao, "Shigeno Yasutsugu," 374-377.
9. *TSSK*, vol. 1, 416; Oketani, *Futabatei Shimei*, 212.
10. Aida, *Kawashima Ō,* 15-17; Watanabe, *Kawashima Yoshiko*, 32.
11. Aida, *Kawashima Ō*, 18-19; *TSSK*, vol. 2, 221-222; *ZTSKKR*, 199; Hirotani, "Pekin keimu gakudō,"93.
12. Aida, *Kawashima Ō*, 24-25; *TSSK*, vol. 2, 226.
13. Oketani, *Futabatei Shimei*, 21; *TSSK*, vol. 2, 226-227; *ZTSKKR*, 199.
14. Peattie, "Japanese Treaty Port Settlements," 183. Note that in fact Japanese before 1896 did not enjoy the same privileges as Westerners in Shanghai.
15. *TSSK*, vol. 2, 227-234.
16. Peattie, "Japanese Treaty Port Settlements," 183.
17. *ZTSKKR*, 200. Note that Arao also found Kawashima an unpleasant fellow: *TSSK*, vol. 2, 240; Watanabe, *Kindai Nit-Chū minshū*, 108.
18. *TSSK*, vol. 2, 240; Watanabe, *Kindai Nit-Chū minshū*,109.
19. Reynolds, "Training Young China Hands," 214-217; *TSSK*, vol. 1, 343-344, 382-395; *TSSK*, vol. 3, 608; Harrell, *Sowing the Seeds*, 22-23.
20. *TSSK*, vol. 2, 241-250.
21. *ZTSKKR*, 201.
22. Keene, *Appreciations of Japanese Culture*, 267-274.
23. *TSSK*, vol. 2, 250-253; *ZTSKKR*, 201; *MHNS*, vol. 4, 457.
24. Kitaoka, "China Experts in the Army," 332; Brooks, "The Gaimushō's China Experts," 378. Parlaying the role of interpreter into jobs of greater responsibility and influence as Kawashima did beginning with his Taiwan posting is not uncommon and reflects a practical reality: if parties to a negotiation are unable to communicate, the person who can bridge the language gap is the one in control. A striking mid-nineteenth century example is that of H.N. Lay, official with the British Consular Service in China. An apprentice interpreter at seventeen, Lay rose quickly through the ranks to become at twenty-seven chief administrator of the powerful Chinese

Imperial Customs Service. [See Spence, *To Change China*, 93-112] On the Chinese side in the same period one is reminded of the *compradores*, Chinese agents for foreign businessmen in China, whose language and entrepreneurial skills often made them as wealthy as their employers. In post-1979 China, too, knowledge of foreign languages, English in particular, has been a way to move up fast in the bureaucracy and private sector.

25. See also the case of Sinologist Kano Naoki in Fogel, "Kano Naoki's relationship to *Kangaku*," 358-371.
26. Peattie, "Japanese Attitudes towards Colonialism," 83; Chen, "Attempt to Integrate the Empire," 247-248. General Nogi has gotten generally low marks for his performance as Taiwan's governor-general. Kamisaka, *Dansō no reijin*, 45. Nogi and Kawashima apparently remained close friends. Aida, *Kawashima Ō*, 53-65; Watanabe, *Kawashima Yoshiko*, 34; *TSSK*, vol. 2, 252-253.
27. *MHNS*, vol. 2, 120, for article authorizing establishment of the Military School in 1874.
28. *TSSK*, vol. 2, 254; Preston, *Boxer Rebellion*, 183-189.
29. Giles, *Siege of the Peking Legations*, 178.
30. *TSSK*, vol. 2, 256-257.
31. Moser, *Foreigners within the Gates*, 71.
32. *TSSK*, vol. 2, 277; Putnam Weale, *Indiscreet Letters from Beijing*, 435; Wakeman, *Perspectives on Modern China*, 78; Preston, *Boxer Rebellion*, 303-304.
33. *TSSK*, vol. 2, 258-262; Hirotani, "Pekin keimu gakudō," 94.
34. *TSSK*, vol 2, 272-276; Hirotani, "Pekin keimu gakudō," 94-95; Kamisaka, *Dansō no reijin*, 48.
35. Oketani, *Futabatei Shimei*, 218.
36. *TSSK*, vol. 2, 274-275; Kawashima, "Bō Futabatei Shimei kun," 209-217; Watanabe, *Kindai Nitchū minshū*, 12; Oketani, *Futabatei Shimei*, 216.
37. *TSSK*, vol. 2, 275-276; Hirotani, "Pekin keimu gakudō," 96-99; Oketani, *Futabatei Shimei*, 209, 220. On the yen equivalents in salaries, see Chapter II of the present work, note 65.
38. *TSSK*, II, 277-280; Wakeman, "Models of Historical Change," 79.
39. Headland, *Court Life in China*, 162 (quote); Rawski, *Last Emperors*, 72-77, 92-93; Chin, *Su Qinwang*, 30; Crossley, *Orphan Warriors*, 173-174. Crossley (174) says, "Because Kang's group made few serious attempts to integrate progressive Manchu energies with their program, the real possibilities for reform in 1898 may forever remain elusive." On Su and the role of Manchu progressives, see also Headland, *Court Life in China*, passim, and Rhoads, *Manchus and Han*, 71.
40. *TSSK*, vol. 2, 281; Chin, *Su Qinwang*, 25-33; *Nikki*, vol. 5, 72; Watanabe, *Kindai Nitchū minshū*, 112-113; Kamisaka, *Dansō no reijin*, 36-37.
41. Putnam Weale, *Shaping of the Far East*, vol. 1, 231-235.
42. *TSSK*, II, 281; Kamisaka, *Dansō no reijin*, 37-38; Watanabe, *Kindai Nitchū*, 112-114.
43. *TSSK*, vol. 2, 277. The position of Commandant of Gendarmerie was traditionally held by princes or heads of the Six Boards. *TSSK*, vol. 2, 281; *Nikki*, vol. 4, 234-235; vol. 5, 119, 131, 138, 140. Konoe had met Yu Lang on his summer 1901 trip to

China. He met Kawashima, probably also for the first time, during that same trip, at a meeting sponsored by the Beijing Tō-A Dōbunkai.

44. For example, see *MHNS*, vol. 11, 242.
45. Watanabe, *Kindai Nitchū*,113-115; *TSSK*, vol. 2, 282-283.
46. *MHNS*, vol. 11, 303, (September 1, 1901); *Nikki*, vol. 4, 233, 277. Natong appears on Ō En's list of Chinese missions (Ō En, *Shinmatsu chūgoku tai-Nichi*, Appendix 1, 5) as having visited Japan in May of 1901 to look at financial institutions. Crossley, *Orphan Warriors*, 193.
47. *TSSK*, II, 285; Hirotani, "Pekin keimu gakudō," 95; Harrell, *Sowing the Seeds*, 38; Reynolds, *China, 1898-1912*, 167-169.
48. Wakeman, "Models of Historical Change,"79.
49. Kawashima, *Tai-Shi narabi ni tai-ManMō*, 19-20.
50. See Chapter II of the present work, n52, for numbers of Russian troops on the Asian front at the time of the Boxer Uprising and after. As noted, a *New York Times* report from December 8, 1901 ("Mobilizing Troops in Manchuria") cites a current British estimate of 200,000 Russian troops, "in Manchuria, in other Chinese provinces, and in Southern Siberia." A *Times* report on the eve of the Russo-Japanese War ("Russian Troops in Manchuria" January 6, 1904) refers to a Russian force of 225,000 which was "ready for service in Eastern Asia" by the end of 1901. Articles are available online at www.nytimes.com/ref/membercenter/nytarchive.html.
51. Chin, *Su Qinwang*, 56.
52. Fairbank, *East Asia*, 468-479; Harrell, *Sowing the Seeds*, 132-139; Okamoto, *Japanese Oligarchy*, 57-102; Putnam Weale, *Re-Shaping of the Far East*, 221-224.
53. Oketani, *Futabatei Shimei*, 219 (quote); Okamoto, *Japanese Oligarchy*, 95.
54. *TSSK*, vol. 1, 742-746.
55. *Nikki*, Suppl. vol., 527, letter from Karachin Prince to Konoe dated August 1903. Note that Konoe stopped recording in his diary in April 1903.
56. Kawashima,"Bō Futabatei Shimei kun," 209-217; Hirotani, "Pekin keimu gakudō," 99.
57. Ryan, *Japan's First Modern Novel*, 1965.
58. See Ryan, *Japan's First Modern Novel,* especially Chapter 3 ("Writing *Ukigumo* and Translating Turgenev"), for Futabatei's waning confidence in his talents as a novelist, feelings that never left him. Kawashima's personal insecurities, on the other hand, so palpable during his disastrous time in China in the 1880s, morphed into brash confidence after his unique China skills were recognized by top brass in the Sino-Japanese War.
59. Chin, *Su Qinwang*, 40; Rhoads, *Manchus and Han*, 91. See Kamisaka, *Dansō no reijin*, 38-39, on Su's posts. Su was appointed minister of the Tibetan and Mongolian Affairs Department after his ouster from the public works post in 1902, then minister of the Department of Civil Affairs (Minzhengbu) from 1907 to 1911.
60. Putnam Weale, *Re-Shaping of the Far East,* vol. 2, 228-229.
61. McCormack, *Chang Tso-lin*, 5; Peter Duus, *Japanese Informal Empire in China*, xxiii, and Myers, "Japanese Attitudes toward Colonialism," 102-106; Bland, *The Pity of It*, 242-242, 246-248; Borg and Okamoto, eds, *Pearl Harbor as History*, 381.

62. Aida, *Kawashima Ō*, 89-92; Watanabe, *Kindai Nit-Chū*, 115-116; *TSSK*, vol. 2, 283-284. See Putnam Weale, *Re-Shaping of the Far East*, vol. 2, 229, for an example of a blood brother relationship in this case between the Empress Dowager's chief eunuch, Li Lianying, and the Russian representative in Beijing. Examples of Chinese and Japanese brotherhood pacts are found also in Fogel, trans., *Travels in Manchuria and Mongolia*, 126.
63. Kamisaka, *Dansō no reijin*, 52-53.
64. Oketani, *Futabatei Shimei*, 100-101.
65. Note that Kawashima had contacts at court other than Prince Su. For Kawashima's dealings over rail development and the state of play in Manchuria/Mongolia post-Russo-Japanese War, see *ZTSKKR*, 203-204; Aida, *Kawashima Ō*, 98-106; Fairbank, *East Asia*, 630, 468-483; Kamisaka, *Dansō no reijin*, 53-54; Putnam Weale, *Re-shaping of the Far East*, vol. 2, 241-24 3; Borg and Okamoto, *Pearl Harbor as History*, 380-381.
66. Rhoads, *Manchus and Han*, 120; *MHNS*, vol. 13, 500-502. See Putnam Weale, *Re-shaping of the Far East*, 290: Yuan, he says ". . . in common with every Chinese official, high and low, is pro-Chinese and pro-nothing else." On advisers at Baoding, see Watanabe, *Kindai Nit-Chū*, 103-105.
67. *MHNS*, vol. 13, 500; Aida, *Kawashima Ō*, 107-110; Rhoads, *Manchus and Han*, 119-120, 149-153.
68. Morrison, *Correspondence*, vol. 2, 685.
69. Young, "The Reformer as a Conspirator," 245.
70. Pearl, *Morrison of Peking*, 223, quotes Morrison as saying, "The police force cannot be too highly praised . . ."; Kamisaka, *Dansō no reijin*, 42; Rhoads, *Manchus and Han*, 155-156; Chin, *Su Qinwang*, 335-337.
71. Rhoads, *Manchus and Han*, 121, 148-149; Reynolds, *China, 1898-1912*, 186-192; Spence, *Search for Modern China*, 254-262.
72. *TSSK* vol. 2, 290-295 (quote on 291).
73. Kawashima, *Tai-Shi narabi ni*, 22.
74. Aida, *Kawashima Ō*, 114; *TSSK*, vol. 2, 291-292.
75. *TSSK*, vol. 2, 293-297. Kawashima's anti-Yuan campaign did not stop at verbal attacks, warnings to official Japan about Yuan's double-dealing, but went so far as plotting how Yuan might be physically barred from returning to Beijing, even assassinated. In one case, Kawashima convinced a young Japan-trained commander in the revolutionary army that the success of the revolution depended on occupying a city on the Peking-Hankow rail line, thus preventing Yuan's progress to the capital. The commander cut off rail service and was promptly killed by Yuan's men. Apparently Prince Su was not informed of these various plots, though Kawashima did consult with Prince Gong in one case. Kawashima claimed that because he thought Su was the most likely of the princes to take power, he was reluctant to risk having Su's name sullied by association with assassination attempts.
76. Aida, *Kawashima Ō*, (Appendix: excerpt from Kawashima, *Tai-Shi kanken* [My Personal Views on China], August 1912), 184-185.
77. Ibid, 186; *TSSK*, vol. 2, 320.

78. *MHNS*, vol. 14, 500-501.
79. On what she calls the "deliberate racism of the nationalist movement," see Crossley, *Orphan Warriors*, 193-197.
80. Spence, *Search for Modern China*, 262-268; Pearl, *Morrison of Peking*, 228-236; Harrell, *Sowing the Seeds*, 216; Jansen, *Japanese and Sun Yat-sen*, 131-133; Rhoads, *Manchus and Han*, 205-228; *MHNS*, vol. 14, 527-528, for articles of abdication.
81. *TSSK*, vol. 2, 299-300; Rhoads, *Manchus and Han*, 205-228.
82. Morrison, *Correspondence*, vol. 2, 715. Morrison noted on January 23, 1912, 706: Liang Bi " . . . is regarded as the most highly equipped officer in the Chinese army, who was for eight years in Japan."
83 Aida, *Kawashima Ō*, 124-140; Morrison, *Correspondence,* vol. 2, 715; Fang, *Qingmo Minchu yangxue,* 8; *TSSK*, vol. 2, 300-303; Kamisaka, *Dansō no reijin,* 57-58.
84. Aida, *Kawashima Ō*, 141-157, 150, 220-226 on relationship with Iwasaki; *TSSK*, vol. 2, 325-329; Kamisaka, *Dansō no reijin*, 62.
85. Paula Harrell, (unpublished paper), "In Refutation of Kang Youwei," 33 (quote); Rhoads, *Manchus and Han*, 293. Crossley, *Translucent Mirror*, 351, suggests that Zhang felt the Manchus could not go "home" but should be granted special territory north of the Yellow River.
86. See Fogel, *Travels in Manchuria and Mongolia*, 71, for land grabbing by Chinese settlers.
87. On Outer Mongolia's independence, see Fairbank, *East Asia*, 788-790. *TSSK*, vol. 2, 325-326, discusses the Karachin Prince's point that since Mongolia was originally not part of China but simply a Qing ally, once the Qing house was gone it should revert to independent status once again.
88. Chin, *Su Qinwang*, 56.
89. McCormack, *Chang Tso-lin*, 17-27; Kamisaka, *Dansō no reijin*, 57.
90. Aida, *Kawashima Ō*, 162 and 172-189 (the latter from Appendix, *Tai-Shi kanken*, 1912).
91. For a biographical sketch of General Staff Col. Matsui Seisuke, see *TSKKR*, vol. 3, 1347-1349; for a bio on General Taga, see *TSSK*,vol. 3, 784-786; for the Su-Kawashima team, see Aida, *Kawashima Ō*, 226-228, and for funds from Iwasaki and Ōkura, see ibid., 225.
92. *TSSK*, vol. 2, 346-348 (quote on 347) + 329-344; Aida, *Kawashima Ō*, 164-167 [and 132-167 for a full account of the first independence movement]; Watanabe, *Kindai Nit-Chū*, 143-144.
93. Jansen, *Japanese and Sun Yat-sen, 188-189*; Wilbur, *Sun Yat-sen*, 28; Young, "Chinese Leaders and Japanese Aid," 136-139.
94. Aida, *Kawashima Ō*, 194, 167; Watanabe, *Kawashima Yoshiko*, 24;
95. Aida, *Kawashima Ō*, 199 passim.
96. Reportedly, it was in 1915, when Yoshiko was eight, that the marriage arrangement was made. Kamasaka, *Dansō no reijin*, 75, 77, 80.
97. Morrison, *Correspondence*, vol. 2, 269. The Morrison quote relates to Kalgan, present day Zhangjiakou in Hebei Province so the "frontier" he speaks of is with Inner Mongolia. Morrison was consumed with the post-1911 fluid situation in Mongolia

and Inner Mongolia and the threat of Russian encroachment. His correspondence is richly informative on the question.

98. Note that Shiba Gorō's brother participated.
99. Aida, *Kawashima* Ō, 214, 219, 383; Kamisaka, *Dansō no reijin*, 76-78; Watanabe, *Kindai Nit-Chū,* 167; Jansen, *Japanese and Sun Yat-sen*, 196-197; Crossley, *Orphan Warriors*, 204.
100. Su's reaction as reported by Kawashima. See Aida, *Kawashima Ō*, 293-294.
101. Aida, *Kawashima Ō*, 384.
102. Kamisaka, *Dansō no reijin*, 19, provides a chart of Su's children, 85; Aida, *Kawashina Ō*, 295.
103. Kamisaka, *Dansō no reijin,* 62-91; Aida, *Kawashima Ō*, 295-299; Chin, *Su Qinwang*, 57-83. Note Yoshiko's role in Bertolucci's famous film, "The Last Emperor."
104. Kawashima, *Tai-Shi narabi ni*, 19-20.
105. Ibid., 37, 32-34.
106. Ibid.,40-42.
107. Ibid., 44. Note: Jansen, *Japanese and Sun Yat-sen*, 199, that Chiang visited Japan in 1927.
108. Kawashima, *Tai-Shi narabi ni,* 24. Kawashima adds: "On the other hand, as a result of schlepping through life for more than 200 years with nothing in their outward selves to distinguish them in character from the Chinese, they have become even more incompetent than the Han people."
109. Ibid., 46.
110. Aida, *Kawashima Ō,* 1935 Nagano speech, 496.
111. Kawashima, *Tai-Shi narabi ni,* 5-6; Aida, *Kawashima Ō*, 1935 Nagano speech, 496ff.
112. Kawashima, *Tai-Shi narabi ni*, 11.
113. Ibid., 54-55.
114. Ibid., 46.
115. Ibid., 56.
116. Ibid., 56, 52.
117. Aida, *Kawashima Ō,* 408. On Puyi, see Spence, *Search for Modern China,* 392 ff.
118. Aida, *Kawashima Ō*, 482-491. Note: Kawashima had an interview with Puyi in March 1932.
119. Ibid., 457, opinion paper to Prime Minister Satō, June 1932.
120. Ibid, 412.
121. See, for example, *Kawashima on ōdō* (kingly way or just government) and *daidō* (principled government) in Aida, *Kawashima Ō,* 441, and Kawashima, *Tai-Shi narabi ni*, 8, 12.
122. Kawashima, *Tai-Shi iken*, 35.
123. Ibid., 1.
124. For a full account of Yoshiko's trial and rumors surrounding her death, see Kamisaka, *Dansō no reijin*, 176-248. On the U.S. interest in tracking Kawashima Yoshiko postwar, I am indebted to Marlene Mayo for sending me the Kawashima

Yoshiko files held at National Archives II in College Park, Maryland and listed as Record Group 319 Box 285, IRR Personal, Counter-intelligence Records, Army.

125. Kamisaka, *Dansō no reijin*, 212.

Notes to Chapter 5

1. Takada, "Ko Ariga hakushi omoide no ki," 101-102; *MHNS*, vol. 3, 53.
2. Roberts, *Mitsui*, 223.
3. Takada, "Ko Ariga hakushi omoide no ki," 102.
4. Marshall, *Academic Freedom*, 32; Beauchamp, *Foreign Employees*, 20; Jones, *Live Machines*, Table 2; Passin, *Society and Education in Japan*, 94-95; Chamberlain, *Things Japanese*, 104; Morse, *Japan Day by Day*, 219.
5. Benfy, *The Great Wave*.
6. Benfy, *The Great Wave*, 75-108; Victoria Weston, *Japanese Painting and National Identity*, 2-8, 22-29, 43-43; *MHNS*, vol. 7, 25; Fenollosa and Ariga, *Tō-A Bijutsushikō,* "Introduction," 20-21; Ariga, "Account of My Winter Hibernation at Shiobara," *GJ* 31:371 (April 15, 1920): 745-746.
7. *MHNS*, vol. 5, 179; Passin, *Society and Education in Japan*, 74; Marshall, *Academic Freedom*, 60-61; Ariga, "Account of My Winter Hibernation at Shiobara," *GJ* 31:371 (April 15, 1920): 745-746; Ariga, "Miscellaneous Thoughts on Current Affairs," *GJ* 8:95 (October 10, 1905): 270-272.
8. *TSKKR*, vol. 2, 713.
9. Takada, "Ko Ariga hakushi omoide no ki,"102-103.
10. Ariga, "On My Return Home,"*GJ* 10:120 (November10, 1907): 105.
11. Smith, *Grant*, 612
12. Ariga, *La Guerre Sino-Japonaise*, 2, 41. For the text of the 1864 Geneva (Red Cross) Convention, see the Avalon Project at Yale Law School, nineteenth century documents: Avalon.law.yale.edu
13. Ariga, *La Guerre Sino-Japonaise*, 2, 41; Koskenniemi, *Gentle Civilizer*, 39; Ariga, *La Croix Rouge*, 13-14; Hutchinson, *Champions of Charity*, 105-138, 205; Kawamata, *History of the Red Cross*, 44-45; Okamoto, *Japanese Oligarchy*, 18-19.
14. Koskenniemi, *Gentle Civilizer,* 280; Ariga, *La Guerre Sino-Japonaise*, xii-xiii
15. Note also that Takahashi Sakuyé, legal adviser to the naval command, wrote a study of the Sino-Japanese War published by Cambridge University Press in 1899. For Ariga's review in praise of Takahashi's work, see "Dr. Takahashi Sakue's *Cases of international law during the Chino-Japanese War*," *GJ* 3:26 (June 1900): 175-178.
16. Ariga, "The Russo-Japanese War and International Law," *GJ* 7:81 (August 20, 1904): 1820.
17. Keene, *Emperor of Japan*, 494-495.
18. Ariga, *La Guerre Sino-Japonaise*, 80-82; Paine, *Sino-Japanese War*, 210-211.
19. Ariga, *La Guerre Sino-Japonaise*, xii, 77-93. Paine (*Sino-Japanese War*, 212*)* is in error when she says that Ariga claimed that since the Chinese "did not adhere to the terms of the Geneva Convention, they got what they deserved." Ariga's statement in

La Guerre Sino-Japonaise, 85-86, states that while Japan could logically argue that because China did not conform to the laws of war, Japan had no responsibility in the Port Arthur affair, in fact since Japan "had resolved to conform to the laws of war, no matter what the actions of China, it is thus a given that she should at least be declared responsible in terms of her own conscience. Furthermore, Japan has constantly sought to entertain relations with civilized nations, respecting them as equals. From this point of view as well, she was held to the obligation of respecting the laws of war, so long as it did not detract from her victories."

20. Kemuyama, "Ariga sensei no omoide," 104.
21. Ariga, *La Guerre Sino-Japonaise*, v-x (quotes on vi, vii, viii); Koskenniemi, *Gentle Civilizer*, 135-136.
22. Ariga, *La Guerre Sino-Japonaise*, ix.
23. Ibid., 5-9.
24. Koskenniemi, 132-133, 155-159, 279-281; Ariga, *La Guerre Sino-Japonaise*, 9. Ariga, always well-apprised of European news, very likely had a subtle message here for contemporary European readers aware of reports of massacres of the Congolese in the tens of thousands by Belgian troops, that just war principles even unilaterally applied did not preclude a victorious outcome.
25. Paine, *Sino-Japanese War*, 177; Ariga, *La Croix Rouge*, 16-17, 65-7; Ariga, *La Guerre Sino-Japonaise*, 105-147; Ariga, *The Red Cross Society of Japan*, 40.
26. Westney, *Imitation and Innovation*; Hutchinson, *Champions of Charity*, 175-191, 201-275.
27. Ariga, "On My Return Home," *GJ* 10:120 (November 10, 1907): 99.
28. Ariga, *La Croix Rouge*, 66; Ariga, "International Conference of the Red Cross" *GJ* 10:112 (March 10, 1907): 132.
29. Ariga, "Reviews," *GJ* 1:10 (November 1898): 4.
30. Ariga, "On Secrecy in Diplomacy," *GJ* 1:2 (March 1898): 36-38; see also Ariga, "Wars from Now On" *GJ* 3:25 (1900): 159.
31. Okamoto, *Japanese Oligarchy*, 11-40
32. Ariga "On Secrecy in Diplomacy,"*GJ* 1:2 (March 1898): 32-42; GJ5, Ariga, "Refashioning Diplomacy," *GJ* 1:5 (June 1898): 96-102; Ariga in Stead, *Japan by the Japanese*, 218
33. Ariga, "On the Foreign Ministry's Adviser Mr. Denison," *GJ* 1:8 (September 1898): 159-165.
34. Ariga, "Reviews," *GJ* 1:10 (November 1898): 1-8
35. Kemuyama, "Ariga sensei no omoide," 104.
36. Ariga, "Wars from Now On," *GJ* 3:21 (1900): 158.
37. Roosevelt, vol. XIII, 338.
38. Ariga, "Discussion of the Philippines," *GJ* 1:7 (August 1898): 140.
39. Ariga, "Ten Big Issues in East Asian Diplomacy," *GJ* 1:6 (July 1898): 111; Ariga, "On Preserving China's Integrity," *GJ* 2:11(January 1899): 187-196.
40. *Nikki*, vol. 2, 15.
41. Ariga, "On China's Reform," *GJ* 1:10 (November 1898): 179-186.
42. Koskenniemi, *Gentle Civilizer*, 278.

43. Hull, *Two Hague Conferences*, 12; Eyffinger, *1899 Hague Peace Conference*, 5.
44. Ariga, "Account of My Journey to the International Peace Conference," *GJ* 2:18 (1899): 727-738; *Nikki*, vol. 2, 321.
45. Ariga, "Account of My Journey to the International Peace Conference," *GJ* 2:18 (1899): 733-738; Ariga, "Proceedings of the International Peace Conference," *GJ* 2:19 (1899): 773. Ariga was officially named a delegate on May 24, 1899. Eyffinger, *1899 Hague Peace Conference*, 5, 104, 125-127, 160-162 (see 160 for quote regarding the Chinese presence at the conference); Hull, *Two Hague Conferences*, 6-9.
46. Ariga, "Commentary on the International Peace Conference," *GJ* 2:19 (1899): 787-790; Ariga, "The Hague Peace Conference: One Success, One Failure," *GJ* 3:21 (1900): 881-882. The article from *Jiji Shimpō* may be found in *MHNS*, "Arms Reduction Failure," vol. 10 (June 1899), 404.
47. Ariga,"The Hague Peace Conference: One Success, One Failure," *GJ* 3:21 (1900): 881-888; Ariga, "Wars from Now On," *GJ* 3:25 (1900): 157-169.
48. Ariga, "Japan's Position Regarding the China Incident," *GJ* 3:30 (1900): 389-392 (quote on 392).
49. See Chapter I of the present work ("Konoe Atsumaro and the Case for Chinese-Japanese Collaboration"); Okamoto, *Japanese Oligarchy*, 48-49; Keene, *Emperor of Japan*, Ch. 51.
50. For example, in an article in *GJ*, "The Facts and Critical Assessment of the So-called Policy of Exchanging Manchuria for Korea," *GJ* 6:70 (October 20, 1903): 327-334, Ariga blasted Japan's Manchuria policy as a series of diplomatic blunders, starting in 1895 with the failure to insist that the Liaodong retrocession agreement include an assurance that no other foreign power would be allowed to occupy the territory. He catalogued how time and again Japan's diplomats had missed the subtleties of Western deal making, in the process unwittingly giving sanction to Russia's growing presence in Manchuria, now a serious threat to Japanese interests. Compare this with the statement of the seven professors, summarized by Okamoto, *Japanese Oligarchy*, 64-65, similar in its analysis of the problem, but stronger in rejecting reciprocal track arrangements. On the six professors and seven professors, see Okamoto, 58-67, and also Marshall, *Academic Freedom*, 8-17.
51. Ariga, "Is the Time for Hostilities Already at Hand?" *GJ* 6:64 (April 20, 1903): 225-233; Ariga, "Critique of Japan's Policy Toward Russia in Manchuria," *GJ* 6:68 (August 20, 1903): 295-301; Ariga, "The Facts and Critical Assessment of the so-called Policy of Exchanging Manchuria for Korea," *GJ* 6:70 (October 20, 1903): 327-334; Ariga, "My Dream Candidate as Japan's Ambassador to Russia," *GJ* 6:71 (November 20, 1903): 397-400. What Ariga had in mind was appointing the highly distinguished former governor of Taiwan, Kabayama Sukenori as special envoy to head a mission, comparable to the 1873 Iwakura Mission, to St. Petersburg for final talks with the Russians. Kabayama, he pointed out, was highly experienced, popular with the public, respected in political circles, and notably reserved in his opinions regarding resolution of the current crisis.
52. Ariga, "My Fourth Correspondence from My Trip to the West," *GJ* 5:53 (June 1902): 354-359; Ariga, "In the Company of International Law Scholars on My

Fifth Trip to the West," *GJ* 5:56 (September 1902): 43-46; Ariga, "International Conference of the Red Cross," *GJ* 10:112 (March 10, 1907): 132; Kemuyama, "Ariga sensei no omoide," 106-107.

53. Ariga, "The Russo-Japanese War and International Law," *GJ* 7:81 (August 20, 1904): 1822.
54. Ibid., 1823-1825.
55. Ariga, "Reflections in the Midst of Actual Combat," *GJ* 7:84 (November 20, 1904): 662-667.
56. Ibid., 665.
57. Ibid., 668.
58. Keene, *Emperor of Japan*, 606-607.
59. Ariga, "New Battlefront at Lushun," *GJ* 8:92 (July 10, 1905): 337-343 (quote on 343).
60. Keene, *Emperor of Japan*, 611; Sharf, "A Well-Watched War," 6-11 (quote p. 9); Ariga, *La Guerre Russo-Japonaise*, 130-152.
61. Ariga, *Extracts from "La Guerre Russo- Japonaise,"* 52-105. Note that these extracts were translated by the staff of the Carnegie Endowment for International Peace in 1942 for "official use during the present war."
62. This would tie in with the army's decision six months later to do a comprehensive survey of the region in preparation for managing the territory postwar. See Matsusaka, *The Making of Japanese Manchuria*, 50 passim.
63. See, for example, Ariga, "A Piece of Advice to China," *GJ* 12:140 (July 10, 1909): 103.
64. Prasenjit Duara, *Sovereignty and Authenticity*, 41-49, 58 (quote); Ariga, *Mandate for Manchuria*, passim.
65. Koskenniemi, *Gentle Civilizer*, 151
66. Ariga, *Mandate for Manchuria*, 86-94. In the book Ariga deals peripherally with the dilemma, then capturing the concern of his fellow international lawyers at the Institut de droit international: how to extend to developing areas the benefits of advanced civilization, which included a belief in international law, without breaching notions of sovereignty and rules-based actions central to that very belief? Or, to put it another way, could imperialism with its implied element of coercion be justified in civilizing mission terms? (Koskenniemi, *Gentle Civilizer*, Chapter II). For Ariga, the inclusion-exclusion, European vs non-European dichotomy faced by his European colleagues translated into how to define a legal context, including application of humanitarian law, for Japan's relations with China-Manchuria, Taiwan, and Korea. In political terms, there were legal precedents aplenty in European practice supporting arrangements that advantaged stronger states over weaker. Ariga's Manchuria mandate proposal was nothing radical. But on the question of exporting civilization, Ariga departed from his European colleagues who tended to work from a hierarchy of more and less civilized states reaching from Europe to Africa and Asia. His was a much more culturally flat world, at least the Asian part of it. He argued that Chinese farmers in Manchuria had a higher standard of morality and respect for authority than their Japanese counterparts

so that it made no sense to try to change local customs there or to settle the area with lower class Japanese. Such efforts in Taiwan and Korea had already proven problematic, he said. Ariga, who was no dove, sounded positively like a soft-power proponent when he suggested that Japan should lead by example, aim for influence over the long term, and entrust development efforts to private, humanitarian organizations, not the government.

67. On the Hibiya Riot, see Okamoto, *Japanese Oligarchy*, 196-223; Ariga, "Miscellaneous Thoughts on Current Affairs," *GJ* 8:95 (October 10, 1905): 268-276. Ariga termed the use of police force against citizens unconstitutional since there was nothing on the books declaring such protest action unlawful.
68. Ariga, *La Guerre Russo-Japonaise*, Title page, 552, 574.
69. Ariga, "On My Return Home," *GJ* 9:98 (January 10, 1906): 22; Ariga, "On My Return to Home," *GJ* 10:120 (November 10, 1907): 100.
70. Ariga, *La guerre Russo-Japonaise au point de vue continental et le droit international.*
71. Ariga, "International Conference of the Red Cross," *GJ* 10:112 (March 10, 1907): 132-143; Ariga, "Third Letter from My Sixth Trip to the West," *GJ* 10:117 (August 10, 1907): 467-469; Ariga, "On My Return Home," *GJ* 10:120 (November 10, 1907): 99-105; Ariga, "Half Month Diplomatic Review," *GJ* 11:122 (January 10, 1908): 1-11. On Ariga as a well-known figure, see Hutchinson, *Champions of Charity*, photos, 210 and 249.
72. Ariga, "On My Return Home," *GJ* 9:98 (January 10, 1906): 23.
73. Ariga, "The Japan-Korea Treaty and the Question of Coercion," *GJ* 9:102 (May 10, 1906): 155-160; Ariga, "Legal Basis for Union with Korea," *GJ* 13:152 (July 1910): 97-102; Ariga, "Basic Issues with Our Union with Korea," *GJ* 13:153 (August 1910): 105-112; Ariga, "Thoughts on a Partnership with Korea," *GJ* 13:154 (September 1910): 119-124. Note that in the three articles written in 1910, Ariga speaks variously of the arrangement with Korea as a "union" (*gōhō)*, apparently a term he coined himself, "partnership" (*gappei*), and "annexation," (*heigō*).
74. Aoyagi, "Leaving My Position as a Writer for China Update," 116.
75. Reynolds, *China, 1898-1912,* 189. Note that the decision to adopt the Japanese constitutional model was made in 1907. Note also in Harrell, *Sowing the Seeds*, 92f, that Ariga's works were translated into Chinese in the 1900-1901 issues of *Translation Journal*, published by Chinese students in Japan. For a detailed, convincing account of China's move to constitutional rule, see Norbert Meienberger, *The Emergence of Constitutional Government in China.*
76. Ariga, "Miscellaneous Thoughts on Current Affairs," *GJ* 8:94 (September 10, 1905): 216. On Ariga's translated works, see Li, "The Role of the Japanese Advisor," 72 fn14.
77. Li, "The Role of the Japanese Advisor," 47-50; Ariga, "Advice to Chinese Students in Japan," *GJ* 11:125 (April 10, 1908): 62-72.
78. Ariga, "Circumstances of My Accepting Employment," *GJ* 17:199 (February 15, 1913): 1-8; Reynolds, *China, 1898-1912*, 188-192; Meienberger, *Emergence of Constitutional Government*, 75-89.
79. Ariga, "A Piece of Advice for China," *GJ* 12:140 (July 10, 1909): 103.

80. "Getsuji bansankai kiji," *GJ* 13:151 (June 1910): 47-53.
81. "Ariga shuhitsu no byōki," *GJ* 14:161 (April 1911): 56; Ariga, "Account of My Winter Hibernation at Shiobara," *GJ* 31:371 (April 15, 1920): 743; Kemuyama, "Ariga sensei no omoide," 108.
82. Ariga, "Attitude of the Japanese Regarding the Disturbances," *GJ* 14:168 (November 1911): 1.
83. See Meienberger, *Emergence of Constitutional Government*; Ichiko, "Political and Institutional Reform, 1901-1911;" Tung, *The Political Institutions of Modern China*; Bergère, *Sun Yat-sen.*
84. Ariga, "On the Late Dr. Morrison," *GJ* 32:377 (July15, 1920): 176-182 (quote 179); Morrison, *Correspondence*, vol. 2, 99.
85 Morrison, *Correspondence*, vol. 2, 100-101; Ariga, "Initial Impressions on Arrival," *GJ* 17:203 (April 15, 1913): 941-942.
86. Aoyagi, "En Seigai komon to shite no ko Ariga hakushi," 71-76; Ariga, "Initial Impressions on Arrival," *GJ* 17:203 (April 15, 1913): 941.
87. Aoyagi, "En Seigai komon to shite no ko Ariga hakushi," 76; Ariga,"Two Weeks after the Formal Opening," *GJ* 17:205 (May 15, 1913): 1066; Pearl, *Morrison of Peking*, 278-279; Morrison, *Correspondence*, vol. 2, 637; on Hirai, see "Peking Takeaways," 7-8. Li, in "The Role of the Japanese Advisor," 52, cites a figure of 189 foreigners in Yuan's advisory group at all levels. Young, *Presidency of Yuan Shih-k'ai*, 169-173, quite correctly makes a distinction between this general group and those few, including Ariga Nagao, who were "close enough to Yuan to feel some of the responsibility"(169) for the fundamental changes in political structure underway.
88. Ariga, "Detailed Account of Activities," *GJ* 31:367 (February 15, 1920): 291; Ariga, "Initial Impressions on Arrival," *GJ* 17:203 (April 15, 1913): 941; Ariga, "My Work during My Stay in Beijing," *GJ* 18:210 (August 1, 1913): 228-229.
89. Ariga,"My Work during My Stay in Beijing," *GJ* 18:210 (August 1, 1913): 228.
90. Reynolds, *China, 1898-1912*, 186-192; Morrison, *Correspondence*, vol. 2, 99; Ariga, "Circumstances of My Accepting Employment" *GJ* 17:199 (February 15, 1913): 2-3; Ariga, "On the Late Dr. Morrison," *GJ* 32:377 (July 1920): 176-177. Ariga was proud of his work. He liked to relate how the 1906 group sought his help after briefings by constitutional experts in London left them in a hopeless muddle. Would he try to reconstruct what the British *might* have said, they asked, and incorporate this along with arguments for centralized government into a draft report to the throne? Two weeks later Ariga had produced a plan for top-down rule patterned after the Meiji constitution. He offered no comment on the final Chinese product, a constitutional monarchy that made more of imperial sovereignty and less of representative institutions than the Meiji original.
91. Several key people on the Japan side urged Ariga to accept the Yuan appointment. Takada Sanae of Waseda University said he proposed Ariga's name. Banzai Rihachirō, Japan's military attaché in China, said he sent Ariga's name to Takada but that nothing was done until former PM Ōkuma and genrō Saionji got involved. See, Takada, "Ko Ariga hakushi omoide no ki," 103-104, and Banzai, "Ariga

hakushi to En Seigai," 111. G.E. Morrison's opinion carried the heaviest weight with Yuan.

92. Ariga, "My Initial Impressions on Arrival," *GJ* 17:203 (April 15, 1913): 940; Reynolds, *China, 1898-1912*, 182; Harrell, *Sowing the Seeds*, 35-42 and *passim*; Okada, "Regarding China's Educational and Legal Compilations," *Taiyō* (August 1, 1909): 50-52; Ariga, *La Chine et la Grande Guerre Européenne*, 1-11.
93. Banzai, "Ariga hakushi to En Seigai," 111-112.
94. Pearl, *Morrison of Peking*, 264.
95. Ariga, "The Present State of Affairs in China" *GJ* 17:206 (June 1, 1913): 1286.
96. See for example Young, *Presidency of Yuan Shih-k'ai*. However, there were some observers at the time who took exception to the prevailing view that China was unfit for representative government. See Sudhindra Bose's comments on Frank Goodnow's article, "Reform in China," appearing in *The American Political Science Review* of May 1915.
97. Ariga, "My Work During My Stay in Beijing," *GJ* 18:210 (August 1, 1913): 230-231; Ariga, "The Constitution of the Republic of China: The Process of Transferring Sovereignty," *GJ* 18:211 (August 15, 1913): 338-347; Ariga, "The Constitution of the Republic of China," *GJ* 18:212 (September 1, 1913): 441-452.
98. Ariga, "The Constitution of the Republic of China," *GJ* 18:212 (September 1, 1913): 452; Ariga, "The Constitution of the Republic of China: The Process of Transferring Sovereignty," *GJ* 18:211 (August 15, 1913): 338-347.
99. Ariga, "The State of Affairs," *GJ* 17:203 (April 15, 1913): 852; Ariga, "Two Weeks After the Formal Opening," *GJ* 17:205 (May 15, 1913): 1065-1068. For excellent discussions of the confusion surrounding and incomplete commitment to the idea of a "liberal republic" on the part of Chinese reformers, revolutionaries and Yuan himself, see Young, *Presidency of Yuan Shih-k'ai*, especially Chapters 4 and 6.
100. Ariga, "China's North-South Accord Policy," *GJ* 18:216 (November 1, 1913): 882-885. For comment on Jefferson, see Russell Short, "Founding Father?" *New York Times Magazine,* February 14, 2010.
101. Ariga, "China's North-South Accord Policy," *GJ* 18:215 (October 15, 1913): 769-777.
102. Ariga, "China's North-South Accord Policy," *GJ* 18:216 (November 1, 1913): 881.
103. Ariga, "Detailed Account of Activities," *GJ* 31:368 (March 1, 1920): 407.
104. Goodnow, "Reform in China," 218.
105. Goodnow, "The Parliament of the Republic of China," 545.
106. As Ernest Young says (*Presidency of Yuan Shih-k'ai,* 150) about leading reform figure Liang Qichao, ". . . his doubts about what a premature adoption of democracy might actually produce were widely shared, among revolutionaries as well as reformers." Aoyagi in "En Seigai komon to shite no ko Ariga hakushi," 71-76, says that Ariga was perceived as being responsible for Yuan's action toward parliament. Li treats this issue in "The Role of the Japanese Advisor," 63-64, though unfortunately the translation on page 64 makes little sense.
107. Ariga, "Taking Preventive Measures," *GJ* 18:213 (September 15, 1913): 553-562; Ariga, "The Constitution of the Republic of China," *GJ* 18:212 (September 1, 1913):

441-452. Note that Ariga's "Taking Preventive Measures" was reproduced as a chapter in Ariga's draft constitution entitled, "Guan yi xian ping" (Kibitzing while watching a game of chess). Ariga, "My Work during My Stay in Beijing," *GJ* 18:210 (August 1, 1913): 232. The title, Ariga explains, refers to a foreigner watching from the sidelines as Chinese constitutional discussion groups north and south battled over the contents of the draft.

108. Ariga, "China's North-South Accord Policy," *GJ* 18:216 (November 1, 1913): 888; Young, *Presidency of Yuan Shih-k'ai*, 174; Ariga, "Taking Preventive Measures," *GJ* 18:213 (September 15, 1913): 559-561.

109. Ariga, "Taking Preventive Measures," *GJ* 18:213 (September 15, 1913): 562.

110. Ariga, "Turkey's Future," *GJ* 18:208 (July 1, 1913): 17.

111. Ariga, "Impressions of the Formal Inauguration,"*GJ* 18:216 (November 1, 1913): 972-976; Pearl, *Morrison of Peking*, 288.

112. Morrison, *Correspondence*, vol. 2, 539-540. Morrison had the meeting with Katō in August 1916 while on vacation in Japan. Katō had been dismissed as foreign minister the previous year.

113. See Ian Nish's excellent biographical sketch, "Katō Takaaki, 1960-1926," 80-91; Chi, *China Diplomacy, 1915-1918*, 1-18, an exceptionally clear account of exceptionally complex negotiations; Dickinson, *War and National Reinvention*, 33-48; and Seki, *Nichi-Ei Dōmei*, 40-56, and passim. Seki offers a fascinating account of Japan's assistance in the Mediterranean. For a discussion of what he terms the "bureaucratic politician," see Robert Scalapino, *Democracy and the Party Movement in Pre-War Japan* (Berkeley: University of California Press, 1962), 195-198.

114. Ariga, "Observations on the Present Situation," *GJ* 20:240 (November 1, 1914): 981-982. Ariga deplored German atrocities committed early in the European conflict, asserting that Japan would never change its policy of adherence to wartime law. On conducting a "civilized" war see Ariga, "International Law in the Aftermath," *GJ* 22:259 (August 15, 1915): 323-330.

115. Ariga, *La Grande Guerre Européenne*, 14; Chi, *China Diplomacy*, 19-21. On assurances to China, see Dickinson, *War and National Reinvention*, 96 and Chi, *China Diplomacy*, 26, and 29-30. Note that Ariga attributed violations of conduct of war standards by German troops to their lack of proper education in wartime law. (Ariga,"Observations on the Present Situation" *GJ* 20:240 [November 1, 1914]: 981-982).

116. Ariga, "We Must Focus on the Role of Diplomacy," *GJ* 20:239 (October 15, 1914): 865-872 (quote on 872).

117. Dickinson, *War and National Reinvention*, 97-102. Dickinson, 100, speaks of Katō's refusal to consider "genrō suggestions for a special envoy of distinguished stature, one close to themselves, to conduct negotiations with China." It is reasonable to speculate that genrō suggestions included Ariga Nagao. On Japan's conduct during the joint Japan-British Jiaozhou operation, see Chi, *China Diplomacy*, 25

118. Ariga, "Questions about Japanese Troop Deployment to Europe," *GJ* 20:241 (November 15, 1914): 1095-1103; Ariga, "Alas! Money and Rice and Maps," *GJ* 20:243 (December 15, 1914): 1323-1326; Ogawa Gōtarō, "Questions for Advocates

of Sending," 147-152; Dickinson, *War and National Reinvention,* 58-83, 97-99. Based on figures given in Niall Ferguson, *The Pity of War,* 106, the £30 million would have been about 40 percent of Britain's 1913 defense expenditures.

119. Chi, *China Diplomacy,* quote, 37, and see for superb clear, complete account of negotiations, 28-61. Dickinson, *War and National Reinvention,* also provides excellent analysis and discussion, Chapter III.
120. On "Asia is not Asia's Asia," see *GJ* article (no author) "Tai-Shi gaikō no yōtei," 249-254 (quote on 250). For a sampling of criticism of Katō diplomacy, see ibid. as well as *GJ* articles (no author) "Tai-Shi kōshō," 648-653; "Tai-Shi kōshō no keika," 695-701; "Tai-Shi kōshō no kiki,"1039-1043; "Gaikō shippai no sekinin,"1161-1166; and also Harada, "Tai-Shi kōshō ni tsuite," 12-17.
121. Ariga, "Reflections," *GJ* 21:254 (June 1, 1915): 1167-1170 (quote on 1170); Chi, *China Diplomacy,* 50-55. Chi, 55, calls Ariga,"the advocate of true Sino-Japanese cooperation."
122. Chi, *China Diplomacy,* 56.
123. Chi, *China Diplomacy,* 53-6l; Young, *Presidency of Yuan Shih-k'ai,* 186-192; Dickinson, *War and National Reinvention,*107-114. Dickinson argues that the Katō-genrō confrontation was less about the substance of foreign policy than who was entitled to make the decisions. Ariga's involvement, which he does not mention, suggests otherwise—that the genrō favored a China policy that was broader based, not exclusively reliant on the Anglo-Japanese Alliance so central to Katō's thinking. See also, Jansen's gold standard account of the 21 Demands, *Japanese and Sun Yatsen,* 183-193, that shows Sun Yatsen and the Chinese revolutionaries all too willing to concede to Japan's demands in exchange for Japanese aid.
124. Young, *Presidency of Yuan Shih-k'ai,* 221.
125. Quote: Morrison, *Correspondence,* vol. 2, 532. Young, *Presidency of Yuan Shih-k'ai,* Chapter 8; Chi, *China Diplomacy,* Chapter III; Dickinson, *War and National Reinvention,* 123-138; Morrison, *Correspondence,* vol. 2, 450-451.
126. Morrison, *Correspondence,* vol 2, 488; Young, *Presidency of Yuan Shih-k'ai,* 219. Li in "The Role of the Japanese Advisor" supports the view that Ariga caved in on the emperor issue. He cites as evidence Banzai Rihachirō's comment in his 1933 *Gaikō jihō* retrospective on Ariga that Ariga welcomed Yuan's plan to become emperor. According to Banzai, Ariga said, "I work for Yuan so if my efforts turn out to be to Yuan's advantage, isn't that a good thing? I can't find much to object to about a good man improving his prospects." Whether Banzai's recollection is accurate is one question, the other whether Ariga meant his words to convey support for Yuan becoming emperor or simply for an expansion of his executive powers. Looking back on his constitution writing role in 1920, Ariga himself blamed the ill-fated movement to make Yuan emperor as the cause of China's failure to implement reforms started under the Yuan presidency. See Ariga, "Detailed Account of Activities," *GJ* 31:368 (March 1, 1920): 390-407; Banzai, "Ariga hakushi to En Seigai," 113; and Li, "The Role of the Japanese Advisor," 48, 64, 78-79, fn74.
127. Banzai, "Ariga hakushi to En Seigai," 113-114; Chi, *China Diplomacy,* 71.

128. The weight of evidence suggests that Ariga's position was close to Morrison's, which was to urge Yuan to move forward to complete meaningful reforms he had initiated as the republic's chief executive. See Morrison's memo to Yuan in Morrison, *Correspondence*, vol. 2, 485-489. Ariga, "Detailed Account of Activities," *GJ* 31:368 (March 1, 1920); Takada, "Ko Ariga hakushi omoide no ki"; Kemuyama, "Ariga sensei no omoide"; Li, "The Role of the Japanese Advisor."
129. Morrison, *Correspondence*, vol. 2, 511.
130. Ariga, "On the Late Dr. Morrison," *GJ* 32:377 (July 15, 1920): 179-180; Morrison, *Correspondence*, vol. 2, 532-533.
131. Ariga, "Detailed Account of Activities," *GJ* 31:368 (March 1, 1920): 23.
132. See Ariga's letter to Morrison about his contract renewal, dated August 8, 1917 and written from Japan, Morrison, *Correspondence*, vol. 2, 620-621.
133. Ariga, *Shina Seikan*. For the book advertisement, see *GJ* 31:365, January 15, 1920.
134. MacMillan, *Peacemakers*, 315-353; Pearl, *Morrison of Peking*, 374. According to Morrison, the Chinese would have invited him to attend the conference, as a foreign adviser to China's delegation, had it not been for their reluctance to include Ariga and Padoux.
135. Ariga, "Account of My Winter Hibernation at Shiobara," *GJ* 31:371 (April 15, 1920): 743-752; Fenollosa, *Tō-A bijutsushikō*, translated by Ariga Nagao; and "Keichō Ariga hakushi,"123.

Notes to Conclusion

1. Jansen, *Making of Modern Japan*, 441.
2. See Kowner, "Between a Colonial Clash and World War Zero," in the excellent set of essays edited by Rotem Kowner, *The Impact of the Russo-Japanese War.*
3. Roosevelt, "The College Graduate and Public Life," *Works of Theodore Roosevelt,* vol. VIII, 36.
4. Jansen, *Japanese and Sun Yat-sen*, 33.
5. See for example the recent set of articles under the heading, "Asia Redux: Conceptualizing a Region for our Times," in *The Journal of Asian Studies*, Vol. 69, No. 4 (November 2010).
6. Harrell, *Sowing the Seeds*, 189-192.
7. Roosevelt, "Expansion and Peace," *The Works of Theodore Roosevelt,* vol. VIII, 336.
8. Original quote in Chapter IV of the present work.
9. Original quote in Chapter IV of the present work.
10. Original quote in Chapter IV of the present work.

11 Young, *Japan's Total Empire*, 55-78.

Bibliography

Abe Hiroshi. *Chūgoku kindai gakkōshi kenkyū* (Research into the history of China's modern schools). Tokyo: Fukumura shuppan, 1993.

____, *Chūgoku no kindai kyōiku to Meiji Nihon* (China's modern education and Meiji Japan). Tokyo: Fukumura shuppan, 1990.

____, editor. *Nit-Chū kyōiku bunka kōryū to masatsu: Senzen Nihon no zai-Ka kyōiku jigyō* (Japanese-Chinese educational and cultural exchange and areas of friction: Japanese educational activities in prewar China). Tokyo: Daiichi shobō, 1983.

Aida Tsutomu and Kawashima Naniwa. *Kawashima Naniwa Ō* (The elderly Mr. Kawashima Naniwa). Tokyo: Bunsuikaku, 1936.

Aoyagi Atsutsune. "En Seigai komon to shite no ko Ariga hakushi" (The late Dr. Ariga as adviser to Yuan Shikai," *GJ* 45:540 (June 1, 1927): 71-76.

____. "Shinkoku jihō shippitsu no ji" (Leaving my position as a writer for China update). *GJ* 9:100 (March 1906): 115-118.

Ariga Nagao and Paul Fauchille. *La Chine et la grande guerre Europée̊ne au point de vue du droit international d'après les documents officiels du gouvernement Chinois.* Paris: A. Pedone, 1920.

Ariga Nagao. *Bunmei sensō hōki* (Laws of civilized war). Tokyo: Kinkōdō, 1904.

____. "Diplomacy." In *Japan by the Japanese,* edited by Alfred Stead, 142-218. London: William Heinemann, 1904.

____. *Extracts from La guerre Russo-Japonaise au point de vue continental et le droit international d'après les documents officiels du Grand Ètat-major Japonais* (section Historique de la guerre de 1904-1905) [English] Washington, DC: Carnegie Endowment for International Peace, Division of International Law, 1942.

____. *Guan yi xian ping* (Kibitzing while watching a game of chess). [n.p.]: 1913.

____. *Hogokoku ron* (Discussion of a protectorate). Tokyo: Waseda Daigaku shuppanbu, 1906.

____. *The Japanese Red Cross Society and the Russo-Japanese War: A Report.* London: Bradbury Agnew, 1907.

____. *Kinji gaikōshi* (History of foreign relations in recent times). Tokyo: Waseda Daigaku shuppansha, 1898.

____. *La Croix Rouge en Extreme-Orient: exposé de l'organisation et du fonctionnement de la Croix-Rouge du Japon.* Paris: A. Pedone, 1900.

____. *La guerre Russo-Japonaise au point de vue continental et le droit international d'après les documents officiels du Grand Ètat-major Japonais (section historique de la guerre de 1904-1905).* Paris: A. Pedone, 1908.

____. *La guerre Sino-Japonaise au point de vue du droit international.* Paris: A. Pedone, 1896.

____. *Manshū inin tōchi ron* (Discussion of a mandate for Manchuria). Tokyo: Waseda Daigaku shuppanbu: Hatsubaimoto hakubunkan, 1905.

____. *The Red Cross Society of Japan: Its Organization and Activity in Time of Peace and War.* St. Louis: Universal Exposition, 1904.

____. *Saikin sanjūnen gaikōshi* (History of foreign relations in the last thirty years). Waseda Daigaku shuppansha, 1914.

____. *Sekijūji jōyaku hen* (Compilation of Red Cross treaties). Tokyo: Nihon Sekijūjisha, 1894.

____. *Shina seikan* (A correct view of China). Tokyo: Gaikō jihōsha shuppanbu, 1918.

Ariga Nagao. Writings from *Gaikō jihō (Revue Diplomatique).* Selection of articles by Ariga Nagao dating from 1898-1920 [irregular, 1898-1906; semimonthly, 1912-1920], and listed in chronological order:

____. "Gaikō himitsu ron" (On secrecy in diplomacy). *GJ* 1:2 (March 1898): 32-42.

____. "Gaikō kaizō ron" (Refashioning diplomacy). *GJ* 1:5 (June 1898): 96-102.

____. "Tō-A gaikō no jūdaimondai" (Ten big issues in East Asian diplomacy). *GJ* 1:6 (July 1898): 103-114.

____. "Fuirippin ron" (Discussion of the Philippines). *GJ* 1:7 (August 1898): 131-141.

____. "Gaikōkan kansei kaisei ron" (On revising the regulations governing the foreign service). *GJ* 1:8 (September 1898): 151-158.

____. "Gaimushō komon Denison-shi ron" (On the Foreign Ministry's adviser Mr. Denison). *GJ* 1:8 (September 1898): 159-165.

____. "Shina kakushin ron" (On China's reform). *GJ* 1:10 (November 1898): 179-186.

____. "Honpō daiichigō ni taisuru shoshinbun no hihyō" (Reviews from various newspapers of the first issue of this journal). *GJ* 1:10 (November 1898): 1-8.

____. "Shina hozen ron" (On preserving China's integrity). *GJ* 2:11 (January 1899): 187-196.

____. "Bankoku heiwa kaigi kikō" (Account of my journey to the International Peace Conference). *GJ* 2:18 (1899): 727-738.

____. "Bankoku heiwa kaigi sadan" (Commentary on the International Peace Conference). *GJ* 2:19 (1899): 787-796.

____. "Bankoku heiwa kaigi kiji" (Proceedings of the International Peace Conference). *GJ* 2:19 (1899): 773-786.

____. "Bankoku heiwa kaigi kiji" (Proceedings of the International Peace Conference). *GJ* 2:20 (1899): 833-843.

____. "Bankoku heiwa kaigi no issei ippai" (International Peace Conference: one success, one failure). *GJ* 3:21 (1900): 881-888.

____. "Kyō igo no sensō" (Wars from now on). *GJ* 3:25 (1900): 157-169.
____. "Shinkoku ni okeru Tenshukyō" (Roman Catholicism in China). *GJ* 3:30 (1900): 1472-1485.
____. "Shinkoku jiken ni okeru Nihon no taido" (Japan's position regarding the China Incident). *GJ* 3:30 (1900): 389-392.
____. "Shinkoku zengosaku" (Remedial measures for China). *GJ* 3:33 (1900): 415-419.
____. "Pekin kakkoku shishin kaigi" (Meeting of the foreign representatives in Peking). *GJ* 3:34 (1900), 427-437.
____. "Seiyū daiichi tsūshin" (My first correspondence from my trip to the West). *GJ* 5:51 (April 1902): 50-54.
____. "Seiyū daiyon tsūshin" (My fourth correspondence from my trip to the West). *GJ* 5:53 (June 1902): 354-359.
____. "Daigo seiyūchū kokusaihōgakusha to no kōsai" (In the company of international law scholars on my fifth trip to the West). *GJ* 5:56 (September 1902): 43-46.
____. "Senki sude ni jukushita ka" (Is the time for hostilities at hand?) *GJ* 6:64 (April 20,1903): 225-233.
____. "Manshū ni kansuru tai-Ro gaikō hihyō" (Critique of Japan's policy toward Russia in Manchuria). *GJ* 6:68 (August 20, 1903): 295-301.
____. " Iwayuru Man-Kan kōkan no jissō to hihyō" The facts and critical assessment of the so-called policy of exchanging Manchuria for Korea). *GJ* 6:70 (October 20, 1903): 327-334.
____. "Yume ni ken-Ro taishi o okuru" (My dream candidate as Japan's ambassador to Russia). *GJ* 6:71 (November 20, 1903): 397-400.
____. "Nichi-Ro kaisen" (Outbreak of war between Japan and Russia). *GJ* 7:74 (February20, 1904): 1489-1496.
____. "Nichi-Ro kōshō tenmatsu hihyō" (A critical assessment of the course of Russo-Japanese negotiations). *GJ* 7:74 (February 20, 1904): 1465-1488.
____. "Kankoku hogoken no shōrai" (The future of protective authority over Korea). *GJ* 7:75(March 20, 1904): 470-474.
____. "Nichi-Ro chōtei dan" (Russo-Japanese mediation talks). *GJ* 7:78 (May 20, 1904): 517-520.
____. "Nichi-Ro sensō to kokusaihō" (The Russo-Japanese War and international law). *GJ* 7:81 (August 20, 1904):1820-1826.
____. "Jissenchū no meisō" (Reflections in the midst of actual combat). *GJ* 7:84 (November 20, 1904): 662-667.
____. "Manshū no byōkon oyobi sono kyūjihō" (The root cause of Manchuria's illness and how to cure it). *GJ* 7:85 (December 20, 1904): 684-687.
____. "Manshū tetsudō seibun no senrei" (Precedents for the making of a Manchurian railway). *GJ* 8:89 (April 10, 1905): 105-109.
____. "Manshū inin tōchi ron no hihyōka ni shashiawasete benkaisu" (In defense of *Manshū inin tōchi ron* with all due respect for my critics). *GJ* 8:90 (May 1905): 125-130.
____. "Ryojun no shin senjō" (New battlefront at Lushun). *GJ* 8:92 (July 10, 1905): 337-343.

____. "Jiji zakkan" (Miscellaneous thoughts on current affairs). *GJ* 8:94 (September 10, 1905): 213-220.
____. "Jiji zakkan" (Miscellaneous thoughts on current affairs). *GJ* 8:95 (October 10, 1905): 268-276.
____. "Manshū no jitsugyō sensō" (Manchuria's business war). *GJ* 8:97 (December 10, 1905): 320-326.
____. "Kichō no ji" (On my return home). *GJ* 9:98 (January 10, 1906): 22-24.
____. "Hogokoku no kenkyū" (A study of protectorates). *GJ* 9:99 (February 10, 1906): 29-36.
____. "Nichi-Kan kyōyaku to kyōhaku mondai" (The Japan-Korea Treaty and the question of coercion). *GJ* 9:102 (May 10, 1906): 155-160.
____. "Kankoku ni okeru Nihon no shihōken" (Japan's judicial powers over Korea). *GJ* 9: 103 (June 10, 1906): 182-188.
____. "Bankoku Sekijūji sōkai" (International Conference of the Red Cross). *GJ* 10:112. (March 10, 1907): 132-143.
____. "Dairoku seiyū daisan shin" (Third letter from my sixth trip to the West). *GJ* 10:117 (August 10, 1907): 467-480.
____. "Kichō no ji" (On my return home). *GJ* 10:120 (November 10, 1907): 99-105.
____. "Nihon no shinyō teiraku" (Decline in Japan's credibility [vis a vis the West]." *GJ* 10:121 (December 10, 1907): 117-128.
____. "Hangetsu gaikōshi" (Half month diplomatic review) *GJ* 11:122 (January 10, 1908): 1-11.
____. "Shinkoku ryūgakusei ni chūkoku" (Advice to Chinese students in Japan). *GJ* 11:125 (April 10, 1908): 62-72.
____. "Shinkoku ni chūkokusu" (A piece of advice for China). *GJ* 12:140 (July 10, 1909): 101-104.
____. "Jiji zakkan" (Miscellaneous thoughts on current events). *GJ* 13:148 (March 1910): 51-54.
____. "Gaikōkan no kyōikuhō kaisei ron" (On revising the standards for educating diplomats). *GJ* 13:149 (April 1910): 55-58.
____. "Kankoku gōhō no hōri" (Legal basis for union with Korea). *GJ* 13:152 (July 1910): 97-102.
____. "Kankoku gōhō no konpon mondai" (Basic issues with our union with Korea). *GJ* 13:153 (August 1910): 105-112.
____. "Kankoku gappei shokan" (Thoughts on a partnership with Korea). *GJ* 13:154 (September 1910): 119-124.
____. "Jiji hyōron" (Comments on current topics). *GJ* 14:161 (April 1911): 49-55.
____. "ChūShin dōran ni taisuru wagaminkan no taido" (The attitude of the Japanese toward the disturbances in central China). *GJ* 14:168 (November 1911): 1-6.
____. "Torukō no unmei" (Turkey's destiny). *GJ* 17:196 (January 1, 1913): 7-16.
____. "Chūka minkoku komon ōhei tenmatsu" (Circumstances of my accepting employment as an adviser to China). *GJ* 17:199 (February 15, 1913): 1-8.
____. "Minkoku kenpō kaigi mae no keisei" (The state of affairs prior to the opening session on China's constitution). *GJ* 17:203 (April 15, 1913): 847-852.

_____. "Nyūen saisho no shokan" (Initial impressions on arrival in Beijing). *GJ* 17: 203 (April 15, 1913): 938-943.
_____. "Chūka minkoku daiichiji kokkai" (The opening session of China's first national assembly). *GJ* 17:204 (May 1, 1913): 955-960.
_____. "Minkoku seishiki kokkai kaikaigo nishūkan" (Two weeks after the formal opening of China's national assembly). *GJ* 17:205 (May 15, 1913): 1065-1069.
_____. "Minkoku no genjō to rekkyō no taido" (The present state of affairs in China and the attitude of the Powers). *GJ* 17:206 (June 1, 1913): 1286-1289.
_____. "Torukō no shōrai to minkoku no zaisei" (Turkey's future and China's financial affairs). *GJ* 18:208 (July 1, 1913): 14-19.
_____. "Pekin taizaichū no yo no jigyō" (My work during my stay in Beijing). *GJ* 18:210 August 1, 1913): 227-232.
_____. "Chūka minkoku kenpō: kakumei no toki ni okeru tōchiken iten no shidai" (The constitution of the Republic of China: the process of transferring sovereignty at the time of the revolution). *GJ* 18:211 (August 15,1913): 338-347.
_____. "Chūka minkoku kenpō" (The constitution of the Republic of China). *GJ* 18:212 (September 1, 1913): 441-452.
_____. "Minkoku kenpō seiteijō shakaitō heigai no yobō" (Taking preventive measures against the harmful influence of socialism in establishing China's constitution). *GJ* 18:213 (September 15, 1913): 553-562.
_____. "Shina nanboku chōwasaku" (China's north-south accord policy). *GJ* 18:215 (October 15, 1913): 769-777.
_____. "Shina nanboku chōwasaku" (China's north-south accord policy). *GJ* 18:216 (November 1, 1913): 880-890.
_____. "Seishiki daisōtō shūninshiki shokan" (Impressions of the formal inauguration ceremony of the president). *GJ* 18:216 (November 1, 1913): 972-976.
_____. "Doitsu ni sakinzeraruru nakare" (We must not let Germany get ahead of us). *GJ* 19:225 (March 15, 1914): 601-603.
_____. "Shina kyōwakoku daisōtō no rikukaigun tōsuiken" (The president of the Chinese Republic's right of supreme command over the army and navy). *GJ* 19:230 (June 1, 1914):1169-1174.
_____. "Morison no Shina ron" (Morrison on China). *GJ* 20:234 (August 1, 1914): 389-391.
_____. "Taisen shūketsu no gaikō ni chūi subeshi" (We must focus on the role of diplomacy in ending the Great War). *GJ* 20:239 (October 15, 1914): 865-872.
_____. "Jikyoku kansatsu i roku" (Observations on the present situation). *GJ* 20:240 (November 1, 1914): 981-984.
_____. "Nihongun Ōshū haken mondai" (Questions about Japanese troop deployment to Europe). *GJ* 20:241 (November 15, 1914): 1095-1103.
_____. "Ā kane to kome to chizu" (Alas! money, rice and maps). *GJ* 20:243 (December 15, 1914):1323-1326.
_____. "Sengo ni taisuru daidōmei no hitsuyō" (The need for a grand alliance after the war). *GJ* 21:244 (January 1, 1915): 1-6.
_____. "Yudayakoku saikō no kōkikai" (Propitious moment to reestablish a Jewish state). *GJ* 21:247 (February 15, 1915): 361-369.

____. "Tsukiyo ni kama o nukaruru nakare" (Don't be caught off guard). *GJ* 21:251 (April 15, 1915): 817-821.

____. "Jukkai" (Reflections). *GJ* 21:254 (June 1, 1915): 1167-1171.

____. "Ōshū taisengo no kokusai hō" (International law in the aftermath of the Great War in Europe). *GJ* 22:259 (August 15, 1915): 323-330.

____. "Shina kenpō seitei jigyō no enkaku" (Detailed account of activities leading to establishment of China's constitution). *GJ* 31:367 (February 15, 1920): 285-296.

____. "Shina kenpō seitei jigyō enkaku" (Detailed account of activities leading to establishment of China's constitution). *GJ* 31: 368 (March 1, 1920): 390-407.

____. "Shiobara fuyugomori no ki" (Account of my winter hibernation at Shiobara). *GJ* 31:371 (April 15, 1920): 743-752.

____. "Yukeru Morison hakushi" (On the late Dr. Morrison). *GJ* 32: 377 (July 15, 1920): 176-182.

"Ariga shuhitsu no byōki," (Editor-in-chief Ariga's illness). *GJ* 14: 161 (April 1911): 56.

Arima Yoriyasu. *Seikai dōchūki* (A journey through the political world). Tokyo: Nihon shuppan kyōdō, 1951.

Bacon, Alice. *Japanese Girls and Women.* Boston and New York: Houghton Mifflin and Company, 1902.

Bailey, Paul. *Reform the People: Changing Attitudes towards Popular Education in Early 20th Century China.*Vancouver: University of British Columbia Press, 1990.

Banzai Rihachirō. "Ariga hakushi to En Seigai" (Dr. Ariga and Yuan Shikai). *GJ* 67:686 (July 1, 1933): 109-115.

Barrett, David P., and Larry N. Shyu, editors. *Chinese Collaboration with Japan, 1932-1945: The Limits of Accommodation.* Stanford: Stanford University Press, 2001.

Beasley, W.G. *Japanese Imperialism, 1894-1945.* Oxford: Oxford University Press, 1987.

____. *The Meiji Restoration.* Stanford: Stanford University Press, 1972.

Beauchamp, Edward, and Akira Iriye, editors. *Foreign Employees in Nineteenth Century Japan.* Boulder, CO: Westview Press, 1990.

"Bei-Ō junkai no zakkan" (Miscellaneous impressions of [Konoe's] tour of America and Europe). *Taiyō* 6:10 (January 3, 1900): 96-97.

Beijing shifan daxue xiaoshi (A history of Beijing Normal College). Beijing: Beijing Shifan Daxue chubanshe, 1984.

Benfey, Christopher. *The Great Wave: Gilded Age Misfits, Japanese Eccentrics, and the Opening of Old Japan.* New York: Random House, 2004.

"Benxiao huan'an Riben Hattori boshi jishi" (Memo on Beijing Normal's banquet in honor of Japan's Dr. Hattori). *Jiaoyu congkan* (The Peking National Normal University Record) 5: 2 (1924): 1-3.

Begère, Marie-Claire. *Sun Yatsen.*Translated by Janet Lloyd. Stanford: Stanford University Press, 1998.

Bird, Isabella L. *Unbeaten Tracks in Japan.* London: John Murray, 1911.

____. *The Yangtze Valley and Beyond.* New York: G.P. Putnam's Sons, 1900.

Bland, J.O.P. *China, the Pity of It.* London: W. Heinemann, 1932.

Borg, Dorothy, and Shumpei Okamoto, editors. *Pearl Harbor as History.* New York:

Columbia University Press, 1973.

Brooks, Barbara. "The Gaimushō's China Experts, 1895-1937." In *The Japanese Informal Empire in China,* edited by Peter Duus, Ramon H. Myers, and Mark R. Peattie, 369-394. Princeton, NJ: Princeton University Press, 1989.

Bu Ping. "Nit-Chū rekishi kyōdō kenkyū no igi to kadai" (The significance and tasks of the Japan-China Joint History Research). *Sekai* (August, 2007): 207-210.

Burkman, Thomas W. *Japan and the League of Nations, 1914-1938.* Honolulu: University of Hawai'i Press, 2008.

Burton, Margaret E. *The Education of Women in China.* New York: Fleming H. Revell Co., 1911.

Cao Rulin. *Yisheng zhi huiyi* (Recollections of a lifetime). Hong Kong: Chunqiu zazhi she, 1966.

Chamberlain, Basil L. *Things Japanese.* London: J. Murray, 1905.

Chang, Iris. *The Rape of Nanking: The Forgotten Holocaust of World War II.* New York: Basic, 1992.

Checkland, Olive. *Humanitarianism and the Emperor's Japan, 1877-1977.* New York: St. Martin's Press, 1994.

Chen, Edward I-te. "The Attempt to Integrate the Empire: Legal Perspectives." In *The Japanese Colonial Empire,* edited by Ramon H. Myers and Mark R. Peattie, 240-274. Princeton, NJ: Princeton University Press, 1984.

Chi, Madeleine. *China Diplomacy, 1914-1918.* Cambridge, MA: East Asian Research Center, Harvard University Press, 1970.

Chiang Monlin. *Tides from the West.* Taipei: World Book, 1963.

Chin Hsiung-pai [Jin Xiongbai]. *Su Qinwang yu Chuandao Fangzi [Kawashima Yoshiko] funu* (Prince Su and Kawashima Yoshiko, father and daughter). Taibei: Xin wan xiang yue kanshe: Zong jing xiao ming de shuju, 1980.

Chu, Samuel C. "Li Hung-chang: An Assessment." In *Li Hung-chang and China's Early Modernization,* edited by Samuel C. Chu and Kwang-ching Liu. Armonk, NY: M.E. Sharpe, 1994.

Coble, Parks M. "China's 'New Remembering of the Anti-Japanese War of Resistance, 1937-1945." *The China Quarterly* 190 (June 2007): 394-410.

Cohen, Paul A. *History in Three Keys: The Boxers as Event, Experience, and Myth.* New York: Columbia University Press, 1997.

The Constitutional Compact: i.e., The Amended Provisional Constitution of the Republic of China, promulgated on 1st May, 1914. Translated by Sao-ke Alfred Sze and T.Y. Lo. Translation revised by Prof. Frank J. Goodnow and Dr. N. Ariga. Peking: *Peking Daily News,* 1914.

Crossley, Pamela Kyle. *Orphan Warriors: Three Manchu Generations and the End of the Qing World.* Princeton, NJ: Princeton University Press, 1990.

____. *A Translucent Mirror: History and Identity in Qing Imperial Ideology.* Berkeley: University of California Press, 1999.

Dickinson, Frederick R. *War and National Reinvention: Japan in the Great War, 1914-1919.* Cambridge, MA: Harvard University Asia Center, Harvard University Press, 1999.

Dikotter, Frank. *The Discourse of Race in Modern China.* Stanford: Stanford University

Press, 1992.

Duara, Prasenjit. "Asia Redux: Conceptualizing a Region for Our Times." *Journal of Asian Studies* 69: 4 (November 2010): 963-989.

____. *Sovereignty and Authenticiy: Manchukuo and the East Asian Modern.* Lanham, MD: Rowman & Littlefield, 2003.

Duke, Benjamin C. *The History of Modern Japanese Education: Constructing the National School System.* New Brunswick, NJ: Rutgers University Press, 2009.

Duus, Peter. *The Abacus and the Sword: The Japanese Penetration of Korea, 1895-1910.* Berkeley: University of California Press, 1995.

Duus, Peter, Ramon H. Meyers, and Mark R. Peattie, editors. *The Japanese Informal Empire in China, 1895-1937.* Princeton, NJ: Princeton University Press, 1989.

Education in Japan: Prepared for the Louisiana Purchase Exposition. Department of Education, Japan, 1904.

Eyffinger, Arthur. *The 1899 Hague Peace Conference: 'The Parliament of Man, The Federation of the World'.* The Hague; London; Boston: Kluwer Law International, 1999.

Eto Shinkichi and Li Tingjiang. *Jindai zai-Hua Riren guwen ziliao mulu* (Catalogue of resources on Japanese advisers in China in modern times). Beijing: Zhong hua shu ju, 1994.

____. *Konoe Atsumaro to Shinmatsu yōjin* (Konoe Atsumaro and leading figures at the end of the Qing). Tokyo: Hara shobō, 2004.

Fairbank, John King. *The Great Chinese Revolution, 1800-1985.* New York: Harper and Row, 1987.

Fairbank, John K., Edwin O. Reischauer and Albert M. Craig. *East Asia: The Modern Transformation.* Boston: Houghton Mifflin Company, 1965.

Fang Zhao-ying. *Qingmo Minchu yangxue xuesheng timinglu chuqi* (Preliminary listing of students abroad in the late Qing-early Republican period). Taipei: Institute of Modern History, Academia Sinica, 1962.

Fenollosa, Ernest F. and Ariga Nagao. *Tō-A bijitsushikō* (An outline history of East Asian art). Tokyo: Fenorosashi kinenkai, 1921.

Ferguson, Niall. *The Pity of War.* New York: Basic Books, 1999.

____. *Empire: The Rise and Demise of the British World Order and the Lessons for Global Power.* New York: Basic Books, 2002.

Fincher, John H. *Chinese Democracy.* New York: St. Martin's Press, 1981.

Fogel, Joshua A. *Articulating the Sinosphere: Sino-Japanese Relations in Space and Time.* Cambridge, MA: Harvard University Press, 2009.

____. "Kano Naoki's Relationship to *Kangaku.*" In *New Directions in the Study of Meiji Japan,* edited by Helen Hardacre with Adam L. Kern, 358-371. New York: Brill, 1997.

____. *The Literature of Travel in the Rediscovery of China, 1862-1945.* Stanford: Stanford University Press, 1996.

____. *Nakae Ushikichi in China: The Mourning of Spirit.* Cambridge, MA: Council on East Asian Studies, Harvard University, 1989.

____. , editor. *The Nanjing Massacre in History and Historiography.* Berkeley: University of

California Press, 2000.
____. "The Nanking Atrocity and Chinese Historical Memory." In *The Nanking Atrocity 1937-38: Complicating the Picture,* edited by Bob Tadashi Wakabayashi, 267-284. New York: Berghahn Books, 2008.
____. *Politics and Sinology: the Case of Naitō Konan.* Cambridge, MA: Council on East Asian Studies, Harvard University, 1984.
Fraser, Andrew. "The House of Peers (1890-1905): structure, groups and role." In *Japan's Early Parliaments, 1890-1905,* edited by Andrew Fraser, R.H.P. Mason, and Philip Mitchell, 7-30. London: Routledge, 1995.
Furuki, Yoshiko. *The White Plum: A Biography of Ume Tsuda.* New York: Weatherhill, 1991.
Futami Takeshi. "Kyōshihōsei gakudō [jingshi fazheng xuetang] no Nihonjin kyōshū" (Japanese instructors at the Beijing School of Law and Politics). *Kokuritsu kyōiku kenkyūjo kiyō*, 115 (March 1988), 75-89.

Gaikō jihō (Revue diplomatique). Tokyo: Gaikō jihōsha, 1898-1986. [irregular, 1898-1906; Semimonthly, 1912-Mar ch 1944.]
"Gaikō shippai no sekinin" (Responsibility for our diplomatic failures). *GJ* 21:254 (June 1, 1915):1161-1166.
Garrett, Valery M. *Chinese Dragon Robes.* Hong Kong/New York: Oxford University Press, 1998.
____. *Mandarin Squares.* Hong Kong/New York: Oxford University Press, 1990. "Getsuji bansankai kiji" (Report on our monthly dinner meeting). *GJ* 13:151 (June 1910): 47-53.
GJ see *Gaikō jihō*
Giles, Lancelot. *The Siege of the Peking Legations.* Nedlands, W.A.: University of Western Australia Press, 1970.
Goodnow, Frank J. "The Parliament of the Republic of China." *The American Political Science Review* 8.4 (November 1914): 541-562.
____. "Reform in China." *The American Political Science Review* 9.2 (May 1915): 209-224.
Gries, Peter Hays. *China's New Nationalism: Pride, Politics, and Diplomacy.* Berkeley: University of California Press, 2004.

Hall, Ivan P. *Mori Arinori.* Cambridge, MA: Harvard University Press, 1973.
Hani Totoko. "Stories of My Life." *Japan Interpreter* 12, 3-4 (summer 1979): 330-353.
Harada Toyojirō. "Tai-Shi kōshō ni tsuite " (Regarding negotiations with China). *GJ* 21:251 (April 15, 1915): 12-17.
____. "Tai-Shi gaikō no isan" (Miscalculations in our China negotiations) (*GJ* 21:254 (June 1, 1915): 1184-1189.
Hardacre, Helen, and Adam L. Kern. *New Directions in the Study of Meiji Japan.* New York: Brill, 1997.
Harrell, Paula. "Guiding Hand: Hattori Unokichi in Beijing." In *Crossing the Yellow Sea: Sino-Japanese Contacts, 1600-1950,* edited by Joshua A. Fogel, 183-192. Norwalk, CT: EastBridge, 2007.
____. "The Meiji 'New Woman' and China." In *Late Qing China and Meiji Japan,* edited

by Joshua A. Fogel, 109-150. Norwalk, CT: EastBridge, 2004.

____. *Sowing the Seeds of Change: Chinese Teachers, Japanese Students, 1895-1905*. Stanford: Stanford University Press, 1992.

Harvard University. Records of President A. Lawrence Lowell, Folder 71, 1914-1917, UAIS.160; Harvard University Catalogue, 1915-1916, HV 20.413. Harvard University Archives.

Hatano Tarō. "Konoe Kazan o meguru Nit-Chū kōshō shiryō" (Historical materials on Konoe Kazan and Sino-Japanese communications). In *Ajia: kako to genzai* (Asia past and present). Tokyo: Kazan kurabu, 1955, 279-306.

Hattori Sensei koki shukuga kinen ronbunshū (A commemorative volume of essays in celebration of Professor Hattori's seventieth birthday). Tokyo: Fuzanbō, 1936.

Hattori Unokichi. *Kōfushi no hanashi* (The story of Confucius). Tokyo: Kyōbunsha, 1927.

____. *Pekin rōjō nikki* (Diary of the siege of Peking). Tokyo: Heibonsha, 1965.

____. *Pekin rōjō nikki* (Diary of the siege of Peking). Tokyo: [s.n.], 1926.

____. *Shina kenkyū* (Studies of China). Tokyo: Kyōbunsha, 1926.

____. "Shinajin kyōiku ni taisuru shoken" (Views on educating the Chinese). *Chūō Kōron* 24: 2 (1909): 36-42.

____. *Shina no kokuminsei to shisō.* (The national character and thought of China). Tokyo: 1926.

____. "Shinkoku jigen" (China update). *Taiyō* 10:12 (September 9, 1904): 89-91.

____. "Shinkoku to kensei" (China and constitutional government). *Taiyō* 15: 8 (1909): 79-80.

____. *Shinkoku tsūkō* (China sourcebook). Tokyo: Sanseido shoten, 1905, 1966.

____. *Tōyō rinri kōyō* (The essentials of East Asian ethics). Tokyo: Dōbun Shoin, 1942.

Headland, Isaac Taylor. *Court Life in China: The Capital, Its Officials and People.* New York: F.H. Revell and Company, 1909.

Hearn, Lafcadio. *Editorials from the Kobe Chronicle.* Tokyo: Hokuseido Press, 1960.

Hirai Seijirō. "Pekin miyage" (Peking takeaways). *Tetsudō jihō* 15:742 (November 29, 1913), 7-8.

Hirano Ken'ichirō. "Chūgoku ni okeru tōitsu kokka no keisei to shōsūminzoku" (Ethnic minorities and the formation of a unified state in China). In *Ajia ni okeru kokumin tōgō: rekishi, bunka, kokusai kankei* (National unity in Asia: history, culture and international relations), edited by Hirano Ken'ichirō et al. Tokyo: Tōkyō Daigaku shuppansha, 1988.

Hirotani Takio. "Pekin keimu gakudō to Kawashima Naniwa" (The Beijing Police Academy and Kawashima Naniwa). *Kokuritsu kyōiku kenkyūjo kiyō* 115. (March 1988): 91-103.

HSK. See *Hattori Sensei koki shukuga kinen ronbunshū.*

Huang Fu-ch'ing [Huang Fuqing]. *Jindai Riben zai-Hua wenhua ji shehui shiye zhi yanjiu* (Research into Japanese social and cultural enterprises in China). Taipei: Zhongyang Yanjiu Yuan, Jindai Shi Yanjiu Suo, 1982.

Hull, William I. *The Two Hague Conferences and Their Contributions to International Law.* Boston: Ginn & Company, 1908.

Hutchinson, John F. *Champions of Charity: War and the Rise of the Red Cross.* Boulder, CO: Westview Press, 1996.

Ichiko, Chuzo [Ichiko Chūzō]. "Political and Institutional Reform, 1901-11." In *The Cambridge History of China,* Vol. 11, *Late Qing, 1800-1911,* edited by John K. Fairbank and Kwang-ching Liu, part 2, 375-415. Cambridge, UK: Cambridge University Press, 1980.

Ichinomiya Misako *see* Kawahara Misako.

Inoue, Shun. "The Invention of the Martial Arts: Kanō Jigorō and Kōdōkan Judo." In *Mirror of Modernity: Invented Traditions of Modern Japan,* edited by Stephen Vlastos, 163-173. Berkeley: University of California Press, 1998.

Iriye, Akira. *China and Japan in the Global Setting.* Cambridge, MA: Harvard University Press, 1992.

____. *Pacific Estrangement: Japanese and American Expansion, 1897-1911.*Cambridge, MA: Harvard University Press, 1972.

_____, editor. *The Chinese and the Japanese.* Princeton: Princeton University Press, 1980.

Jansen, Marius B. *The Japanese and Sun Yatsen.* Cambridge: Harvard University Press, 1954.

____. "Konoe Atsumaro." In *The Chinese and the Japanese,* edited by Akira Iriye. Princeton: Princeton University Press, 1980.

____. *The Making of Modern Japan.* Cambridge: Harvard University Press, 2000.

Japan, Ministry of Foreign Affairs Archives (*Gaikō shiryōkan),* documents related to selected Japanese advisers in China, 1902-1915. Tokyo: Ministry of Foreign Affairs.

Japanese National Commission for UNESCO. *The Role of Education in the Social and Economic Development of Japan.* Tokyo: Institute for Democratic Education, 1966.

Johnston, Reginald. *Twilight in the Forbidden City.* Wilmington, DE: Scholarly Resources, Inc., 1973.

Judge, Joan. "The Ideology of 'Good Wives and Wise Mothers': Meiji Japan and Feminine Modernity." In Late-Qing China." In *Sagacious Monks and Bloodthirsty Warriors: Chinese Views of Japan in the Ming-Qing Period,* edited by Joshua A. Fogel, 218-248. EastBridge, Norwalk, CT: EastBridge, 2001.

____. *The Precious Raft of History: The Past, the West, and the Woman Question in China.* Stanford: Stanford University Press, 2008.

Judt, Tony. "The past is another country: myth and memory in post-war Europe." In *Memory and Power in Post-War Europe,* edited by Jan-Werner Muller, 157-183. Cambridge: Cambridge University Press, 2002.

Kamisaka Fuyuko. *Dansō no reijin: Kawashima Yoshiko den* (A beautiful woman in male attire). Tokyo: Bungei shunjū, 1984.

Kanō Jigorō. *Watakushi no shōgai to jūdō* (My life and judo). Edited by Otaki Tadao. Tokyo:Tokyo: Shinjinbutsu ōraisha, 1972.

Kanō Jigorō. Edited by the Kanō Sensei Denki Hensankai (Committee to Compile the Biography of Professor Kanō). Tokyo: Kōdōkan, 1964.

Kanō Jigorō chosakushū (Collected works), Vol. 3. Tokyo: Gagatsu shobō, 1983.

Katō Nihei. *Kanō Jigorō: sekai taiiku shijō ni kagayaku* (Kanō Jigorō: leading light in world sports history). Tokyo: Shōyō, 1964.

Katsumi Usui. *Nihon kin-gendai jinmei jiten* (A biographical dictionary of modern and contemporary Japan). Tokyo: Yoshikawa kōbunkan, 2001.

Kawahara Misako [Misaoko]. *Karachin ōhi to watakushi* (The princess of Karachin and I). Tokyo: Fuyū shobō, 1969.

____. *Mōko miyage* (Remembrances of Mongolia). Tokyo: Jitsugyō no Nipponsha, 1909.

Kawamata Keiichi. *The History of the Red Cross Society of Japan.* Tokyo: 1919.

Kawashima Naniwa. "Bō Futabatei Shimei kun o omou" (Recollections of the late Mr. Futabatei Shimei). *Chūō Kōron* 50:12 (1936): 209-217.

____. *Kawashima Naniwa Sensei tai-Shi iken* (Professor Kawashima Naniwa's Views on China). Tokyo: Higashi hankyū kyōkai, 1941.

____. *Shina no byōkon* (The root causes of China's illness). Tokyo: Higashi hankyū kyōkai, 1943.

____. *Tai-Shi narabi ni tai-Man-Mō no kenponteki keirin* (Crafting basic policies to govern China and the Manchuria/Mongolia region). Tokyo: [n.p., top secret material], 1926.

____. *Tai-Shina kanken* (My personal views on China). Tokyo: [n.p.], 1913. Kawashima Yoshiko File from National Archives II: record Group 319, Box 285, IRR Personal, Counter-intelligence Records, Army. College Park, Maryland.

Keene, Donald. *Appreciations of Japanese Culture.* New York: Kodansha International, 1981.

____. *Emperor of Japan: Meiji and His World, 1852-1912.* New York: Columbia University Press, 2002.

____. *Modern Japanese Diaries.* New York: Henry Holt and Company, 1995.

"Keichō Ariga hakushi" (Condolences for Dr. Ariga). *GJ* 34:400 (July 1, 1921): 123.

Kemuyama Sentaro. "Ariga sensei no omoide" (Recollections of Professor Ariga). *GJ* 67:686 (July 1, 1933): 104-108.

"Kichō shitaru Konoe Kō" (Prince Konoe on his return home). *Taiyō,* 5:6 (October 5, 1899): 47-51.

Kitaoka Shin'ichi. "China Experts in the Army." In *The Japanese Informal Empire in China, 1895-1937.* Edited by Peter Duus, Ramon H. Myers, and Mark R. Peattie, 330-368. Princeton: Princeton University Press, 1989.

____. "Insights into the World: Future tasks in study of Japan-China history," April 19, 2010 www.yomiuri.co.jp/dy/columns/commentary/20100419dy01.htm

____. "A Look Back on the Work of the Joint Japanese-Chinese History Research Committee." *Asia Pacific Review* (May, 2010): 6:20.

____. "Nit- Chū rekishi kyōdō kenkyū no shuppatsu" (Start of the Japan-China Joint History Research). *Gaikō Forum* 20 (May, 2007): 14-20.

Kokuryūkai, editor. *Tō-A senkaku shishi kiden* (Records and biographies of pioneer patriots in East Asia). Tokyo: Hara shobō, 1966.

Konoe Atsumaro nikki (Diary of Konoe Atsumaro). Konoe Atsumaro Nikki Kankōkai, editor. 5 volumes and supplemental volume of selected writings. Tokyo: Kajima kenkyūjo shuppankai, 1968.

Konoe Atsumaro. *Hokkaidō shiken* (My personal views on Hokkaido). Tokyo: Akaishi teizō, 1902.

Konoe Fumimaro. "Chichi no koto" (Things about my father). In *Seidanroku* (Setting the record straight). Edited by Itō Takeshi. Tokyo: Chikura shobō, 1936.

Konoe Kazan Kō. Konoe Kazankai, editor/publisher. Tokyo: 1924.

Koskenniemi, Martti. *The Gentle Civilizer of Nations: The Rise and Fall of International Law 1870-1960.* Cambridge, UK; New York: Cambridge University Press, 2002.

Kowner, Rotem. *The Impact of the Russo-Japanese War.* London: Routledge, 2007.

Kudō Takeshige. *Konoe Atsumaro-kō.* Tokyo: Dainichisha zōban, 1938.

Kunimatsu Fumio. *Waga Man-Shi nijūnen no kaiko* (Recollections of my twenty-five years in China and Manchuria). Tokyo: Shin Kigensha, 1961.

Kuropatkin, Aleksei N. *The Russian Army and the Japanese War: Being Historical and Critical Comments on the Military Policy and Power of Russia and on the Campaign in the Far East.* Edited by Ernest D. Swinton. London: J. Murray, 1909.

Lee, Sophia. "The Foreign Ministry's Cultural Agenda for China: the Boxer Indemnity." In *The Japanese Informal Empire in China, 1895-1937,* edited by Peter Duus, Ramon H. Myers, and Mark R. Peattie, 272-306. Princeton, NJ: Princeton University Press, 1989.

Lewis, Ida-Belle. *The Education of Girls in China.* New York: Teachers College, Columbia University, 1919.

Li, Fei Fei, Robert Sabella, and David Liu, editors. *Nanking, 1937.* Armonk, NY: M.E. Sharpe, 2002.

Li, Lillian M., Alison J. Dray-Novey, and Haili Kong. *Beijing: From Imperial Capital to Olympic City.* New York: Palgrave Macmillan, 2007.

Li Tingjiang. "Shinhai kakumei jiki ni okeru Nihonjin komon" (Japanese advisers in China at the time of the 1911 Revolution). *Ajia Kenkyū* 39:1 (December 1992).

____. "The Role of the Japanese Advisor in Early Republican China: A Consideration of Ariga Nagao." *Twentieth Century China,* 23:2 (April 1998).

Lincicome, Mark E. *Principles, Praxis, and the Politics of Educational Reform in Meiji Japan.* Honolulu: University of Hawai'i Press, 1995.

Liu, Kwang-ching. "Politics, Intellectual Outlook, and Reform: the T'ung-wen Kuan Controversy of 1867." In *Reform in Nineteenth Century China,* edited by Paul A. Cohen and John E. Schrecker, 87-100. Cambridge, MA: Harvard University Press, 1976.

Mackie, Vera. *Creating Socialist Women in Japan: Gender, Labour, and Activism, 1900-1937.* New York: Cambridge University Press, 1997.

MacKinnon, Stephen R. *Power and Politics in Late Imperial China.* Berkeley: University of California Press, 1980.

MacMillan, Margaret. *The Peacemakers: The Paris Conference of 1919 and Its Attempt to End War.* London: J. Murray, 2002.

Marshall, Byron K. *Academic Freedom and the Japanese Imperial University, 1868-1939.* Berkeley: University of California Press, 1992.

Mason, R.H.P. "Foreign affairs debates, 1890-1891." In *Japan's Early Parliaments, 1890-1905.* Edited by Andrew Fraser, R.H.P. Mason and Philip Mitchell, 98-156. London: Routledge, 1995.

Matsusaka, Yoshihisa Tak. *The Making of Japanese Manchuria, 1904-1932.* Cambridge, MA: Harvard University Asia Center, Harvard University Press, 2001.

McClain, James L. *Japan: A Modern History.* New York: W.W. Norton & Company, 2002.

McCormack, Gavan. *Chang Tso-lin in Northeast China, 1911-1928: China, Japan, and the Manchurian Idea.* Stanford: Stanford University Press, 1977.

Mehl, Margaret. "Private Academies for Chinese Learning (*Kangaku juku)* in the Meiji Period." In *Late Qing China and Meiji Japan,* edited by Joshua A. Fogel, 87-107. Norwalk, CT: EastBridge, 2004.

MHNS See Nakayama Yasuaki, editor. *Shimbun shūsei Meiji hennenshi.*

Ministry of Foreign Affairs of Japan (MOFA). Final Report of Phase One of the Japan-China Joint History Research Project (February 2010). Available in Japanese at http://www.mofa.go.jp/mofaj/area/china/pdfs/rekishi_kk_j-2.llpdf and https://memoryreconciliation.wordpress.com/

Mitsui Kunitarō. *Okumura Ioko.* Tokyo: Chōbunkaku, 1944.

Morris, Edmund. *The Rise of Theodore Roosevelt.* New York: Ballentine Books, 1979.

Morrison, George Ernest. *The Correspondence of G.E. Morrison.* 2 vols. Edited by Lo Hui-min. Cambridge, UK: Cambridge University Press, 1976-1978.

Morse, Edward S. *Japan Day by Day.* Boston: Houghton Mifflin Company, 1917.

Moser, Michael J. *Foreigners within the Gates: The Legations at Peking.* Hong Kong/New York: Oxford University Press, 1993.

Naitō Torajirō (Konan). "Shina dōran hiken" (My humble opinion on the disturbances in China). GJ 26:304 (July 1, 1917): 8-17.

Nakajima, Kuni. "Naruse Jinzō." In *Ten Great Educators of Modern Japan.* Compiled and edited by Benjamin C. Duke, 67-85. Tokyo: University of Tokyo Press, 1989.

Nakayama Yasuaki, editor. *Shimbun shūsei Meiji hennenshi* (Meiji history through newspapers), Vols. 1-12. Tokyo: Zaisei keizai gakkai, 1936. *Nikki.* See *Konoe Atsumaro nikki.*

Ninagawa Arata. "Shina gaikō no shippai o kanashimu" (Deploring the failure of our China diplomacy). *GJ* 21:246 (February 1, 1915): 276-279.

Nish, Ian H. *Alliance in Decline: A Study in Anglo-Japanese Relations, 1908-23.* London: University of London, The Athlone Press, 1972.

____. "Katō Takaaki, 1860-1926." In *Japanese Envoys in Britain, 1862-1964,* compiled and edited by Ian Nish, 80-91. Folkstone, Kent: Global Oriental, 2007.

____. *"Japanese Expansionism."* In *Imperialism and After: Continuities and Discontinuities.* Edited by Wolfgang J. Mommsen and Jurgen Osterhammel, 83-89. Boston: Allen and Unwin, 1986.

____. *Japanese Foreign Policy in the Interwar Period.* Westport, CT: Praeger, 2002.

____. *Japan's Struggle with Internationalism: Japan, China, and the League of Nations, 1931-3.* London; New York: K. Paul International, 1993.

Ō En [Wang Wan]. *Shinmatsu Chūgoku tai-Nichi kyōiku shisatsu no kenkyū* (Research into educational study tours to China at the end of the Qing period). Tokyo: Kyūko shoin, 1998.

Ogawa Gōtarō. "Nihongun tai-Ōshū haken ronsha ni tadasu" (Questions for advocates of sending Japanese troops to Europe). *GJ* 21:245 (January 15, 1915): 147-152.

____. "Tai-Shi kōshō ni tsuite" (On negotiations with China). *GJ* 21:251 (April 15, 1915): 822-827.

Ogawa Yoshiko. "Shinmatsu no kindai gakudō to Nihon joshi kyōshū: Kanton Joshi Shihan Gakudō o chūshin ni" (Late-Qing modern schools and Japanese women teachers: chiefly the Guangdong Female Normal School). In *Oyatoi Nihonjin kyōshū no kenkyū: Ajia no kyōiku kindaika to Nihonjin* (Studies of Japanese contract teachers: modernization of Asian education and the Japanese), special issue of *Kokuritsu kyōiku kenkyūjo kiyō* (March 1988): 105-114.

Oka Yoshitake. *Konoe Fumimaro.* Translated by Shumpei Okamoto and Patricia Murray. Lanham, MD: Madison Books, 1992.

Okada Asatarō. "Shinkoku no kyōiku oyobi hōsei hensan ni tsuite" (Regarding China's educational and legal compilations). *Taiyō (*August 1, 1909): 50-52.

Okamoto, Shumpei. *The Japanese Oligarchy and the Russo-Japanese War.* New York: Columbia University Press, 1970.

Oketani Hideaki. *Futabatei Shimei to Meiji Nippon* (Futabatei Shimei and Meiji Japan). Bungei hunjū, 1986.

Ōkubo Takaaki. *Okumura Ioko shōden* (Brief biography of Okumura Ioko). Tokyo: Ōzorosha, 1990 [originally published: Tokyo: Aikoku Fujinkai, 1908].

Ōkubo Toshiaki, Tanaka Akira and Matsudaira Norimasa. *Kuge Konoe-ke, kuge Takatsukasa-ke, kuge Sanjō-ke.* Tokyo: Mainichi Shinbunsha, 1990.

Ōmori Chikako. "Tō-A Dōbunkai to Tō-A Dōbun Shoin: sono seiritsu jijō, seikaku, oyobi katsudō " (Tō-A Dōbunkai and Tō-A Dōbun Shoin: their founding circumstances, character, and activities). 19:6 *Chōsa kenkyū hōkoku sōsho/Ajia keizai kenkyūjo* (June 1978): 76-92.

Ono Kazuko. *Chinese in a Century of Revolution, 1850-1950.* Translated and edited by Joshua A. Fogel. Stanford: Stanford University Press, 1989.

____. "Shimoda Utako to Hattori Unokichi" (Shimoda Utako and Hattori Unokichi). In *Kindai Nihon to Chūgoku* (Modern Japan and China), edited by Takeuchi Yoshimi and Hashikawa Bunzō, 201-221.

Ōtsuka Yutaka. "Chūgoku kindai kōtō shihan kyōiku no hōga to Hattori Unokichi" (The beginnings of modern higher normal education in China and Hattori Unokichi). *Kokuritsu kyōiku kenkyūjo kiyō* 115 (March 1988): 45-62.

Outlines of the Modern Education in Japan. Tokyo: Department of Education, May 1893.

Paine, S.C.M. *The Sino-Japanese War of 1894-1895: Perceptions, Power, and Primacy.* Cambridge, UK; New York: Cambridge University Press, 2003.

Passin, Herbert. *Society and Education in Japan.* New York: Bureau of Publications, Teachers College, Columbia University, 1965.

Pearl, Cyril. *Morrison of Peking.* Singapore: Penguin Books, 1970.

Peattie, Mark R. "Japanese Attitudes Toward Colonialism." In *The Japanese Colonial Empire, 1895-1945.* Edited by Ramon H. Myers and Mark R. Peattie, 80-127. Princeton, NJ: Princeton University Press, 1984.

____. "Japanese Treaty Port Settlements in China." In *The Japanese Informal Empire in China, 1895-1937.* Edited by Peter Duus, Ramon H. Myers, and Mark R. Peattie,

166-209. Princeton, NJ: Princeton University Press, 1989.

Preston, Diana. *The Boxer Rebellion.* New York: Walker and Company, 2000.

Putnam Weale, B.L. [pseud]. *Indiscreet Letters from Peking.* New York: Dodd, Mead and Company, 1907.

____. *The Re-shaping of the Far East.* London: Macmillan and Co., 1905.

Rawski, Evelyn Sakakida. *The Last Emperors: A Social History of Qing Imperial Institutions.* Berkeley: University of California Press, 1998.

Reynolds, Douglas R. *China, 1898-1912: The Xinzheng Revolution and Japan.* Cambridge, MA: Council on East Asian Studies, Harvard University, 1993.

____. "Training Young China Hands: Tōa Dōbun Shoin and Its Precursors, 1886-1945." In *The Japanese Informal Empire in China, 1895-1937.* Edited by Peter Duus, Ramon H. Myers, and Mark R. Peattie, 210-271. Princeton: Princeton University Press, 1989.

Rhoads, Edward J.M. *Manchus and Han: Ethnic Relations and Political Power in Late Qing and Early Republican China, 1861-1928.* Seattle: University of Washington Press, 2000.

Roberts, John G. *Mitsui: Three Centuries of Japanese Business.* New York: Weatherhill, 1989.

Roosevelt, Theodore. *The Works of Theodore Roosevelt.* Vols. XIII and XVIII. New York: Charles Scribner's Sons, 1926.

Rose, Barbara. *Tsuda Umeko and Women's Education in Japan.* New Haven: Yale University Press, 1992.

Rose, Caroline. *Sino-Japanese Relations: Looking to the Past, Facing the Future?* London and New York: RoutledgeCurzon, 2005.

Ryan, Marleigh G. *Japan's First Modern Novel: Ukigumo of Futabatei Shumei.* New York: Columbia University Press, 1967.

Sanetō Keishū. *Chūgokujin Nihon ryūgaku shi* (A history of Chinese students in Japan). Tokyo: Kuroshio shuppan, 1960.

Sato Saburō. "Kō-A kai ni kansuru ikkōsatsu" (An inquiry into the Revive Asia Society). *Yamagata Daigaku kiyō* 4 (1951): 399-410.

Seidensticker, Edward. *Low City, High City.* New York: Knopf, 1983.

Seki Eiji. *Nichi-Ei Dōmei: Nihon gaikō no eikō to chōraku* (The Anglo-Japanese Alliance: the glory and decline of Japanese diplomacy). Tokyo: Gakushū kenkyūsha, 2003.

"Sen kyūhyaku jūsan nen" (1913). *GJ* 17:196 (January 1, 1913): 1-6.

Shiba Gorō. *Pekin rōjō* (Siege of Peking). Tokyo: Heibonsha, 1965.

Shimoda Utako sensei den (Biography of Professor Shimoda Utako). Tokyo: Ko Shimoda Kōchō sensei denki hensanjo, 1943.

Shimoda Utako. *Ryōsai to kenbo* (Good wives and wise mothers). Tokyo: Fuzanbō, 1912.

____. *Shinsen kaseigaku* (Updated home economics). Tokyo: Kinkōdō shoseki kabushiki kaisha, 1902.

Shoji, Jun'ichiro. "Briefing Memo: Outlook for the Japan-China Joint History Research Committee." *The National Institute for Defense Studies News* 127 (December, 2008): 1-5.

Sievers, Sharon L. *Flowers in Salt: The Beginnings of Feminist Consciousness in Modern Japan.*

Stanford: Stanford University Press, 1983.
Shao, Dan. "Princess, Traitor, Soldier, Spy." In *Crossed Histories: Manchuria in the Age of Empire,* 82-119. Edited by Mariko Asano Tamanoi. Honolulu: Association for Asian Studies and University of Hawai'i Press, 2005.
Sharf, Frederic A., and James T. Ulak. *A Well-Watched War: Images from the Russo-Japanese Front, 1904-1905.* Newbury, MA: Newburyport Press, 2000.
Smith, Arthur H. *China in Convulsion.* New York: Fleming H. Revell Company, 1901.
Smith, Jean Edward. *Grant.* New York: Simon & Schuster, 2001.
Spence, Jonathan. *The Search for Modern China.* New York: W.W. Norton & Company, 1990.
____. *To Change China: Western Advisers in China, 1620-1960.* New York: Penguin Books, 1980.
Stead, Alfred, editor. *Japan by the Japanese.* London: William Heinemann, 1904.
Strand, David. *Rickshaw Beijing.* Berkeley: University of California Press, 1989.

Tachi Sakutarō. "Ariga hakushi ni tsuki omoidazuru mama ni" (Things that come to mind about Dr. Ariga). *GJ* 67:686 (July 1, 1933): 13-17.
____. "Kokumin shugi to gaikō" (Nationalism and foreign relations) *GJ* 21:254 (June 1915): 1171-1179.
____. "Monrō-shugi to Kyokutō" (Monroe-ism and the Far East). *GJ* 14:164 (July 1911): 95-100.
____. "Shin Monrō-shugi" (New Monroe-ism). *GJ* 21:247 (February 15, 1915): 370-382.
"Tai-Shi kōshō" (Negotiations with China). *GJ* 21:254 (June 1, 1915): 1251-1261.
"Tai-Shi kōshō tenmatsu" (Details of the negotiations with China). *GJ* 21:253 (May 15, 1915): 1148-1160.
"Tai-Shi kōshō no kiki" (Crisis in negotiations with China). *GJ* 21:253 (May 15, 1915): 1039-1043.
"Tai-Shi kōshō" (Negotiations with China). *GJ* 21:251 (April 15, 1915): 866-874.
"Tai-Shi kōshō" (Negotiations with China). *GJ* 21:250 (April 1, 1915): 749-756.
"Tai-Shi kōshō no keika" (The course of negotiations with China). *GJ* 21:250 (April 1, 1915): 695-701.
"Tai-Shi kōshō" (Negotiations with China). *GJ* 21:249 (March 15, 1915): 648-653.
"Tai-Shi kōshō" (Negotiations with China). *GJ* 21: 248 (March 1, 1915): 535-539.
"Tai-Shi gaikō no yōtei" (Secret to success in our China policy). *GJ* 21:246 (February 1, 1915): 249-254.
Takada Sanae. "Ko Ariga hakushi omoide no ki" (Recollections of the late Dr. Ariga). *GJ* 46:543 (July 1927), 101-105.
Takahashi Sakuyé. *Cases of International Law during the Chino-Japanese War.* Cambridge: At the University Press, 1899.
Takeuchi Yoshimi and Hashikawa Bunzō, editors. *Kindai Nihon to Chūgoku* (Modern China and Japan). Tokyo: Asahi Shinbunsha, 1974.
Tam, Yue-him. "Meiji Japan and the Educational and Language Reforms in Late Ch'ing China." In *The Ambivalence of Nationalism: Modern Japan between East and West.* Edited by James W. White, Michio Umegaki, and Thomas R.H. Havens, 61-77.

Lanham, MD: University Press of America, 1990.

Tanaka, Stefan. *Japan's Orient: Rendering Pasts into History.* Berkeley: University of California Press, 1993.

Tao, Demin. "The Influence of the Tongcheng School on Meiji Japan." In *Late Qing China and Meiji Japan,* edited by Joshua A. Fogel, 151-163. Norwalk, CT: EastBridge, 2004.

____. "Nishimura Tenshū's Journey to the Yangtze Basin." In *Sino-Japanese Studies* 1:4 (October 1991): 28-38.

____. "Shigeno Yasutsugu as an advocate of 'Practical Sinology'." In *New Directions in the Study of Meiji Japan,* 373-382. Edited by Helen Hardacre with Adam L. Kern. New York: Brill, 1997.

Teow, See Heng. *Japan's Cultural Policy toward China, 1918-1931.* Cambridge, MA: Harvard University Asia Center, Harvard University Press, 1999.

Tō-A Dōbun Shoin Daigaku shi (A history of the Tō-A Dōbun College). Tokyo: Shanghai Friendship Society, 1955.

Tō-A Dōbunkai, editor. *Tai-Shi kaiko roku* (Memoirs about China). 3 vols. Tokyo: Hara shobō, 1968.

____. *Zoku tai-Shi kaikoroku* (Supplement to memoirs about China). Tokyo: Hara shobō, 1941.

Torii Ryūzō. *Torii Ryūzō zenshū* (Collected works of Torii Ryūzō). Tokyo: Asahi Shinbunsha, 1975.

Townsend, Susan. *Yanaihara Tadao and Japanese Colonial Policy: Redeeming Empire.* Richmond, Surrey: Curzon Press, 2000.

Trevor-Roper, Hugh. *Hermit of Peking: The Hidden Life of Sir Edmund Backhouse.* New York: Knopf, 1977.

TSSK (Tō-A senkaku shishi kiden). See Kokuryūkai, ed.

TSKKR (Tai-Shi kaiko roku). See Tō-A Dōbunkai, ed.

Tung, William L. *The Political Institutions of Modern China.* The Hague: M. Nijhoff, 1964.

Wakabayashi, Bob Tadashi, editor. *The Nanking Atrocity 1937-38: Complicating the Picture.* New York: Berghahn Books, 2007.

Wakeman, Frederic, Jr. " Models of Historical Change: The Chinese State and Society, 1839-1989." In *Perspectives on Modern China,* edited by Kenneth Lieberthal et al., 68-102. Armonk, NY: M.E. Sharpe, 1991.

Wang Jiajian. *Qingmo Minchu wo guo jingcha zhidu xiandaihua de liche*ng (The process of modernizing our police system in late Qing early Republican China). Taibei: Taiwan shangwu yinshuguan, 1984.

Wang Xiangrong. *Shinkoku oyatoi Nihonjin* (Japanese contract specialists in China). Japanese translation of *Riben jiaoxi* by Takeuchi Minoru. Tokyo: Asahi shinbunsha, 1991.

____. *Zhongguo de jindaihua yu Riben* (China's modernization and Japan). Hunan: Hunan People's Publishing House, 1987.

Watanabe Ryūsaku. *Hiroku Kawashima Yoshiko: sono shōgai no shinsō to nazo* (The inside story of Kawashima Yoshiko: the basic truths and unsolved mysteries of her life). Tokyo: Bancho shobō, 1972.

____. *Kindai Nit-Chū minshū kōryū* (Unofficial history of modern interactions between the Japanese and the Chinese). Tokyo: Yūsankaku shuppan, 1981.

Westney, Eleanor D. *Imitation and Innovation: The Transfer of Western Organizational Patterns to Meiji Japan.* Cambridge, MA: Harvard University Press, 1987.

Weston, Timothy B. *The Power of Position: Beijing University, Intellectuals, and Chinese Political Culture, 1898-1929.* Berkeley: University of California Press, 2004.

Weston, Virginia. *Japanese Painting and National Identity: Okakura Tenshin and His Circle.* Michigan Monograph Series in Japanese Studies, no. 45, 2004.

Wilbur, C. Martin. *Sun Yatsen: Frustrated Patriot.* New York: Columbia University Press, 1976.

Wilson, Sandra. *The Manchurian Crisis and Japanese Society, 1931-33.* London and New York: Routledge, 2002.

Wu Rulun. *Dongyu Ribao yibian* (Translations from the Japanese on [Wu's] trip to Japan). Sanetō Keishū Collection, no. 53.

Xiao Chaoran. *Beijing Daxuexiao shi* (History of Beijing University). Beijing: Beijing University Press, 1988.

Yamamuro, Shin'ichi. *Manchuria Under Japanese Dominion.* Translated by Joshua A. Fogel. Philadelphia: University of Pennsylvania Press, 2006.

Yamane Yukio. *Kindai Chūgoku no naka no Nihonjin* (Japanese in modern China). Tokyo: Kenbun shuppansha, 1994.

_____, editor. *Kindai Nit-Chū kankeishi kenkyū nyūmon* (An introduction to the study of the history of Sino-Japanese relations). Tokyo: Kenbun shuppan, 1992.

Yan Ansheng. *Nihon ryūgaku seishinshi: kindai Chūgoku chishikijin no kiseki* (History of the spirit behind overseas study in Japan: traces of Chinese intellectuals in Japan). Iwanami shoten, 1991.

Yang Xuechen and Zhou Yuanlian. *Qingdai Baqi wanggong guizu xingshuaishi* (A history of the rise and fall of the Eight Banners princes and nobles during the Qing period). Shenyang: Liaoning renmin chubanshe, 1986.

Yokoyama Kendō. *Kanō sensei den* (Biography of Professor Kanō). Tokyo: Oda Nobutada, 1941.

Yosano Akiko. *Travels in Manchuria and Mongolia: A Feminist Poet from Japan Encounters Prewar China.* Translated by Joshua A. Fogel. New York: Columbia University Press, 2001.

Yoshida, Takashi. *The Making of the Rape of Nanking: History and Memory in Japan, China, and the United States.* New York: Oxford University Press, 2006.

Yoshikawa Kōjirō, editor. *Tōyōgaku no sōshishatachi* (Pioneers of Asian Studies). Tokyo: Kōdansha, 1976.

Young, Ernest P. "Chinese Leaders and Japanese Aid in the Early Republic." In *The Chinese and The Japanese.* Edited by Akira Iriye, 124-139. Princeton, NJ: Princeton University Press, 1980.

____. *The Presidency of Yuan Shih-k'ai: Liberalism and Dictatorship in Early Republican China.* Ann Arbor: University of Michigan Press, 1977.

____. "The Reformer as a Conspirator: Liang Ch'i-ch'ao and the 1911 Revolution." In *Approaches to Modern Chinese History,* 239-267. Berkeley: University of California Press, 1967.

Young, Louise. *Japan's Total Empire: Manchuria and the Culture of Wartime Imperialism.* Berkeley: University of California Press, 1998.

ZTSKKR (Zoku tai-Shi kaiko roku). See Tō-A Dōbunkai, ed.

Index

Z

About the Author

Paula Harrell (Ph.D. Columbia University) is a China-Japan scholar specializing in twentieth century and contemporary history. In addition to teaching at the University of Maryland and Dickinson College, she worked for a decade as a management specialist on World Bank-financed projects in China. In 2008 Harrell joined the adjunct faculty at Georgetown University (SCS) where she offers courses on twenty-first century China in historical perspective. Her publications include *Sowing the Seeds of Change: Chinese Students, Japanese Teachers, 1895-1905* (Stanford University Press, 1992).

Weatherhead East Asian Institute

Studies of the Weatherhead East Asian Institute Columbia University

Selected Titles

(Complete list at: http://www.columbia.edu/cu/weai/weatherhead-studies.html)

Redacted: The Archives of Censorship in Postwar Japan, by Jonathan E. Abel. University of California Press, 2012.

Occupying Power: Sex Workers and Servicemen in Postwar Japan, by Sarah Kovner. Stanford University Press, 2012.

Empire of Dogs: Canines, Japan, and the Making of the Modern Imperial World, by Aaron Herald Skabelund. Cornell University Press, 2011.

Russo-Japanese Relations, 1905-17: From enemies to allies, by Peter Berton. Routledge, 2011.

Realms of Literacy: Early Japan and the History of Writing, by David Lurie. Harvard University Asia Series, 2011.

Planning for Empire: Reform Bureaucrats and the Japanese Wartime State, by Janis Mimura. Cornell University Press, 2011.

Passage to Manhood: Youth Migration, Heroin, and AIDS in Southwest China, by Shao-hua Liu. Stanford University Press, 2010.

Imperial Japan at its Zenith: The Wartime Celebration of the Empire's 2,600th Anniversary, by Kenneth J. Ruoff. Cornell University Press, 2010.

Behind the Gate: Inventing Students in Beijing, by Fabio Lanza. Columbia University Press, 2010.

Postwar History Education in Japan and the Germanys: Guilty Lessons, by Julian Dierkes. Routledge, 2010.

The Aesthetics of Japanese Fascism, by Alan Tansman. University of California Press, 2009.

The Growth Idea: Purpose and Prosperity in Postwar Japan, by Scott O'Bryan. University of Hawai'i Press, 2009.

National History and the World of Nations: Capital, State, and the Rhetoric of History in Japan, France, and the United States, by Christopher Hill. Duke University Press, 2008.

Leprosy in China: A History, by Angela Ki Che Leung. Columbia University Press, 2008.

Kingdom of Beauty: Mingei and the Politics of Folk Art in Imperial Japan, by Kim Brandt. Duke University Press, 2007.

Mediasphere Shanghai: The Aesthetics of Cultural Production, by Alexander Des Forges. University of Hawai'i Press, 2007.

Modern Passings: Death Rites, Politics, and Social Change in Imperial Japan, by Andrew Bernstein. University of Hawai'i Press, 2006.

The Making of the "Rape of Nanjing": The History and Memory of the Nanjing Massacre in Japan, China, and the United States, by Takashi Yoshida. Oxford University Press, 2006.